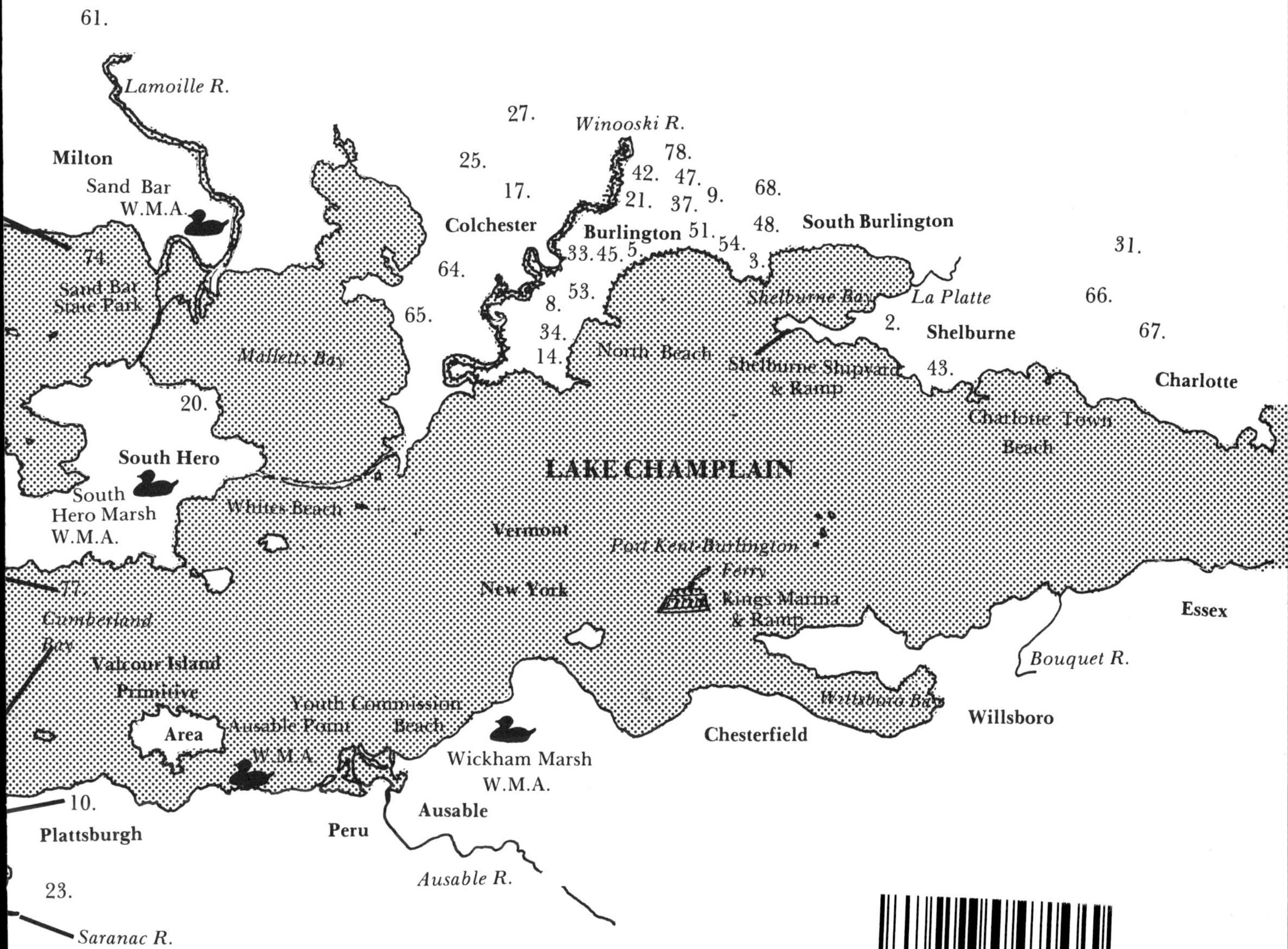

40. S. McIntyre
41. D. McNally
42. I. Melendy
43. E. Menges
44. S. Mitchell
45. O. Moreau
46. W. Nautel
47. C. Novotny
48. F. Owen
49. L. Papineau
50. J. Phillips
51. F. Patno
52. R. Peake
53. J.T. Penrose, Jr.
54. R.F. Perry
55. R. Poquette
56. C. Porter
57. R. Pudvar
58. C. Putnam
59. A. Rocheleau
60. H. Rochester
61. F. Russell
62. J. Senesak
63. A. Scales
64. B. Sharrow
65. R. Thayer
66. G. Thompson
67. G. Thompson, Jr.
68. A. Toutant
69. G. Tremblay
70. M. Vantine
71. A.L. Way
72. A. Way
73. E. Way
74. I. Wells
75. A. Willett
76. J. Willett
77. J. Wright
78. L.G. Wright

Decoys of Lake Champlain

Dr. Loy S. Harrell

Schiffer Publishing Ltd

West Chester, Pennsylvania 19380

Cover: Painting by Lachlan Field, Cornwall, Vermont.
Taken from a photograph dated October 11, 1882, of The
Sand Bar, Lake Champlain, Vermont.

Library of Congress Catalog Number: 86-61296.

Printed in the United States of America.
ISBN: 0-88740-075-2
Published by Schiffer Publishing Ltd.
1469 Morstein Road, West Chester, Pennsylvania 19380

This book may be purchased from the publisher.
Please include $1.50 postage.
Try your bookstore first.

Dedication

This book is dedicated to both my family, whose patience allowed me to venture forth evenings and weekends in pursuit of facts and photos and to those creative folk artists, whose very talents demanded that they be documented.

Acknowledgments

I owe most to my indulgent and creative wife, Rae. Her knowledge and artistic talent lent itself well to my own naive sense of esthetics. Thank you for the encouragement of my mother and my sister Pat, and for my daughter Heather's typing. I am dedicated to David Harrington for Lake Champlain history of decoys and most of my "leads". If I were obliged to dedicate this book to one person, it would be David. My thanks to Peter Mallett for his research of William Maxfield; to James Aiken for traveling from Michigan with his Wellington and Bacon decoys; to Gary Guyette for guidance in discrimination enabling me to pick and choose wisely; to Phillip DeLari-scheliere for his knowledge of "the locals"; to Joseph Duggan for parting with and giving me my first "Bacon" and for his long time collecting experiences; to Ruth and Frank Gage for the "Salls rig", to Herb Prakelt for his knowledge and some superb decoys; to J. Grier Clarke and Sanders Milens for their photographic expertise; to John Ouellet as my Anglo-French guide on forays into Canada and to Bob Shaw for pointing out my first Lake Champlain decoy and encouragement to put Lake Champlain decoy folk art on the map.

Introduction

My introduction to *Decoys of Lake Champlain* was accidental. In pursuit of a resource to identify a newly purchased decoy, I found one available publication. It was published in 1961, by the Shelburne Museum, Shelburne, Vermont (which houses one of the most important collections of decoys in the world) and titled *Decoys at Shelburne Museum*. In this publication there were only three to four references to Lake Champlain decoys and carvers. Yet the Lake is one of the largest fresh water bodies in North America and a major migratory flyway. Of significant mention in the museum text and worthy of quotation is a narrative report by the French explorer Baron Lahontan made in September, 1687. This incidentally, is the first written record of use of decoys in North America.

"In the beginning of September, I set out in a canow upon several rivers, marshes and pools that disembogue in the Champlain Lake, being accompany'd with thirty or forty of the savages that are very expert in shooting and hunting, and perfectly well acquainted with the proper places for finding waterfowl, deer and other sallow beasts. The first spot we took up was upon the side of a marsh or fen, of four or five leagues in circumference: and after we had fitted up our huts, the savages made huts upon water in several places. These huts were made of the branches and leaves of trees and contained three or four men. For a decoy they have the skins of geese, bustards and ducks, dryed and stuffed with hay. The two feet being made fast with two nails to a small place of light plank, which float around the hut. The place being frequented by wonderful numbers of geese, ducks, bustards, teals and an infinity of other waterfowls — see the stuffed skins swimming with their heads erected as if they were alive. They repair to the same place and so give the savages an opportunity of shooting them either flying or upon the water, after which the savages get into their canows and gather them up".

The next recorded historical facts of duck hunting on Lake Champlain are found in an article in the Burlington, Vermont Free Press dated November 10, 1883. Described, were the use of live decoys at the Sand Bar area of Malletts Bay, Vermont. The article also quoted a Grand Isle hunter who stated "I usually shoot four to five hundred ducks a year".

No other pertinent information has been apparently collected since that time. Hence the concept of *Decoys of Lake Champlain* was given birth and impetus.

Lake Champlain with the exception of the Great Lakes, is the largest of the deep, coldwater lakes in the United States. It is located along the boundry between the states of New York and Vermont, and extends northward into the Province of Quebec; southward to Whitehall, New York and connects via the Champlain Canal with the Hudson River. The lake is one hundred and nine miles long and has a surface area of four hundred and forty square miles. The shore line extends five hundred and eighty seven miles affording many sites for both waterfowl nesting and feeding. As such, significant wildlife management areas (W.M.A.) stretch the length of the lake beginning in Missisquoi Bay at the northern end. The State of Vermont established Mud Creek W.M.A. in Alburg, Vermont and Maquam Bay W.M.A. in Swanton, Vermont in 1953 and 1953 respectively. The Maquam Bay W.M.A. is located next to the Missisquoi Waterfowl Refuge, owned and operated by the U.S. Fish and Wildlife Service. The oldest W.M.A. is the Sandbar area of Malletts Bay, Vermont which is located in the town of Milton. It was established in 1920 and is noted as one of the finest hunting areas on the lake. Other areas are, Little Otter Creek W.M.A. in Ferrisburg; Dead Creek in Addison, Vermont which is the largest, 2,578 acres, and the major resting area for migratory Canada geese; and East Creek W.M.A. in Orwell, Vermont. On the New York or western side of the lake are located the Kings Bay W.M.A. in Champlain, N.Y.; and Ward Marsh W.M.A. in Whitehall, N.Y.

Resting, feeding and breeding in these areas are thousands of migratory ducks and geese. Most all major puddle ducks including mallards, blacks, pintails, teals and wood ducks are found on the lake. Divers, including goldeneye or whistlers, redheads, bluebills, canvasbacks and mergansers are also seen along with major flocks of Canadian geese.

It is of little wonder then that waterfowl hunting has been prevalent on the lake for over three hundred years. The use of decoys were necessary to attract the flying birds close enough to shoot from the hunters blind. They were made from locally available material such as cedar, pine and basswood. The decoys were created by local craftsmen, many of whom were boat builders, for their own use and also sold to local hunters. Design was influenced by artistic inclination, ethnic origin and use. Many decoys found near the Canadian end of the lake have French-Canadian influence; i.e. heavy head and wing carving, significant of the St. Lawrence River area. More traditionally however is the "Bacon" look; simplistic lines and smooth surfaces. George H. Bacon (1861-1925) decoys are considered the "classic" style of the lake and so influenced most carvers from the late 1800's to the present day.

This book not only is a reference to the more than seventy carvers found on the lake beginning in 1830 but an effort to amalgamate the effort of present day carvers to establish the "Lake Champlain look". Every major migratory area in the country and their decoys have a peculiar identifying quality beginning with the inletted heads of the Maine Coast, the hollow two piece construction of Barnegat Bay, the raised primaries of the Delaware River decoys to the painted eye decoys of the Chesepeake Bay.

Decoys of Lake Champlain will hopefully aid collectors, dealers and anyone interested in identifying decoys and give impetus to the historical significance of an important folk art.

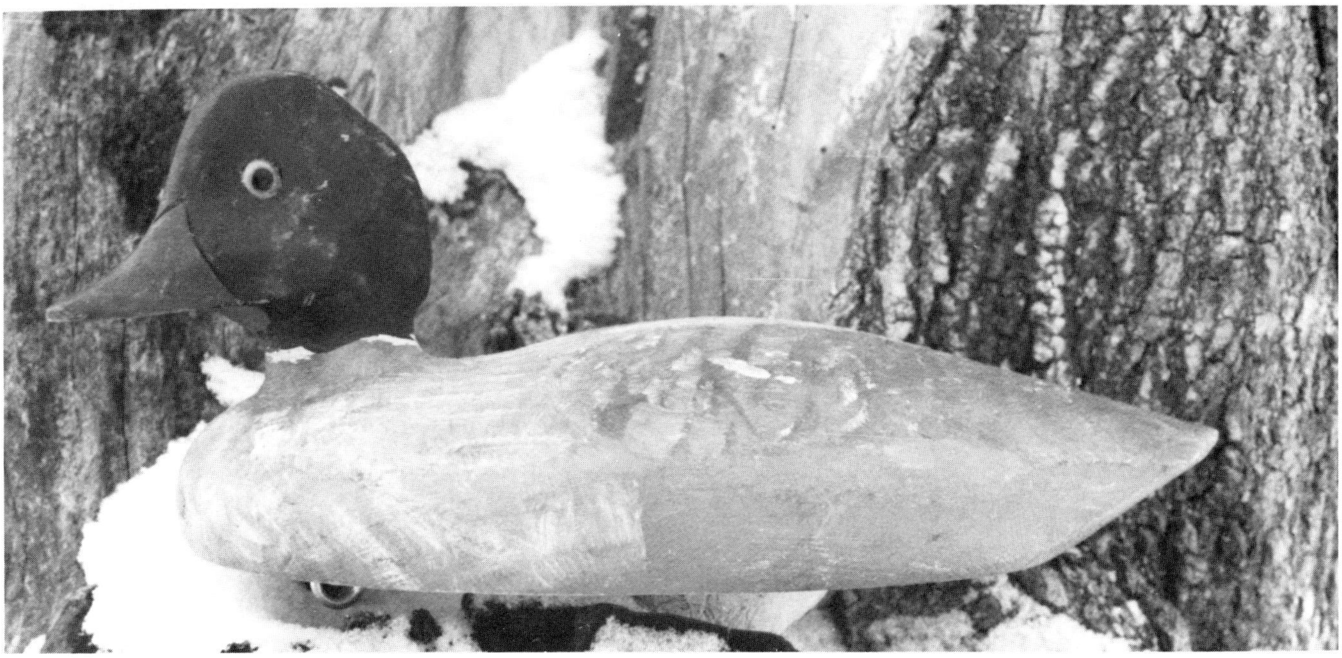

Goldeneye hen by John "Dick" Adams, Grand Isle, Vermont. Ca. 1950. Solid cedar, original paint, collection of Dick Adams.

John "Dick" Adams 1935 — Grand Isle, Vermont started carving as a boy scout to qualify for a merit badge in 1948. Since that beginning Dick has carved hundreds of working and decorative birds. He has won numerous competitions and today carves only decoratives. Adams' attributes being strongly influenced by his father, and Archie Bodette (Page 23) (Note similarity of whistler (Page 23) to Bodette's work). Adams decoys are further noted for his relief style and strong paint.

Greenwing teal drake by Dick Adams, Grand Isle, Vermont. Decorative style, preening. Solid cedar ca. 1965. Collection of Dick Adams.

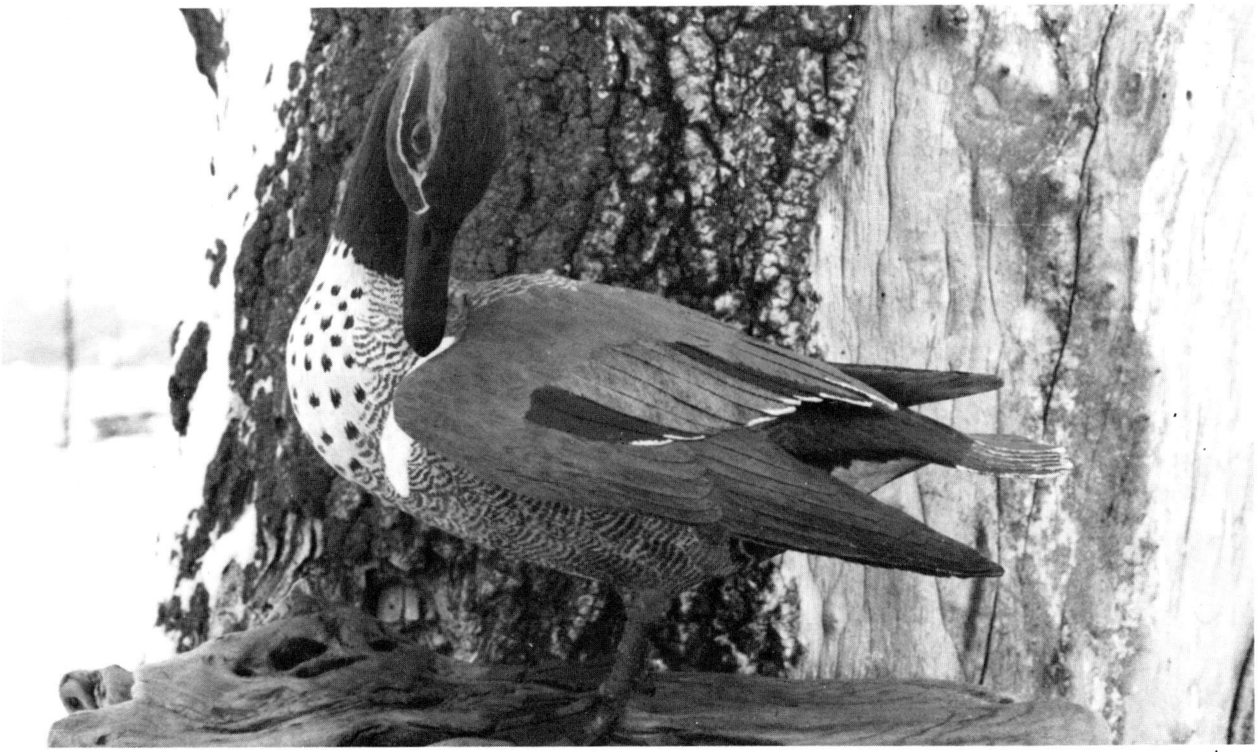

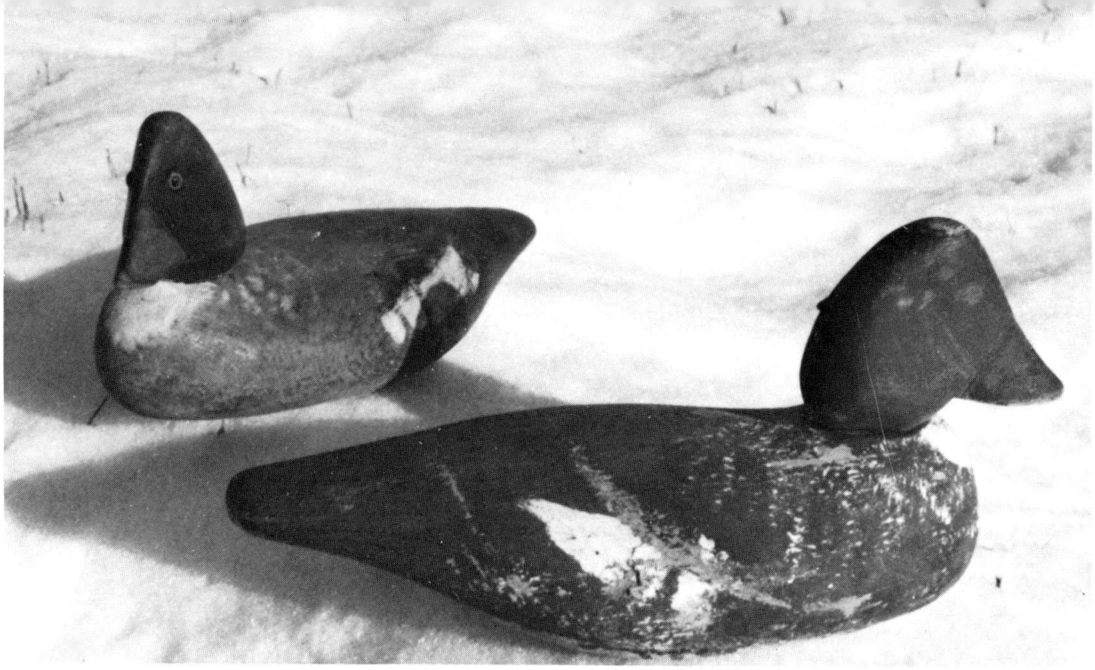

Goldeneye hens by Wellington Aiken ca. 1905, solid pine, painted eyes, and original paint. Collection of Loy S. Harrell.

Wellington Aiken 1879-1954. Hunted over by his son Robert Aiken M.D. Former Health Commissioner, State of Vermont. Wellington, a 1901 graduate of The University of Vermont and later a Professor Emeritus in English, was influenced by the style and paint of George Bacon (Page 12). Simple body style with wedge shaped heads are recognized as peculiar to Lake Champlain. Part of the treasured possession of the Aiken family include decoys by both their grandfathers and George Bacon.

James W. Aiken 1943 — Shelburne, Vermont. James the grandson of Wellington Aiken, grew up in the tradition of duck hunting on Lake Champlain and carving his own rig. As a physician he still finds time to actively carve. His whistlers are hollow basswood and pine construction and stamped J.W.A.

Goldeneye drake by James W. Aiken.

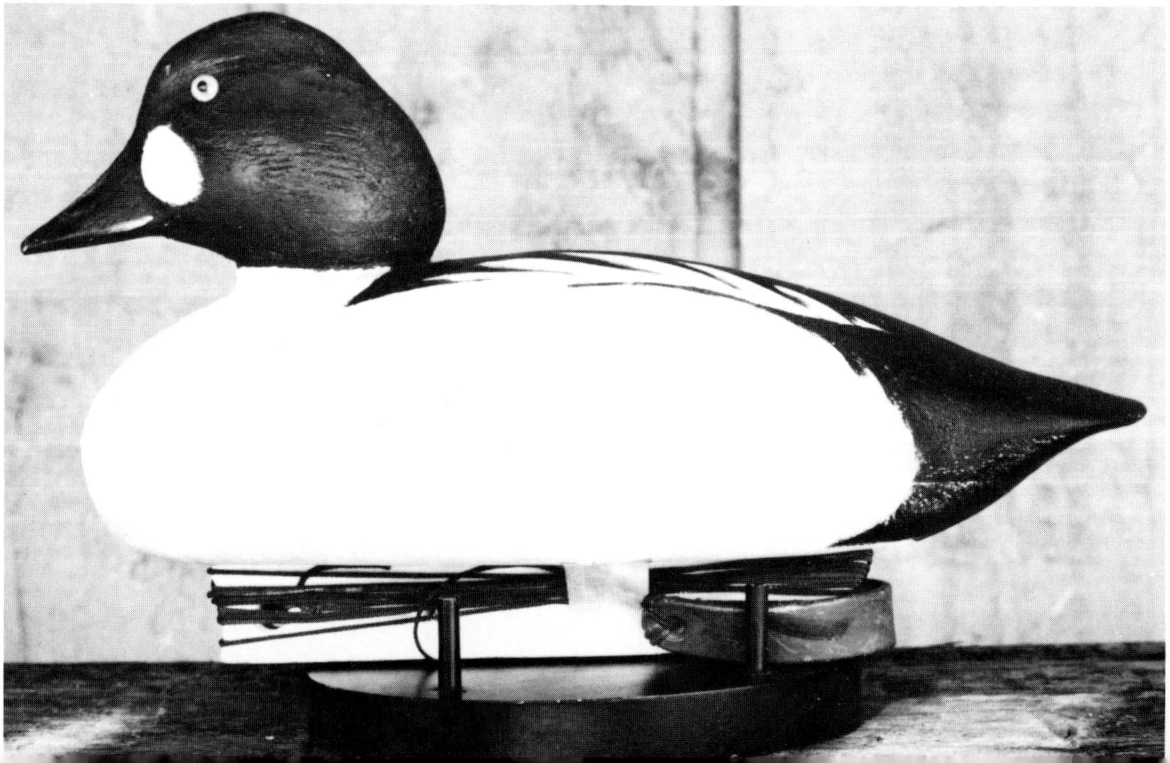

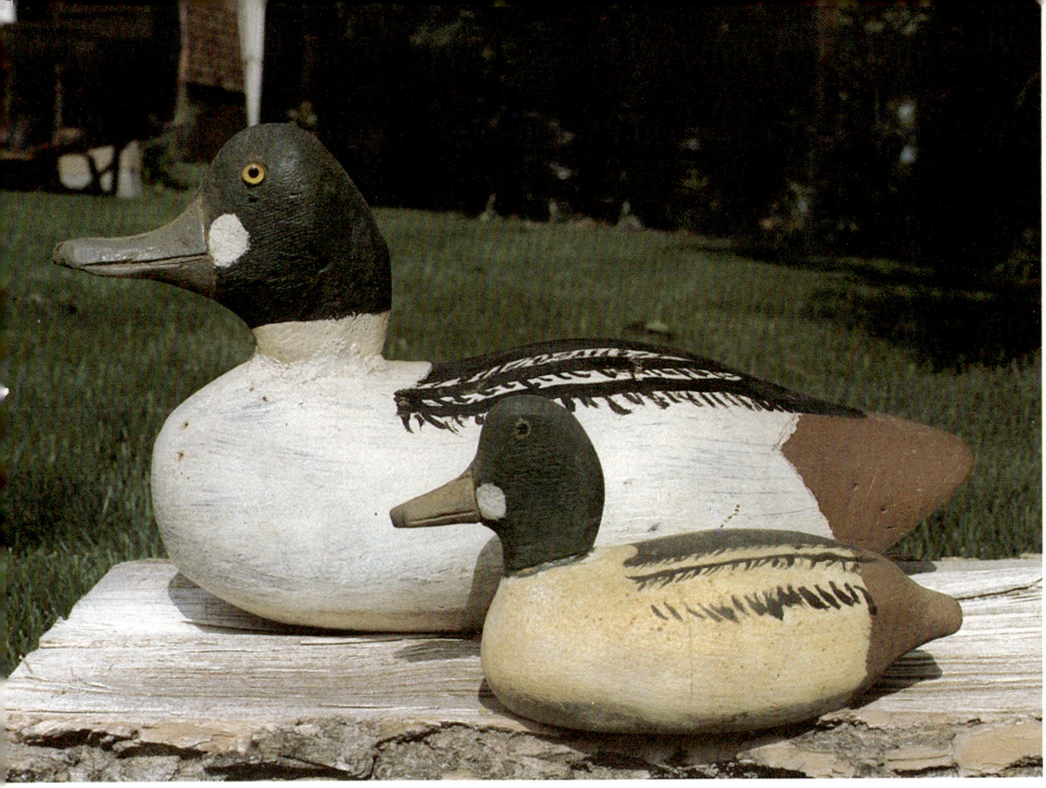

Goldeneye drake by Stanley Averill, Champlain, New York. Solid cedar, original paint. Ca. 1940. Working drake, collection of James Averill — Miniature, collection of Loy S. Harrell.

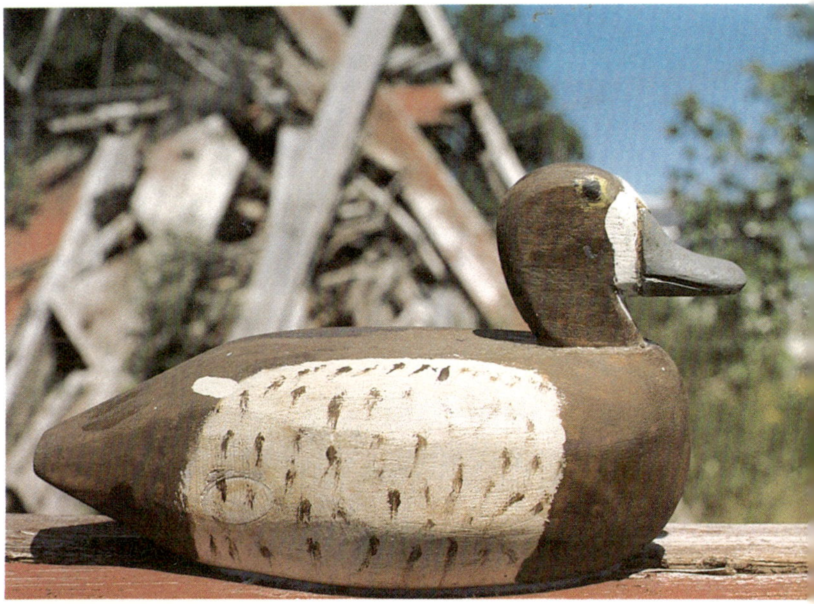

Bluebill hen by Stanley Averill. 1/3 size. Original paint. Collection of R. Cheeseman.

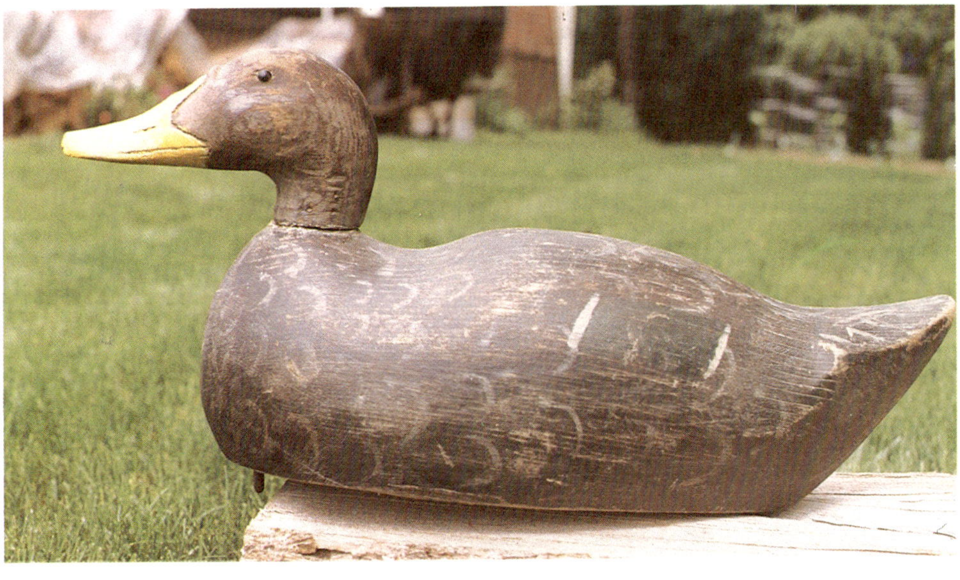

Black duck by Stanley Averill, Champlain, New York. Solid cedar, ca. 1945. This decoy, as well as his other blacks, are very similar to Mason premier grade. Collection of James Averill.

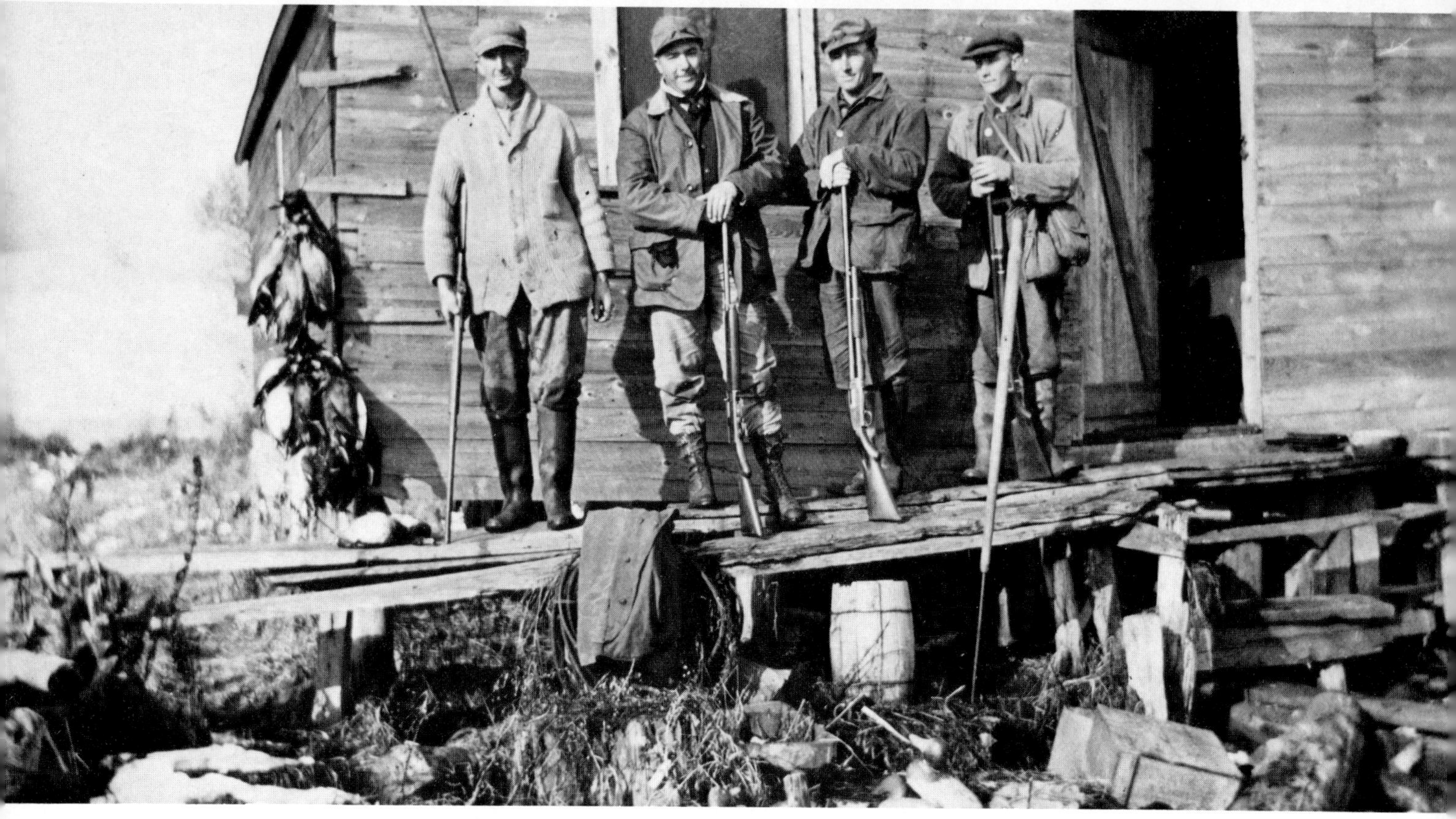

Hunting "shack", Stoney Point, New York, Lake Champlain ca. 1917. (Note days shooting results hanging on left side). Pictured second from left is James Averill 1846-1928 and at his left side, Stanley Averill 1900-1982. Photo courtesy of James Averill.

Stanley Averill 1900-1982 Champlain, New York. Averill was known to spend many cold winter evenings next to his wood stove carving decoys using discarded cedar telephone poles. He sculptured hundreds of blacks, whistlers and bluebills. Stanley was the hunting companion of his father James and both carved decoys for their rig which was used primarily at Point Au Fer, and Stoney Point, Lake Champlain, New York. Averill's decoys appear hand hewn and "folky". All working birds had glass eyes. Averill worked forty-one years at Sheridon Iron Works, Champlain, New York.

Bluebill hen by Stanley Averill, Champlain, New York. Solid cedar, glass eyes, original paint ca. 1945. Collection of James Averill.

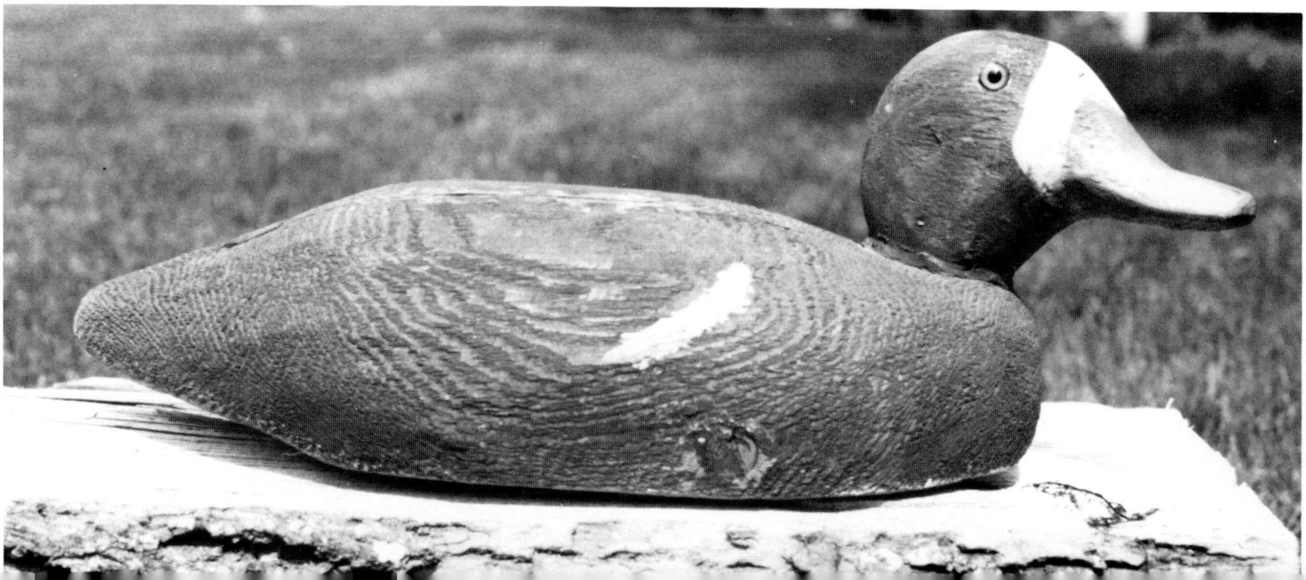

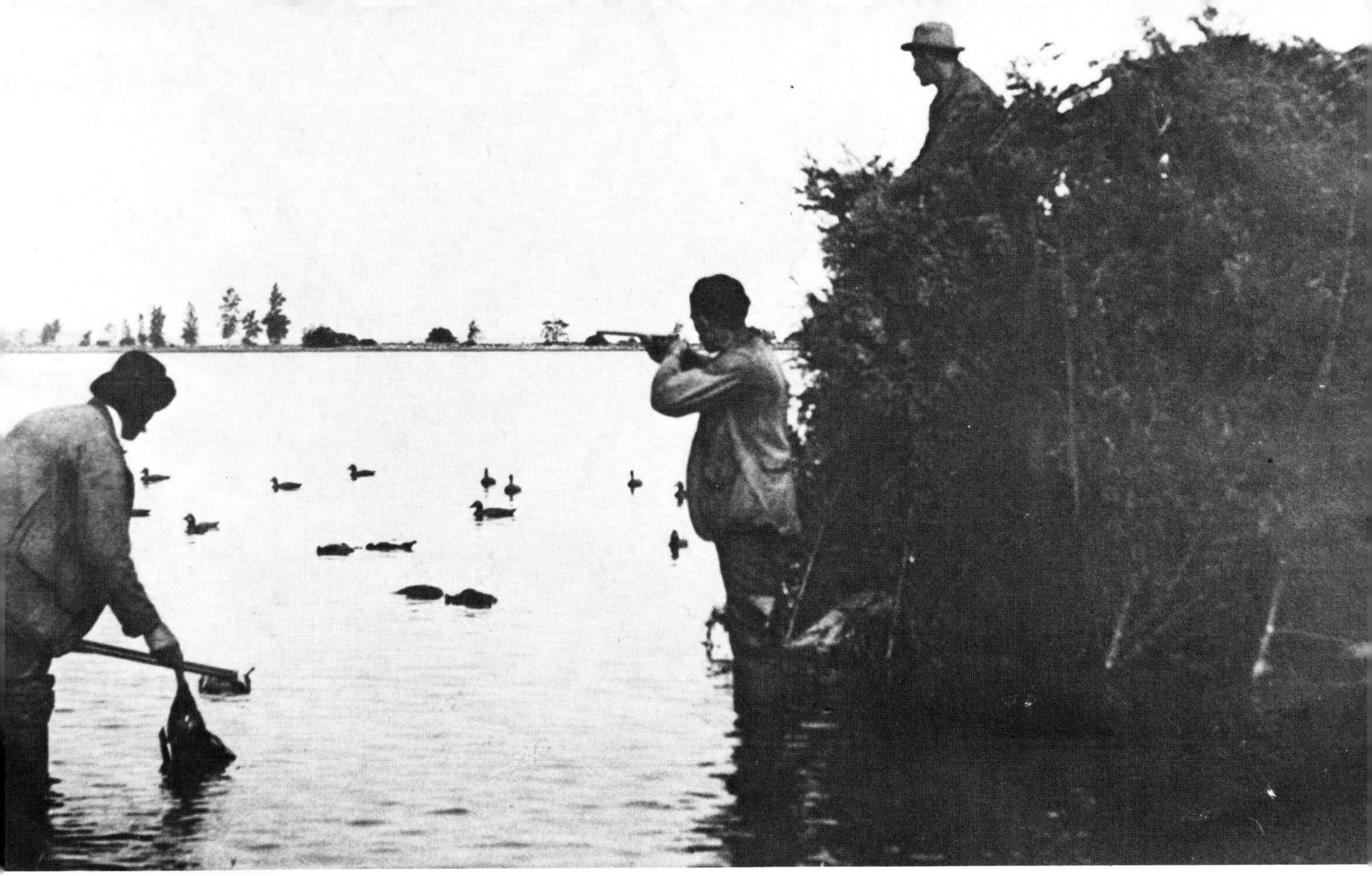

Photograph taken at mouth of Lamoille river, Sand Bar, Lake Champlain, Vermont. Dated Oct. 11, 1882. Left to right: George Bacon, E.E. Bean, and R. Richards. Note Bacon decoys and apparent ease which ducks are decoyed in. Photograph courtesy of Arthur Toutant.

George H. Bacon 1861-1925, Burlington, Vermont, decoys are considered the most collectible and valued of all Lake Champlain carvers. His decoys are featured in the world renowned collection of the Shelburne Museum, Shelburne, Vermont. Bacon influenced most Lake Champlain carvers and the "Bacon style" is associated with the area. Bacon, who lived on Converse Court, Burlington, worked at the Blodgett Company where he sold decoys and guided many of the corporate directors. He also made and sold decoys to "Whites Sporting Goods" store in Burlington during the early 1900's.

Simple, smooth style and paint, (Bacon used a worn whisk broom to apply white stippling to his hen whistlers), the characteristic wedge shaped heads, small glass eyes, three to four inch tear drop lead weight, leather loop to secure the anchor line and a cork plug in the dowel opening are all requisites for an authentic Bacon decoy. His bluebills are often found with "G.H. Bacon" stencilled on the bottom. Bacon carved twenty hen whistlers for every two drakes. Because hens and drakes look closely alike for the first two years and their migratory habits on Lake Champlain, Bacon felt the need to carve mostly hens. Several hundred whistlers and close to seventy bluebills were carved. Only one Bacon black duck is known to the author. Bacon also made and patented fishing lures. In the author's collection is a spinner marked "G.H. Bacon 1900."

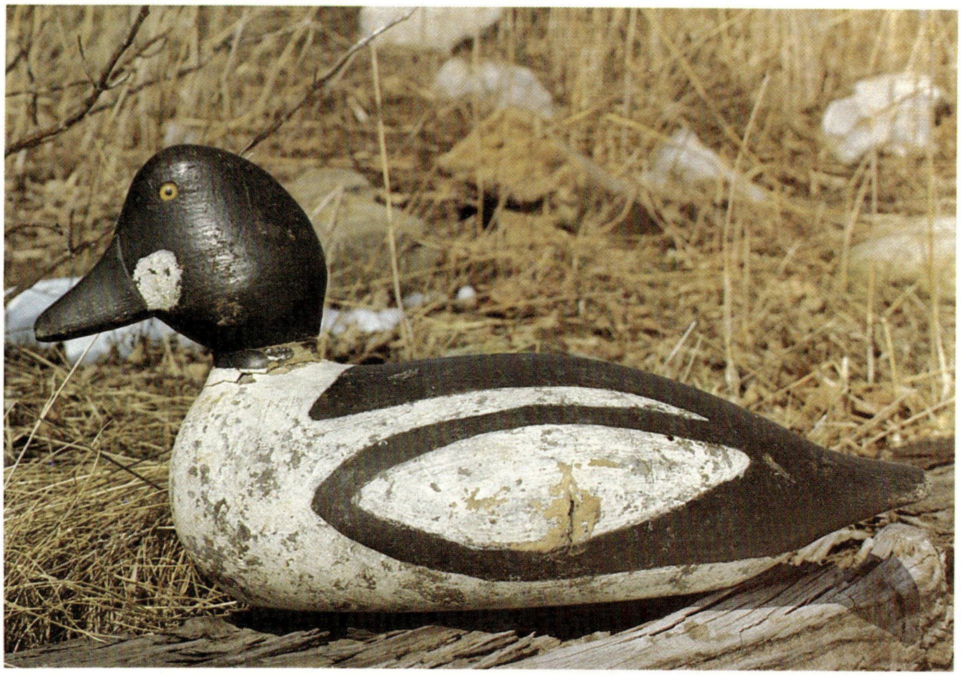

Opposite page top:
Goldeneye hen by George Bacon. This decoy is from the Henry Salls, 1873-1970, Frank Gage, 1910-rig, Colchester, Vermont. It is signed "A.G. Fournier, Burlington, Vermont." Fournier is listed in the 1915 Burlington City Directory as a tailor and merchant of mens wear with his store on Cherry Street. George Bacon worked then at Nelson Jones Grocery on College Street near Fournier whom he hunted with. Decoy body is probably a special order Mason. It is uncertain whether Bacon designed this decoy after a Mason special order or perhaps the Mason was designed from Bacon's model. Collection of Loy S. Harrell.

Goldeneye drake by George Bacon, Burlington, Vermont. Signed R.L. Patrick (1876-1953) former owner of Blodgett Co. and dated "88" on weight. Original paint. Has unusual wedge between head and body to give alert appearance. Collection of Loy S. Harrell.

Goldeneye hen by George Bacon. Original paint, mint condition. Ca. 1910. Rare low head style. Collection of Loy S. Harrell.

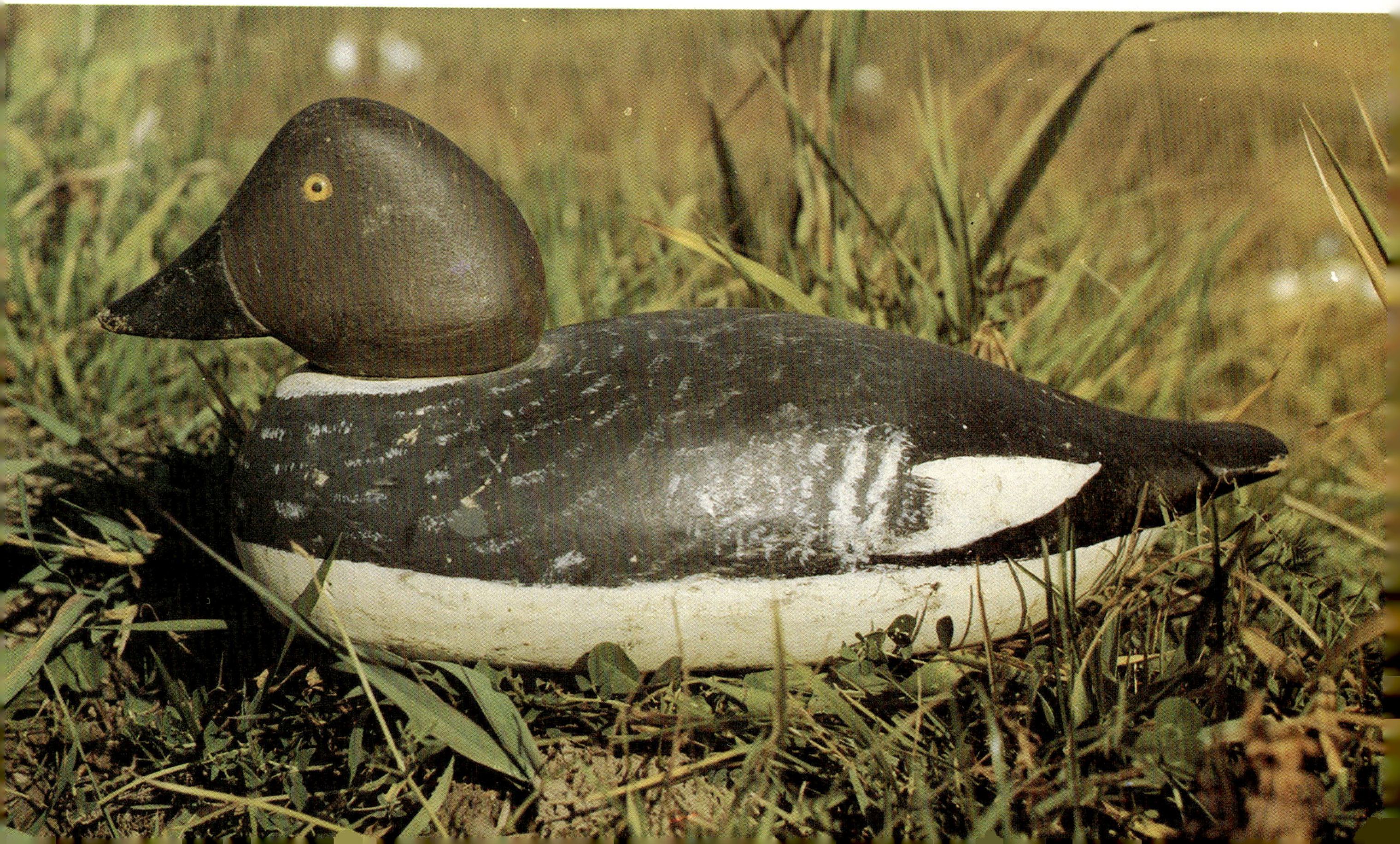

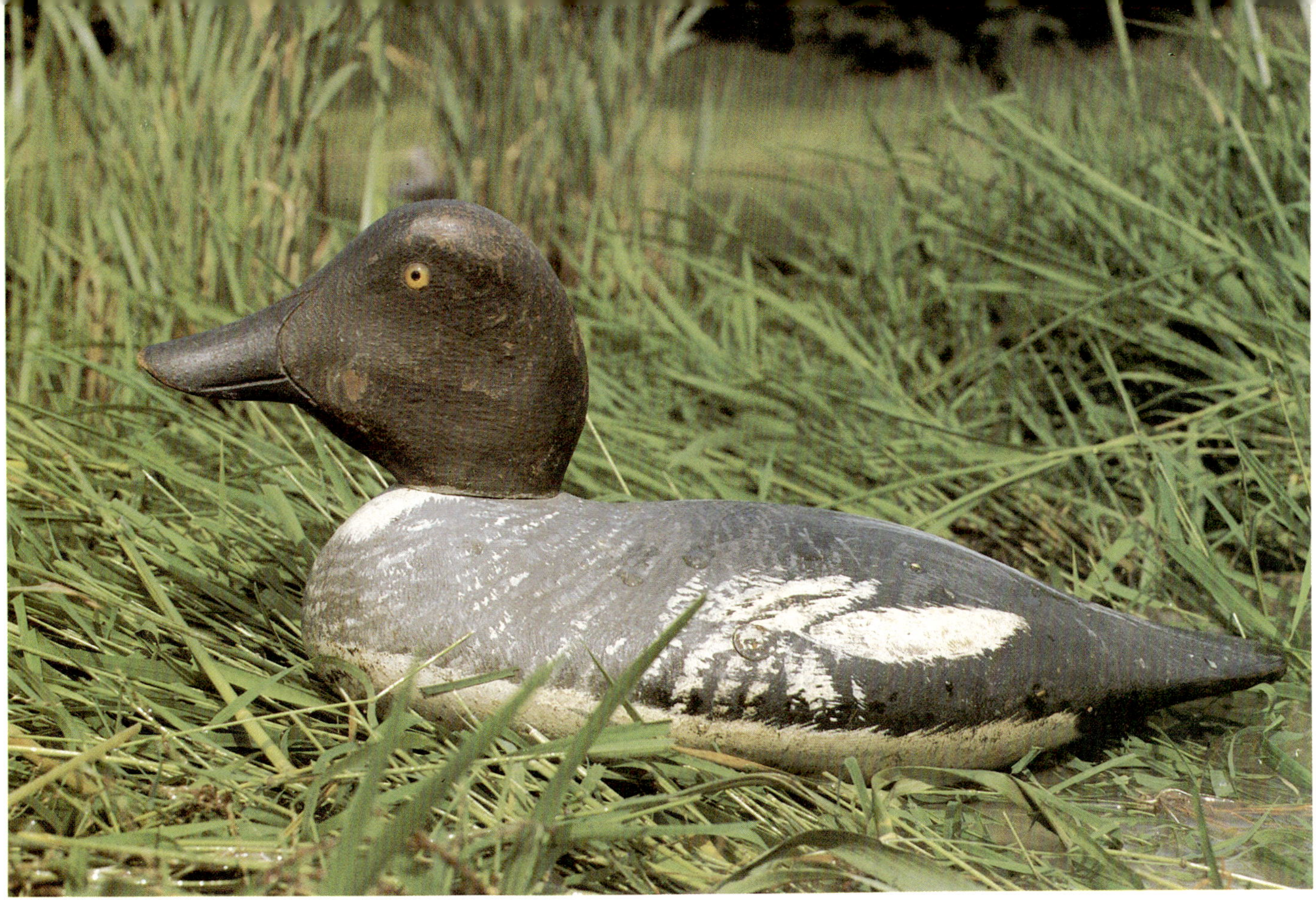

Bluebill by George Bacon, early style ca. 1885. Original paint and solid body. Used in marshes near sand bar park, Lake Champlain. Formerly in Roy Bull collection.

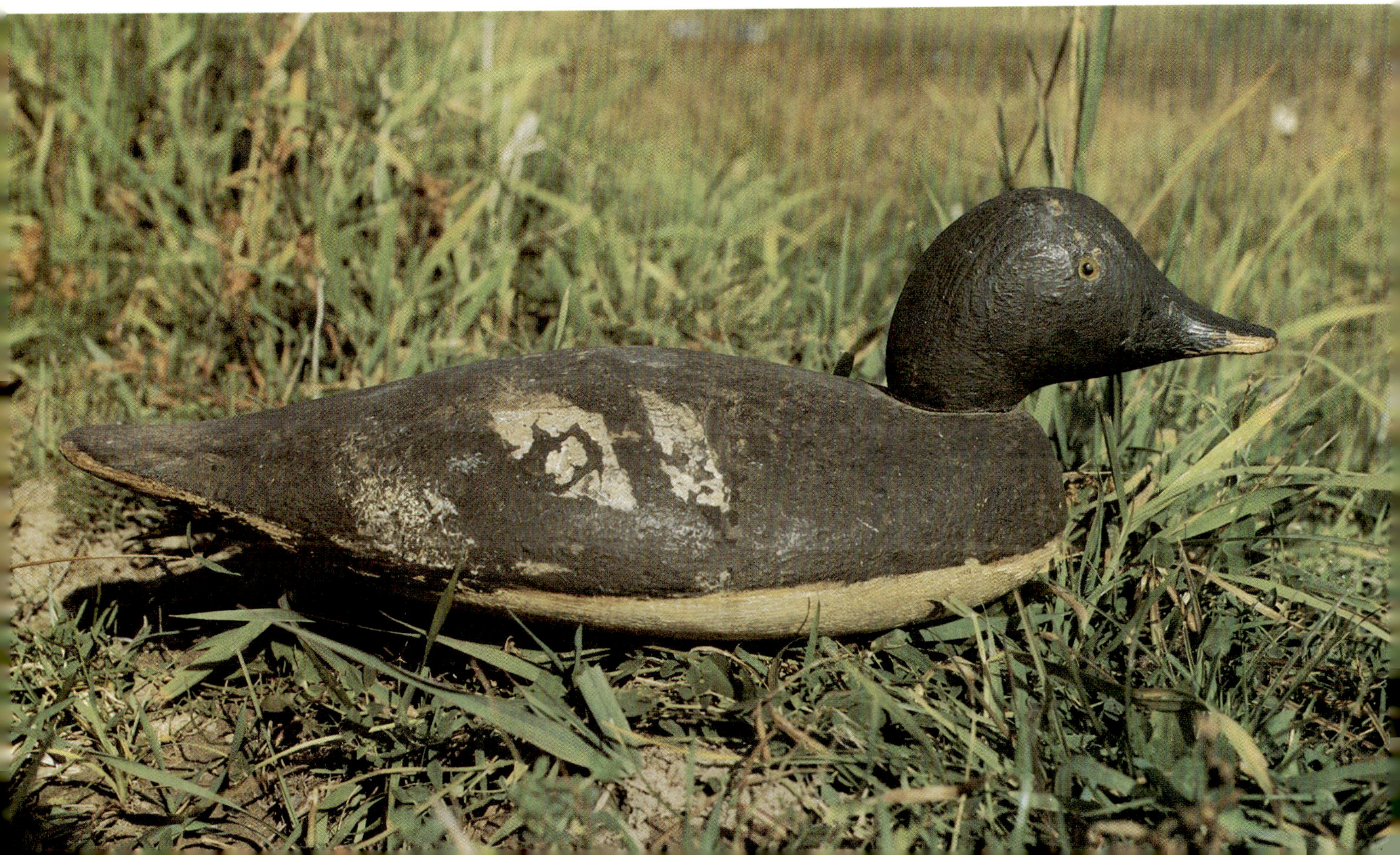

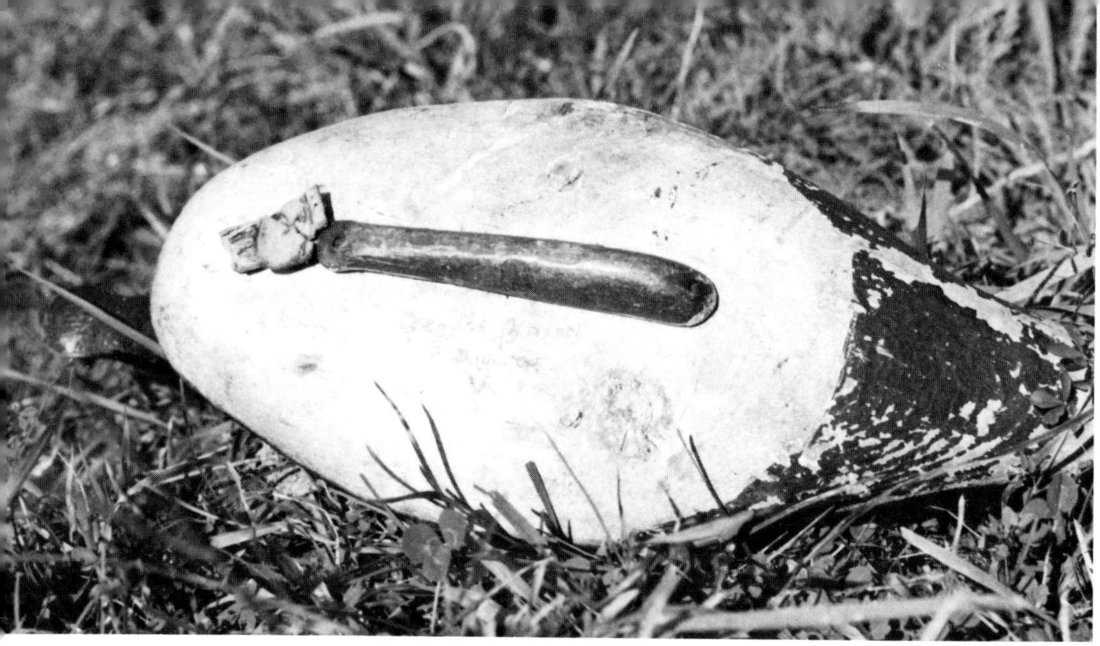

Botton view of Bacon bluebill (Page 13). Note characteristic tear drop weight, leather thong and cork plug.

Bluebill drake by George Bacon, Burlington, Vermont. Original paint, solid pine, and glass eyes. Ca. 1900. Collection of James W. Aiken.

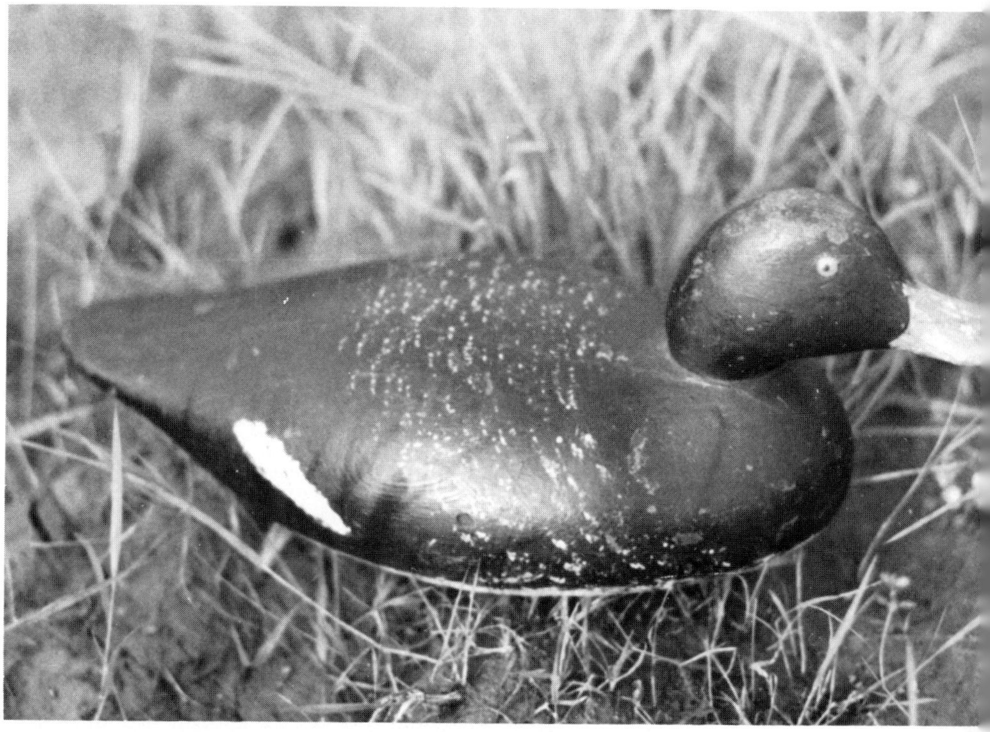

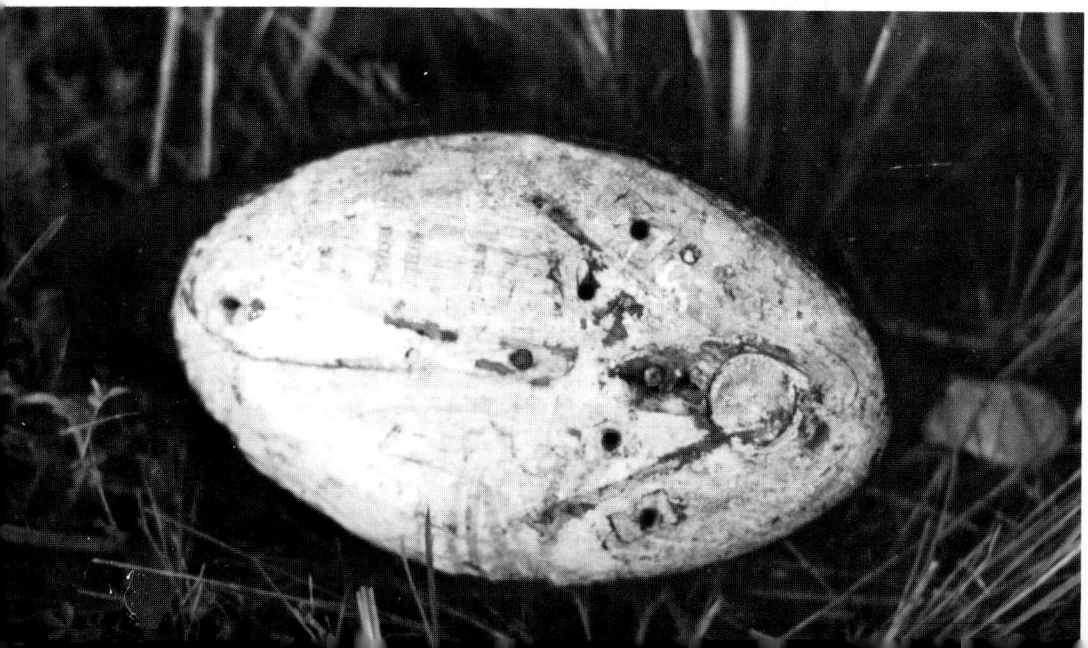

Bottom view of bluebill. George Bacon (above) stenciled *G.H. Bacon*. Note outline of weight and cork plug.

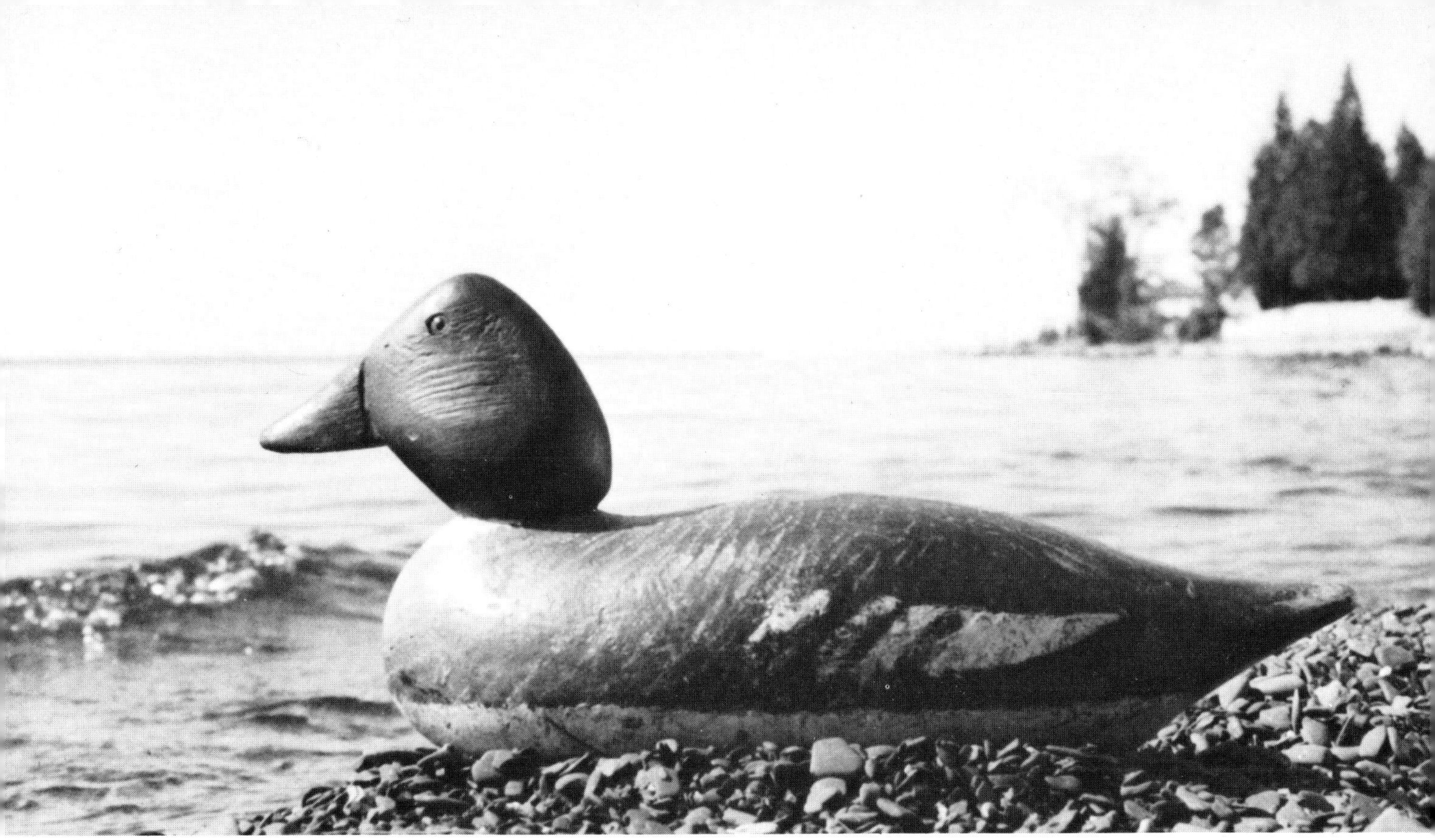

Goldeneye hen by George Bacon. Original paint ca. 1900. Collection of David Hoag. Photo taken from western shore of Grand Isle, Vermont.

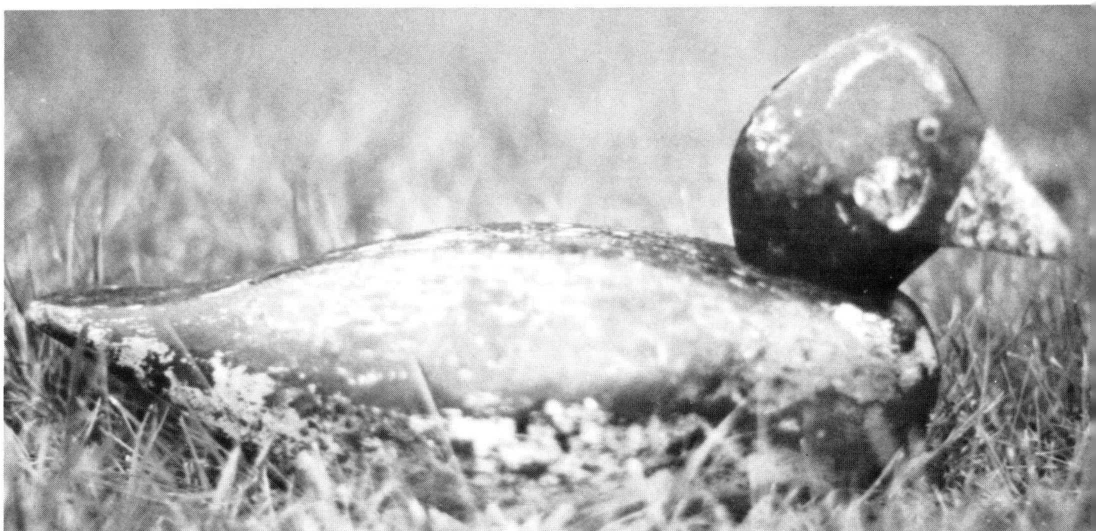

Rare goldeneye drake by George Bacon. Old repaint taken down to original. Collection of Daniel Beauregard.

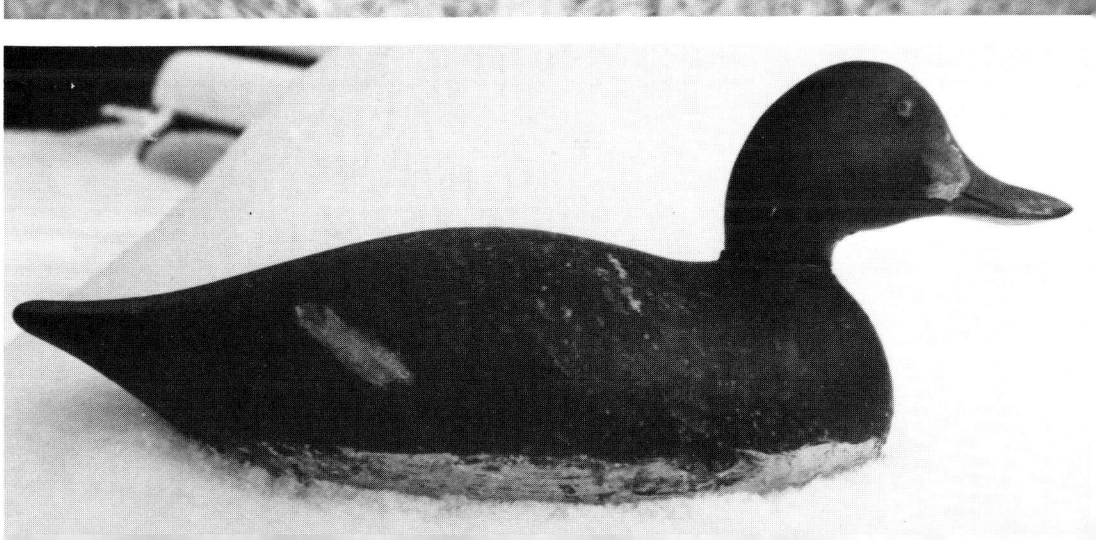

Scaup by George H. Bacon — stenciled "G.H. BACON" on bottom. Original paint. Collection of Jeb Sharrow.

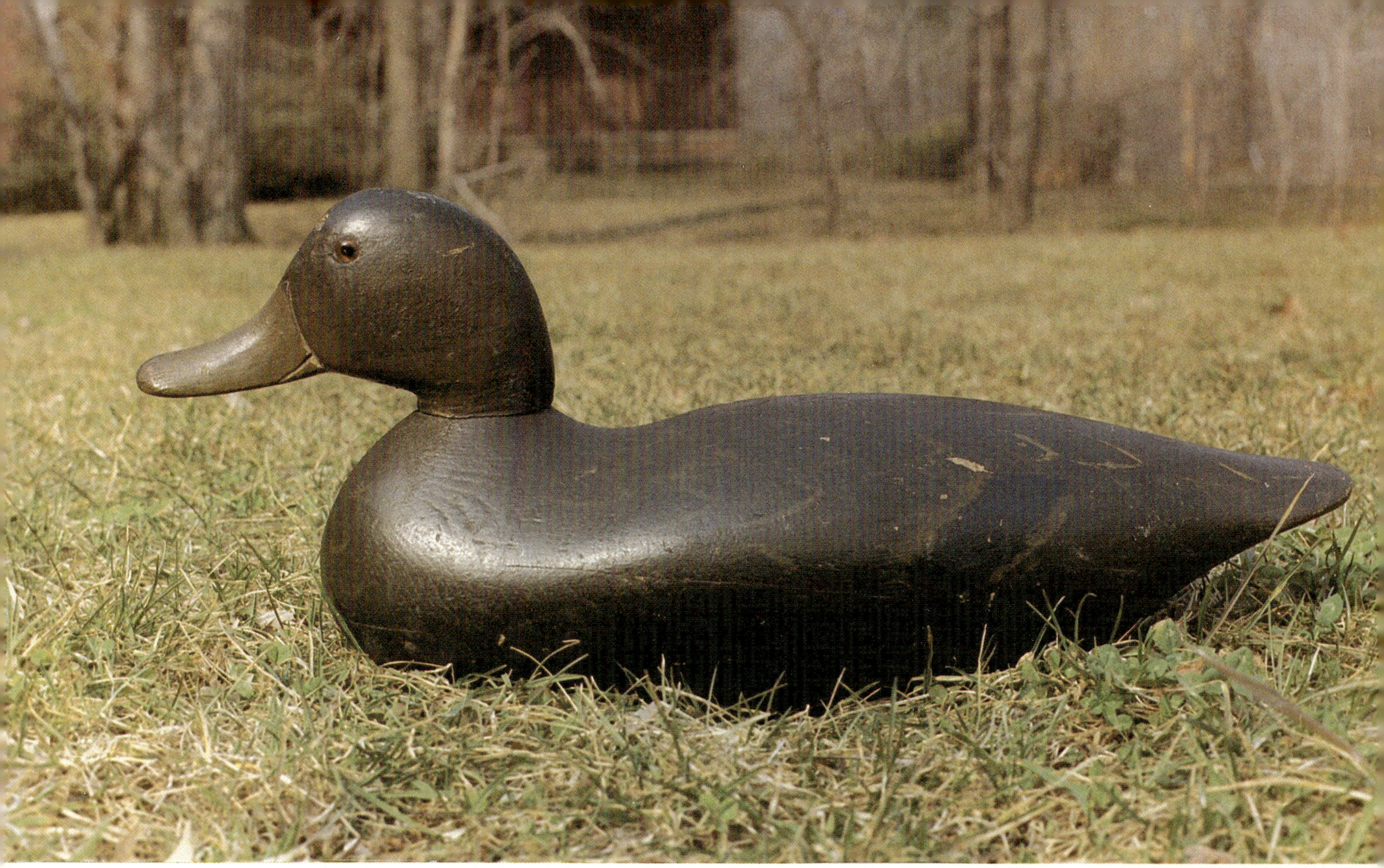

Black duck by George Bacon. This decoy was formerly in the collection of Charles "Dusty" Farnum who was associated with the Dorset House, Shelburne Museum. Body is a Mason while head style and paint are assuredly by Bacon. A rare decoy. Collection of John and Daniel Farnum.

Goldeneye pair by George H. Bacon ca. 1915. Made for "Whites Sporting Goods." Collection of Loy S. Harrell.

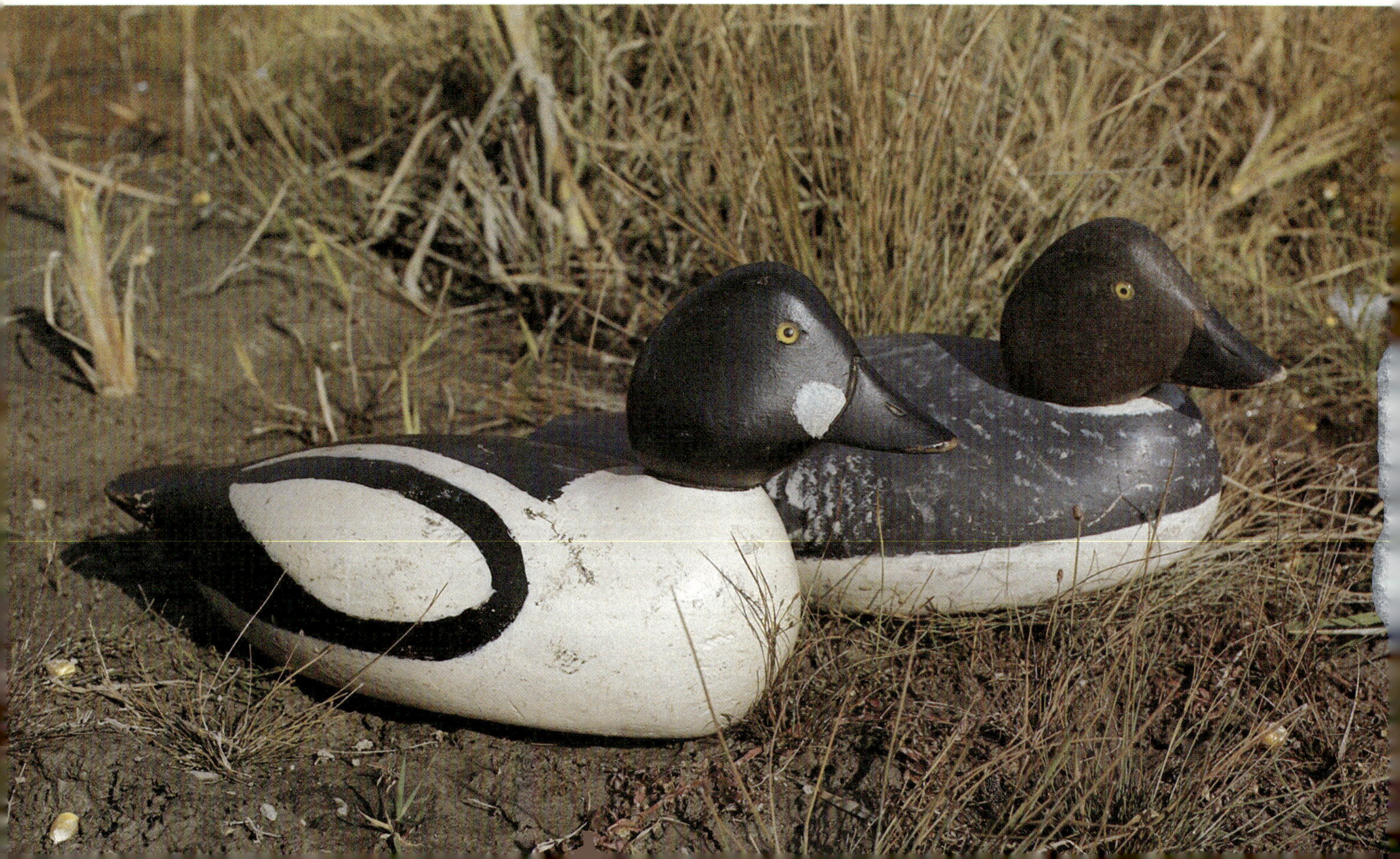

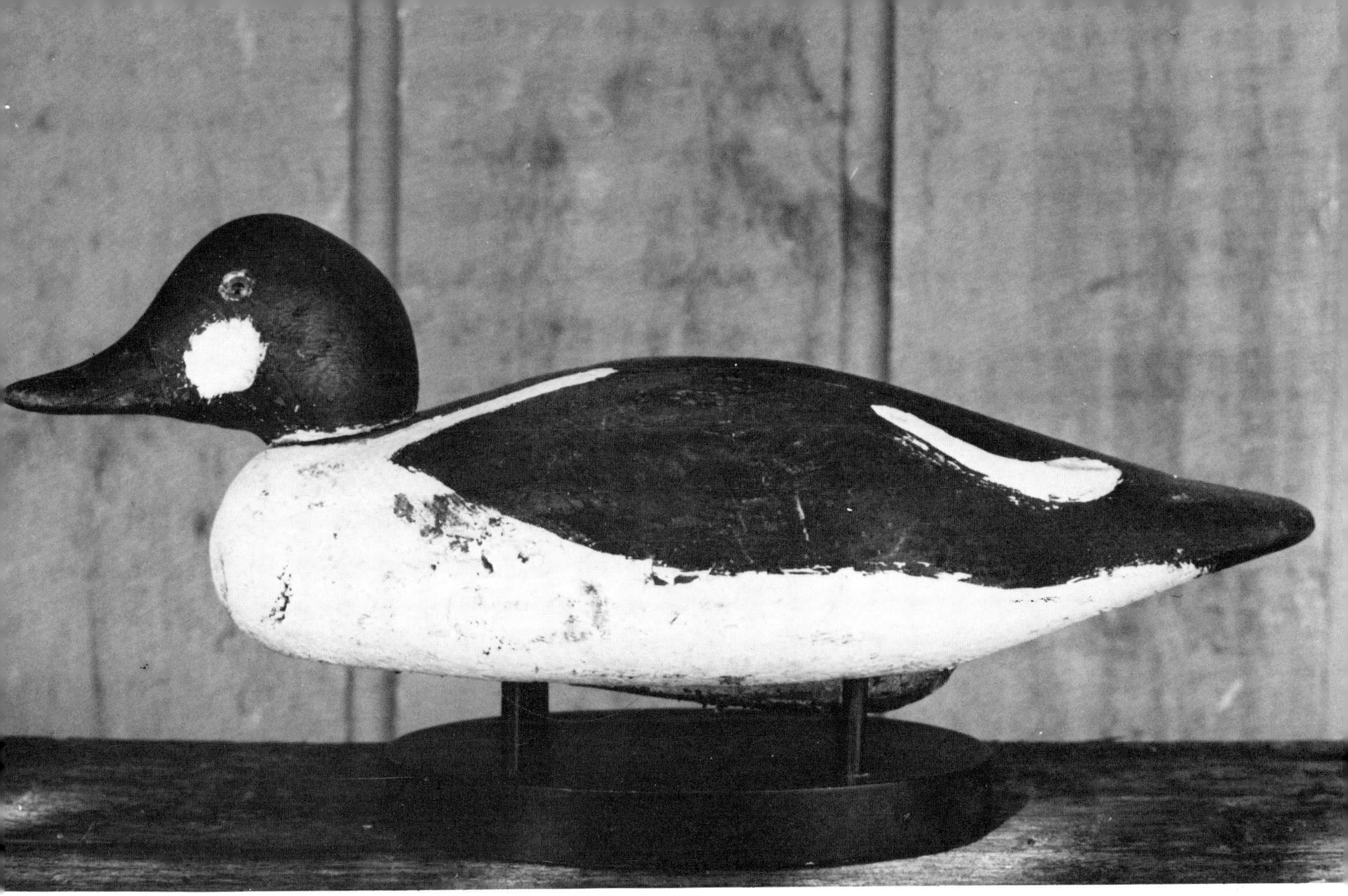

Goldeneye drake by George H. Bacon. Old repaint, originally painted as a scaup. Ca. 1915.

Goldeneye drake by George H. Bacon ca. 1890. Taken down to original paint. Heavier body style than his later carvings. Collection of William Mercia.

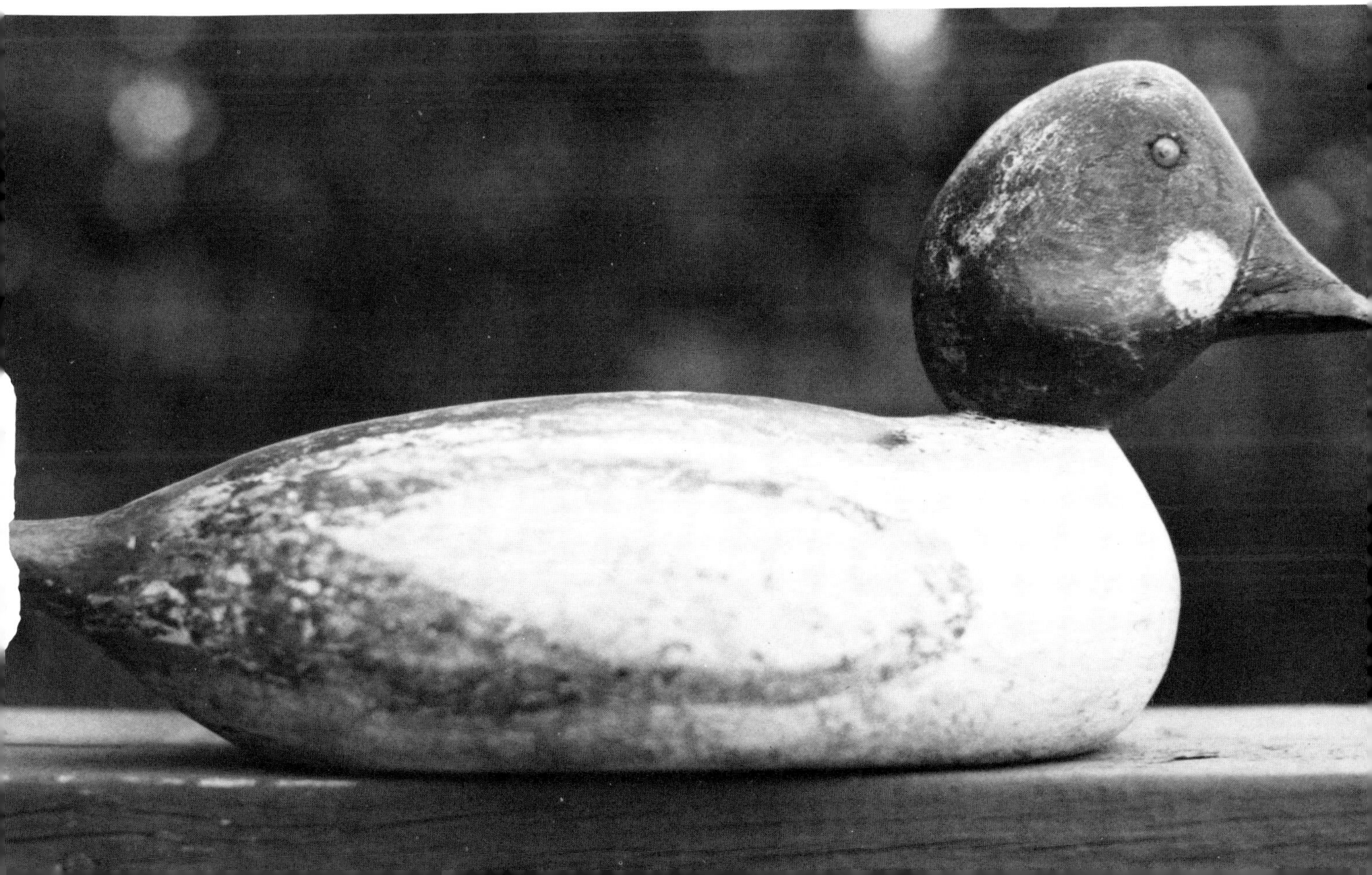

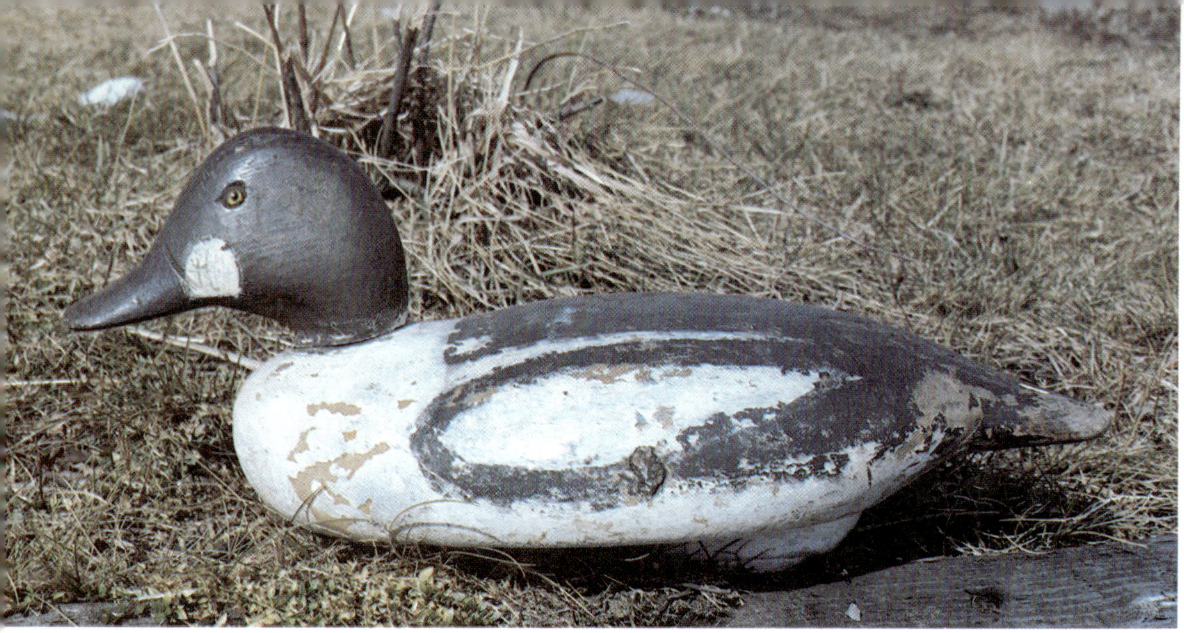

Goldeneye drake. This decoy was no doubt painted by George Bacon. Occasional birds of various body forms are found with Bacon paint or eyes. Branded on bottom "C.E. IRVING", noted Burlington area gunner who was a close friend of Bacon.

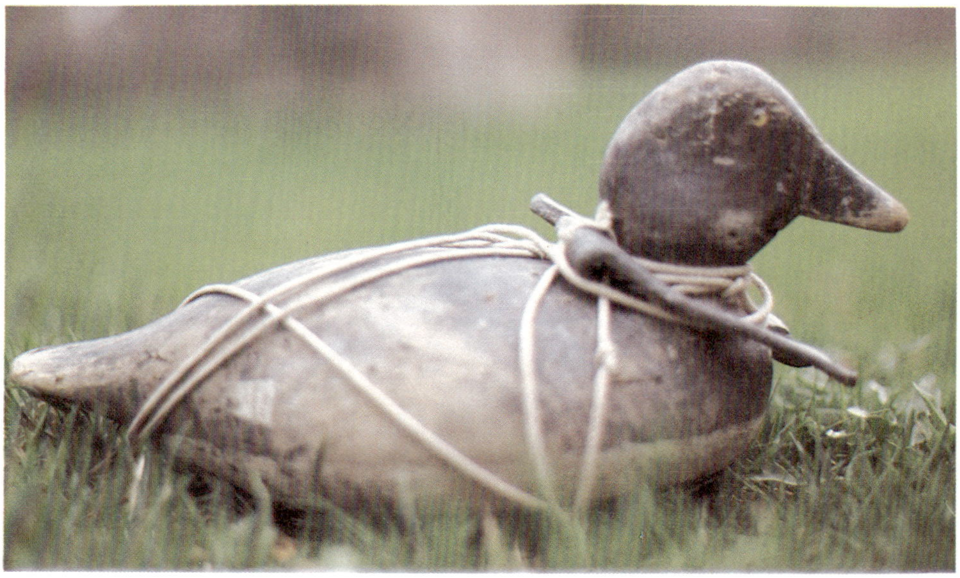

Goldeneye hen by George H. Bacon from the rig of George Spear, Grand Isle, Vermont. Spear dug this decoy from a gunny sack for the photograph.

Bluebill hen by George Bacon. Taken down to original paint. Ca. 1910. Collection of Loy S. Harrell.

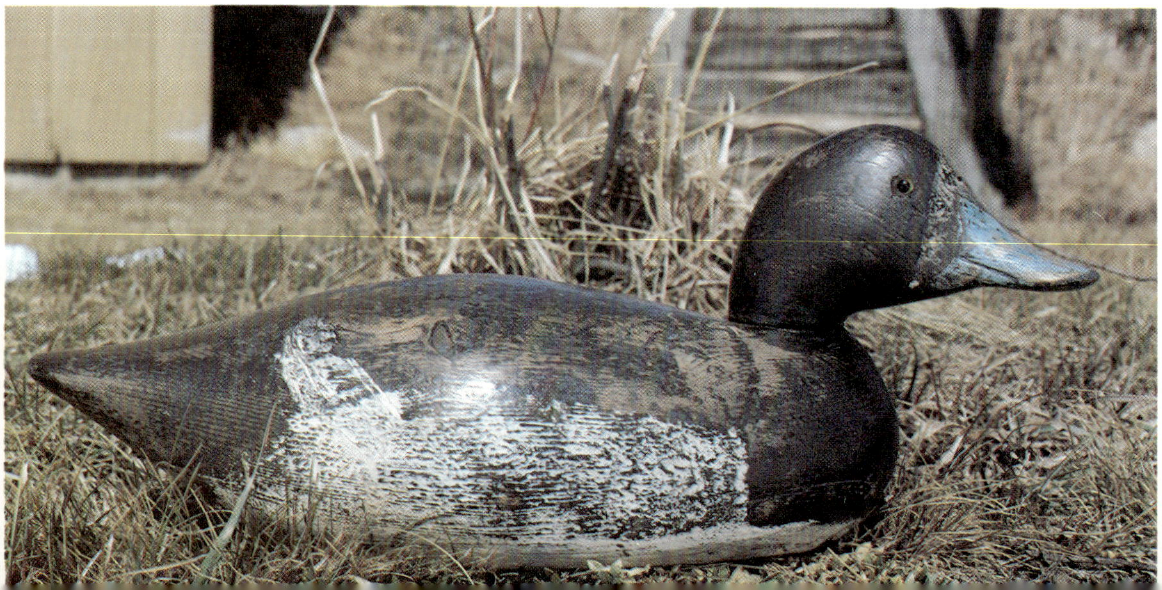

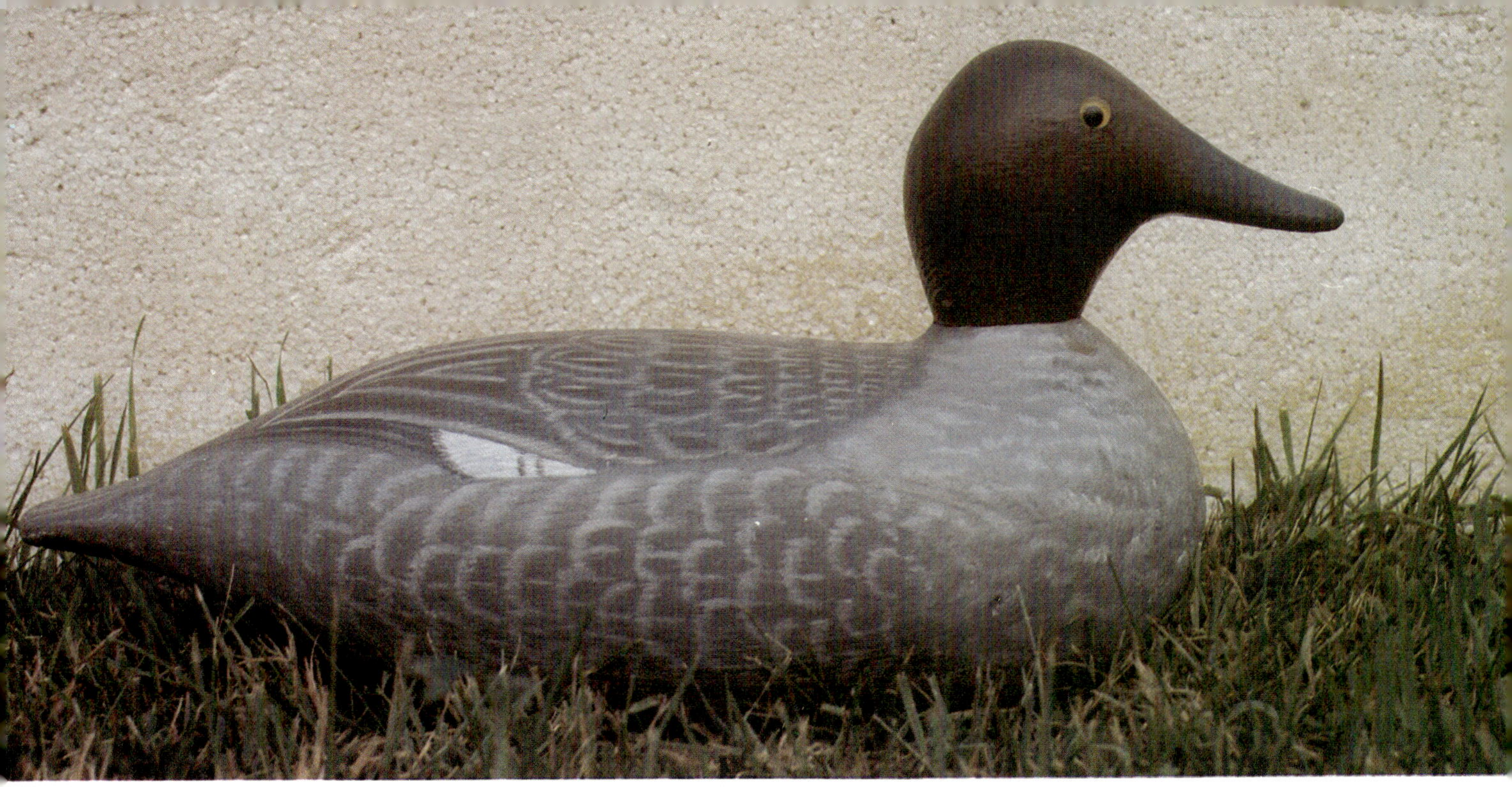

Goldeneye hen by Frank X. Baraby, Milton, Vermont. This decoy was repainted by Robert Lasher. Carved ca. 1910. Collection of George Baraby.

Frank X. Baraby 1883-1973 a tin smith by trade, Baraby was always well known for "whittling something". He grew up in St. Albans and Milton, Vermont, and was an avid hunter and fisherman. His decoys were roughed out of basswood and cedar and refined with a draw-shave. Baraby carved three to four hundred duck decoys and many fish decoys.

A characteristic of his duck decoys is a rectangular and recessed poured weight. His carvings are a real plus for any collection.

Group of six fish decoys made by F.X. Baraby. Used on upper Lake Champlain for ice fishing ca. 1925. Collection of Frank Baraby.

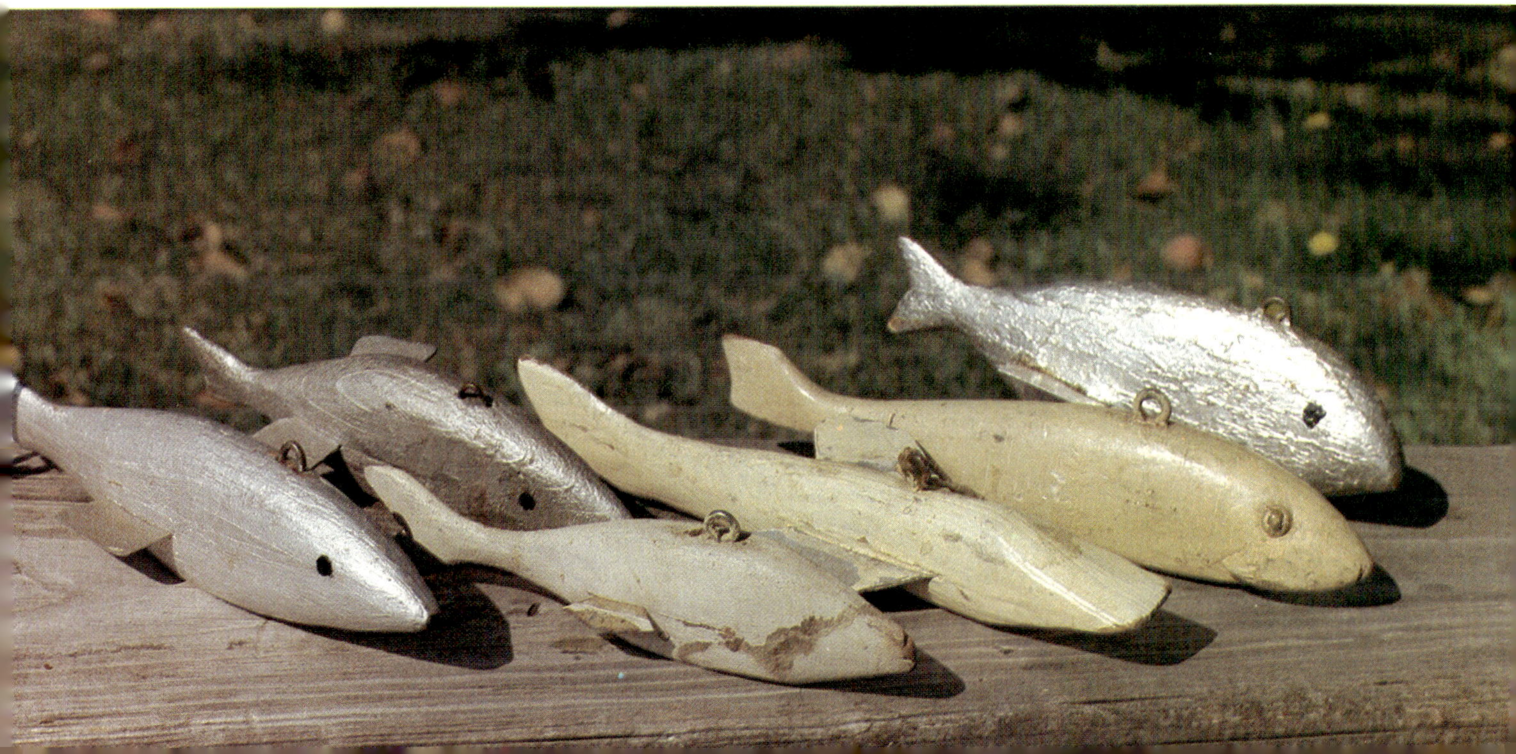

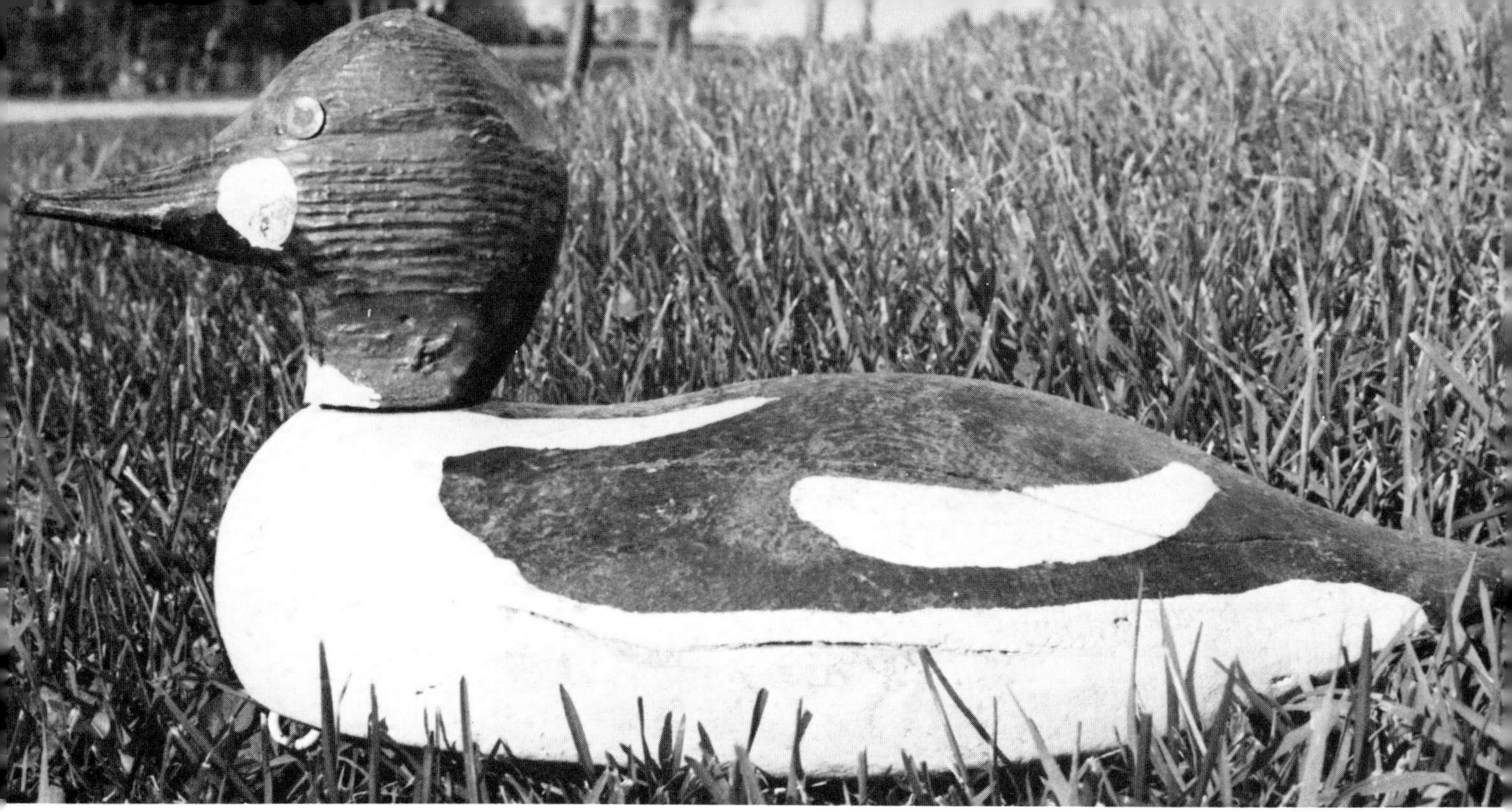

Goldeneye drake by Walla Bruley, Isle La Motte, Vermont.
Ca. 1940, old repaint. Collection of Douglas Patenaude.

Walla Bruley 1906-1958, Isle La Motte, Vermont. Situated in the northeast area of Lake Champlain, Isle La Motte lies in the middle of the migratory flyway. For its residents, duck hunting is a way of life. Bruley was no exception and while confined most of his life to a wheelchair carved many duck and fish decoys. He also made fishing lures and sold them commercially throughout the islands. Bruley was never known to go fishing and come home empty-handed.

Fish decoy by Walla Bruley ca. 1945.

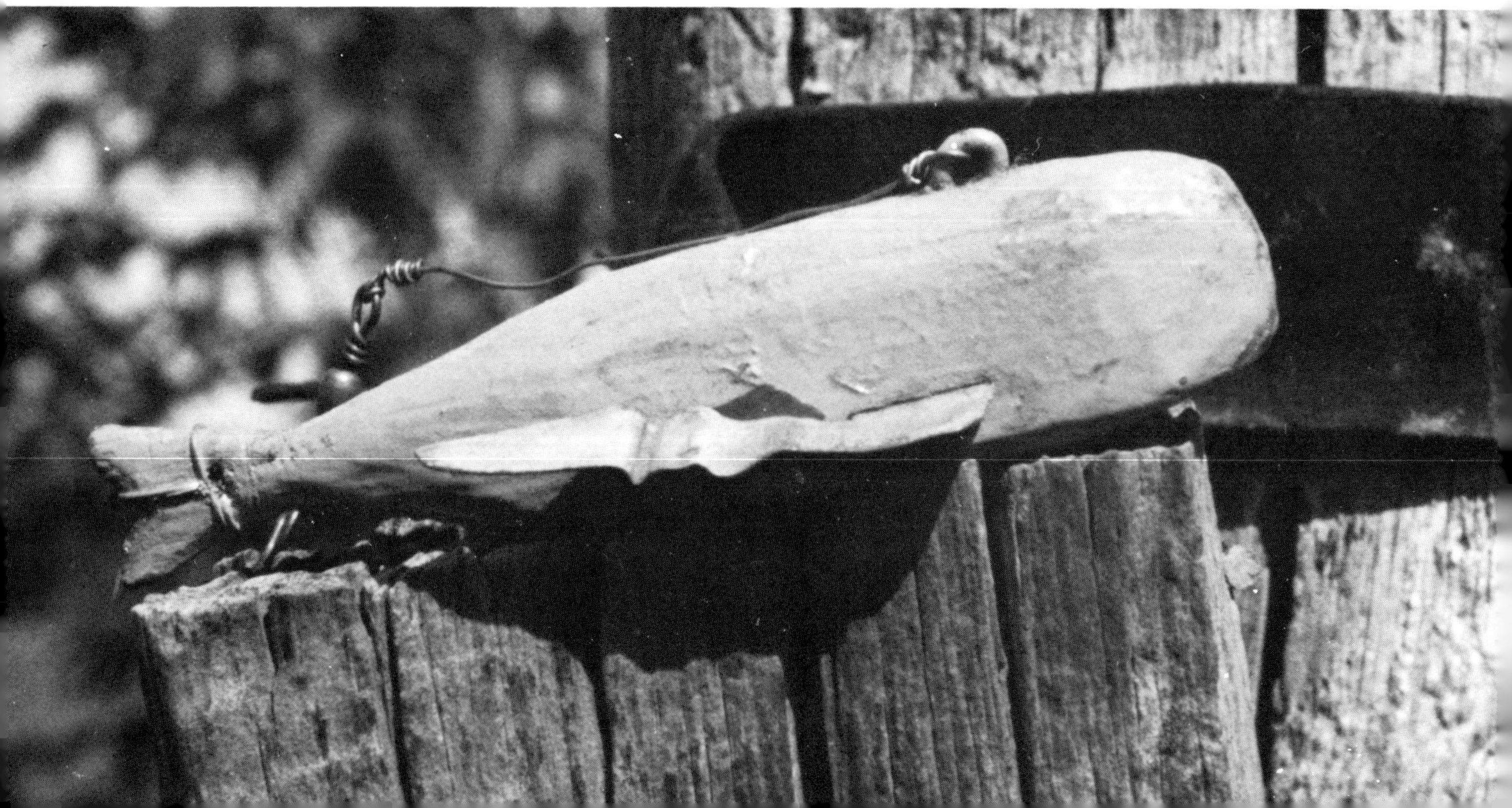

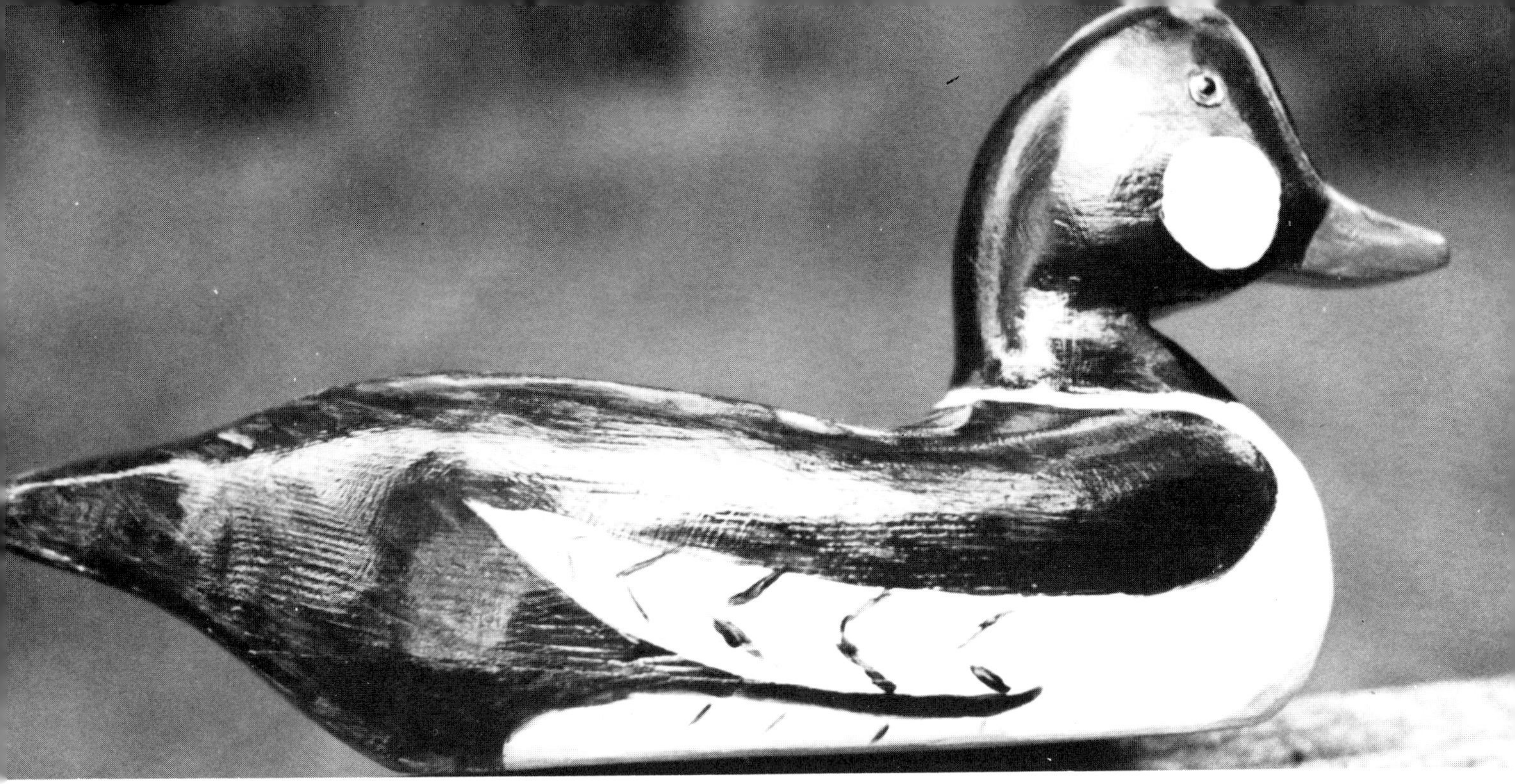

Goldeneye drake by Bertrand Beaubriand ca. 1950.

Bertrand Beaubriand 1910- Port Henry, New York carved numerous decoys including decoratives. This photograph was taken at his home overlooking the southwest shores of Lake Champlain.

Ernest A. Benway 1894-1944 Burlington, Vermont, was a carpenter and loom-fixer by trade. He carved decoys to hunt over at the west shore of South Hero, Vermont. His bluebills are diminutive, with tack eyes. A dowel is inserted through the top of the head and all are branded "EB" on the bottom. He made almost one hundred blocks between 1930-1940.

Bluebill hen by Ernest A. Benway, Burlington, Vermont ca. 1933. Original paint, tack eyes. Collection of Loy S. Harrell.

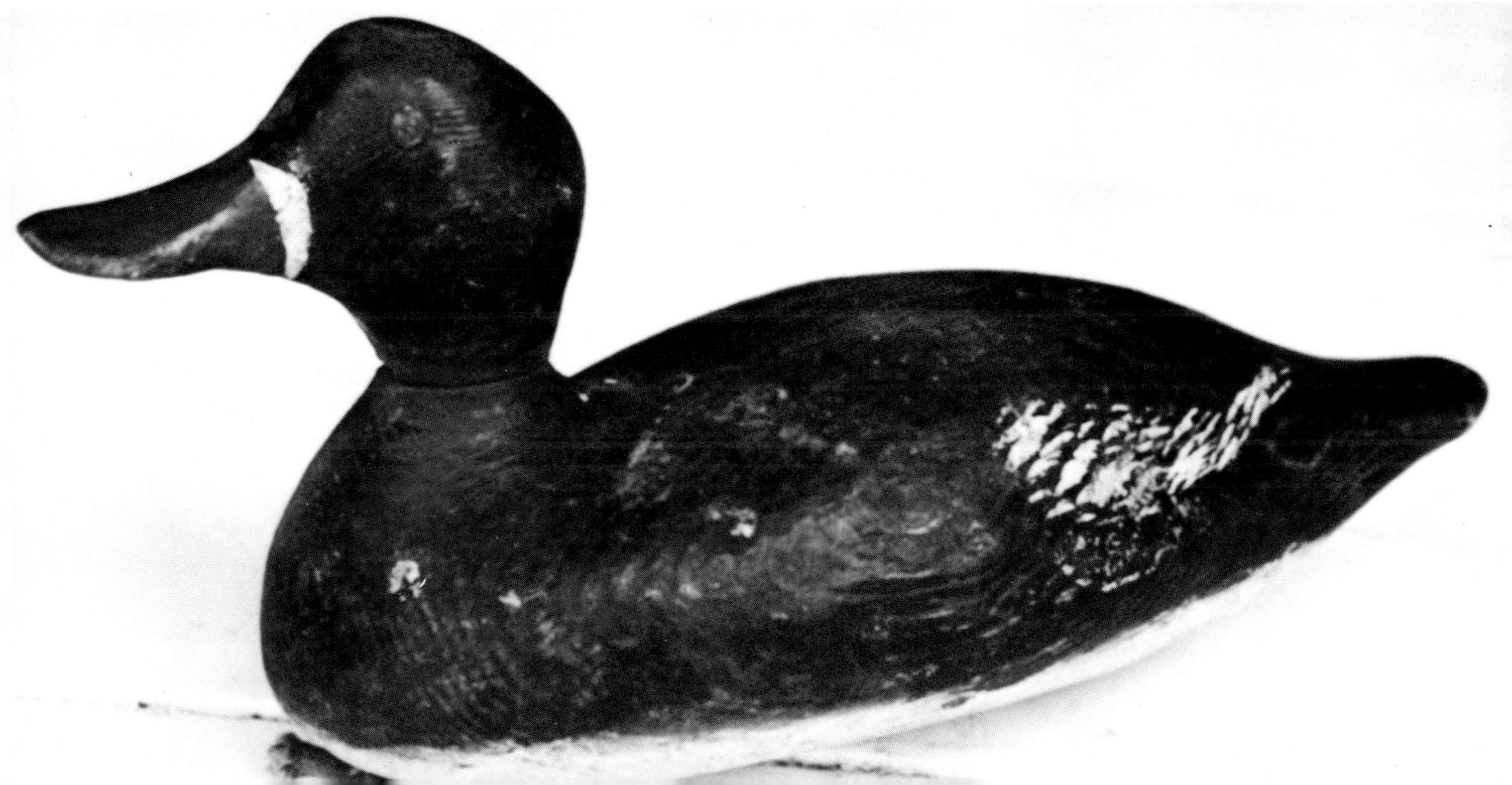

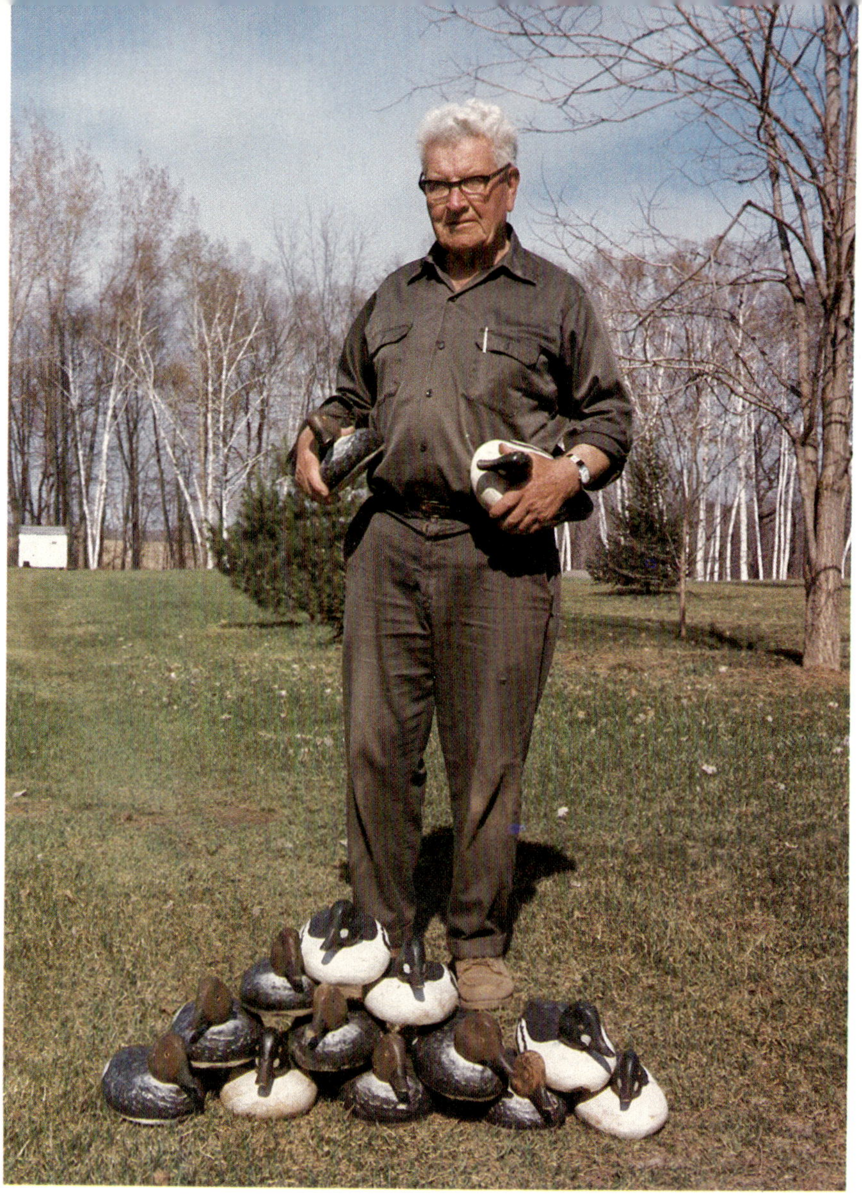

Archibald "Archie" Bodette 1900-1982, West Addison, Vermont. Born on the family farm in West Addison, which borders Lake Champlain, gave Bodette a life long opportunity to study duck and goose migrations and their behavior. He built his blind on the edge of the farm and eventually made what he called the "Perfect Decoy". His early birds were narrow and thick. (He later told his nephew Raymond, who now runs the farm, that they "weren't stable and iced up too soon".) After 1940 he carved flatter, wider birds with a more esthetic appearance. All decoys are characterized by an elliptical weight secured with a brass screw and dowled from the bottom up through the head. Earlier forms are often confused with Bacon decoys and have been seen at auctions so identified. Bodette worked thirty-four years at Weeks School; Vergennes, Vermont. He ran the carpentry shop and "one of the cottages". It was here that he made his decoys which numbered over four hundred. All were whistlers and no blacks or bluebills have been attributed to Bodette. He sold them to any interested hunter and the goldeneye hen (Page 23) originally cost five dollars. Bodette decoys are still available to the collector with a watchful eye and make a splendid addition to any collection. Photograph was taken in 1980 at the Bodette farm by Paul Casson, a collector and historian from Hyannis, Massachusetts.

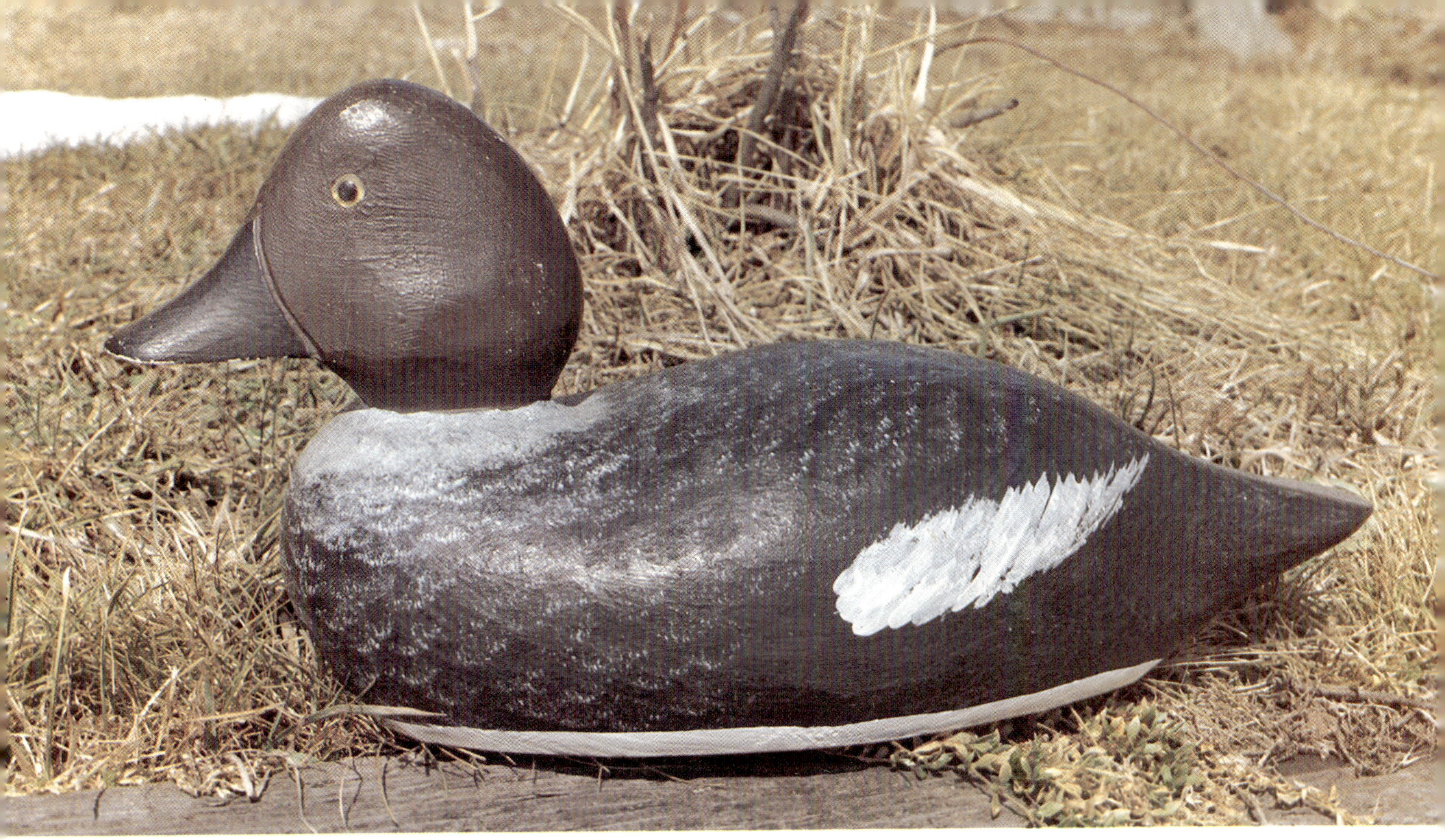

Goldeneye hen by Archie Bodette ca. 1935. Mint original paint. Note the "Bacon influence".

Goldeneye drake by Archie Bodette ca. 1955. Original paint. Photographed at the west edge of the Bodette farm. Collection of William Mercia.

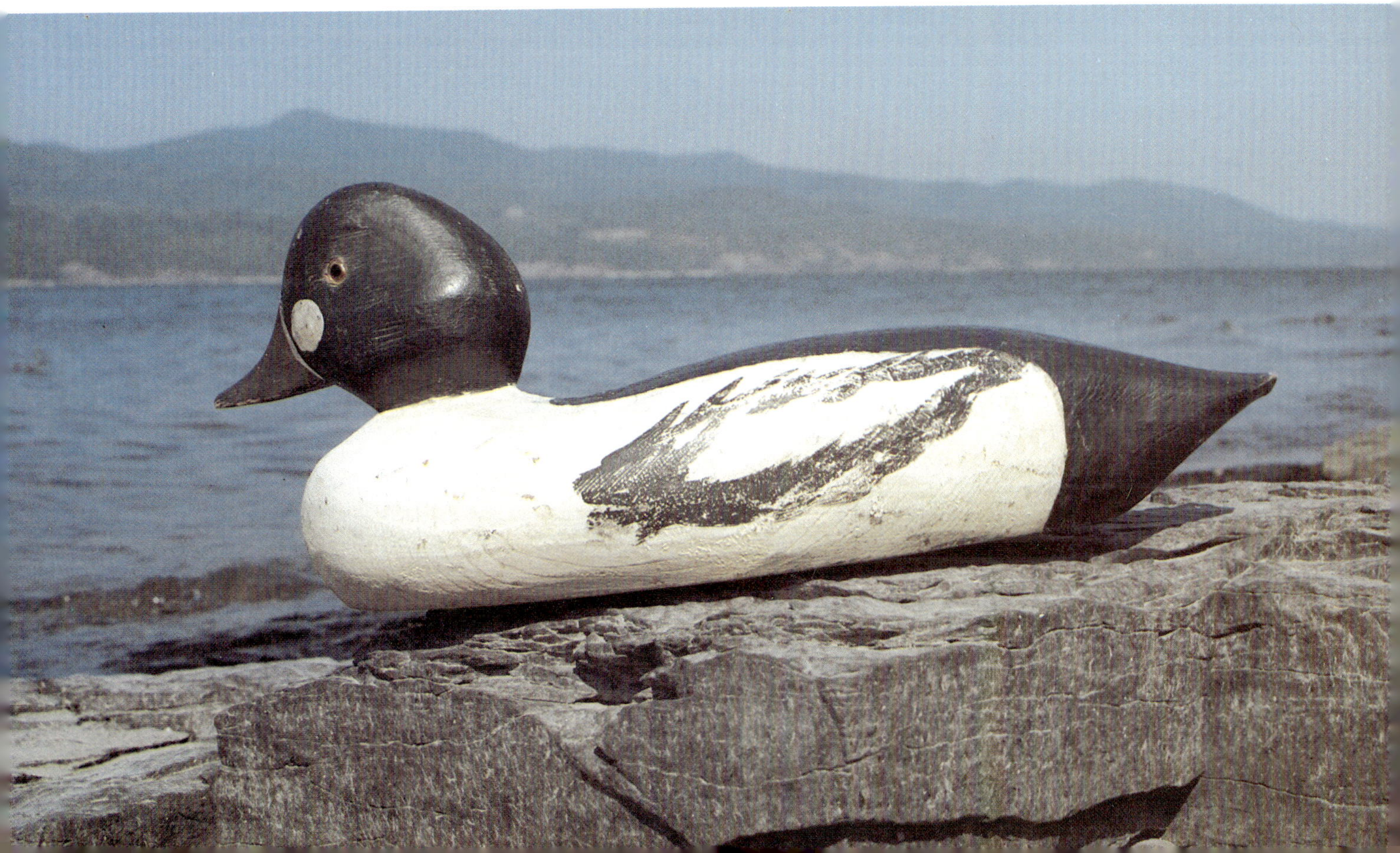

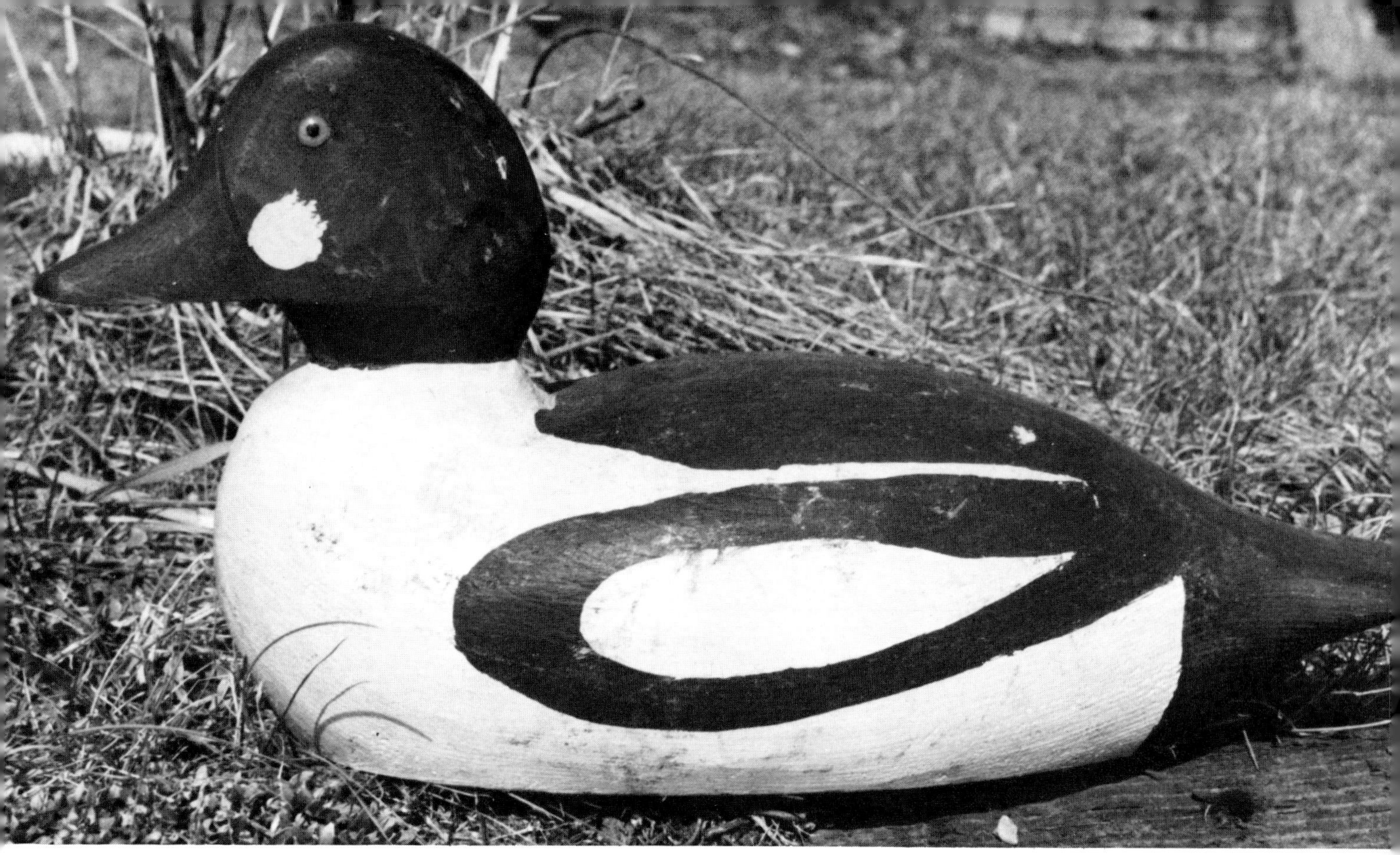

Goldeneye drake by Archie Bodette ca. 1935. Original paint. His "earlier form". Collection of Loy S. Harrell.

Goldeneye hen by Archie Bodette ca. 1960. Original paint. Collection of Patricia Mayo.

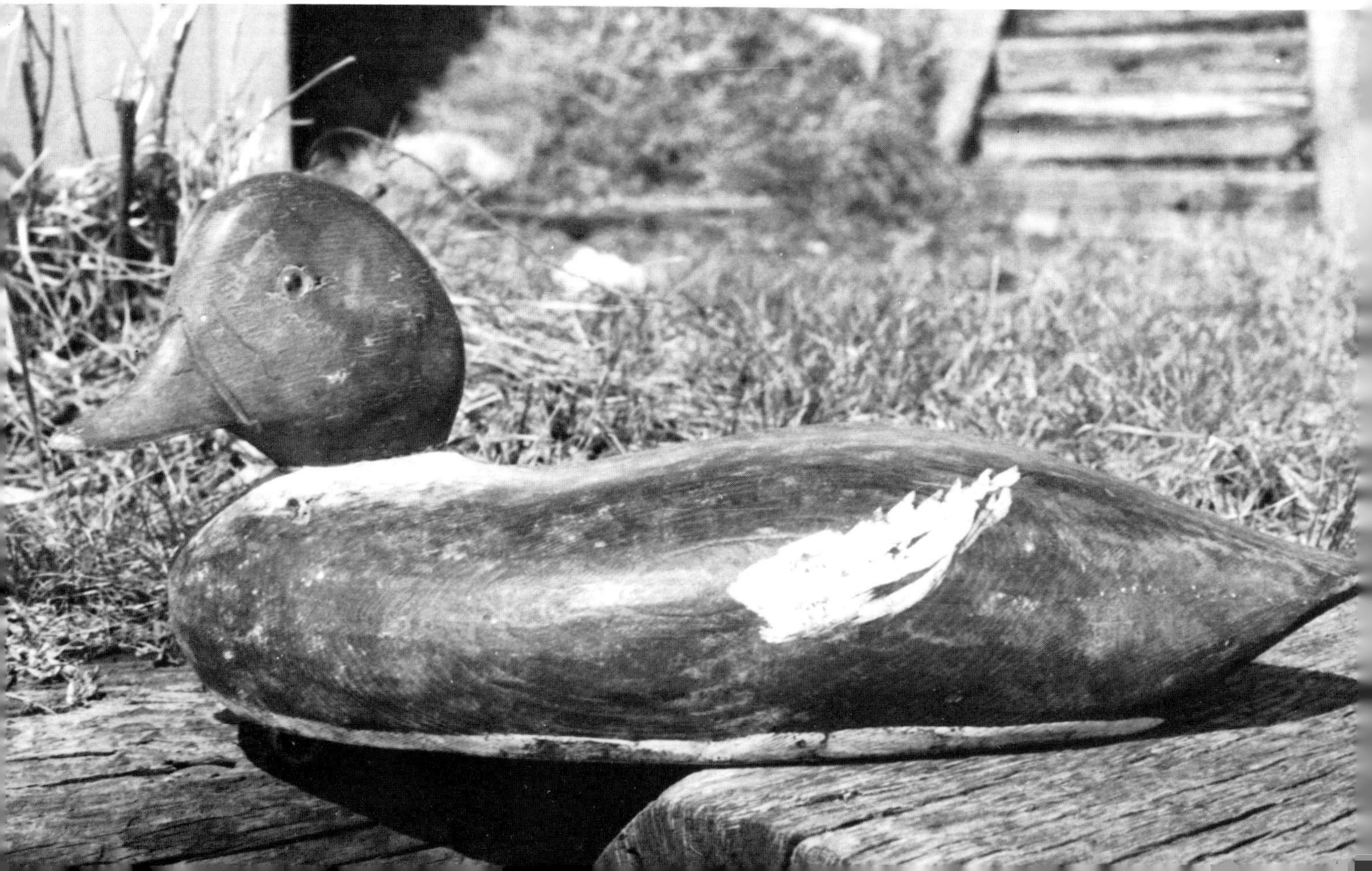

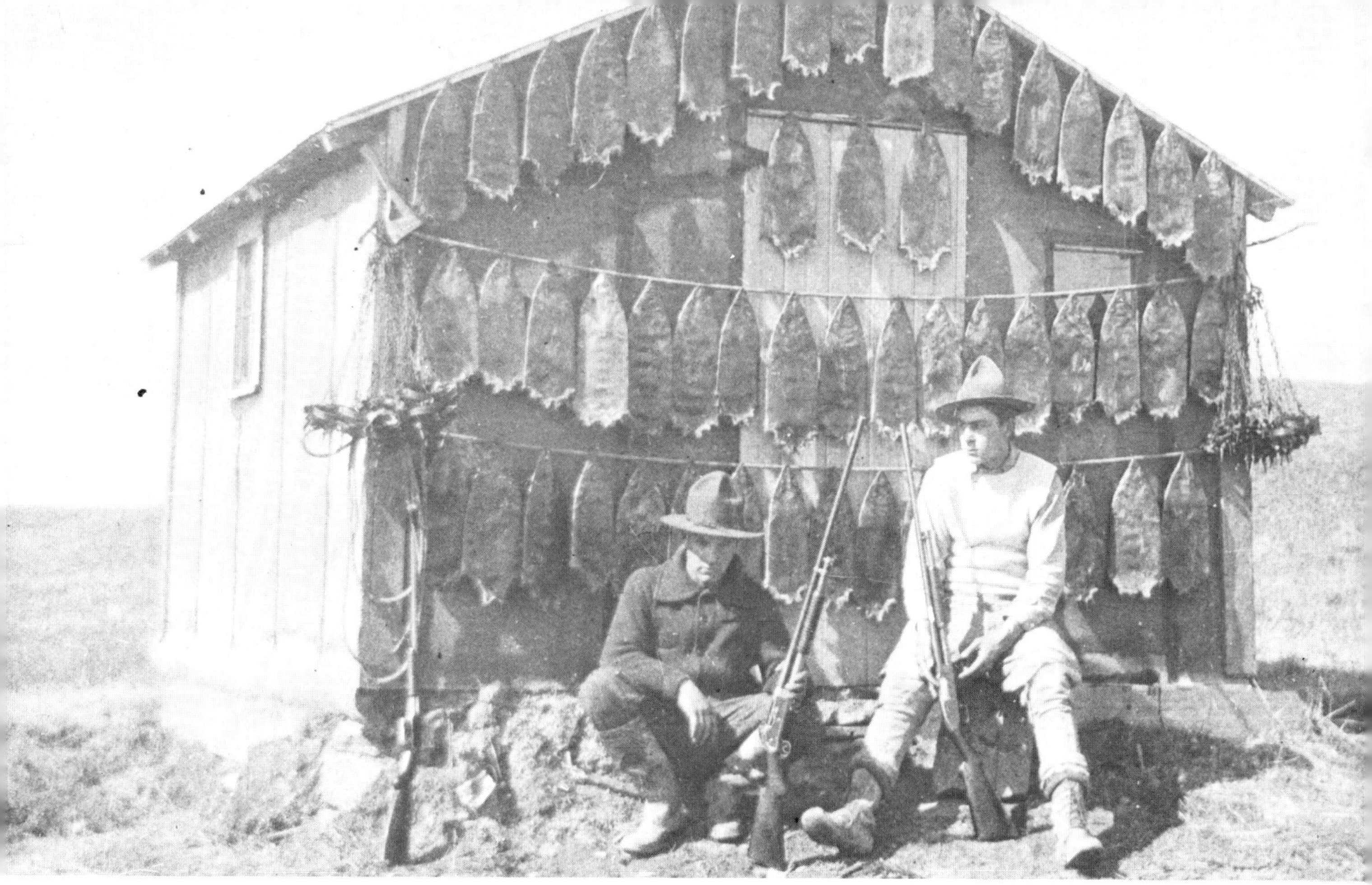

Hospital Creek Camp, Addison, Vermont, 1917. Left to right; Archie Bodette and John Adams with bounty of muskrat pelts. Bodette is holding his Winchester Model II.

Working Bodette whistlers from the rig of Douglas Mulac.

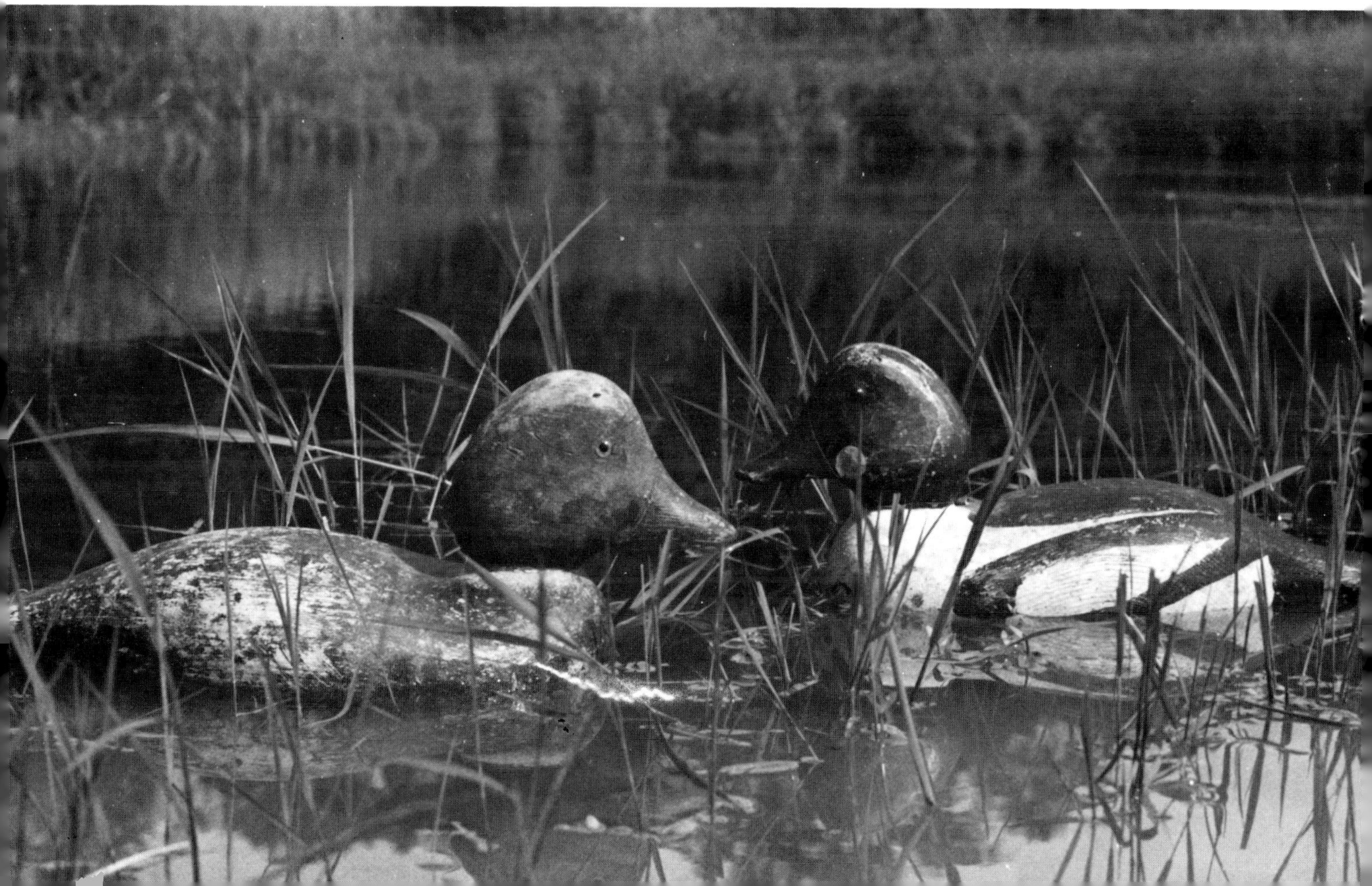

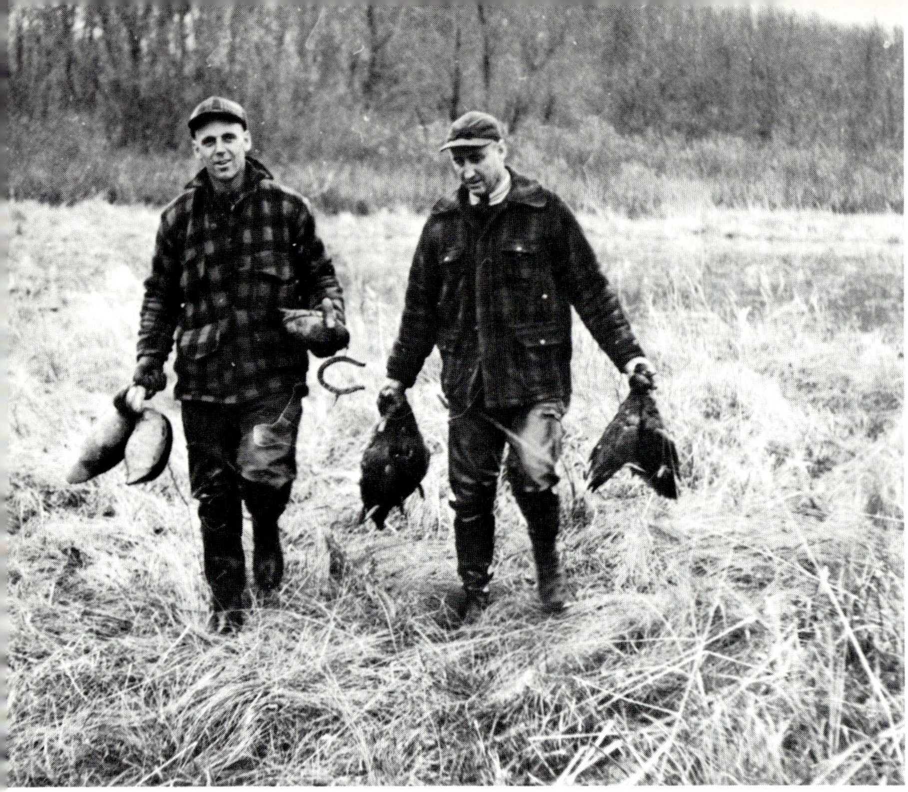

Gilbert Bohannon (left) and Wiggie Church, also a game warden and his frequent hunting companion, returning from a mornings hunt (ca. 1936). Note Bohannon decoys.

Pictured left to right are Ike Sollace, from Shoreham, Vermont, Bohannon and Harry Molton, from Montpelier, Vermont. October 14, 1934. Almost forty ducks including many canvasbacks in days bag. Times have changed! Courtesy of Marie Bohannon.

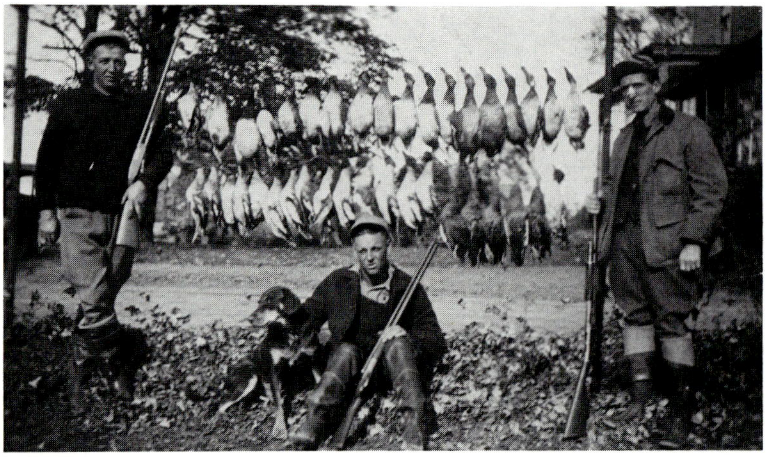

Canada goose by Gilbert Bohannon ca. 1945. Balsa body, pine head, original paint. Collection of Daniel Beauregard.

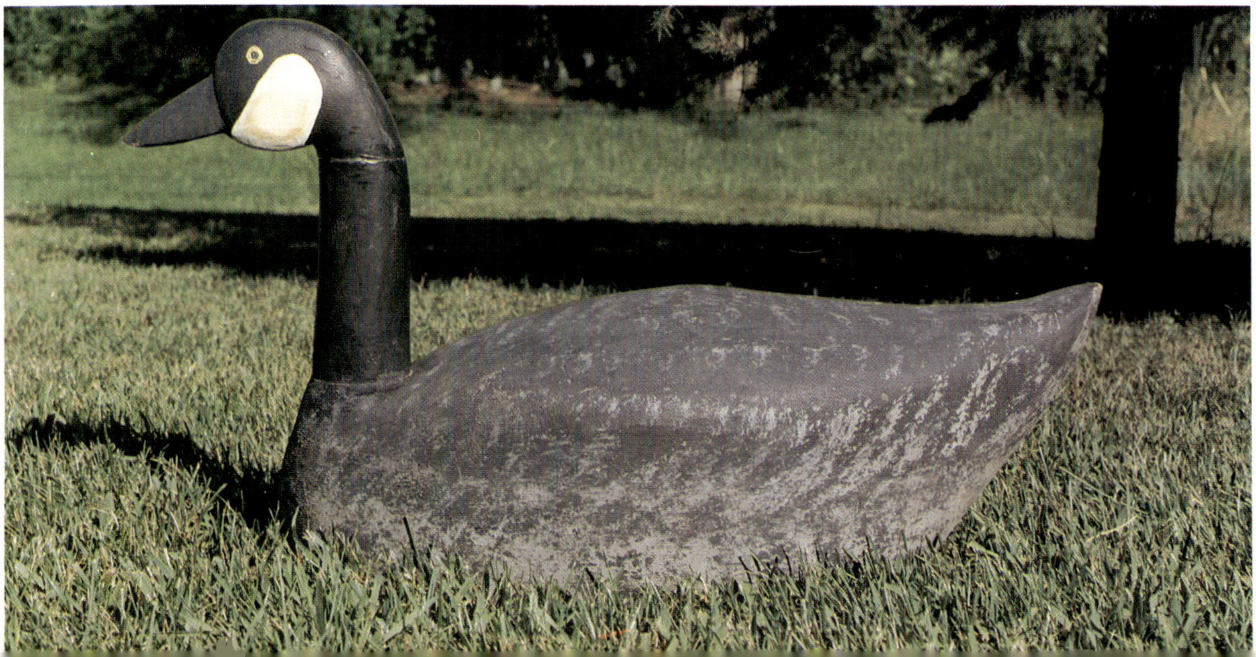

Bluebill drake by Gilbert Bohannon ca. 1940. Original paint. Collection of Loy S. Harrell.

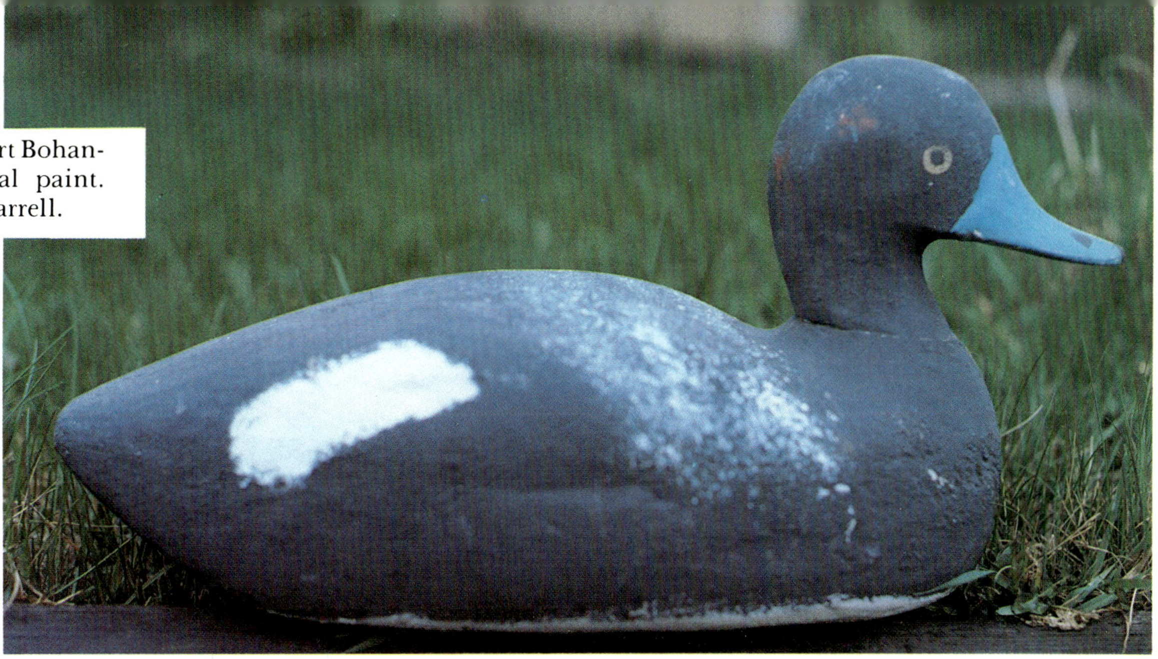

Gilbert Ray Bohannon 1902-1983 Alburg Springs, Vermont.. Bohannon was a game warden, State of Vermont from 1933 to 1967. His love of the outdoors and knowledge of the upper end of Vermont made him a natural for the job. Duck hunting was at his back door in Campbell's Bay and he carved decoys to fill his rig. He also traded and bought decoys from G. Tremblay, his close neighbor.

Wendal Carpenter 1914- Colchester, Vermont. Carpenter, a retired construction foreman, hunted and carved decoys with his close friend Ford Patno (Page 93). They hunted at the "Sand Dunes" in Colchester, Vermont where Carpenter had his camp. He carved almost one hundred blacks and whistlers from cedar driftwood found along the lake.

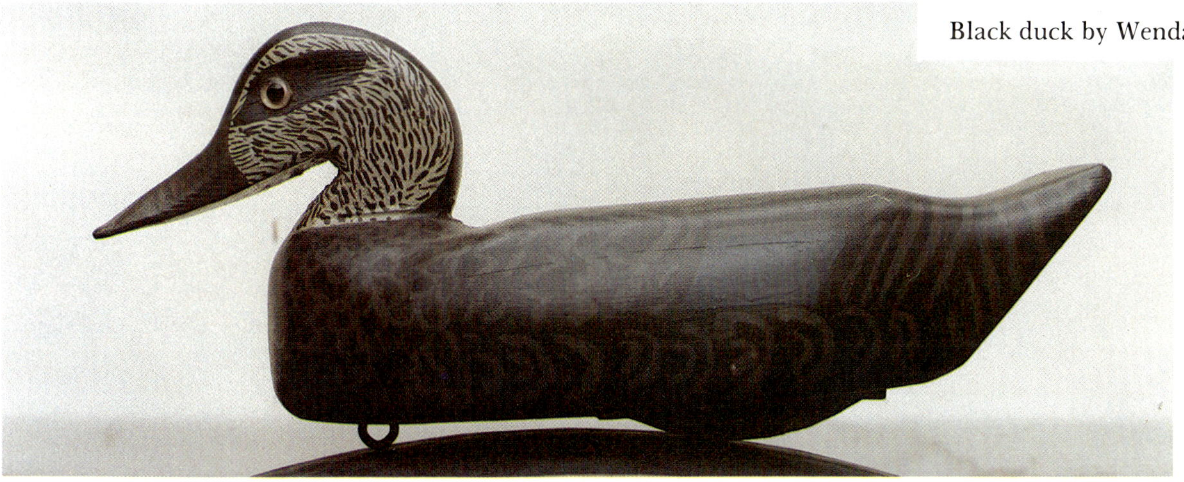

Black duck by Wendal Carpenter.

Whistler hen carved ca. 1965 by Wendal Carpenter.

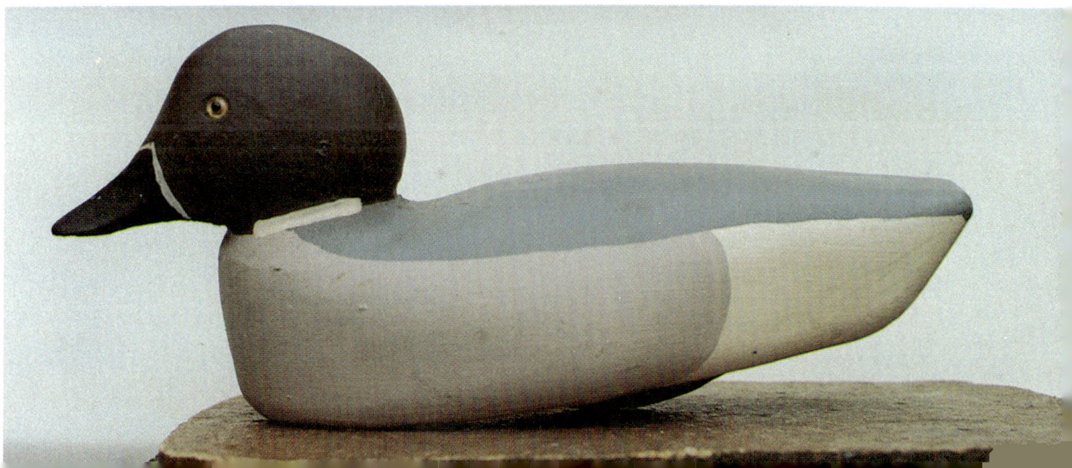

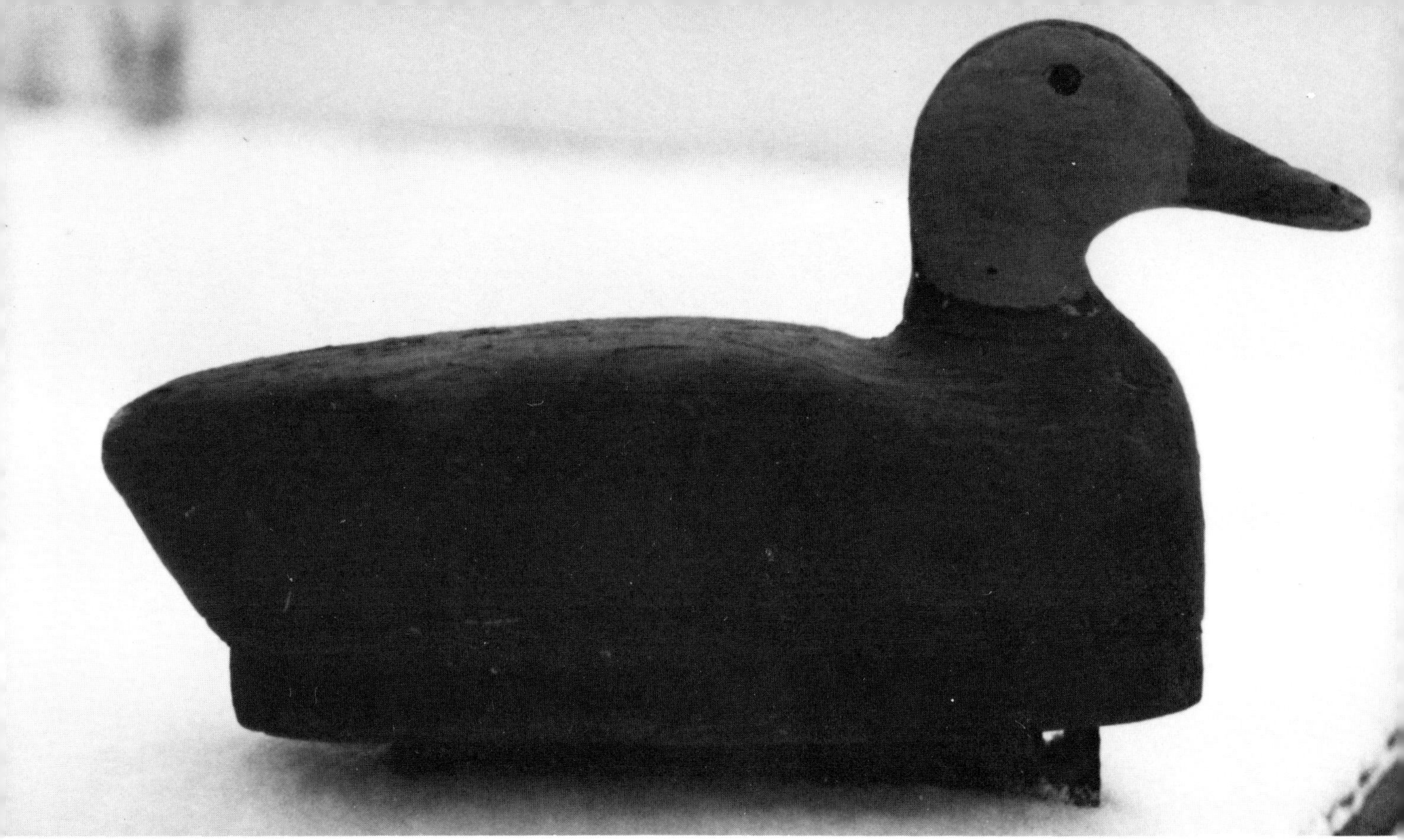

Black duck by Ralph Blow, Burlington, Vermont. Ca. 1960. Collection of Jack Biggie.

Goldeneye drake by Robert Cyrus Booth. 1894-1981, Plattsburgh, New York. One of five dozen made, ca. 1935 and hunted over in Kings and Indian Bay, Lake Champlain. Collection of Christopher Booth.

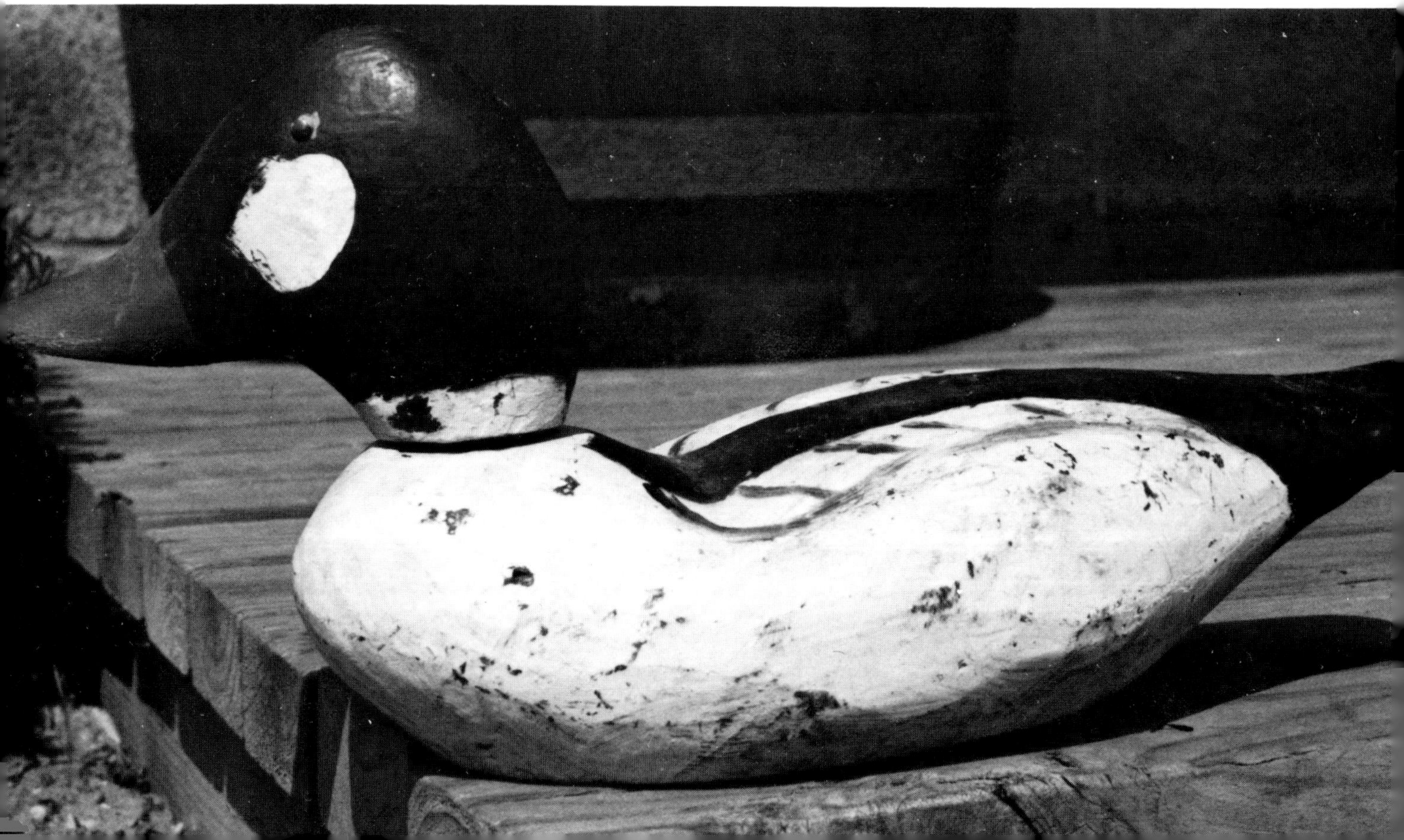

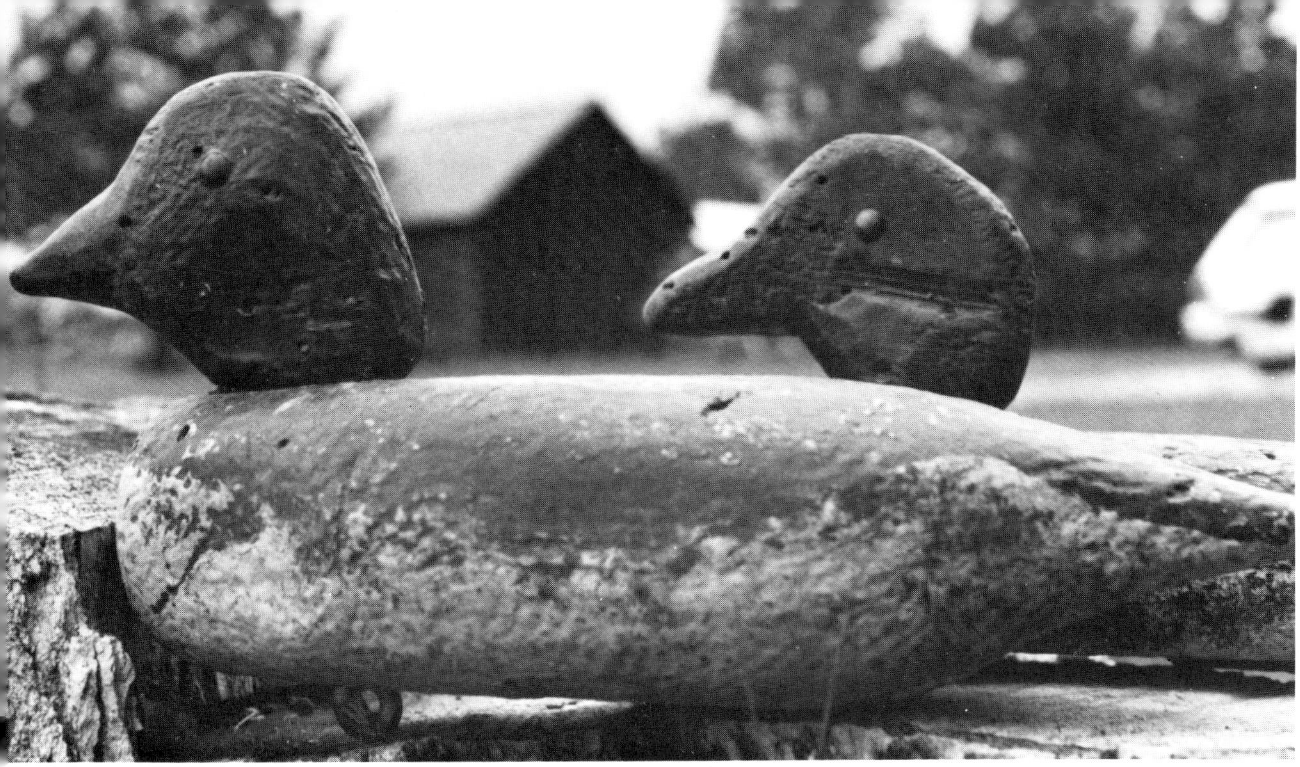

Goldeneye hens by Paul Choiniere carved ca. 1945.

Paul Choiniere 1923- Rouses Point, New York hunted over his decoys at Catfish Bay, part of his family farm on Lake Champlain. Choiniere, Assistant Warden, St. Albans, Vermont Correctional Center also was one of the last persons to have a license to fish commercially on Lake Champlain. His decoys are carved with a hand axe and have tack eyes.

Ronald Curler 1939- West Ferrisburg, Vermont. Curler worked with Archie Bodette at Weeks School which accounts for the similarity between his carving and Bodettes. Curlers' heads are secured with a brass screw and his paint style is different from Bodettes work. Curler carved during the 1950's and 1960's.

Goldeneye drake by Ronald Curler.

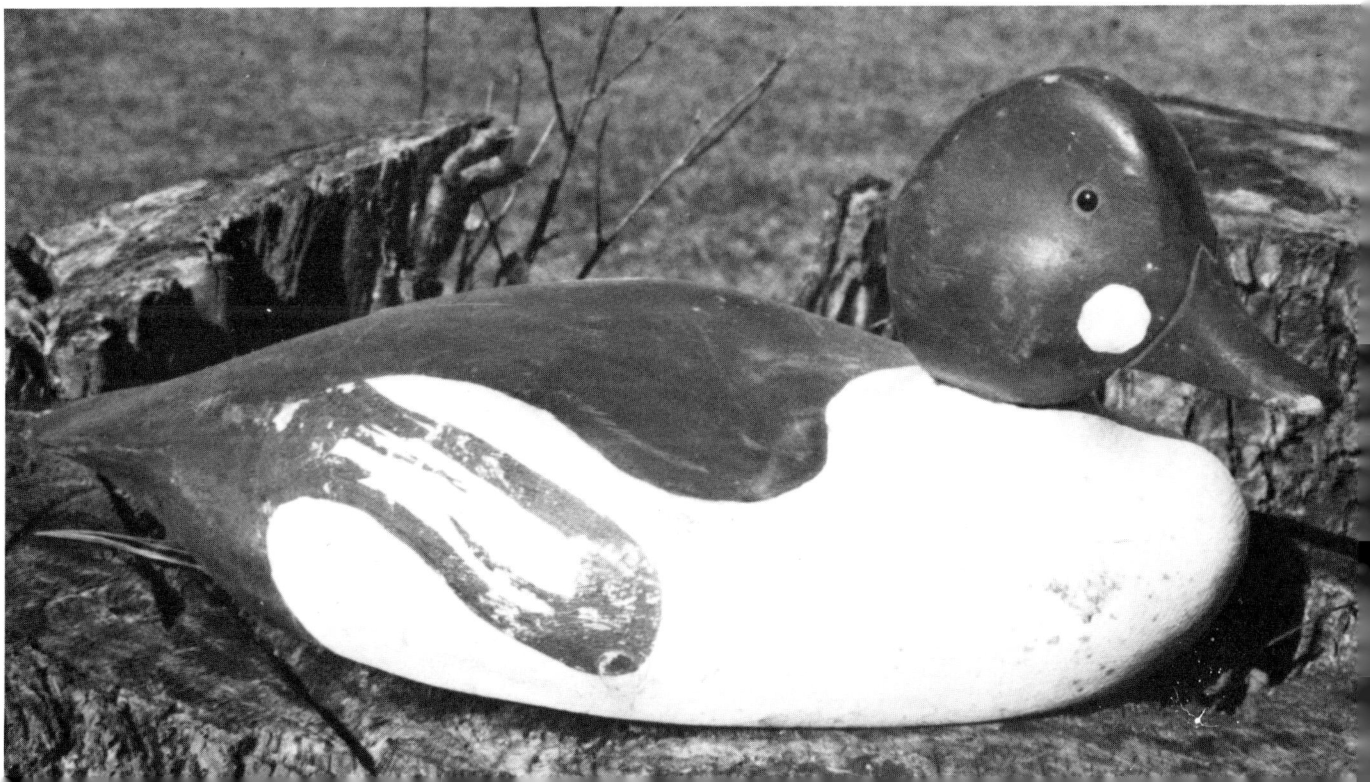

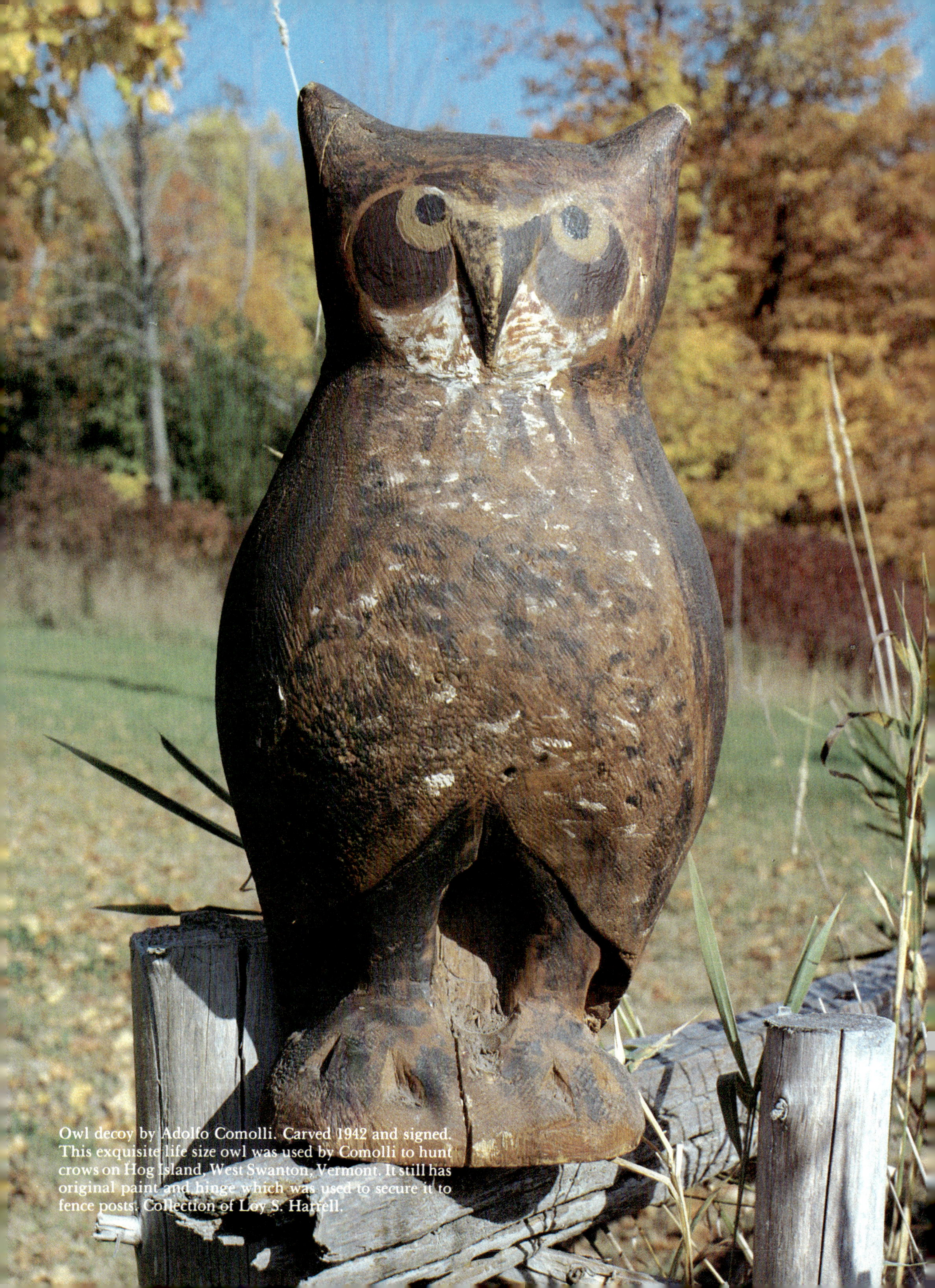

Owl decoy by Adolfo Comolli. Carved 1942 and signed. This exquisite life size owl was used by Comolli to hunt crows on Hog Island, West Swanton, Vermont. It still has original paint and hinge which was used to secure it to fence posts. Collection of Loy S. Harrell.

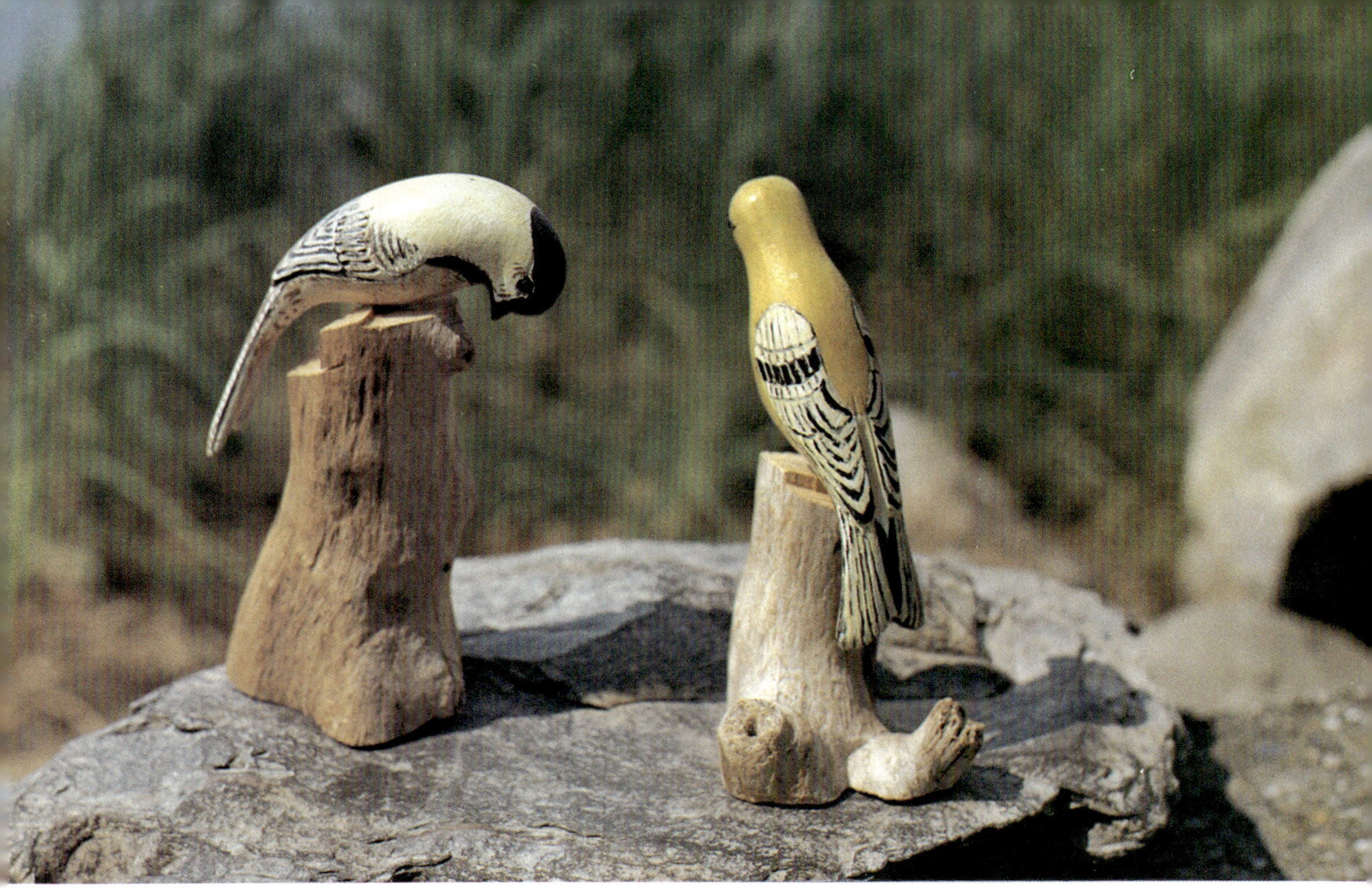

Decorative songbirds by Adolfo Comolli. Original paint Collection of Edward Comolli.

Rig of bluebills by Adolfo Comolli carved 1940. Photo taken on Campbells Bay, Hog Island, Vermont.

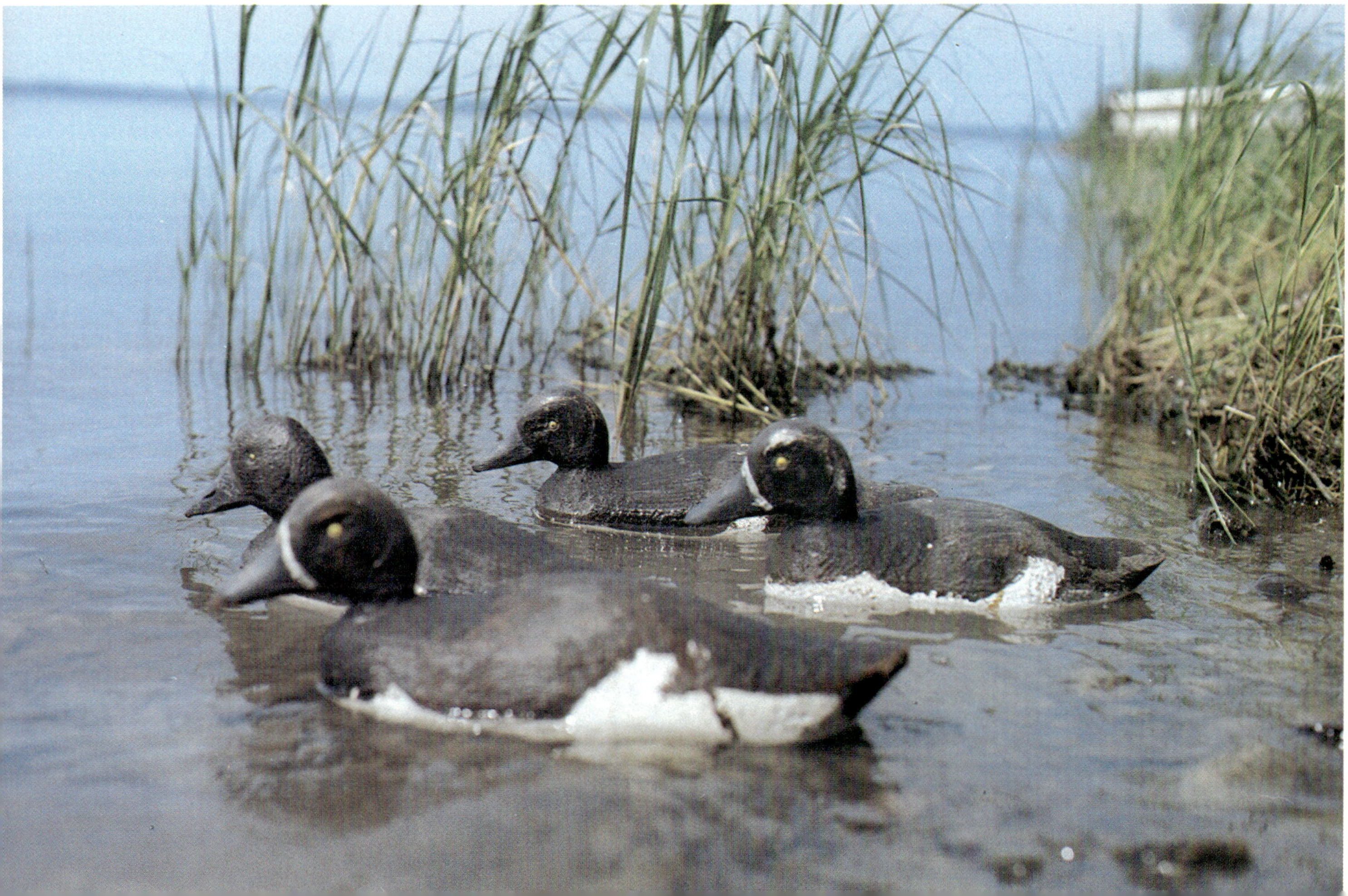

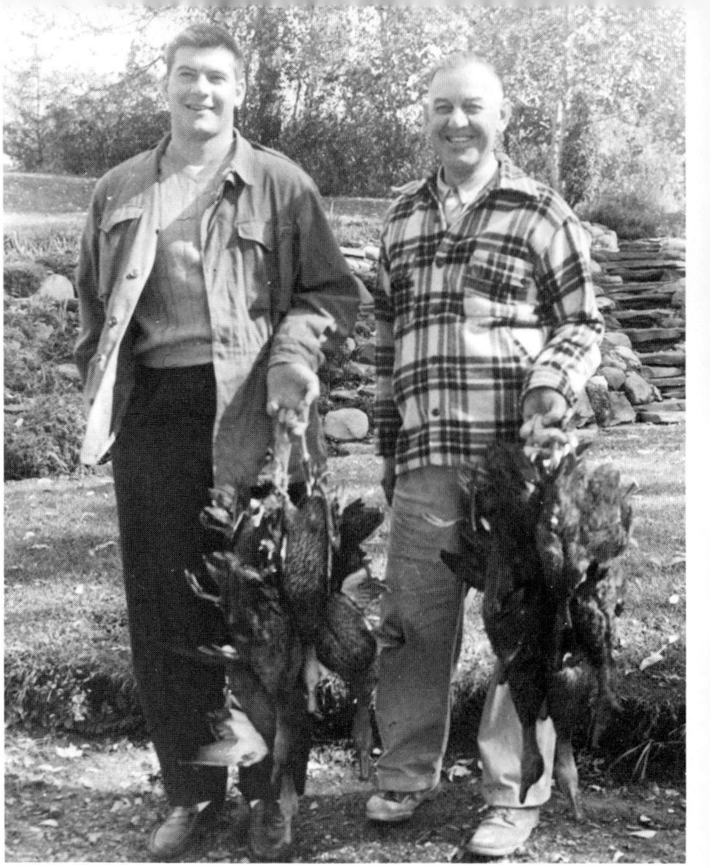

Edward Comolli, left, with his father Adolfo, November 7, 1952. Days bag of blacks and mallards. Photo courtesy of Edward Comolli.

Adolfo Comolli 1894-1965, Barre and Hog Island, West Swanton, Vermont. Hog Island, where the family camp is located, is on the edge of the Missisquoi Wildlife Refuge and bordered by Campbells Bay. This area is the first stopover for migratory blacks, bluebills and whistlers. As a respite from the rigors of running Comolli and Company Granite Works, Barre, Vermont, Adolfo hunted and carved decoys. His blacks were carved out of cork he obtained from refrigerator truck lining and his whistlers and bluebills from discarded cedar telephone poles. Over one hundred decoys still are used by his son Edward who inherited his father's rig.

Bluebill drake by Adolfo Comolli ca. 1940. Note weight made from granite polishing scrolls.

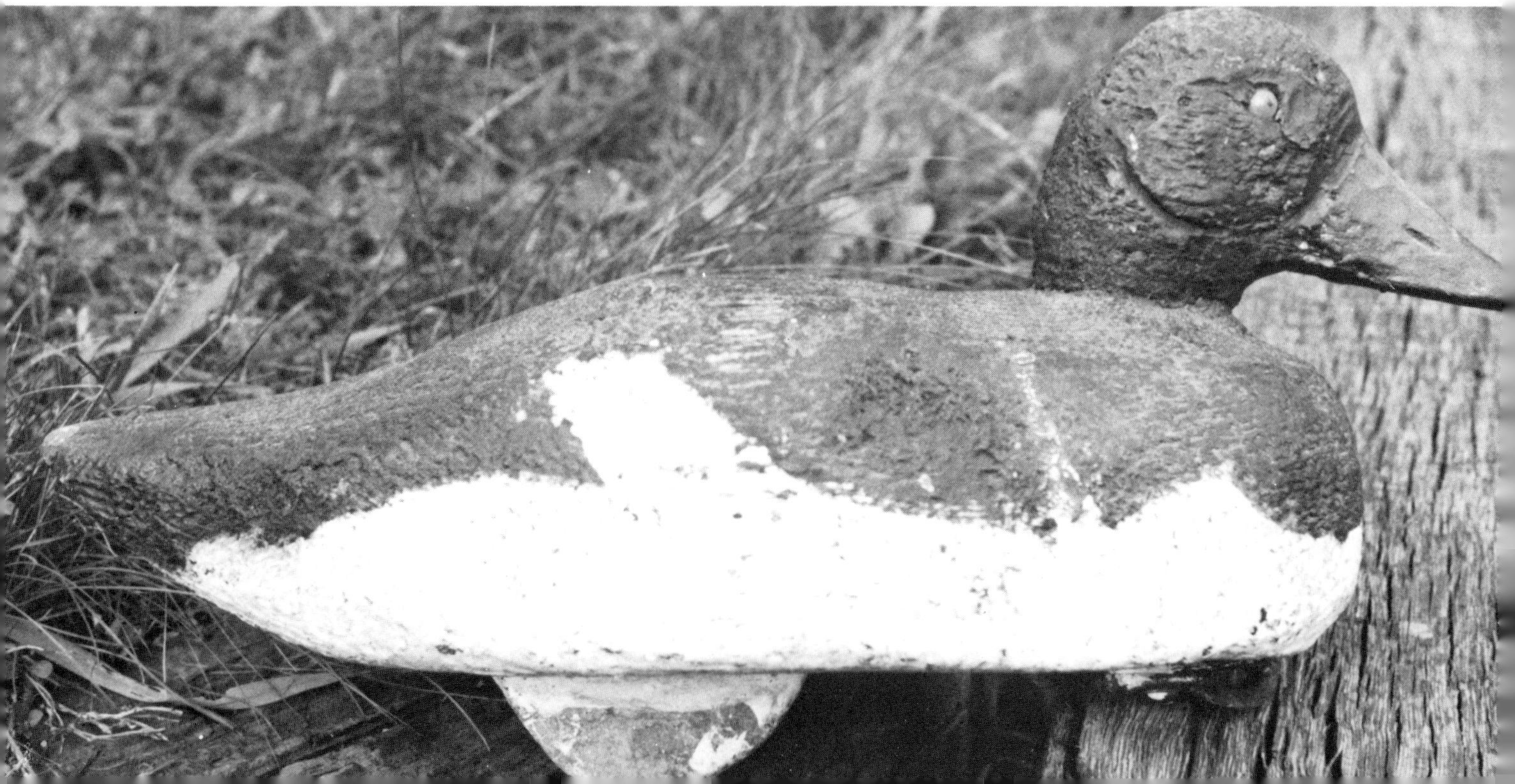

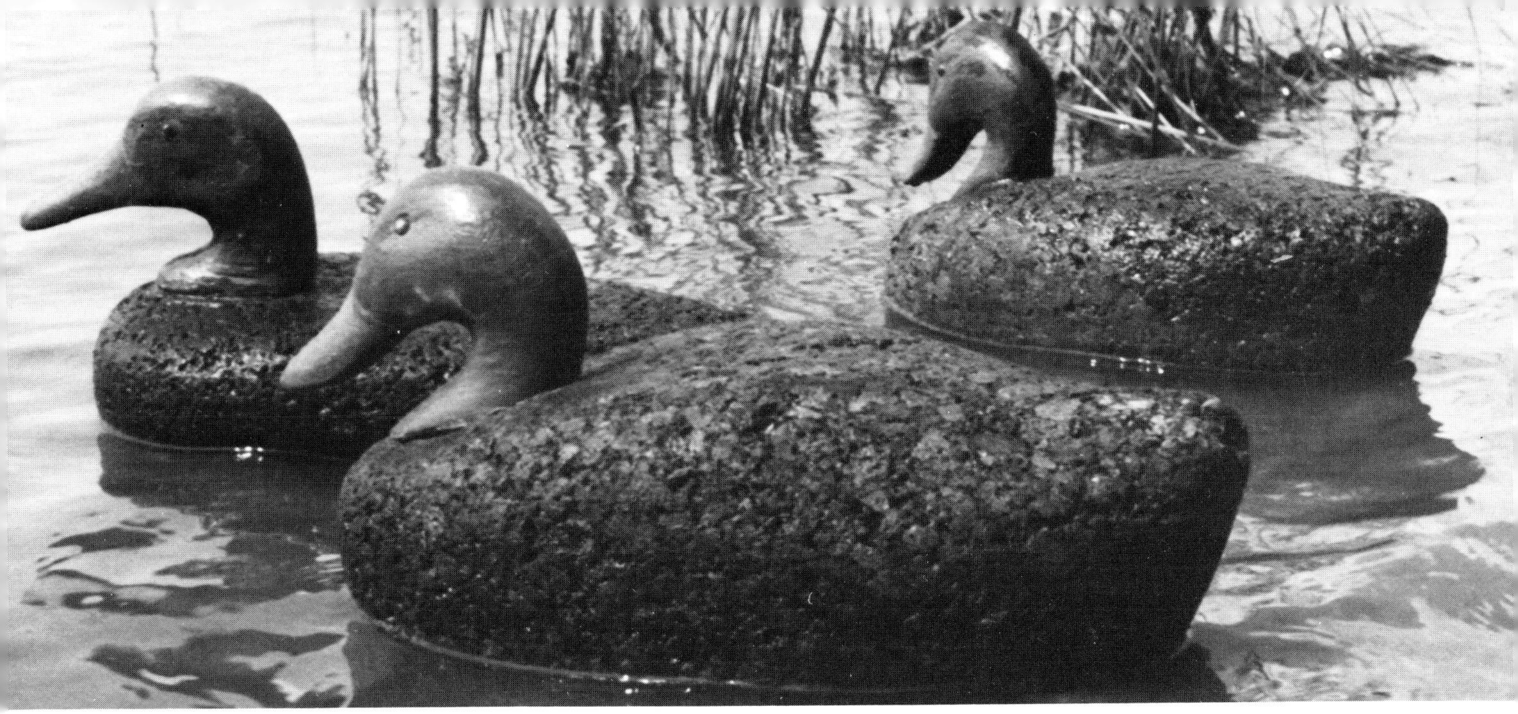

Black ducks by Adolfo Comolli, cork body, wood base, pine heads and glass eyes. Photo taken at Campbells Bay.

Peter E. Costello 1948- Essex, Vermont, is considered one of the northeast top carvers. Influenced by vacations on Plum Island, Massachusetts, Wildlife Preserve, Costello majored in wildlife biology in college. He worked for a number of years as Chief Technician at the kidney dialysis unit at the Vermont Medical Center, Burlington, Vermont. But his calling was to carve and in 1978 he became a full time carver. Costello carved his first decoy in 1972 and thereafter his decoys and miniatures were shown and sold all over New England. He won several first place awards with his mallards and for his working divers-buffleheads. He has carved almost four hundred miniatures and three hundred blacks, whistlers, pintails and widgeons. Construction varies from cork to hollowed cedar. Costello now lives in Florida and is busy carving fish as awards for big game fishing tournaments.

Whistler hen by Peter Costello, early cork body, flat style. Collection of Frank C. Herschede.

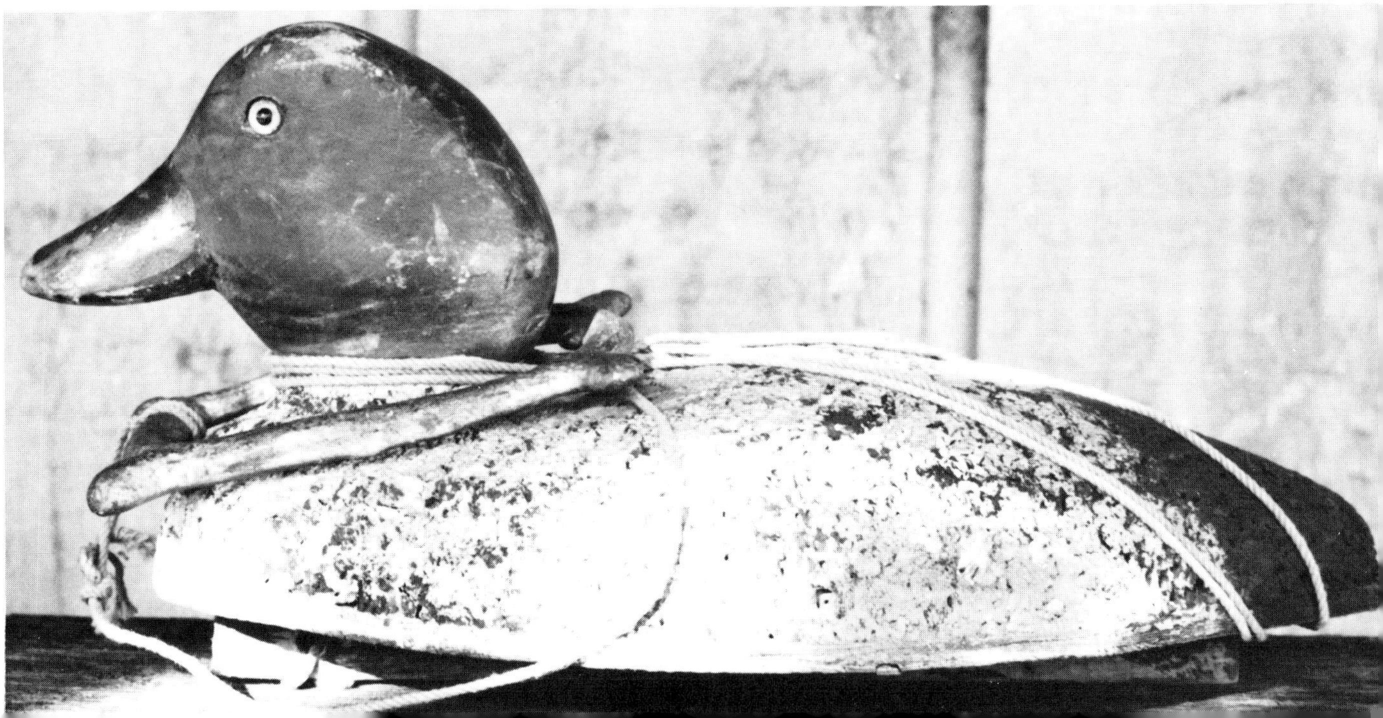

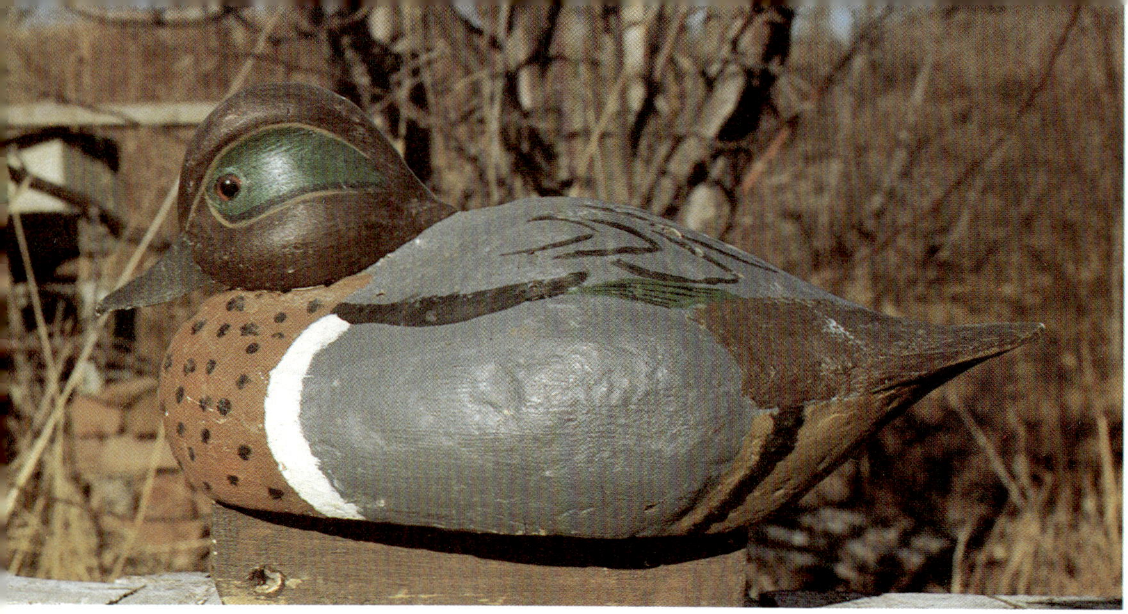

Greenwing teal drake by Peter Costello ca. 1970. Cork body, wood keel and head. Collection of William Coates.

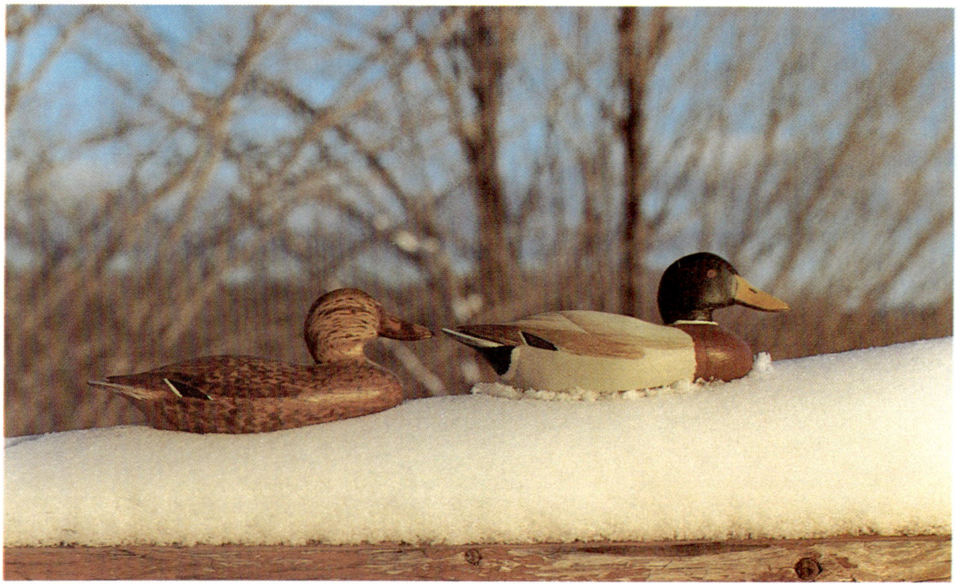

Pair of mallard miniatures by Peter Costello signed and dated. From the collection of Glen A. Wright.

Black duck by Peter Costello ca. 1970. Collection of William Coates.

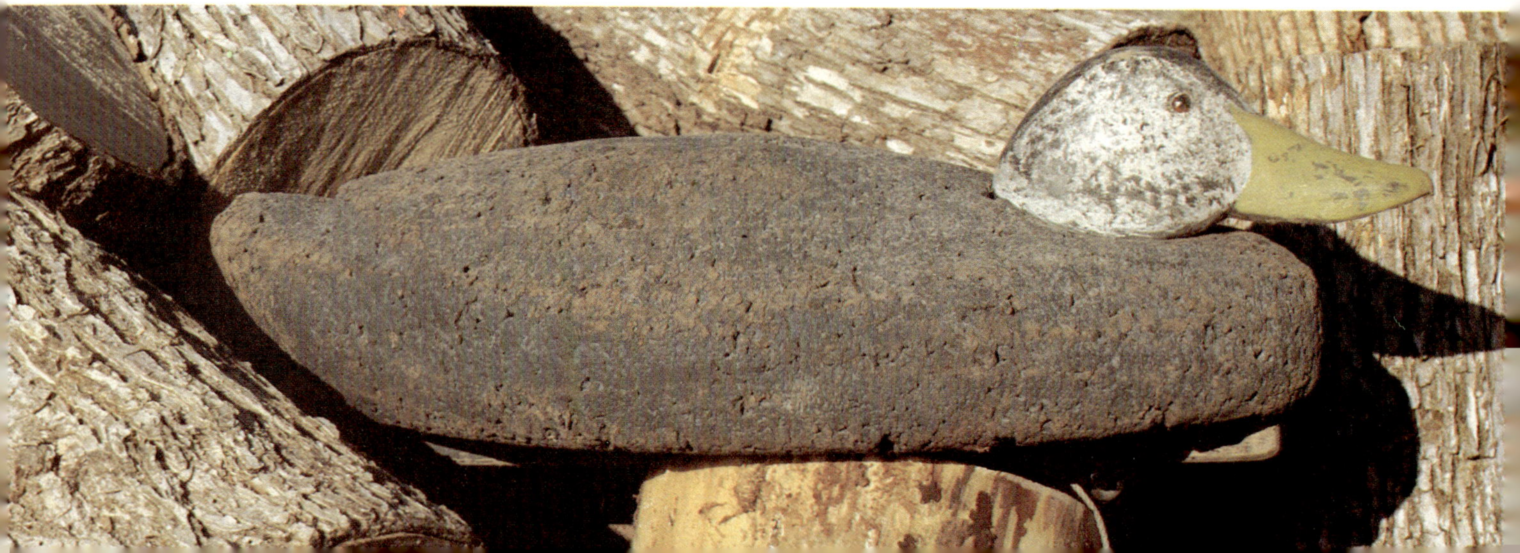

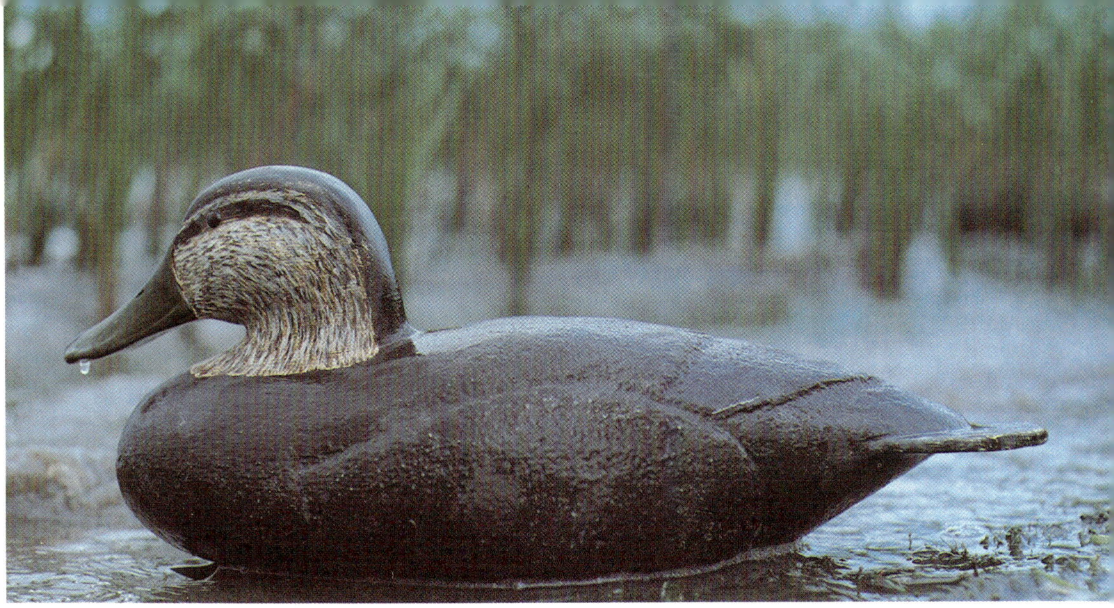

Black duck by Keith Dolbeck. Original paint.

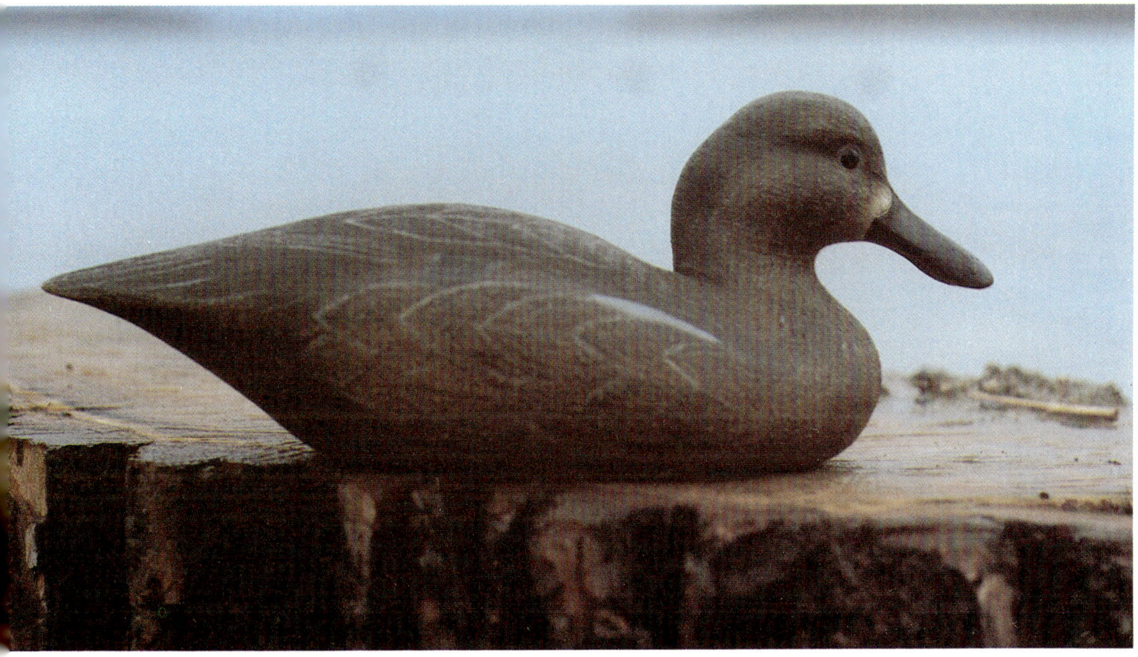

Bluewing teal hen by Keith Dolbeck. Hollow, as are all his decoys. Original paint.

Wood duck drakes by Keith Dolbeck in their natural setting.

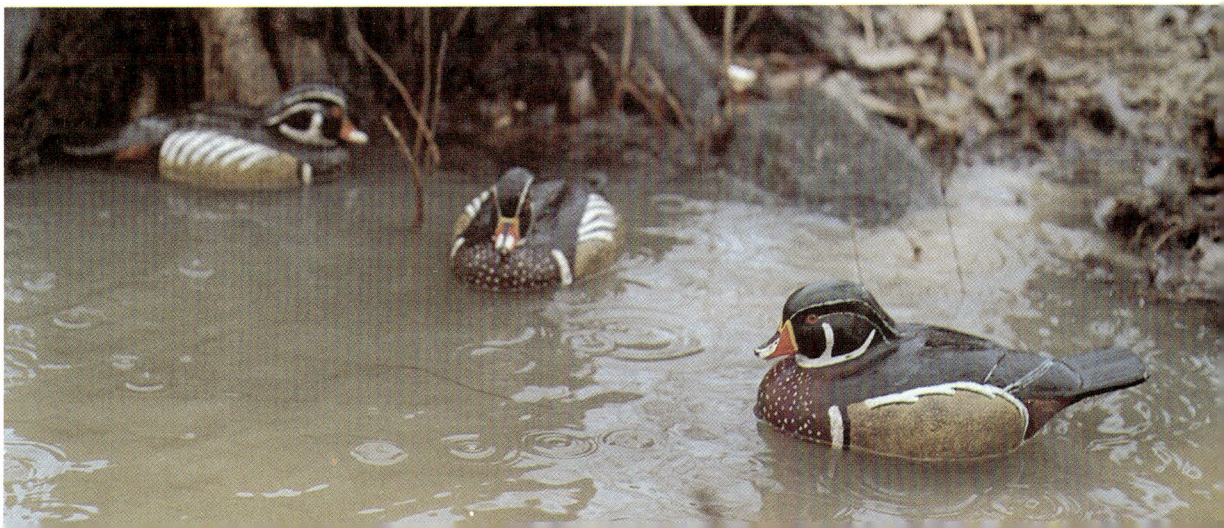

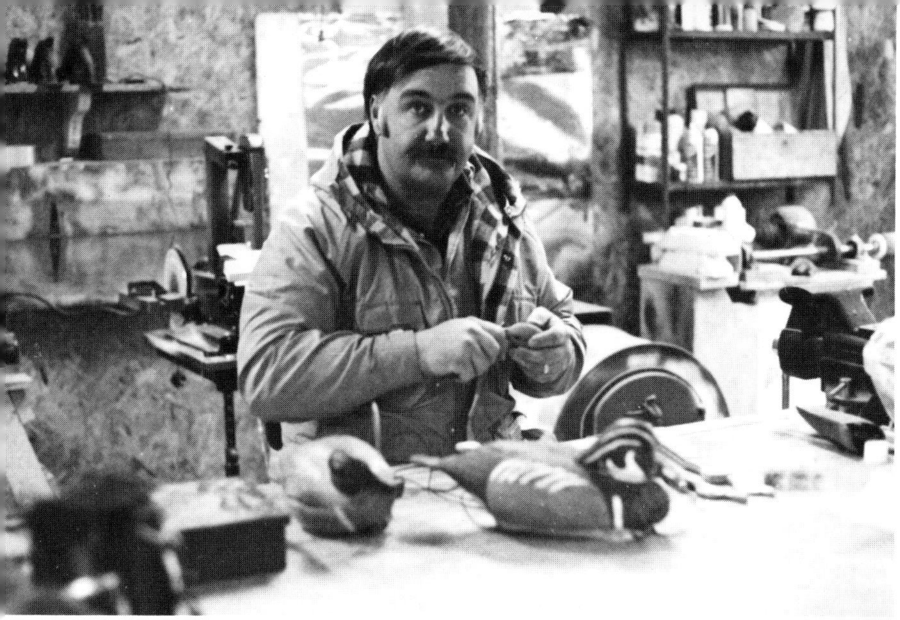

Keith Dolbeck, Ticonderoga, New York. Ca. 1984, in his workshop.

Keith Dolbeck 1948- Wilsons Bay, Ticonderoga, New York. Presently one of the most active decoy carvers on Lake Champlain, Dolbeck is at home on the edge of Wilson's Bay. From his workshop he is a student of all species of ducks and geese which visit the lake. When the author visited Dolbeck, several hooded mergansers, a pair of American mergansers and ten to twenty whistlers were within sight of his workshop. With a background of taxidermy and work for the New York State Dept. of Conservation, Dolbeck has a "natural feel" for the decoy. His carvings have won many prizes and awards for their authenticity as hunting decoys. He has carved twenty to thirty woodducks, the same number of blacks, bluebills and whistlers and ten plus mergansers to use as confidence birds. Further, Dolbeck is the only carver on Lake Champlain to carve almost forty teal for his own hunting rig. He claims that his background as part Abnaki Indian (his grandfather married an Abnaki named "Spring" in the early 1800's) makes him a natural hunter. He is surrounded by six important marshes; *Wilsons Bay* where Lake George empties into Lake Champlain, *East Creek*, Vermont, a ten mile marsh, so revered by the Abnaki Indians for its hunting and fishing that they established a buriel ground there; *Winter-Dale Marsh,* New York, (formerly Widow-Deal), Miller Marsh north of International Paper Mill, New York, with good growth of bull rush and wild celery, *Chatter Marsh,* New York and *Nigger Marsh,* New York. A visit to Dolbeck's home and workshop is a thrilling and enlightening experience whether to talk ducks or swap decoys.

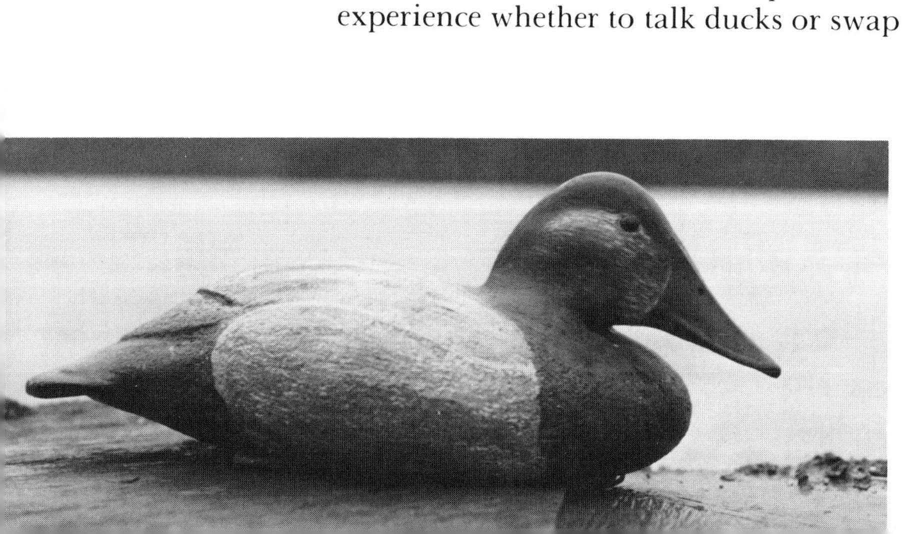

Canvasback hen by Keith Dolbeck ca. 1975. Original paint.

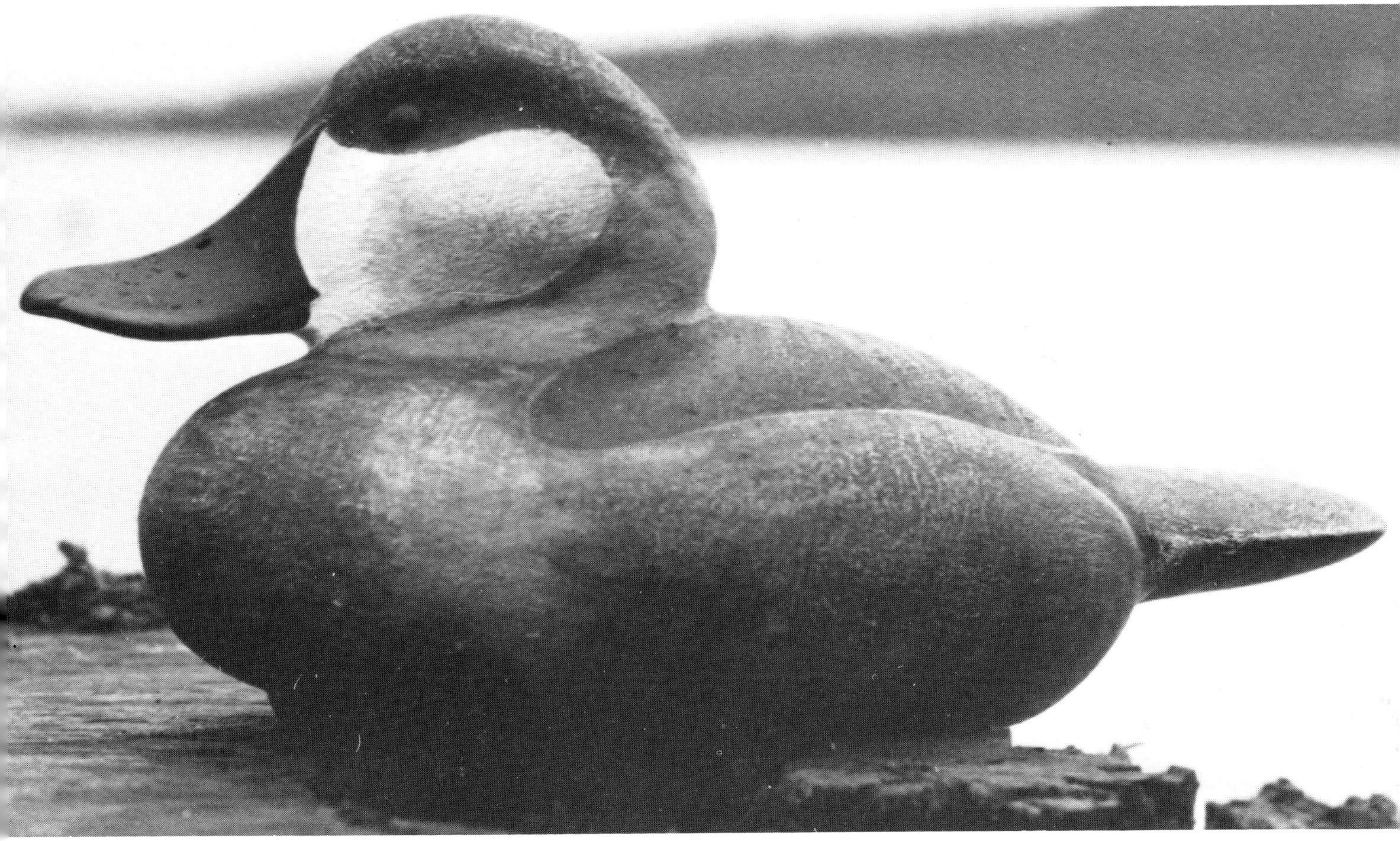

Ruddyduck drake by Keith Dolbeck. 1st place in Michigan hunting decoy contest.

Pintail hen by Keith Dolbeck. Hollow cedar body, basswood head, and original paint.

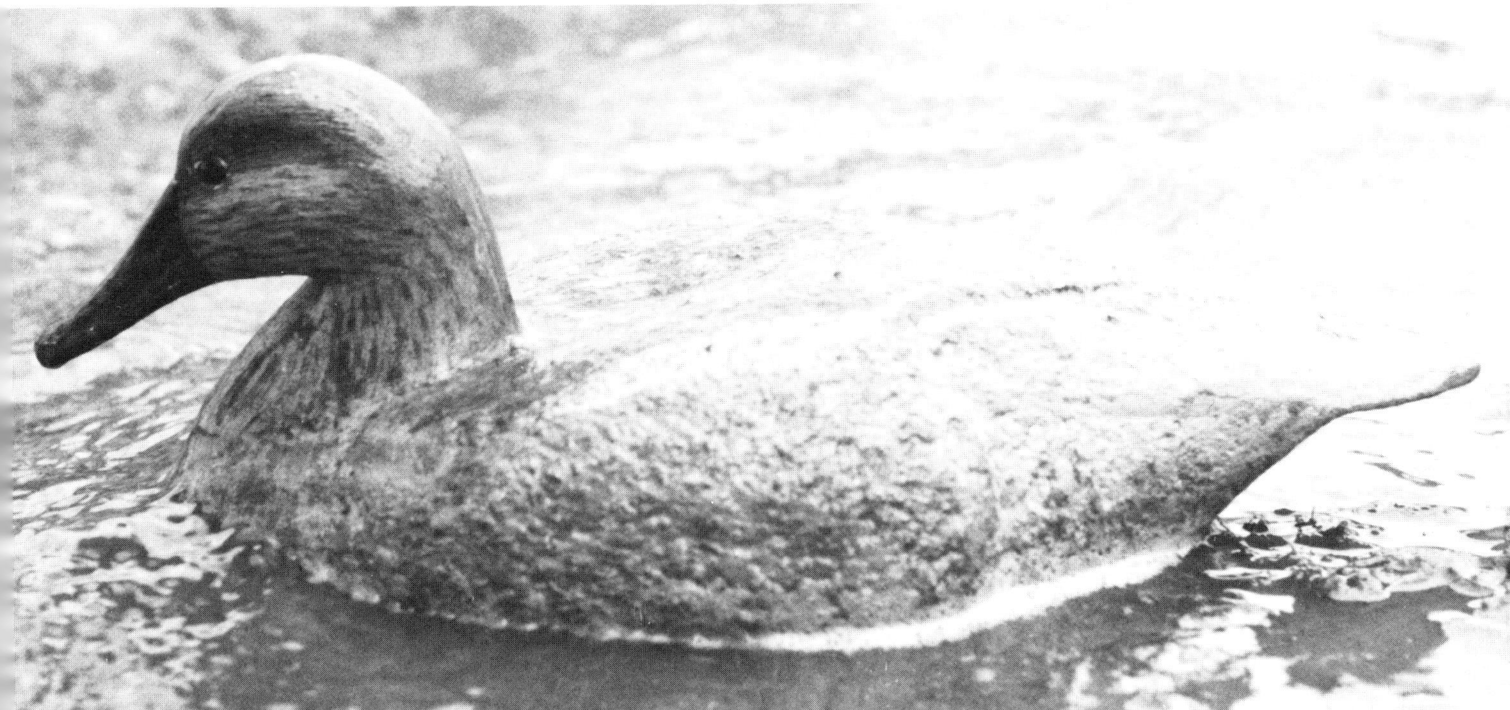

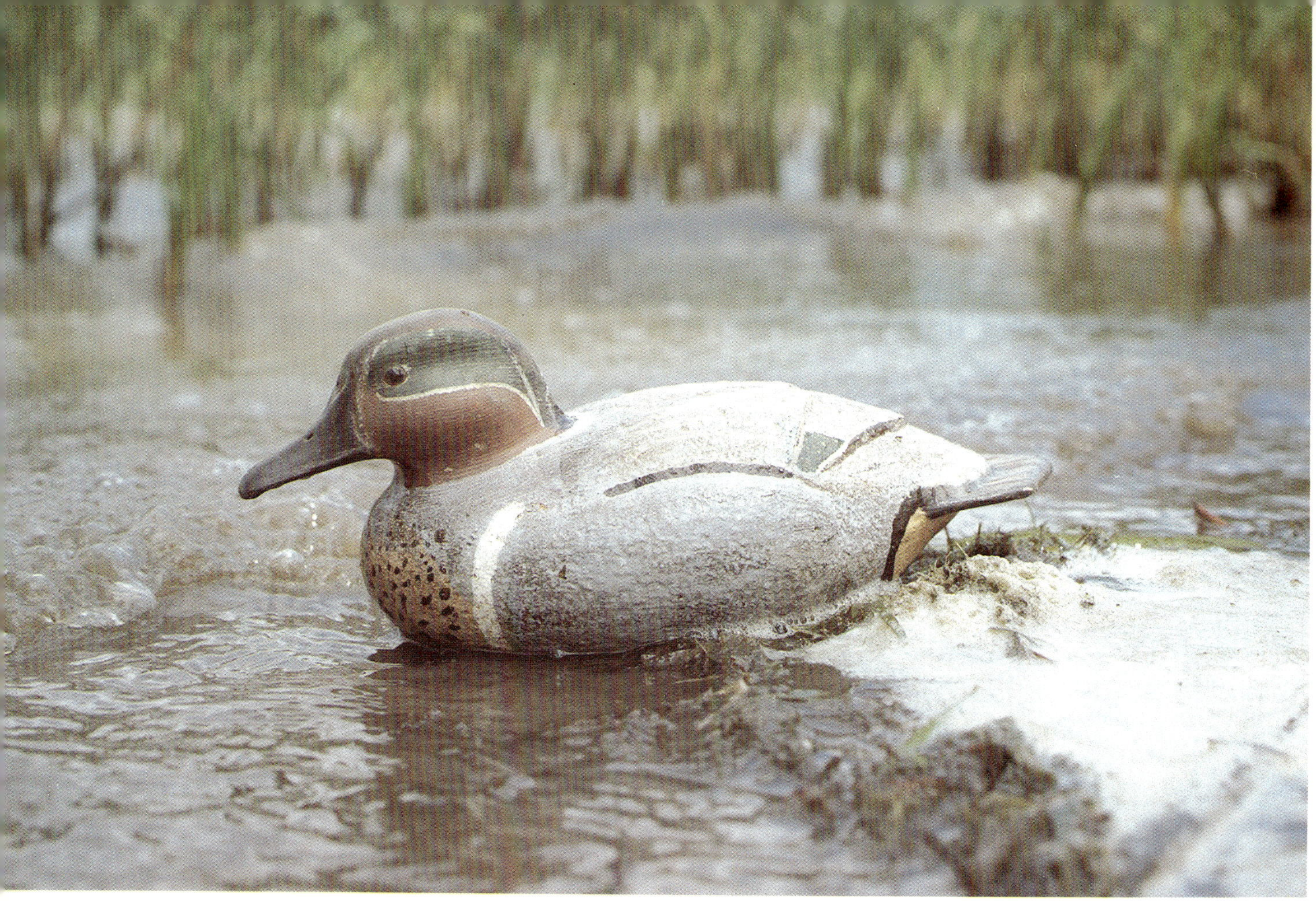

Greenwing teal by Keith Dolbeck. Original paint.

Goldeney hen by Keith Dolbeck ca. 1980. Original paint.

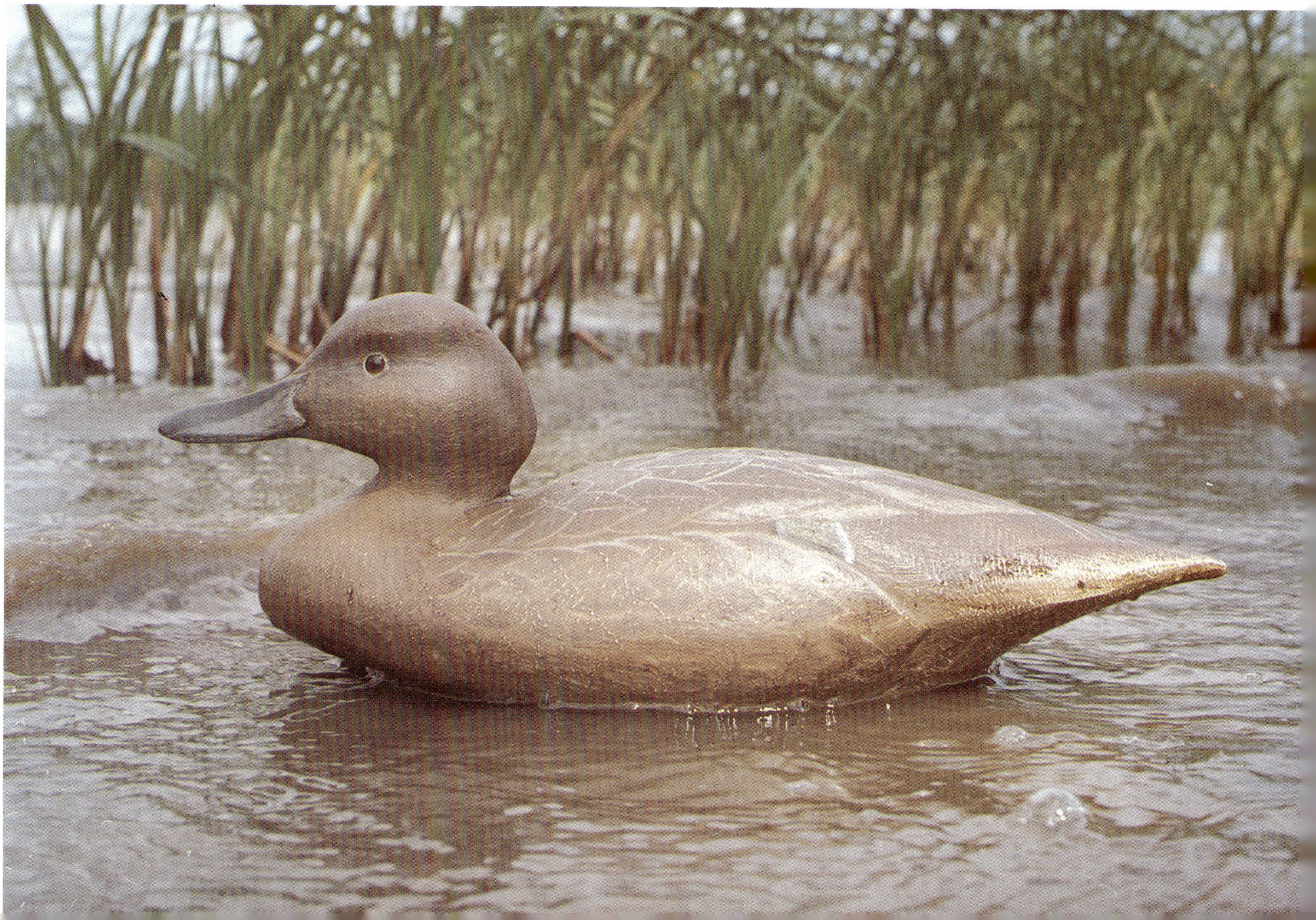

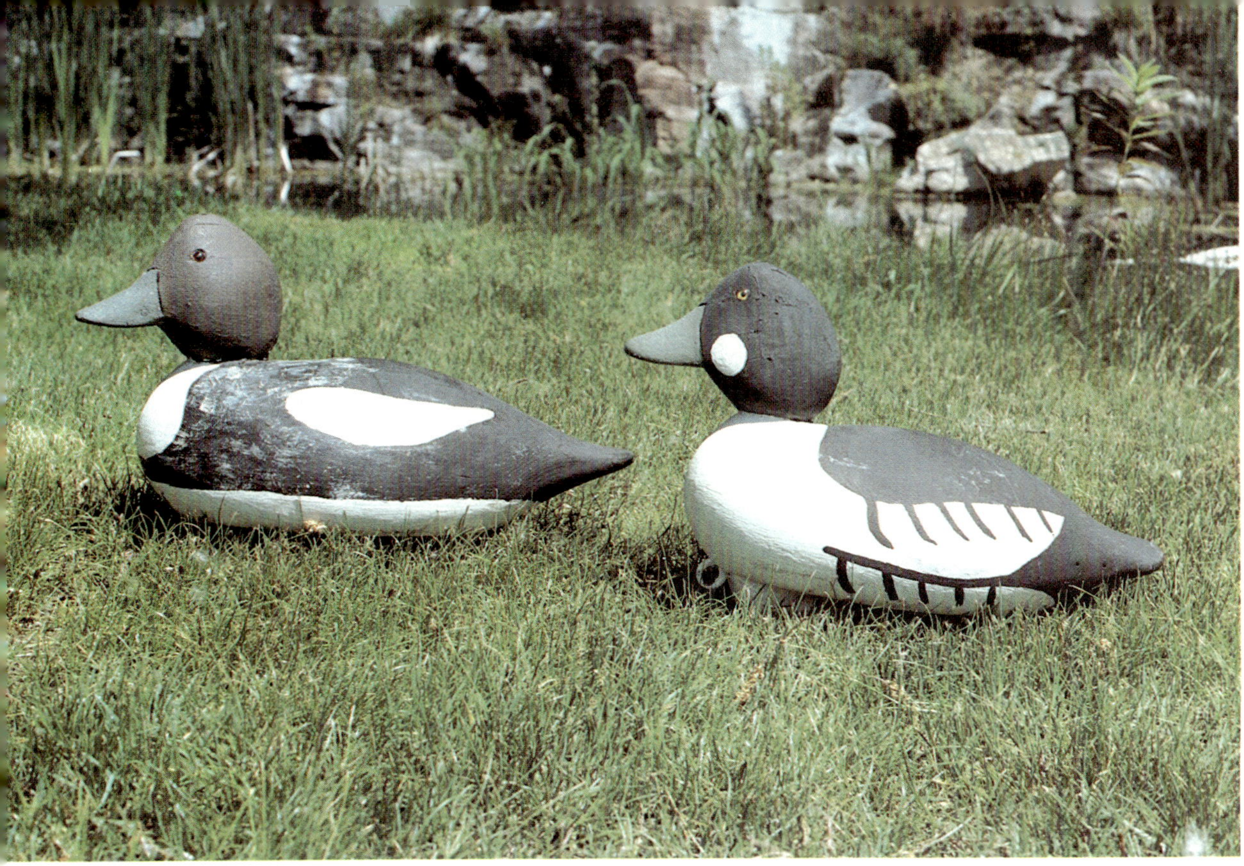

Goldeneye hen and drake by Lloyd Durbrow. Hollow, original paint. Ca. 1955.

Lloyd Durbrow 1926- Burlington, Vermont. After moving to Vermont in 1946 Durbrow began duck hunting and subsequently carving decoys. He carved many whistlers and blacks with hollow, pine construction. Durbrow states he was influenced by Charles "Shang" Wheeler style.

Black ducks by Lloyd Durbrow ca. 1958. Styled after "Shang" Wheeler.

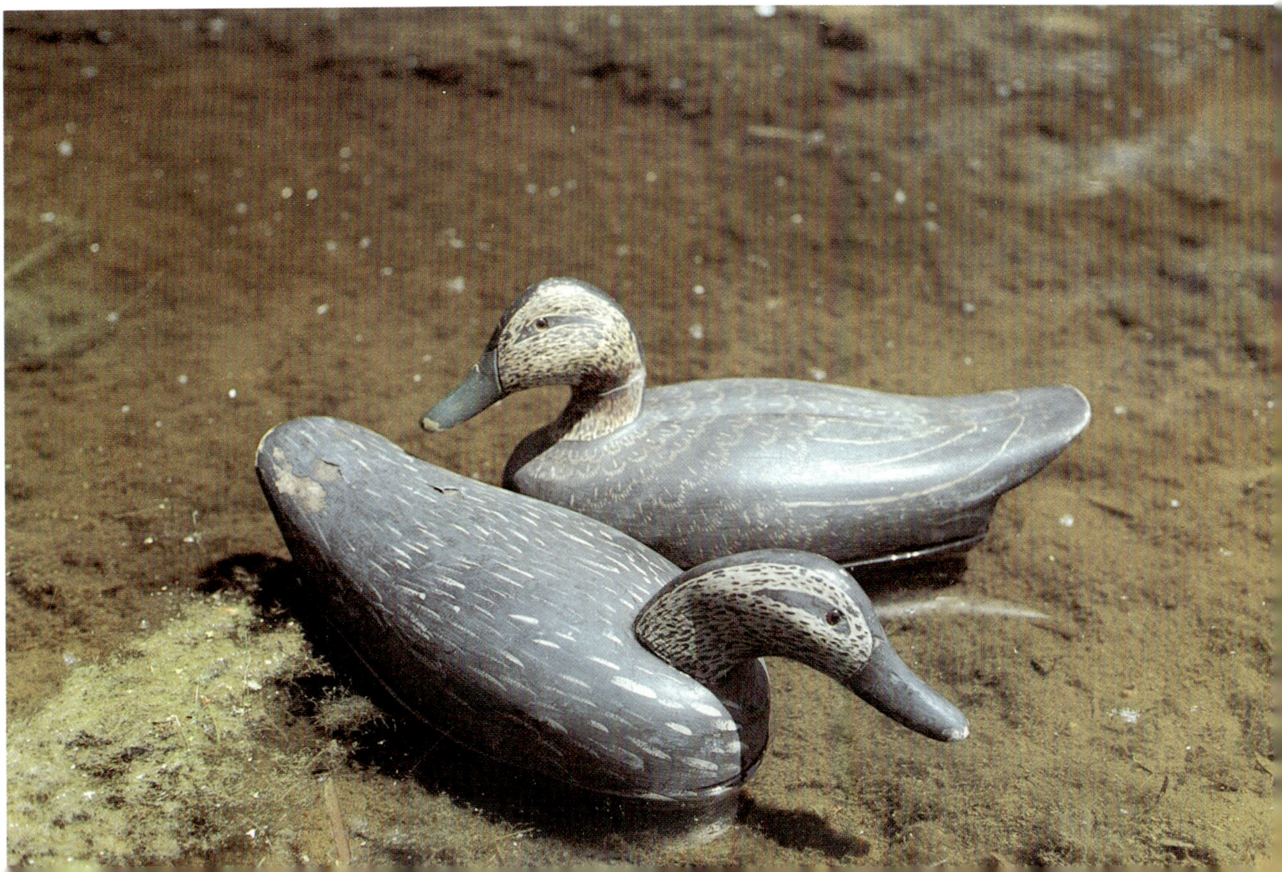

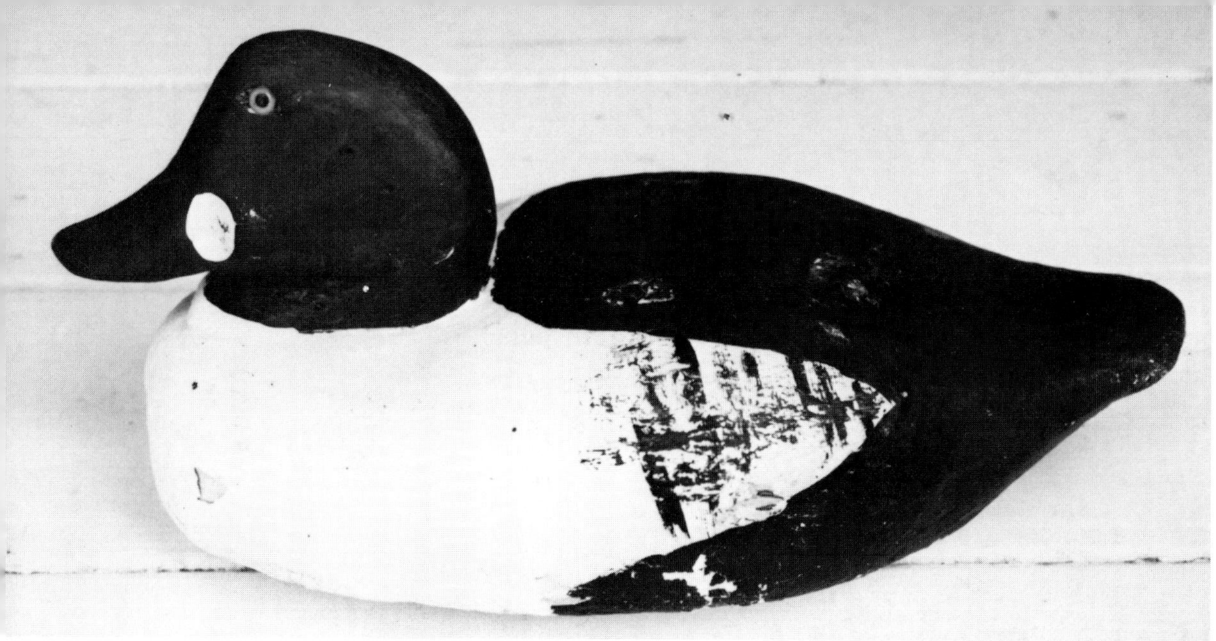

Goldeneye drake by Everett Dubuque, South Hero, Vermont. Balsa body, glass eyes, ca. 1970.

Everett Dubuque 1941- South Hero, Vermont, has carved almost one hundred goldeneyes, both cedar and balsa construction. Dubuque held the last sturgeon fishing license on Lake Champlain and was instrumental in the pilot program of commercial eel fishing.

Lorenzo "Bazoo" Duval 1916-1976 Swanton, Vermont. Duval not only carved decoys but built boats which he used and sold on the lake.

Donald J. Fasking 1929- Plattsburgh, New York. Fasking originally began carving decoys to hunt with while living in Wisconsin. His grandfather, John Accola, (1871-1955) was a noted carver from Prarie Du Sac and Fasking was influenced by his work. Fasking carved many bluebills and teals for his gunning rig. He later began carving competitively and has won seven awards at the Ward Foundation Championships in Salisbury, Maryland. Fasking is now actively carving and teaches classes in the art of decoy carving in the Plattsburg area. His decoys are hollow, cedar construction and have keels.

Goldeneye hen by Lorenzo "Bazoo" Duval. Carved ca. 1935, photographed on the Missisquoi River.

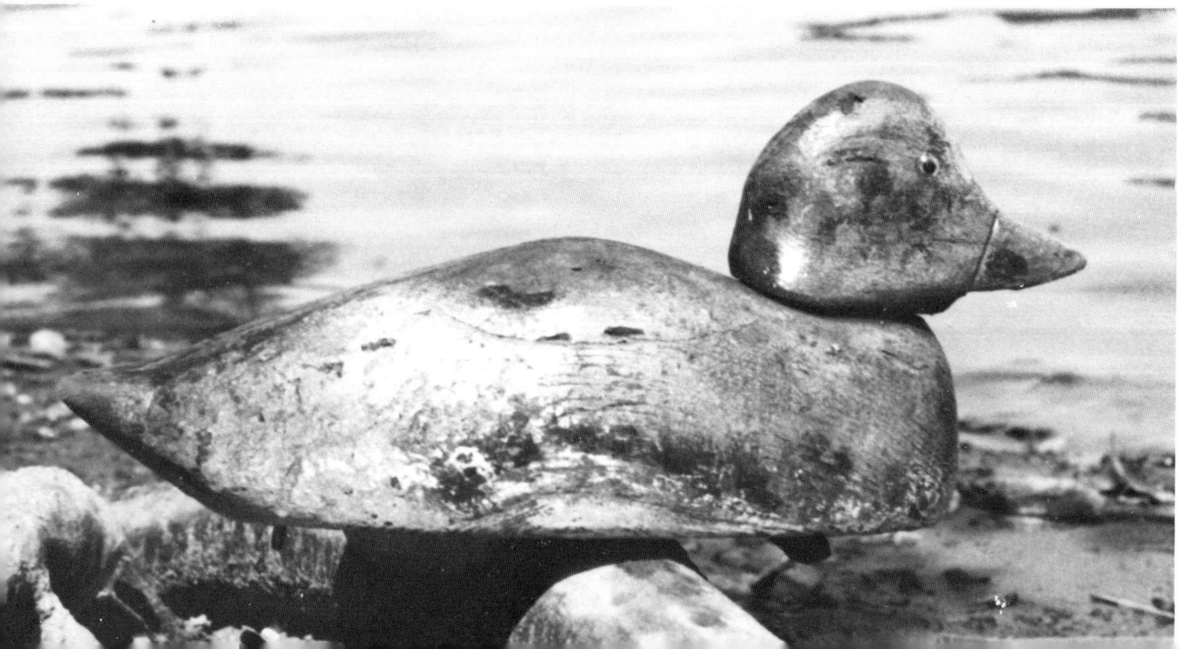

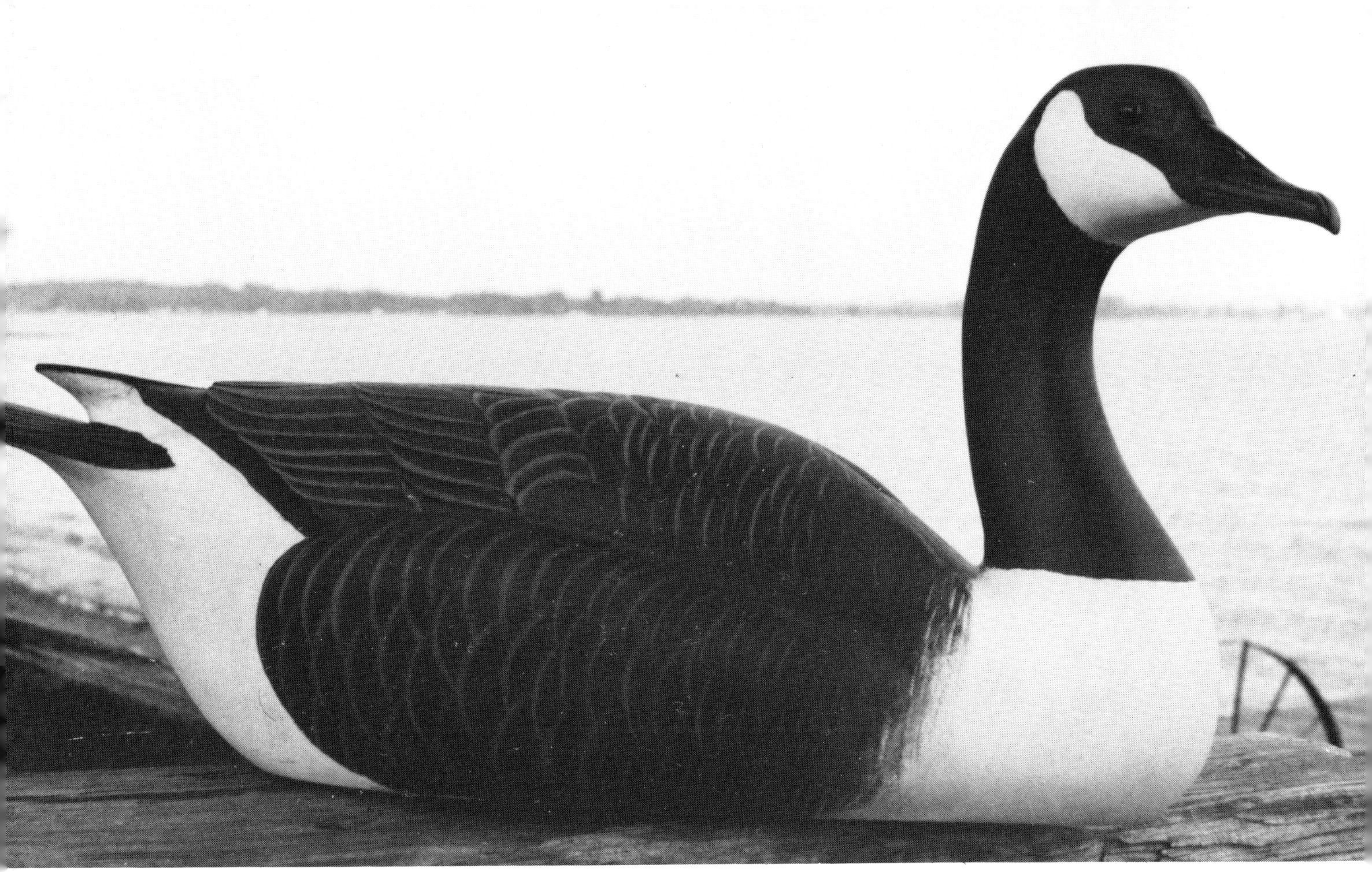

Canada goose by Donald J. Fasking, Plattsburgh, New York. Hollow, original acrylic paint. Designed as a floater. Collection of Mary Lou Lynch.

Bluebill drake by Donald Fasking ca. 1980. Original paint.

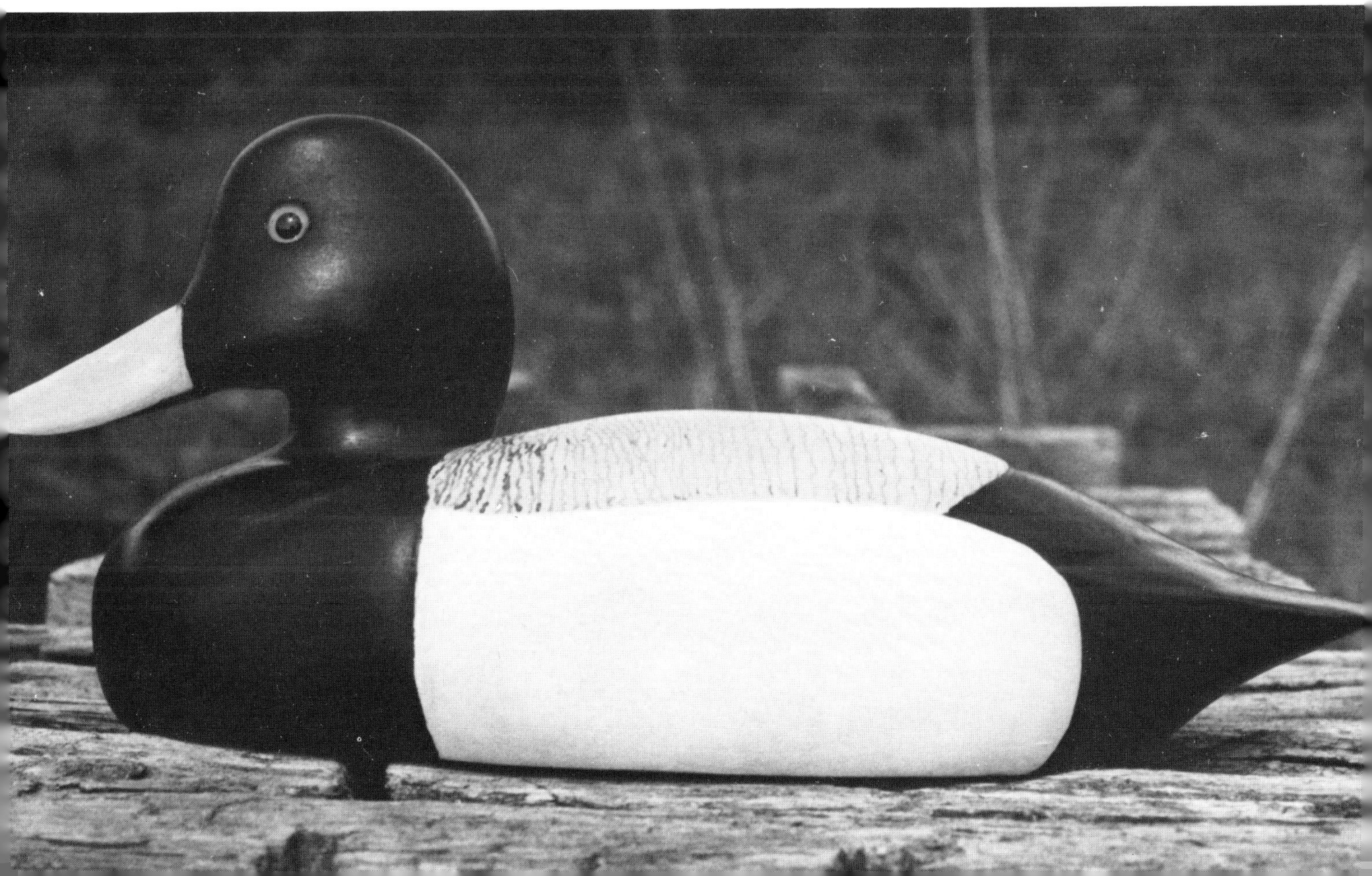

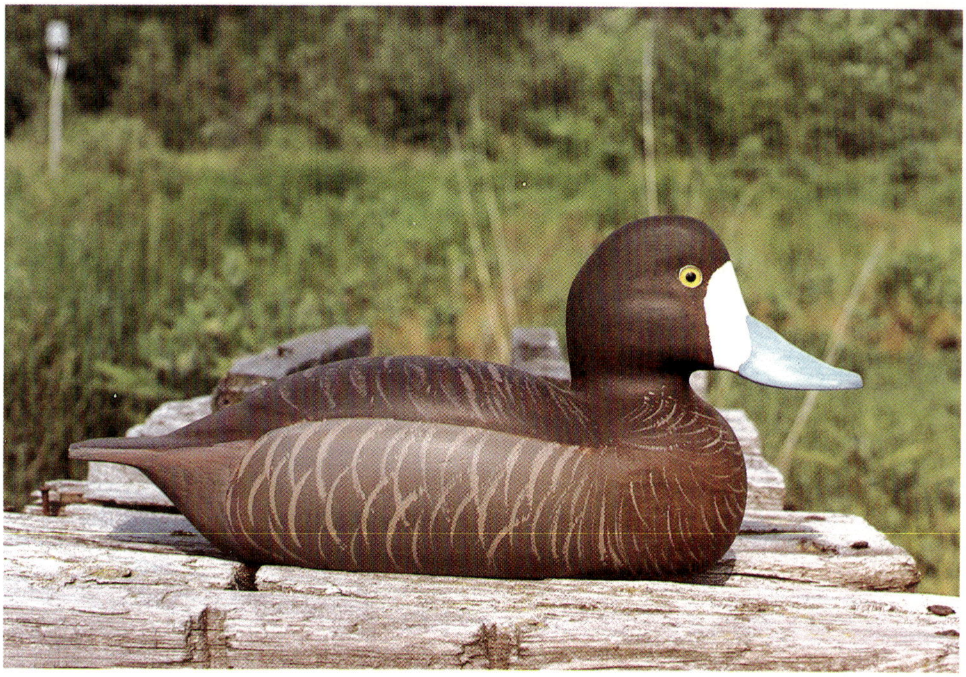

Scaup hen by Donald Fasking. Original paint, ca. 1980.

Black bellied plover, by Donald Fasking. Original paint, cedar construction. Collection of Loy S. Harrell.

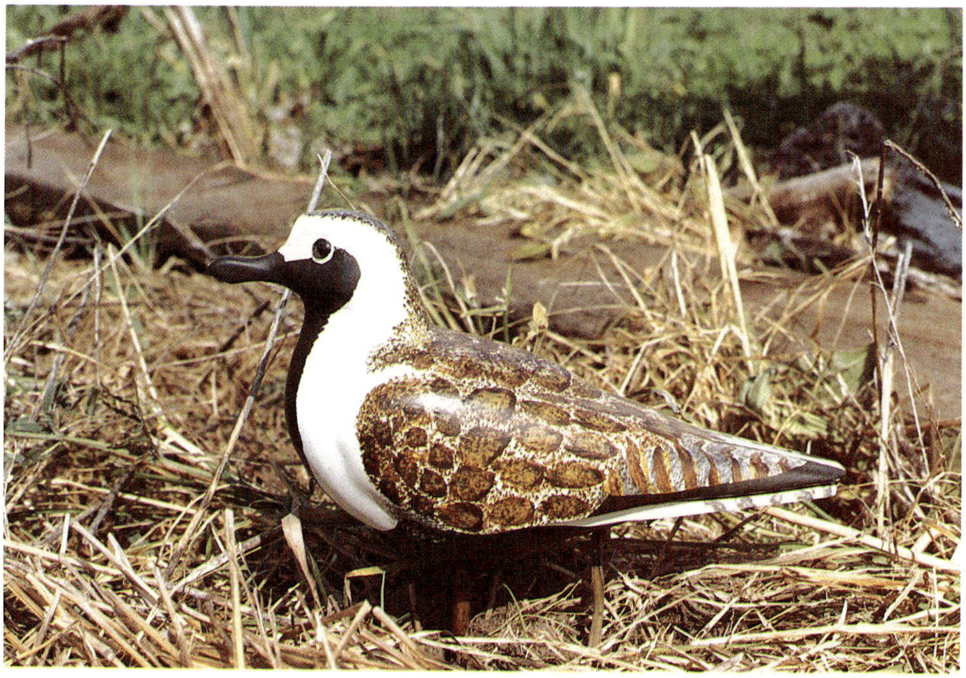

Douglas L. Field 1949- Cornwall, Vermont. Field, now a sheep rancher in Australia grew up in Cornwall, a short distance from the edge of Lake Champlain. He hunted in Shoreham and Bridport along the south-east shore. Field's creative talents became apparent in his carvings. He carved over fifty decoys using white cedar and oil paints. Strongly influenced by his artist father, Field's decoys are artistic gems and any collector or hunter would be remiss to hunt over them and risk damage to their finish.

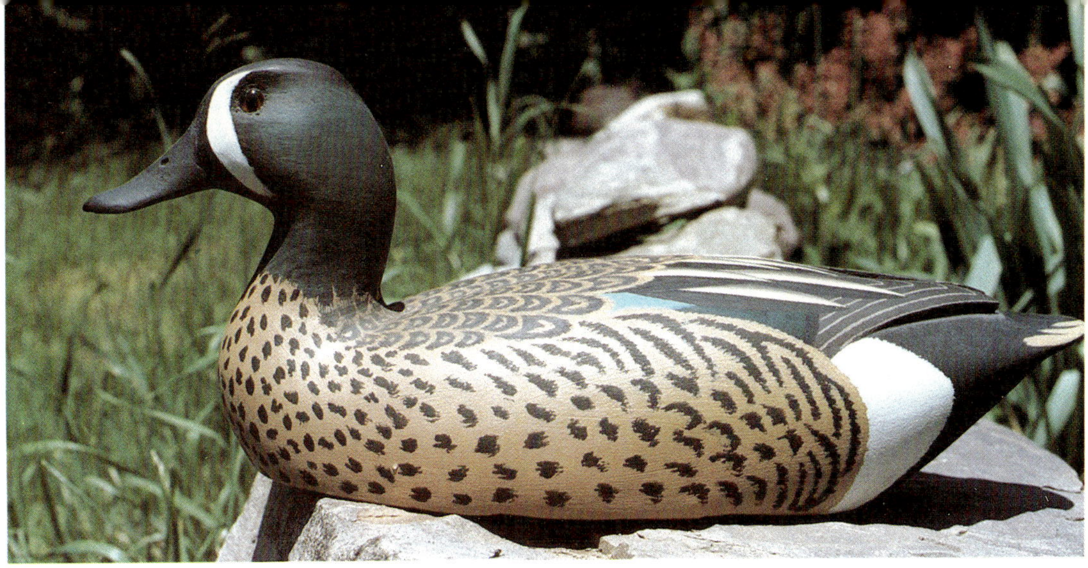

Bluewing teal drake by Douglas Field ca. 1980. Original paint. Collection of Loy S. Harrell.

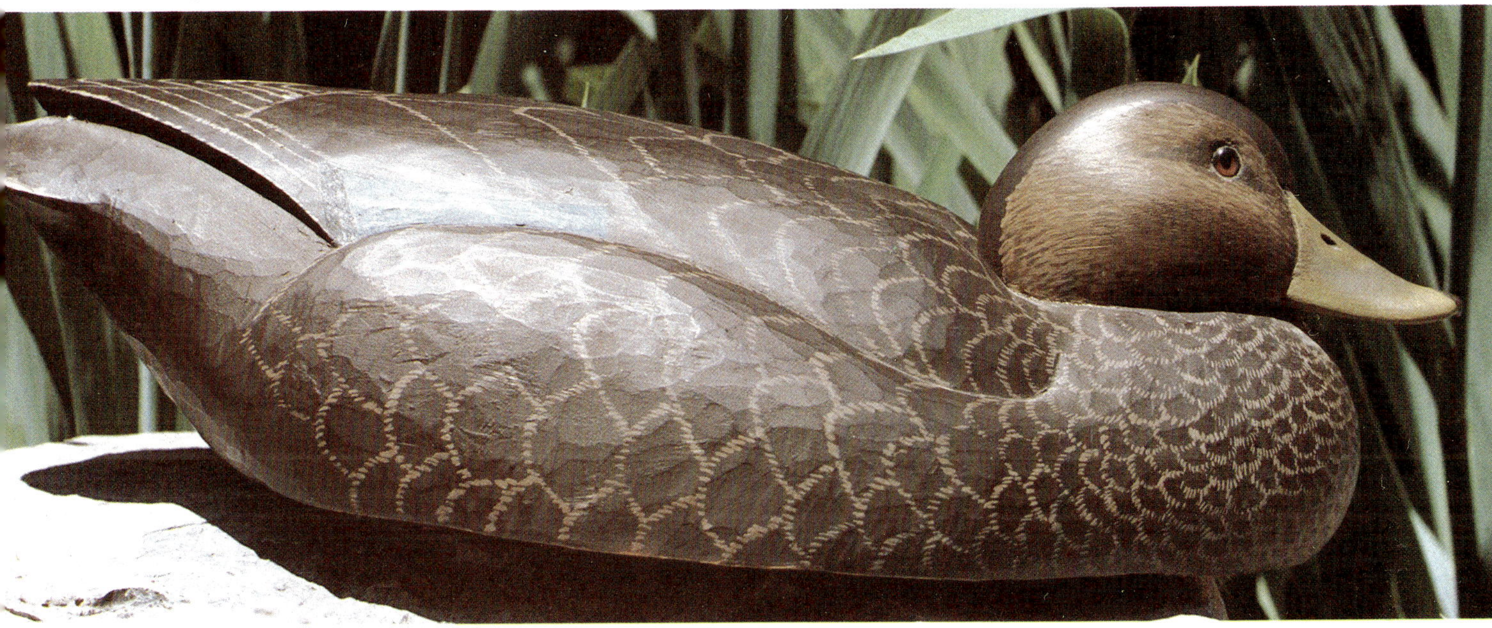

Black duck by Douglas Field. Original paint ca. 1980. Collection of Lachlan and Martha Field.

Canvasback drake by Douglas Field. Chip carved surface, original paint.

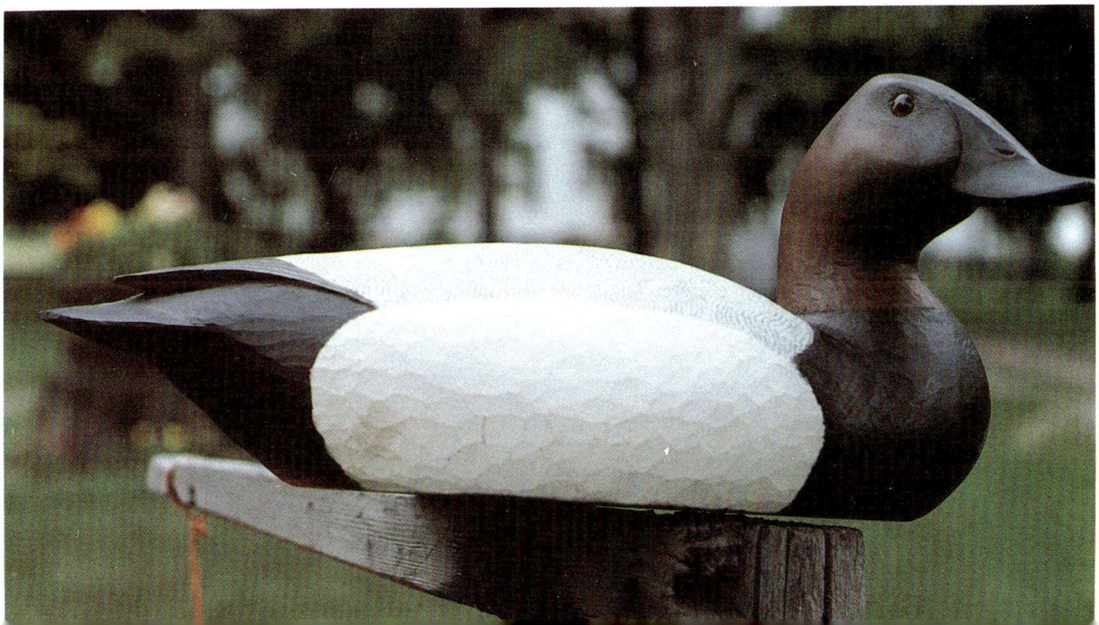

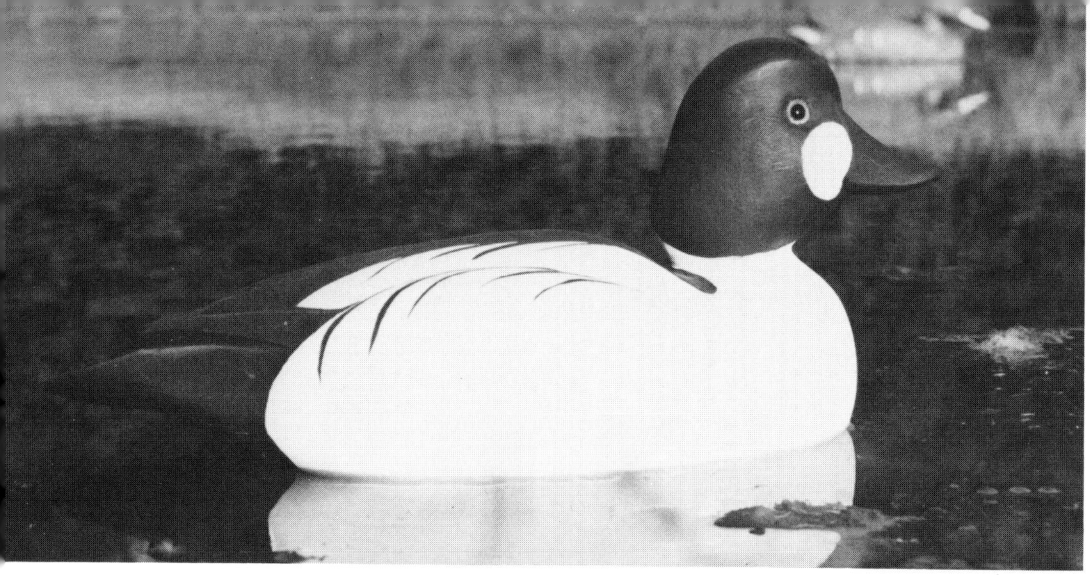

Goldeneye drake by Douglas Field. Glass eyes, original paint. Ca. 1980. Collection of Loy S. Harrell.

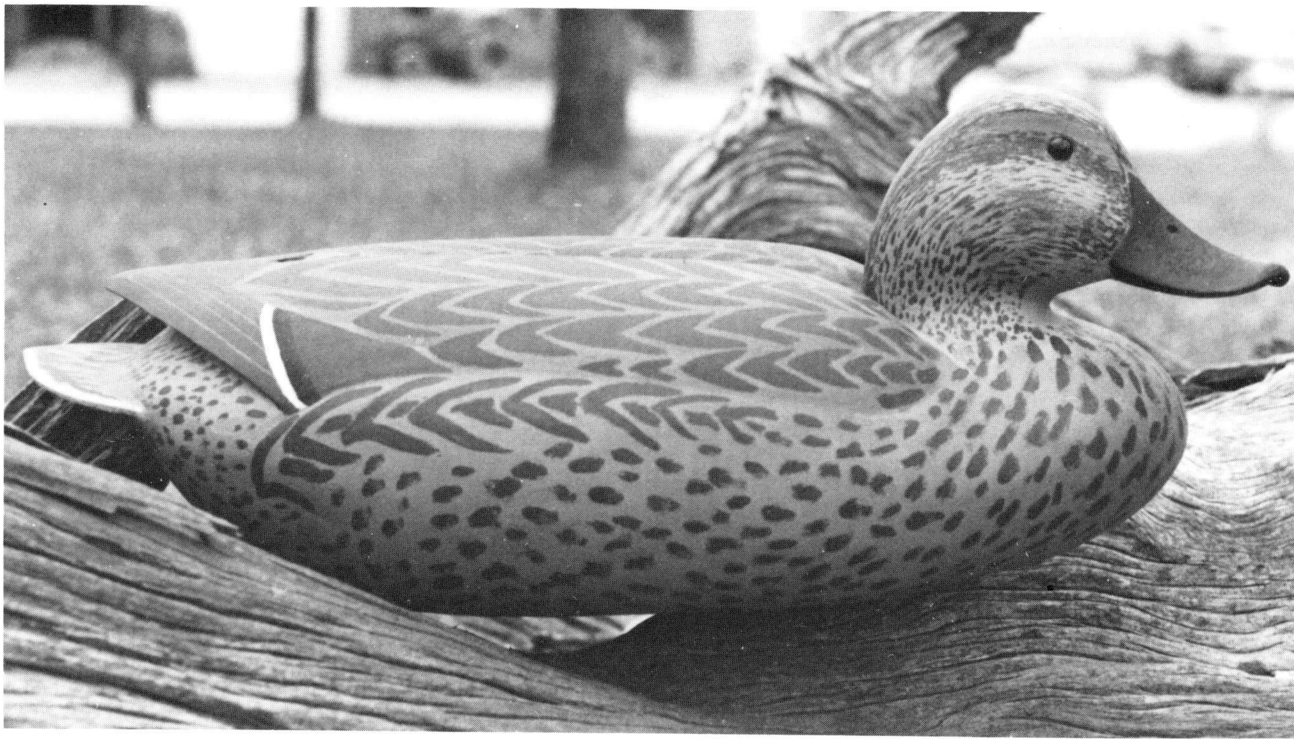

Mallard hen by Douglas Field. Collection of Edwin and Lucille James.

Mallard drake by Douglas Field. Original paint. Collection of Edwin and Lucille James.

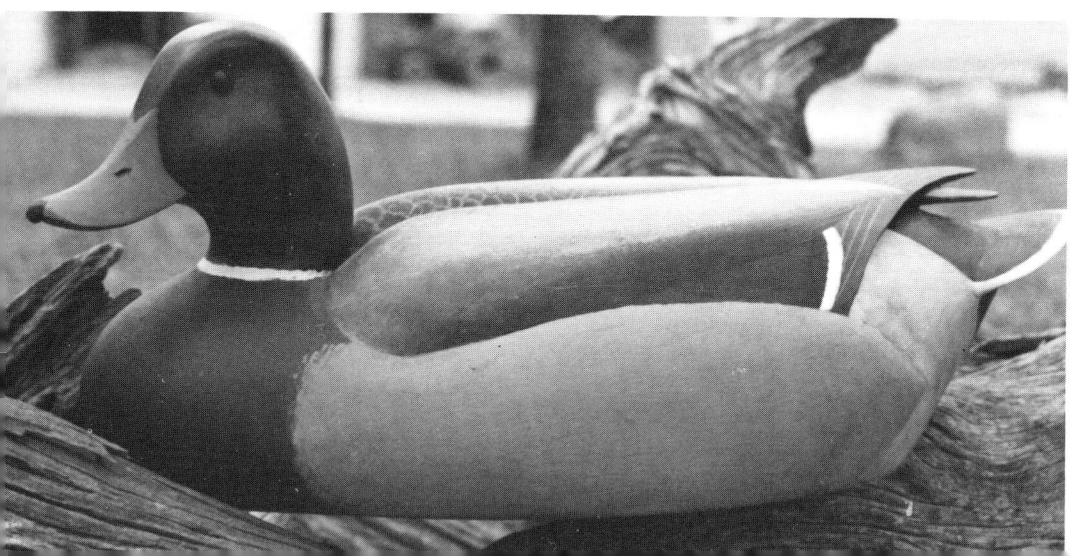

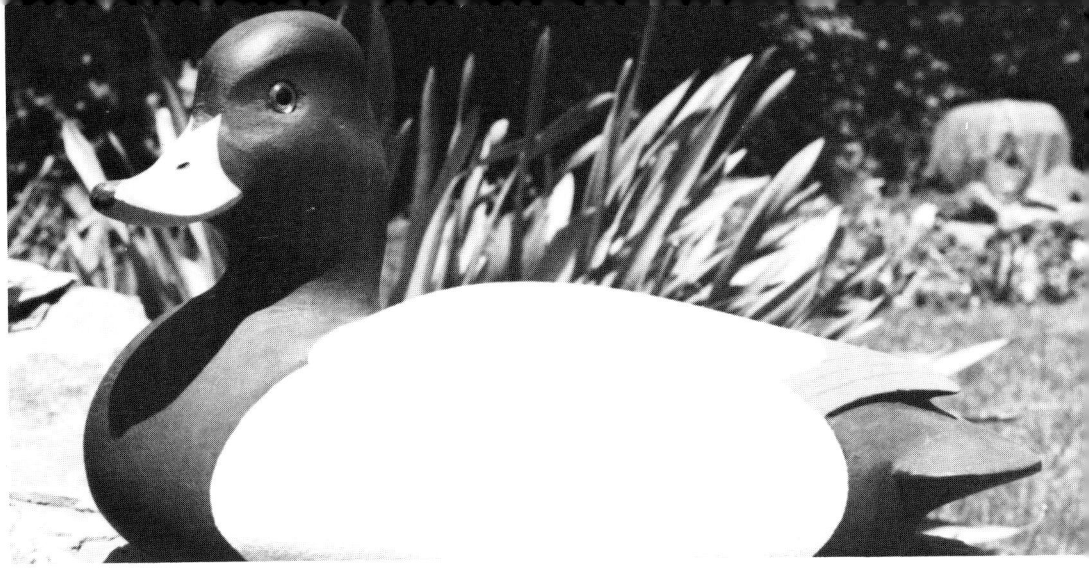

Bluebill drake by Douglas Field ca. 1980.

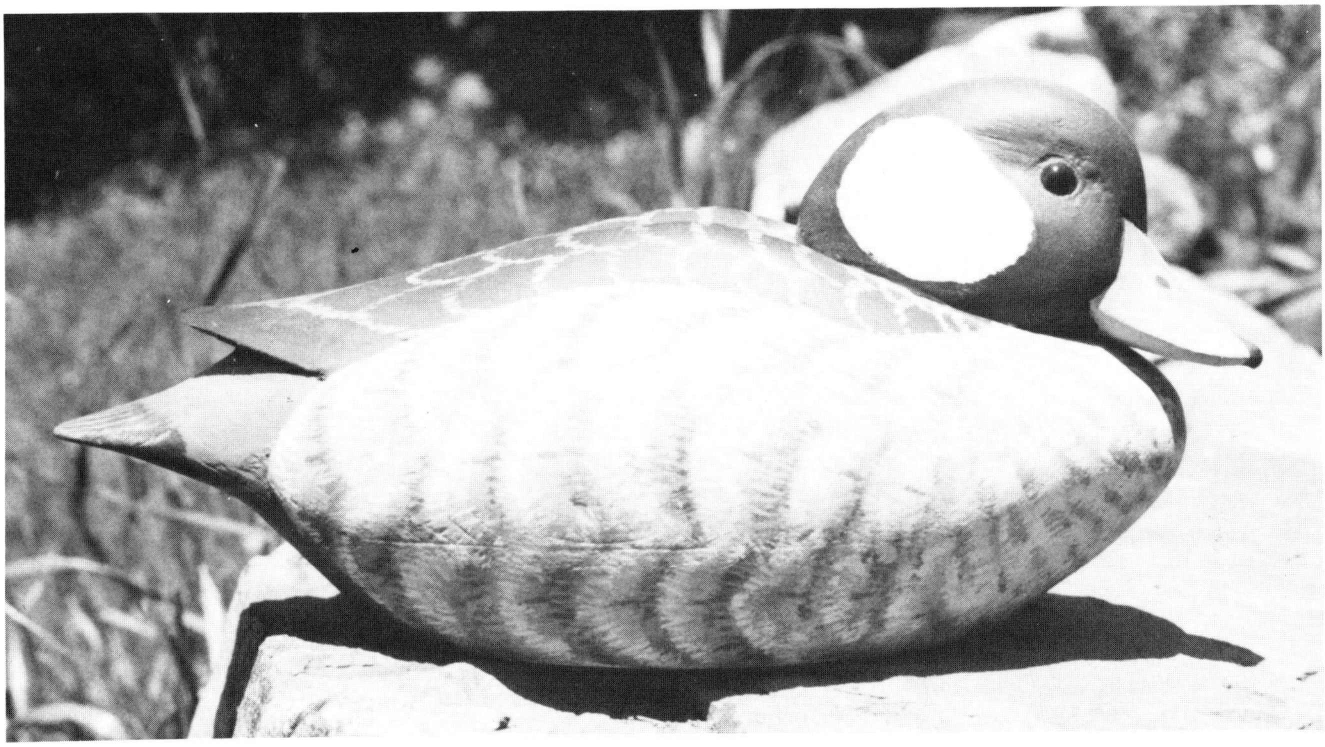

Bufflehead drake by Douglas Field, Cornwall, Vermont. Original paint. Ca. 1978.

Goldeneye hen, low head by Douglas Field. Original paint (a beautiful decoy). Collection of Lachlan Field.

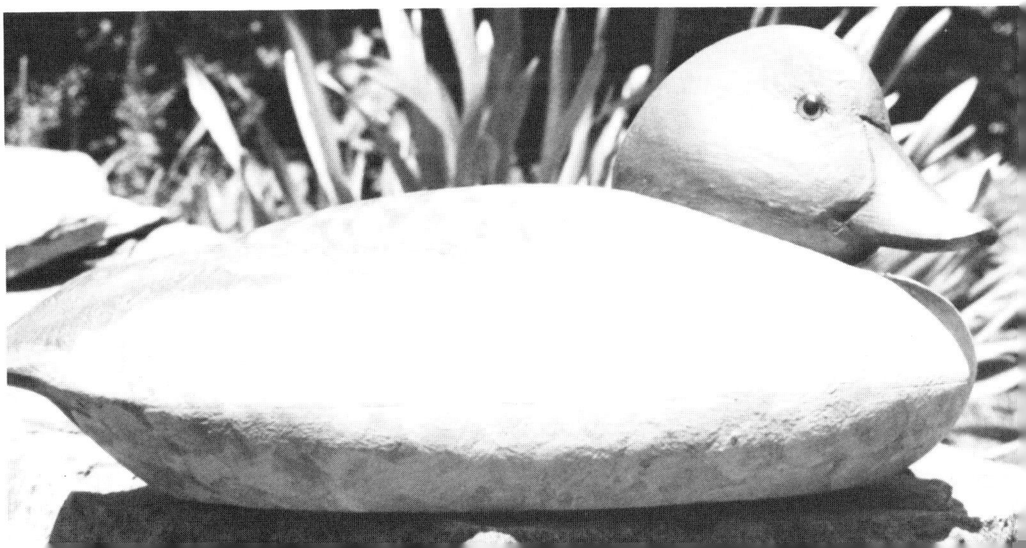

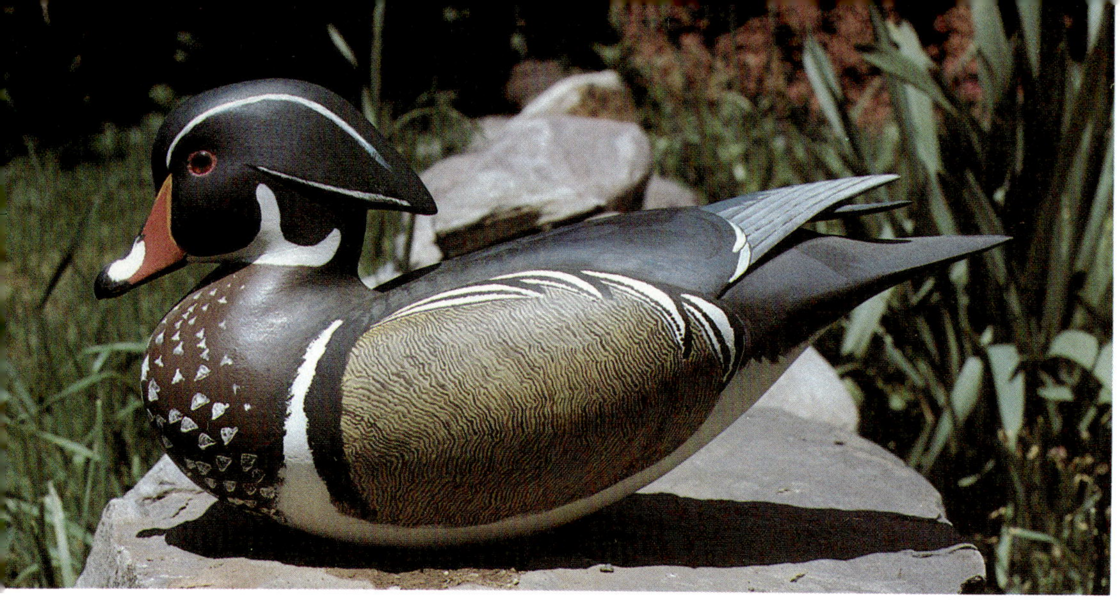

Woodduck drake by Douglas Field. Decorative style.
Collection of Lachlan Field.

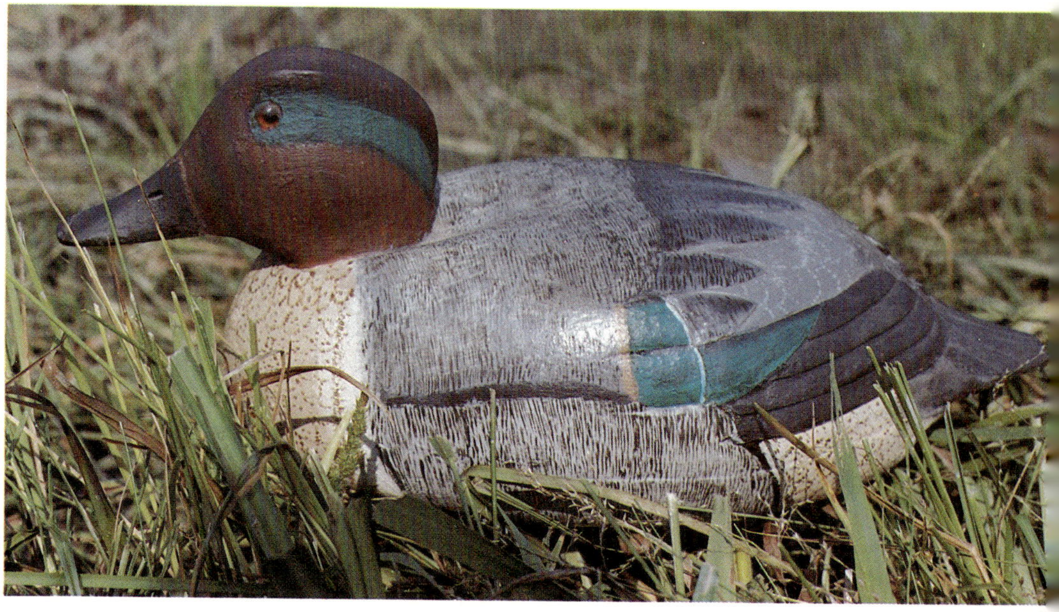

Greenwing teal drake by Phillip Gregory. Original paint.
Collection of Loy S. Harrell.

Greenwing teal hen by Phillip Gregory. Collection of
Jane Gregory.

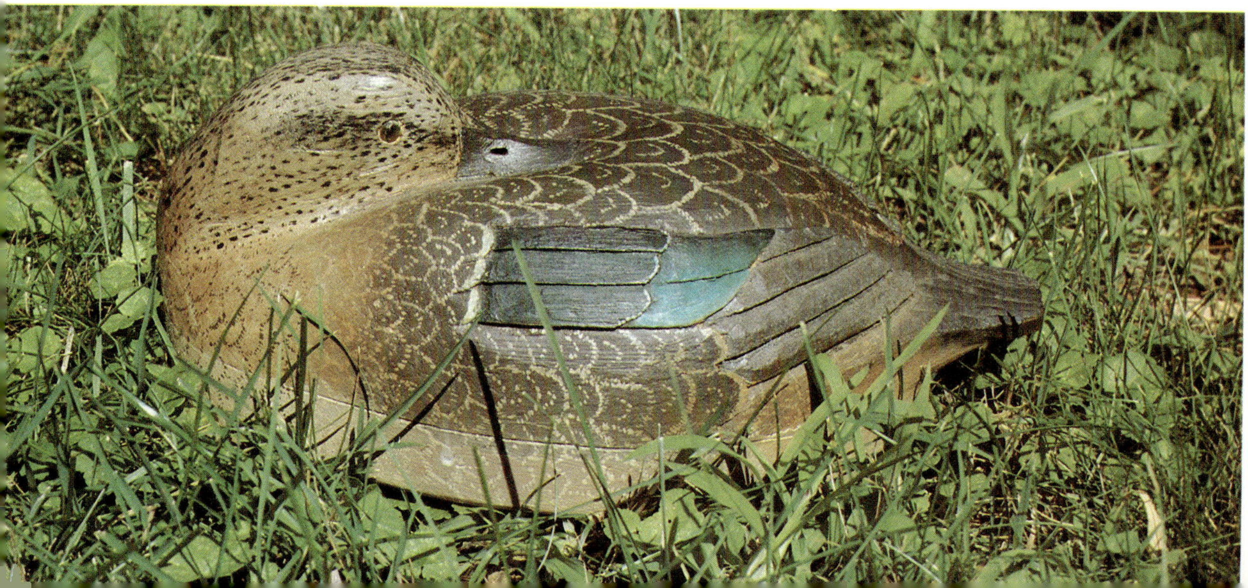

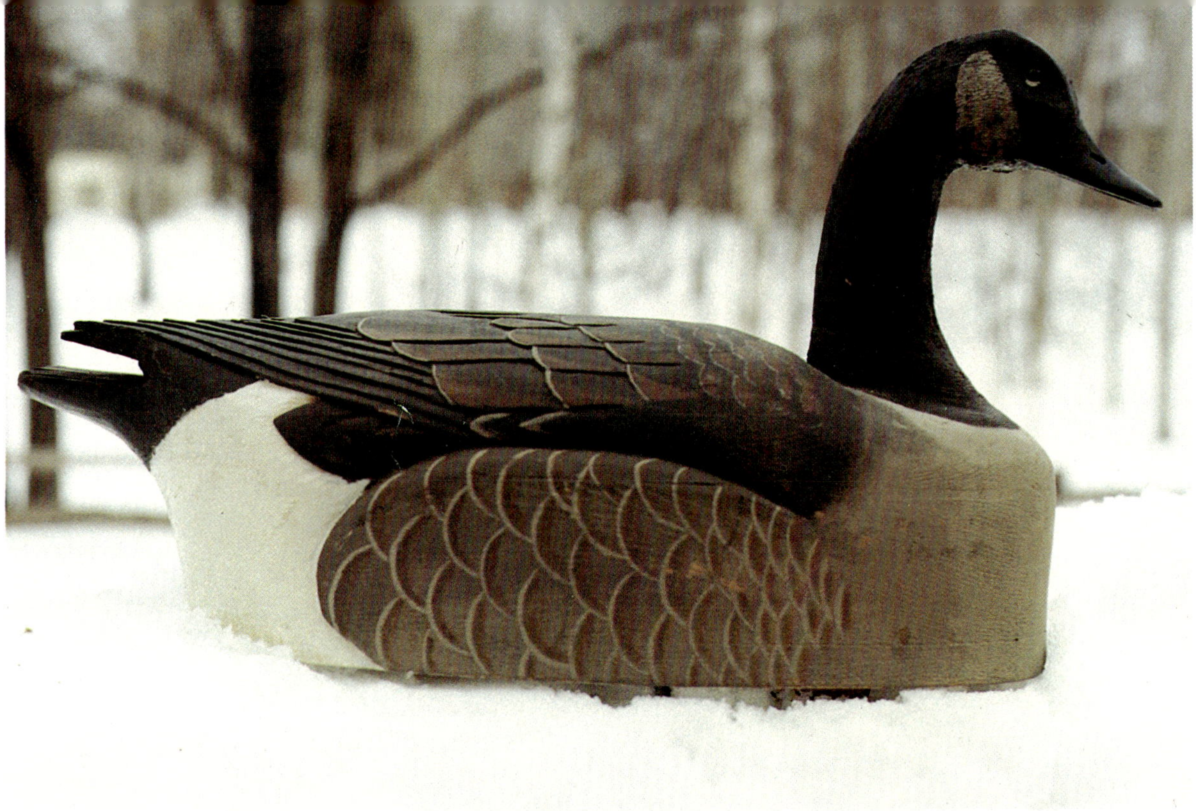

Canada goose by Phillip Gregory ca. 1962. Hollow, pine construction with raised feather carving. Used as a floater collection of Jane Gregory Rubin.

Phillip Gregory 1911-1969. Essex Junction, Vermont. A Canada goose and black duck decoy were given to the Shelburne Museum in 1969 by the Gregory family as a tribute to this mans wonderful carvings. He was born in Lyndonville, Vermont and at age twenty began to carve working decoys which he used primarily at the Sand Bar, Lake Champlain. His hunting companions, Rupert King and Russ Merriman were also carvers and active hunters. In 1960, Gregory attended a decoy show at the Shelburne Museum and according to his wife, Jane, "he was off to the races". In effect, his creative, lifelike decoys began to unfold. He became dedicated to carving working decoys that were as close to the real thing as possible, yet sturdy enough to gun over. His rigs are all hollow, cedar and pine construction. When he died in 1969, Gregory had an inventory of almost one hundred decoys. Many are in private collections. But the majority are still held by his family.

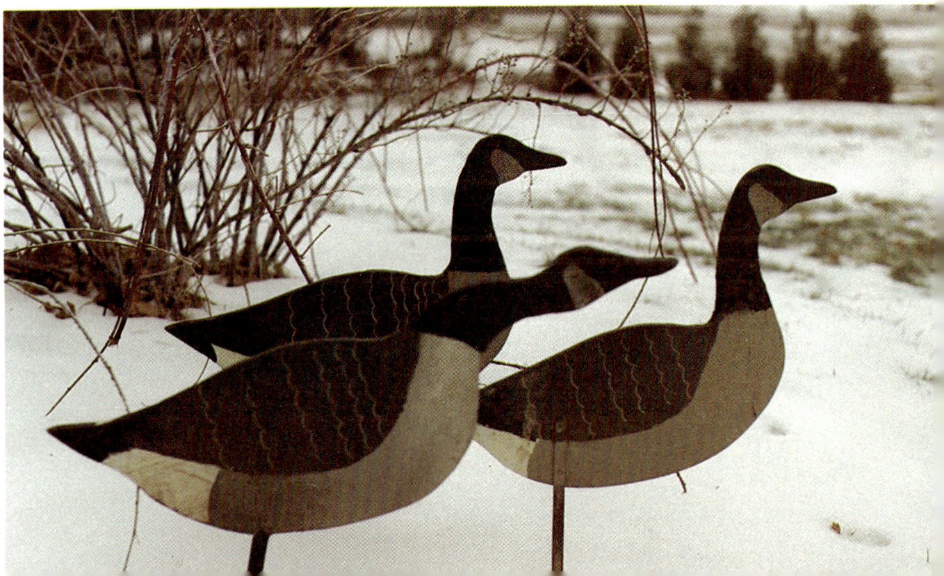

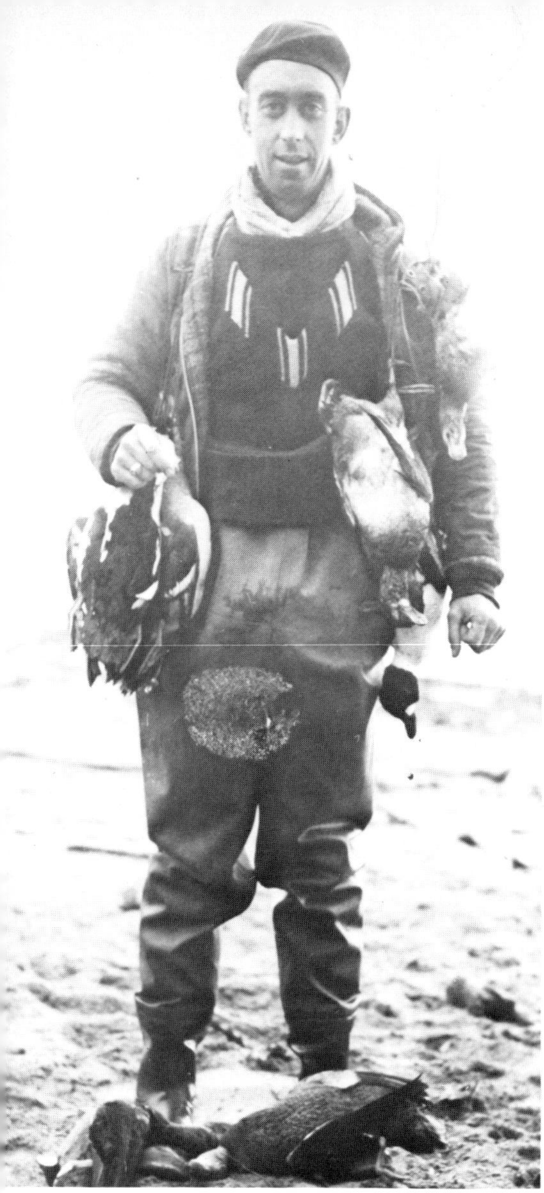

Phillip "Pete" Gregory 1942 at Sand Bar Marsh, Milton, Vermont.

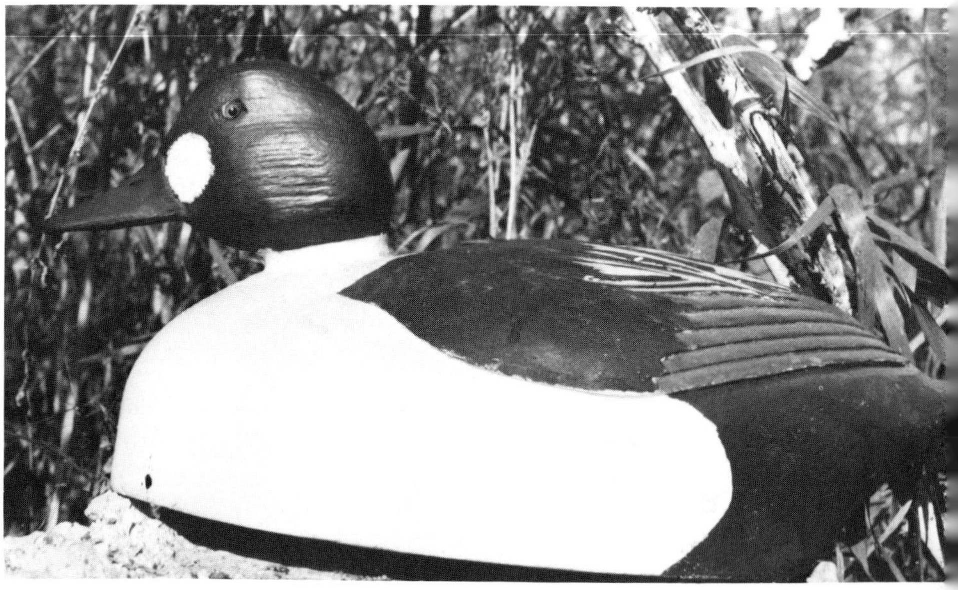

Bluebill drake by Phillip Gregory. Collection of Jane Gregory Rubin.

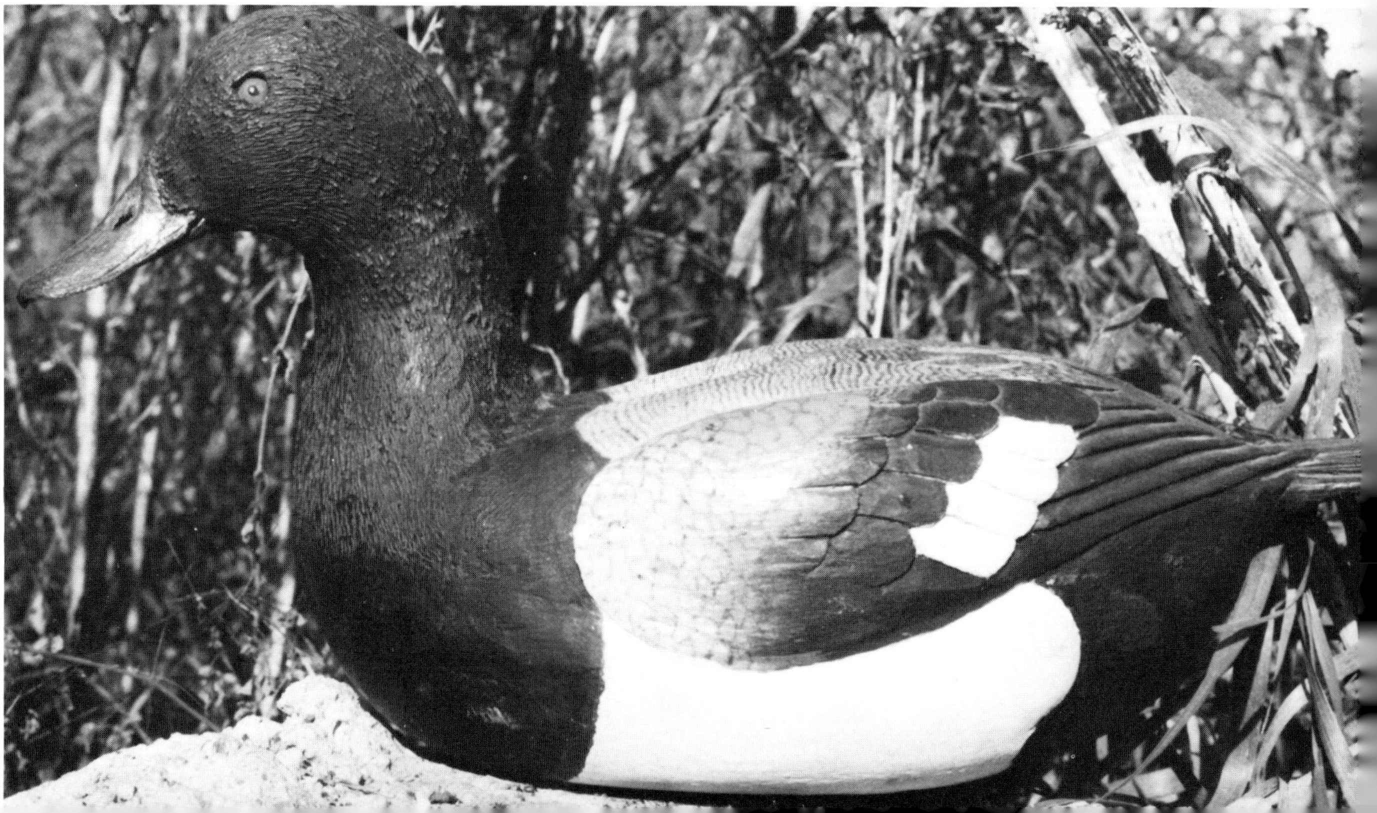

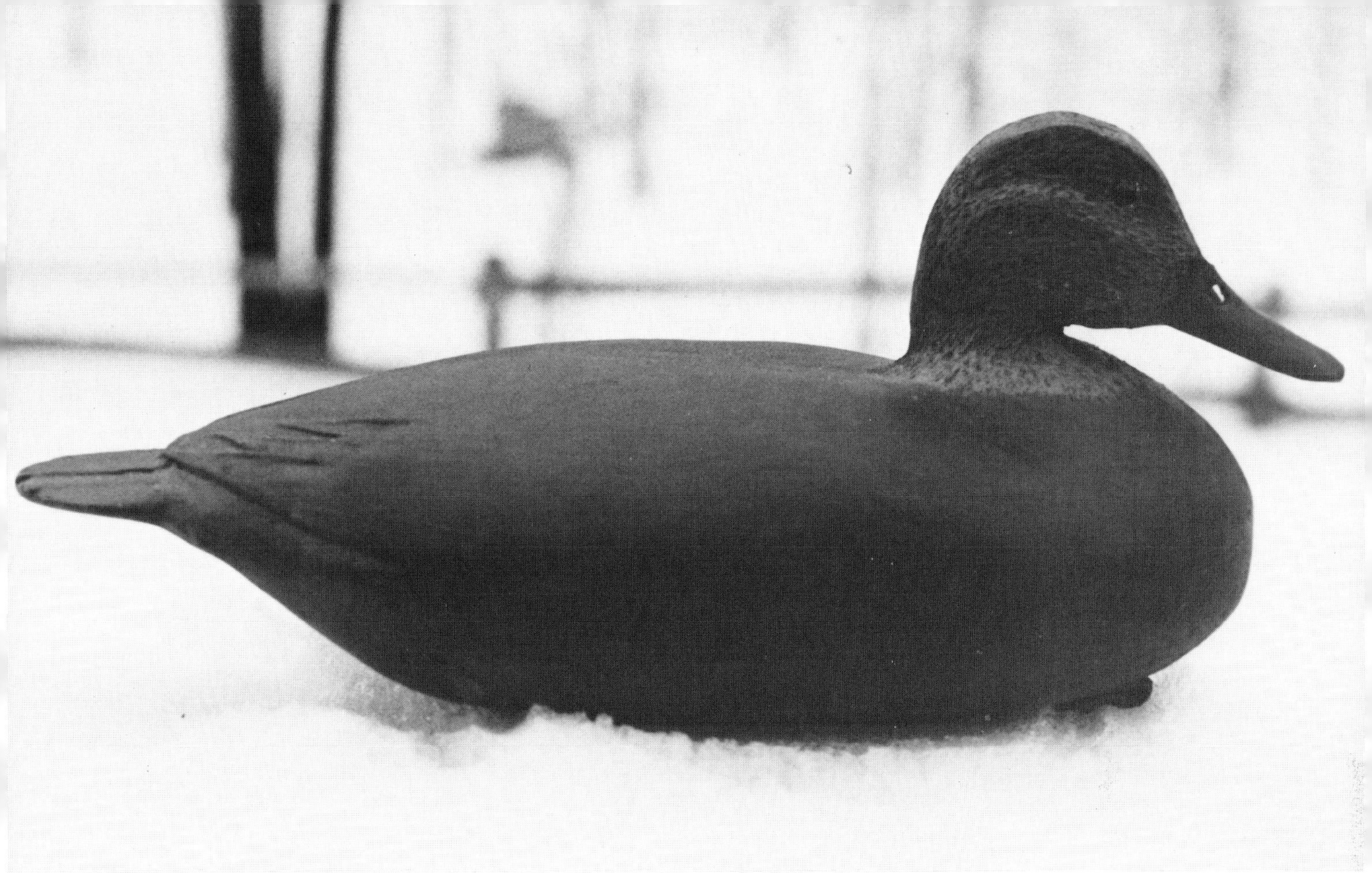

Black duck by Phillip Gregory ca. 1960. Working original paint.

Pintail drake by Phillip Gregory, carved as a working decoy. Original paint. Collection of Jane Gregory.

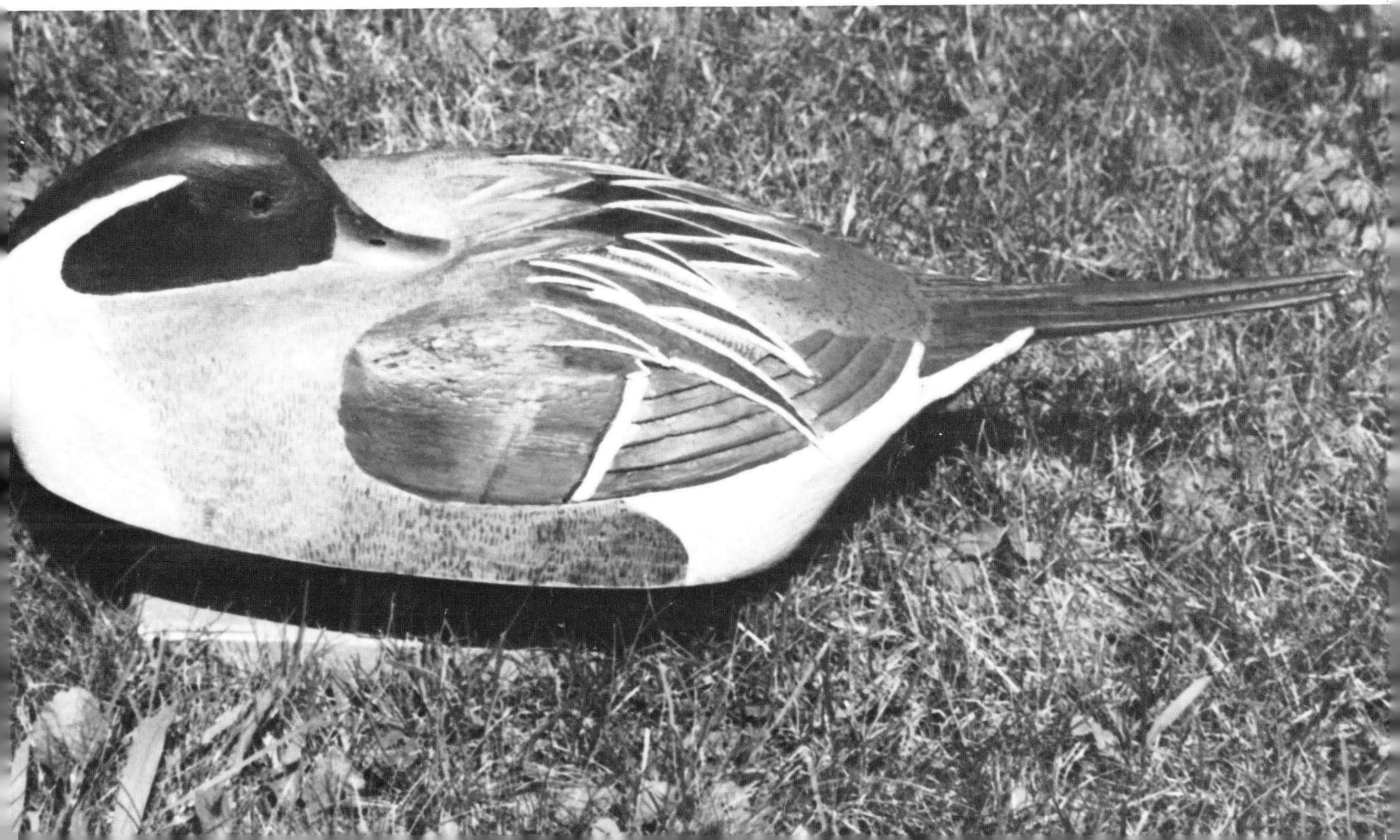

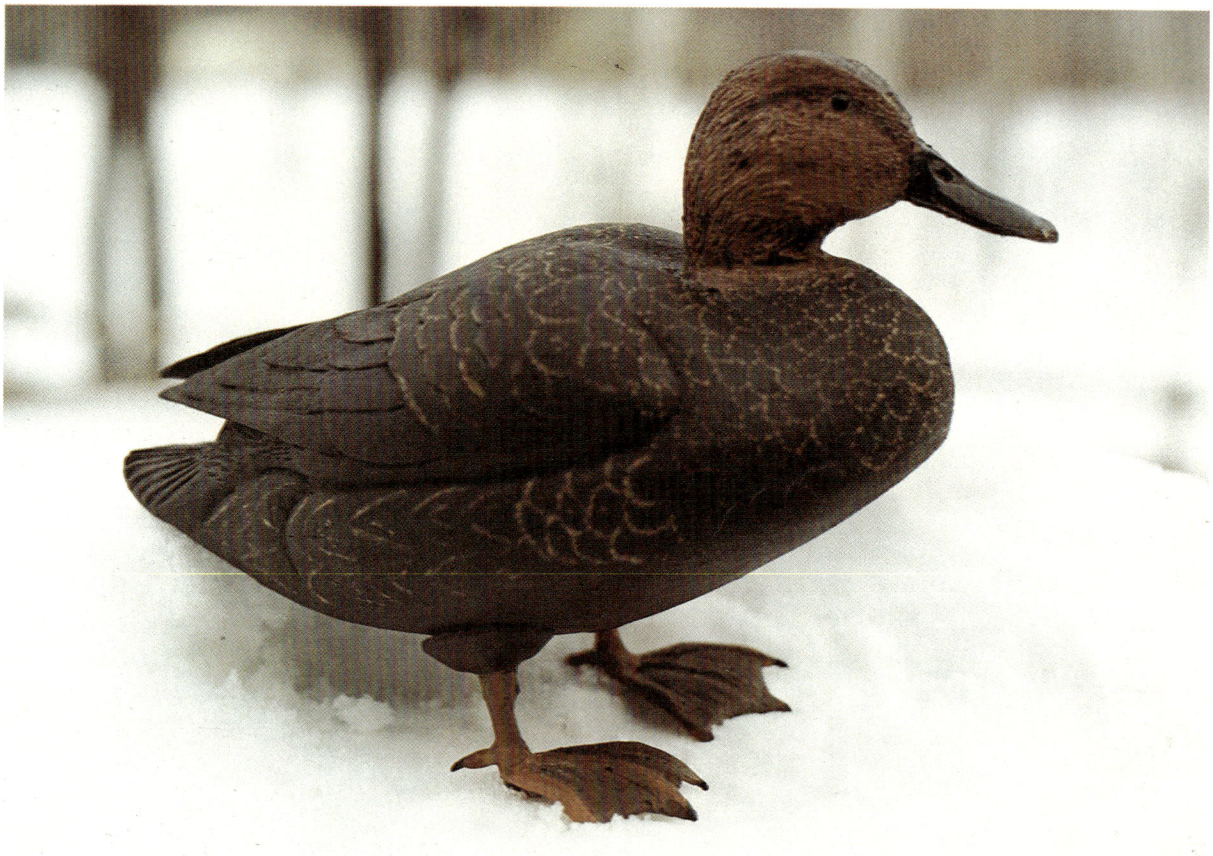

Black duck by Phillip Gregory. Pine, decorative ca. 1965.

Woodduck drake by Phillip Gregory. Original paint, working decoy ca. 1963. Collection of Jane Gregory.

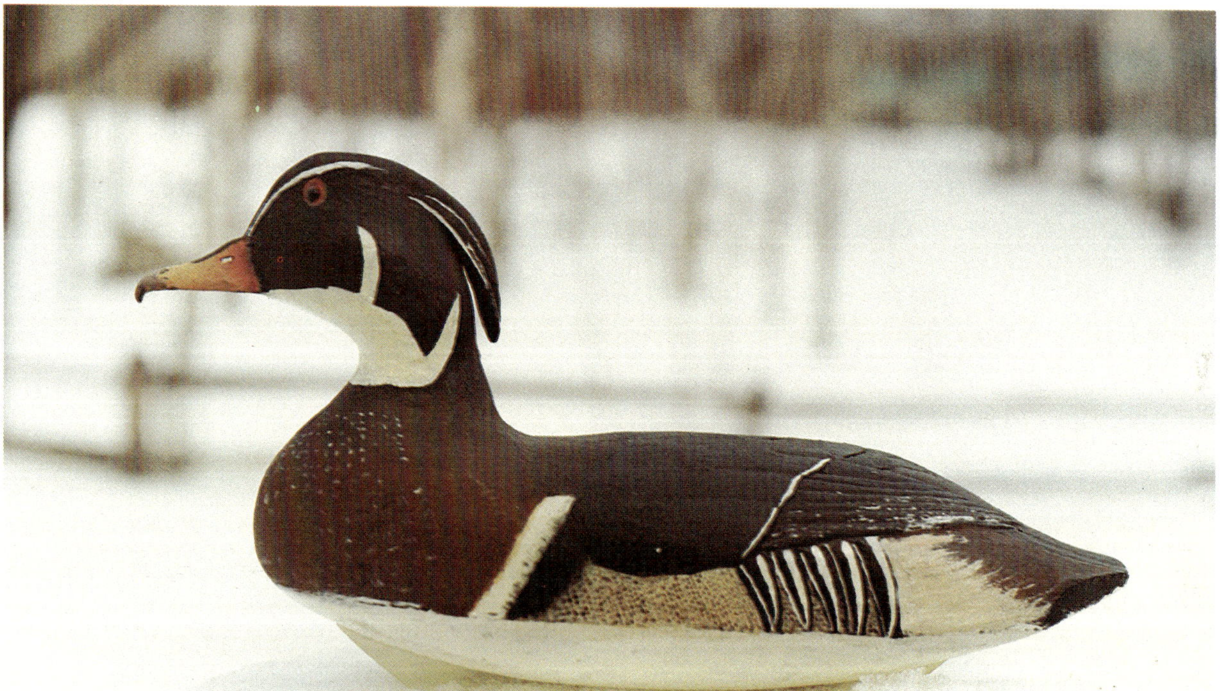

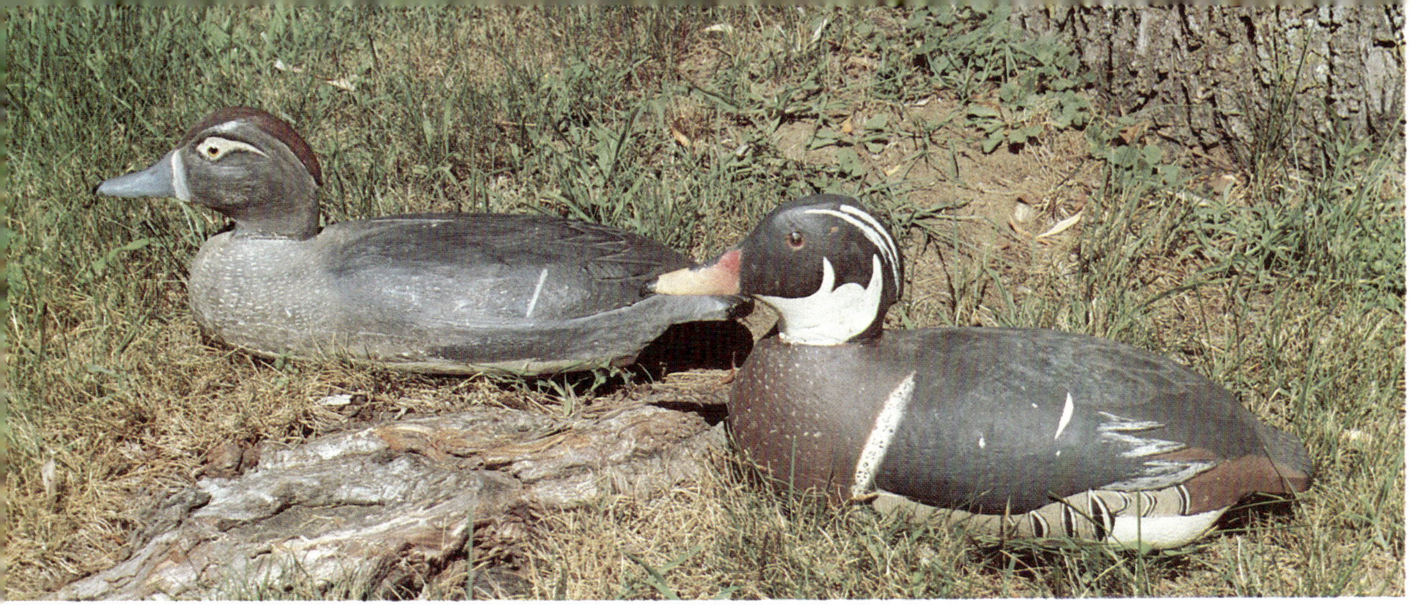

Woodduck hen and drake by Phillip Gregory ca. 1950.

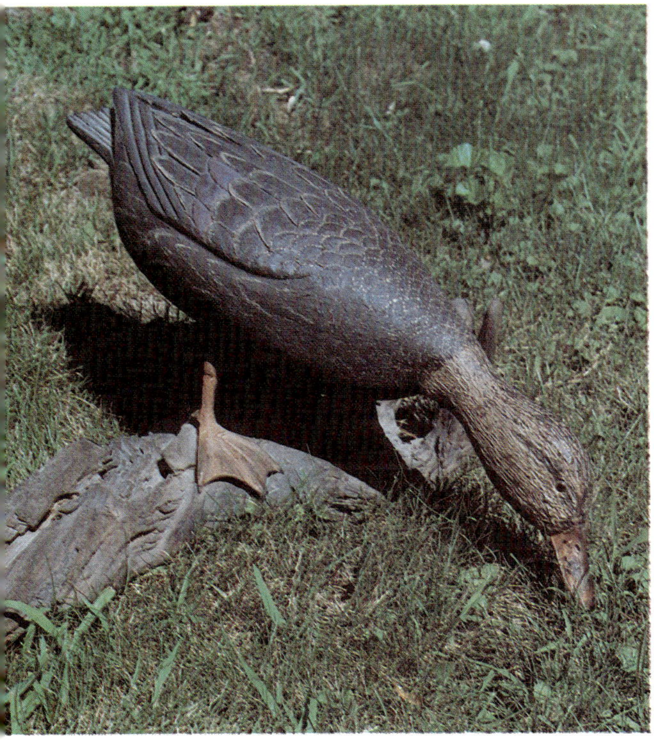

Black duck feeding by Phillip Gregory ca. 1960. Original paint, hollow with raised carving.

Blue goose by Phillip Gregory. Decorative with raised carving, original paint.

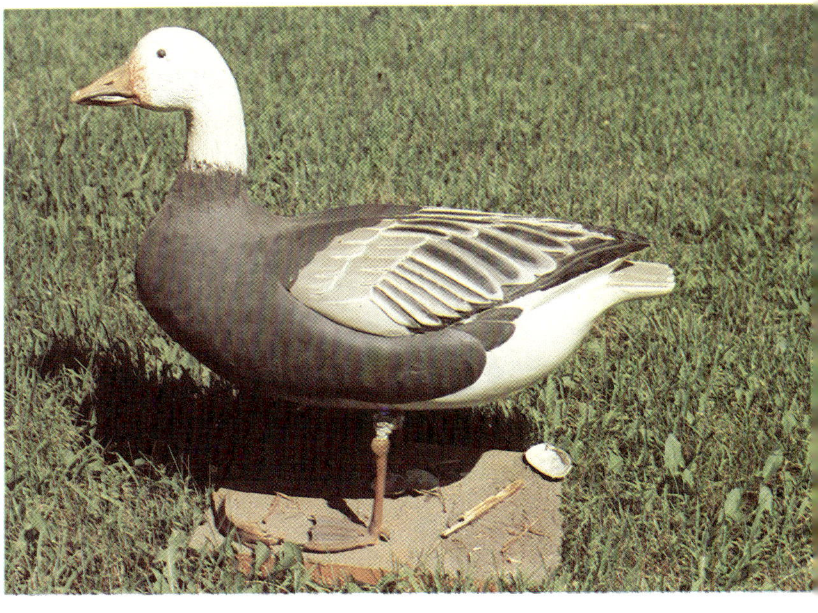

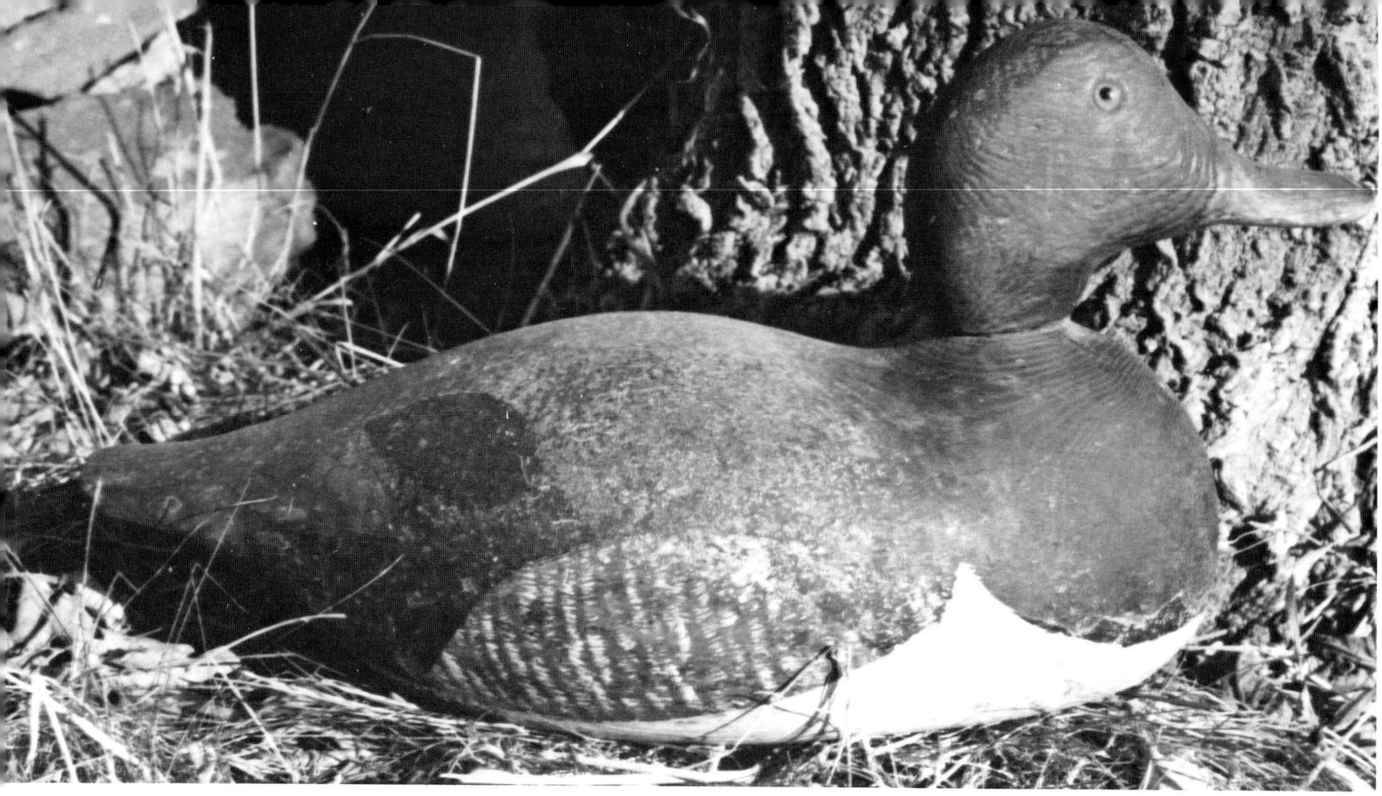

Bluebill drake by Eldon B. Griffith. Ca. 1945. Original working paint. Collection of William Coates.

Eldon B. Griffith 1898-1978, Vergennes, Vermont. Griffith's decoys are simplistic yet easily identified by their style and strong paint. His earlier ones are "folky" in nature with elongated, wide bills. The prominent head quickly suggests a Griffith decoy and those shown depict his style changes. Griffith worked as the town clerk of Vergennes during the 1950's to late 1960's. Little is known as to the quantity of decoys he made and finding one is a rare treat.

Whistler drake by Eldon B. Griffith, ca. 1940. Original paint. Working decoy. Collection of Loy S. Harrell.

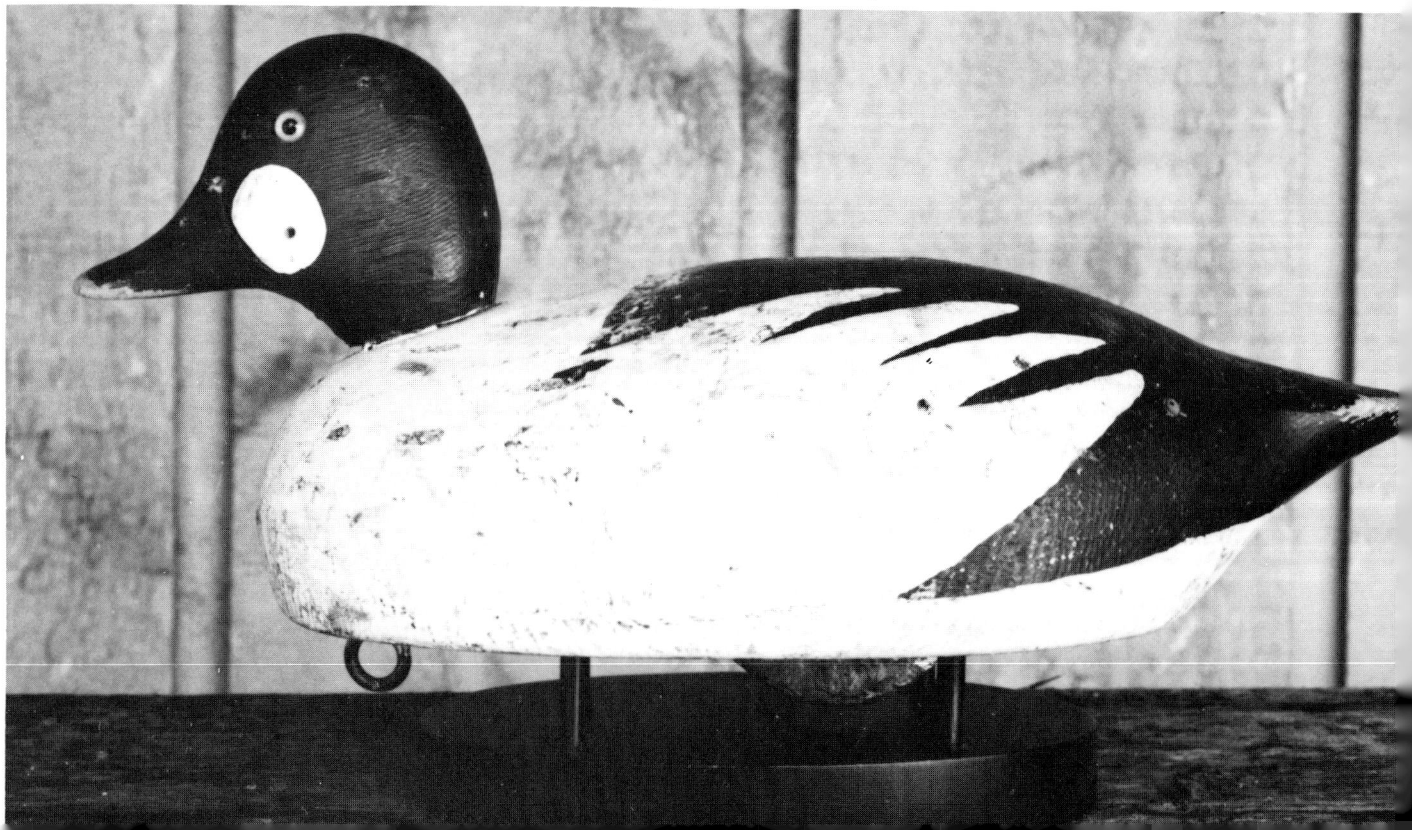

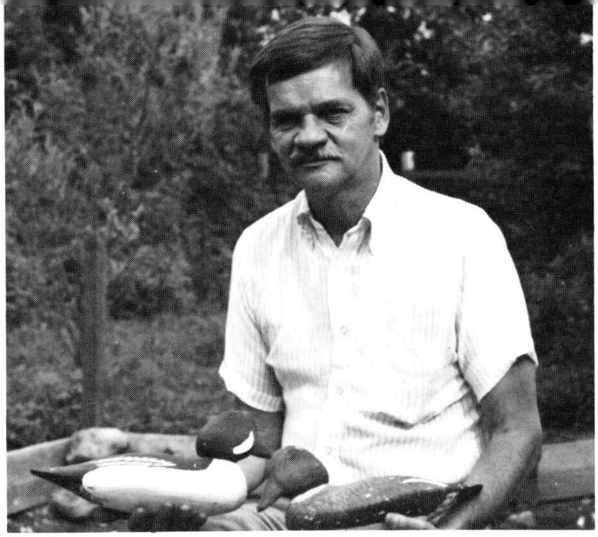

David Harrington at his aviary 1984. Holding pair of immature goldeneyes.

David Harrington 1934- Underhill Center, Vermont, once described by David Webster, former curator of the Dorset House, as "The last of the old time decoy makers". Harrington's decoys rank with the finest ever made. His versatility in style is illustrative of a man seeking perfection in his art form. From early cork rigs to more sophisticated hollow decoys, his birds are all geared for lake hunting. Harrington grew up on the lake and George Hard, former athletic director at Burlington High School, referred to David as "the best hunter at this school". (He and his brother, Darwin, were usually late for school during duck season). Harrington began carving in 1963 after "being inspired by a show at the Shelburne Museum". He carved mostly pine and cedar birds. Claiming "basswood is poor because it will rot at the site of scarring". All birds are painted with flat leadbase paint. Harrington states he carved over three hundred whistlers and several dozen drake bluebills. He doesn't recall painting hen bluebills because "the color of the drake lightens up the rig to make it more visible". He claims he can "paint a whistler hen in five minutes using the Bacon stippling method". Harrington's decoys and miniatures became in great demand and in 1969 he opened a sporting goods store in Winooski, Vermont which featured his work. However, in 1978 Harrington tragically lost his eyesight due to advanced diabetes and he had carved his last decoy. Today he lives with his family in Underhill and has contributed invaluable information and historical facts to this writer. He still welcomes conversation about the "Good Old Days".

Bluebill hen by Eldon Griffith. Original paint, glass eyes, note head style. One of a pair. Collection of Joseph Duggan.

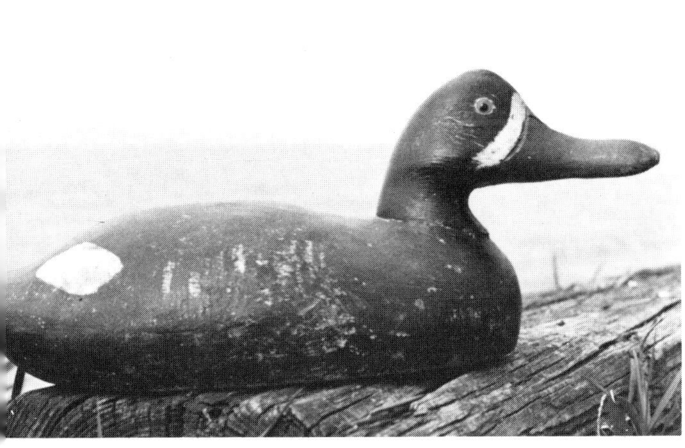

Bluebill drake sleeper by Eldon Griffith. Original paint. Collection of William Coates.

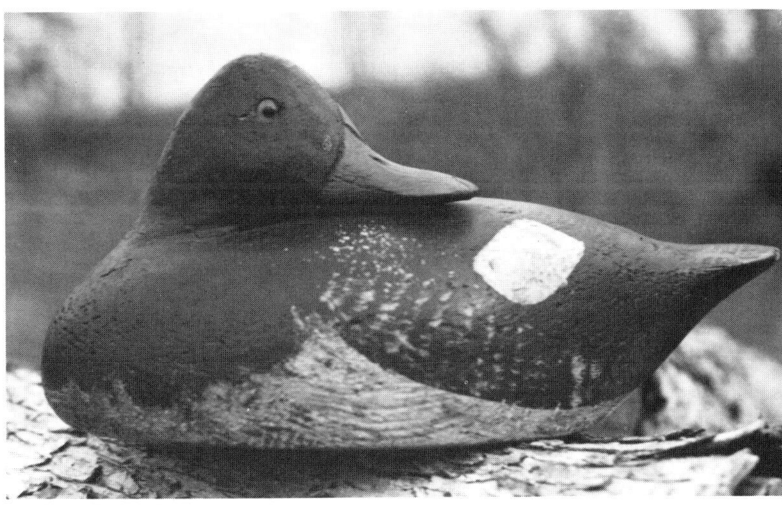

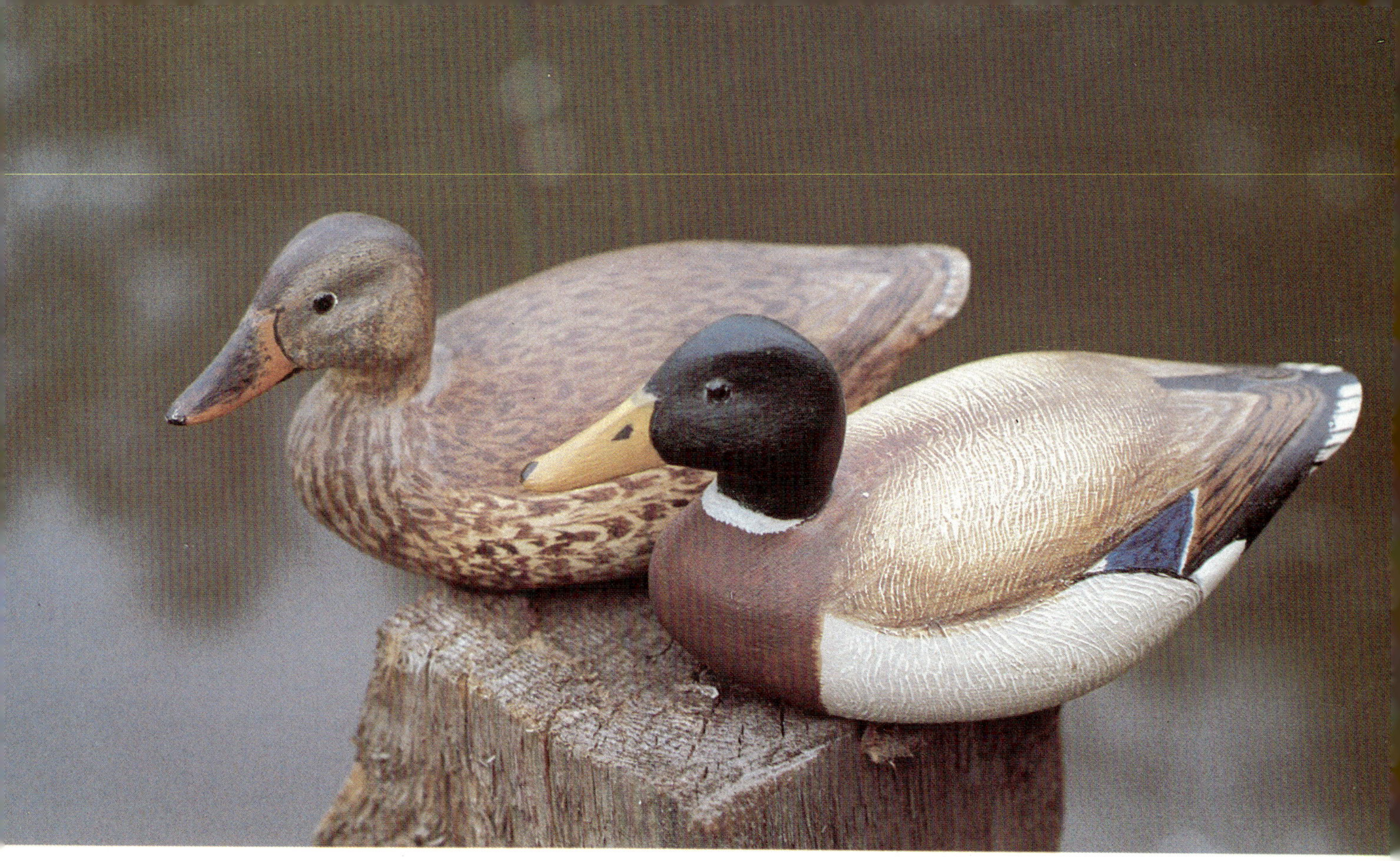

Pair of miniature mallards by David Harrington. Signed and original paint. Harrington made several hundred miniatures. Note exquisite paint work.

Whistler hen and miniature by David Harrington, original paint. Signed by Harrington. Collection of Loy S. Harrell.

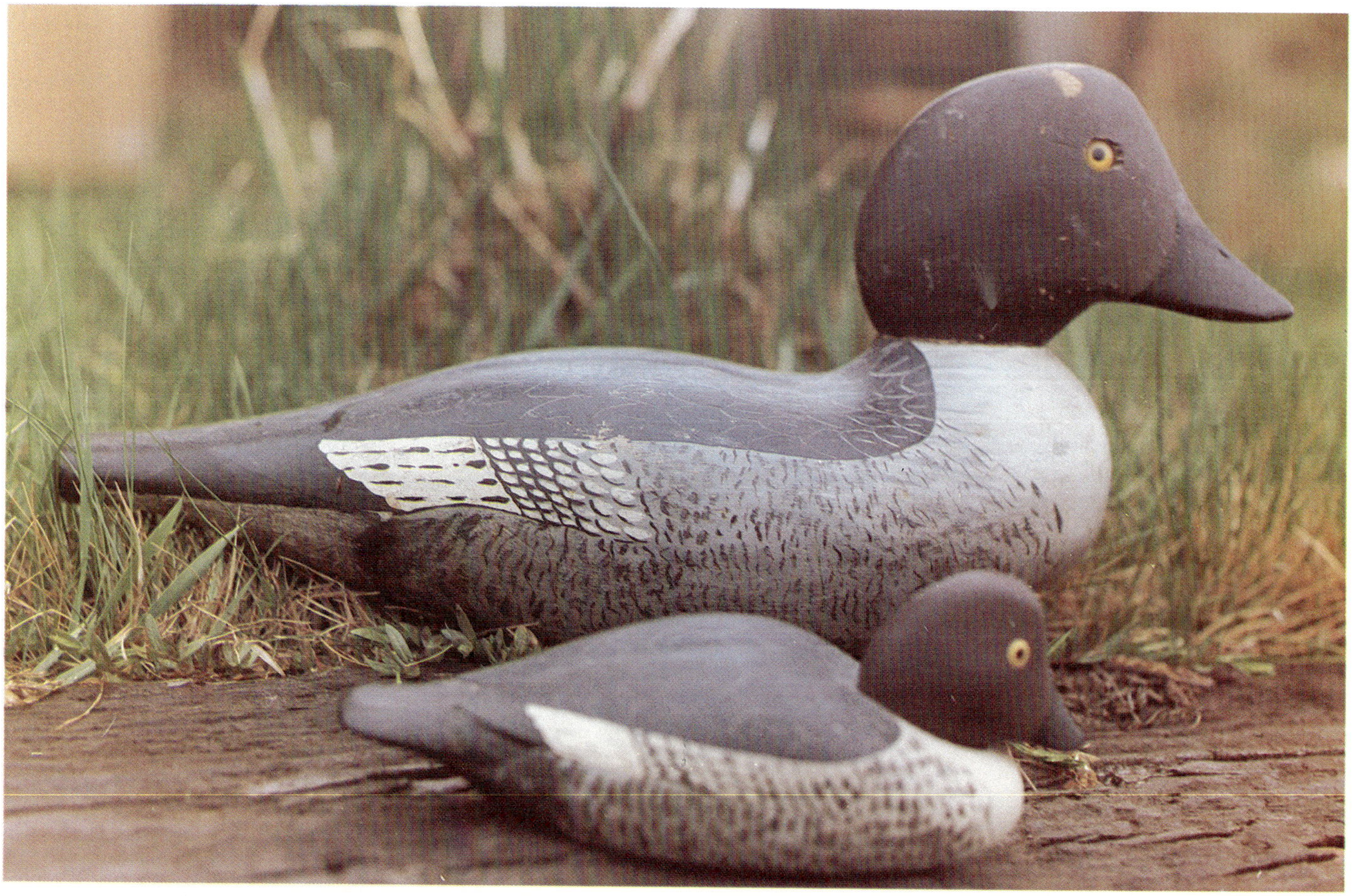

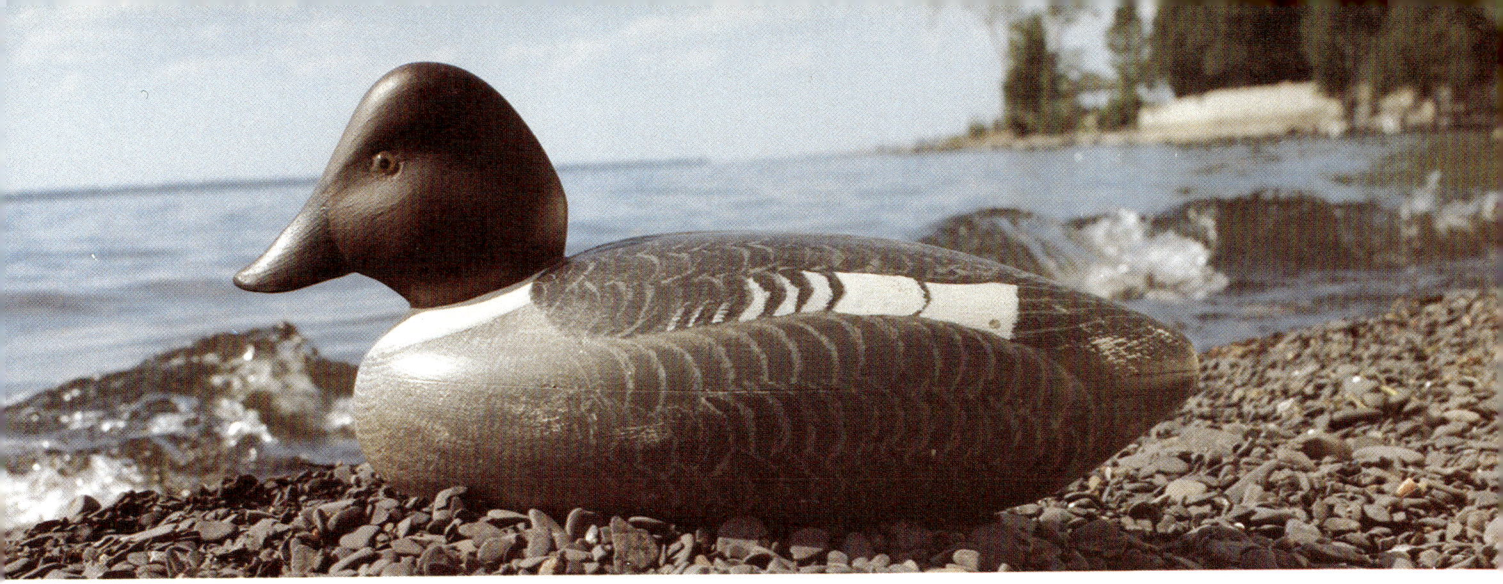

Goldeneye hen by David Harringon, early style ca. 1969. Original paint. Collection of David Hoag.

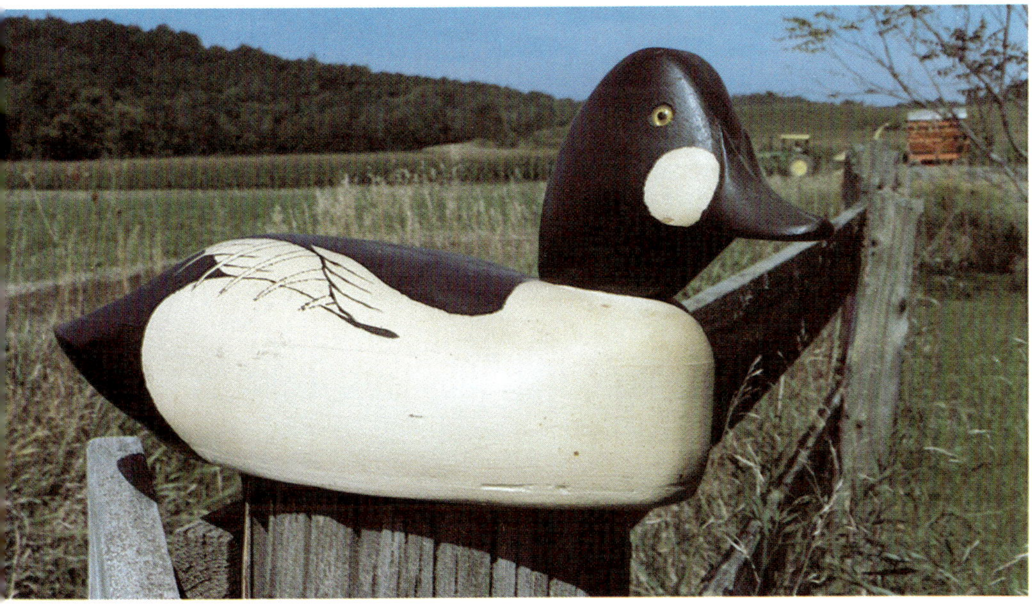

Goldeneye drake by David Harrington, three piece construction, and original paint. Collection of Tom Holloway.

Hooded merganser by David Harrington, a working decoy in original paint. Collection of the carver.

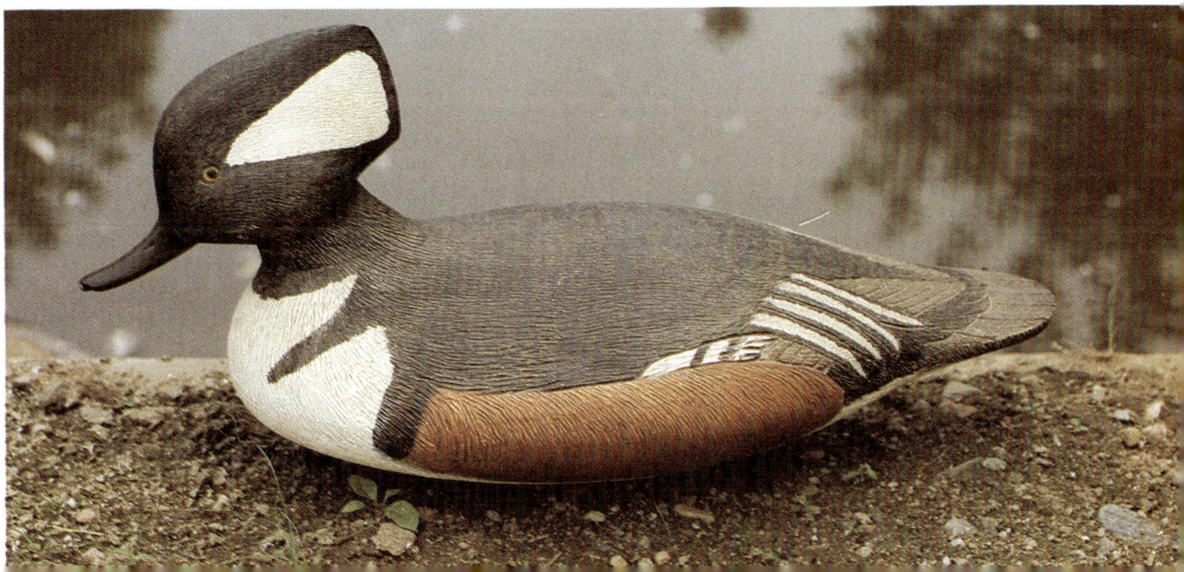

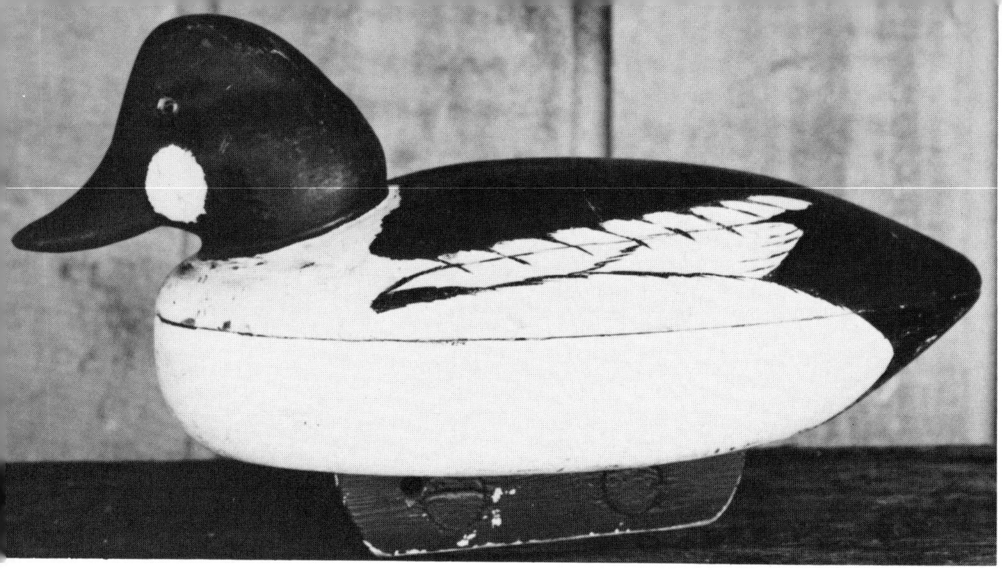

Whistler drake by David Harrington, hollow, original paint, leaded keel and glass eyes. Collection of Loy S. Harrell.

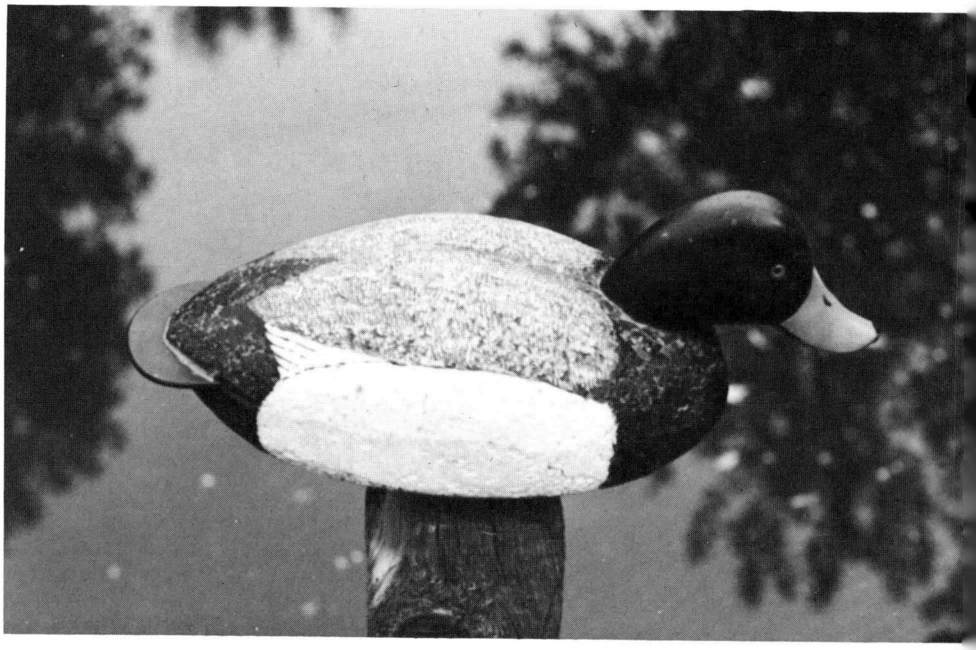

Bluebill drake by David Harrington. Original paint with tail insert, smooth head style. Signed and dated 1971.

Bluebill drake by David Harrington. Solid feeder. Note change in style between this decoy and page 57. (This is the only one of this style).

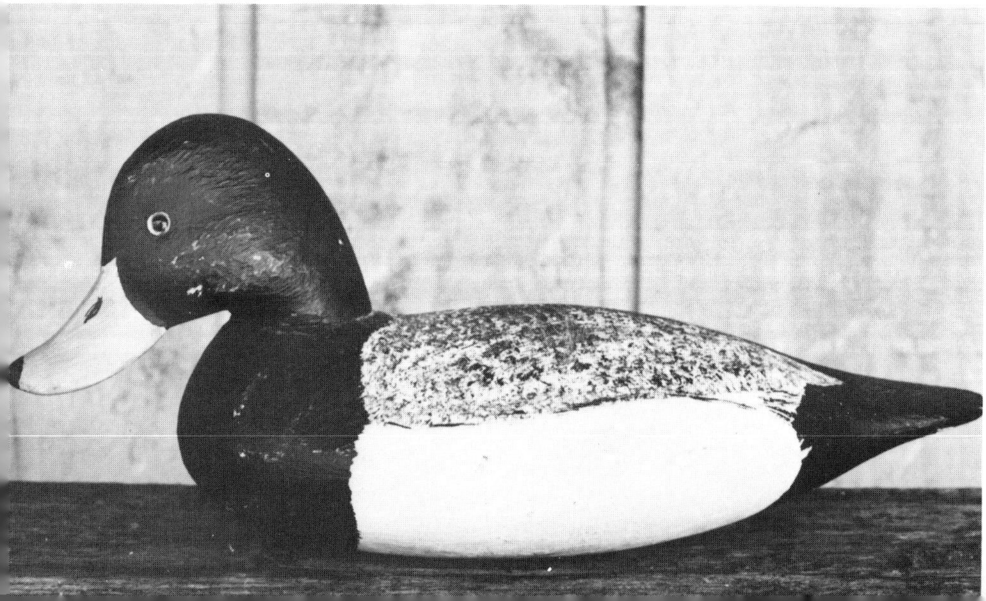

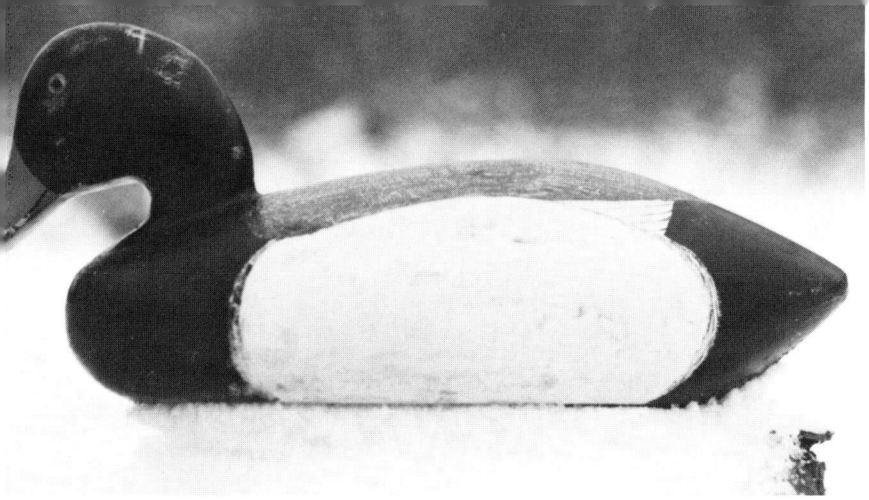

Bluebill drake by David Harrington. Hollow, feeding position.

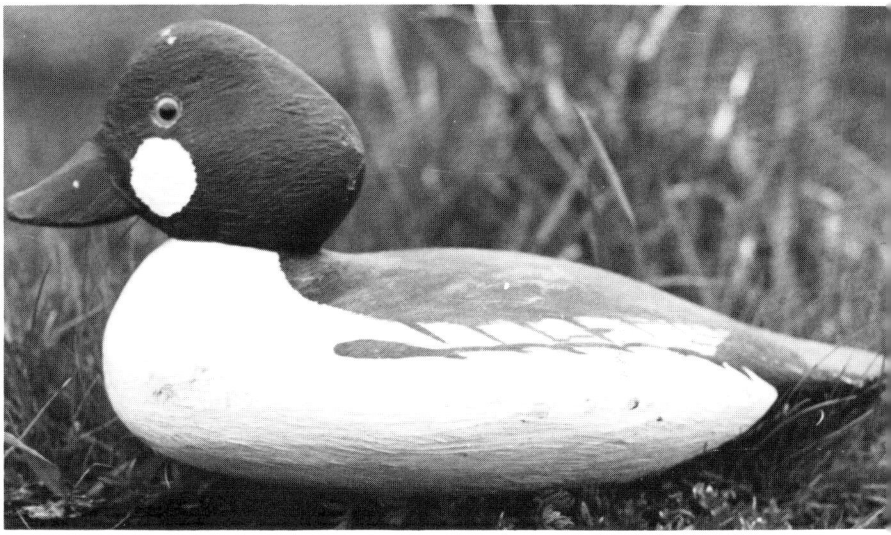

Goldeneye drake by David Harrington. Original paint, solid cedar. Body and head rasping to simulate relief. Collection of Colby Wood.

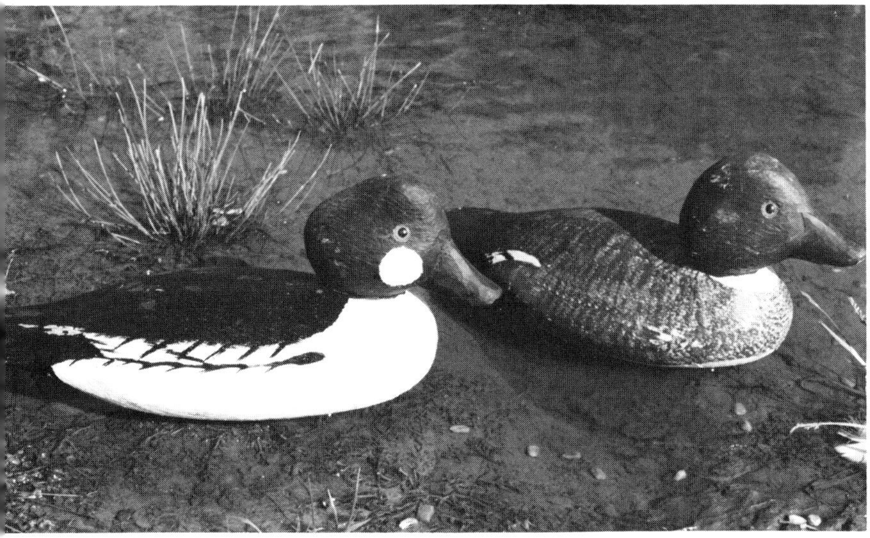

A pair of Harrington whistlers in their natural setting. These decoys are characteristic of his work. Both have surface rasping.

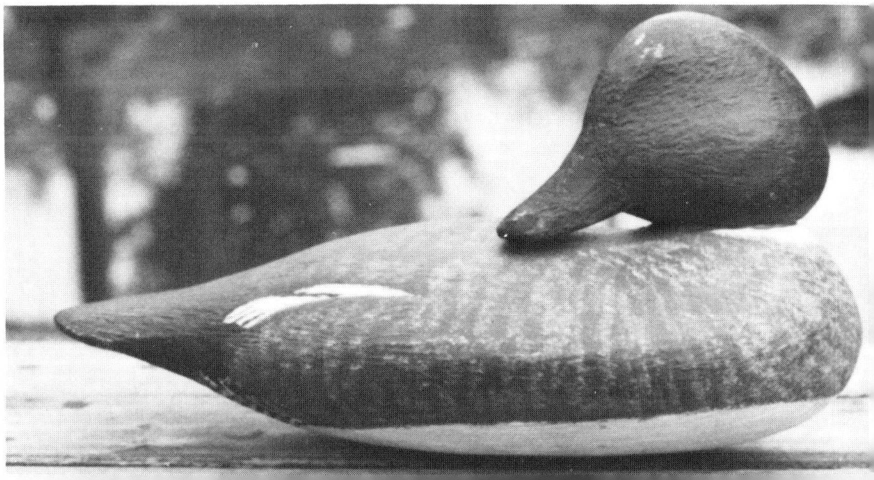

Preening Harrington goldeneye, no eyes, original paint. Many of his decoys were made without glass eyes. In background is Harrington's aviary.

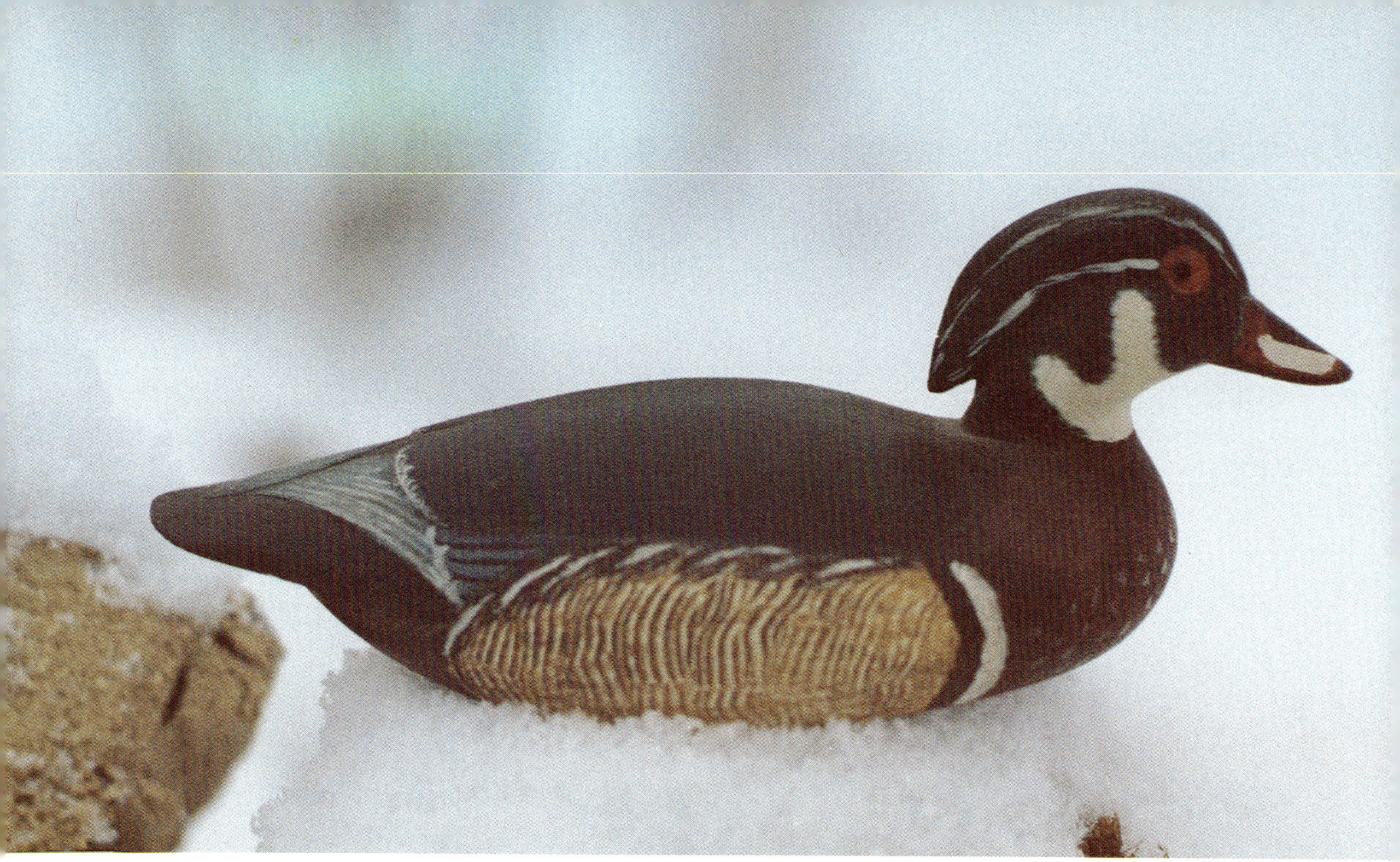

Woodduck drake miniature by David Harrington. Ca. 1970. Original paint.

Redhead drake by Captain John "Daddy" Holly, 1818-1892, Havre De Grace, Maryland. Original paint and keel. Ca. 1890. Six of his decoys were recently found at a home in the Vermont Islands. These decoys point out the wide variety of decoys found on Lake Champlain. They were hunted over by two brothers during the early 1900's.

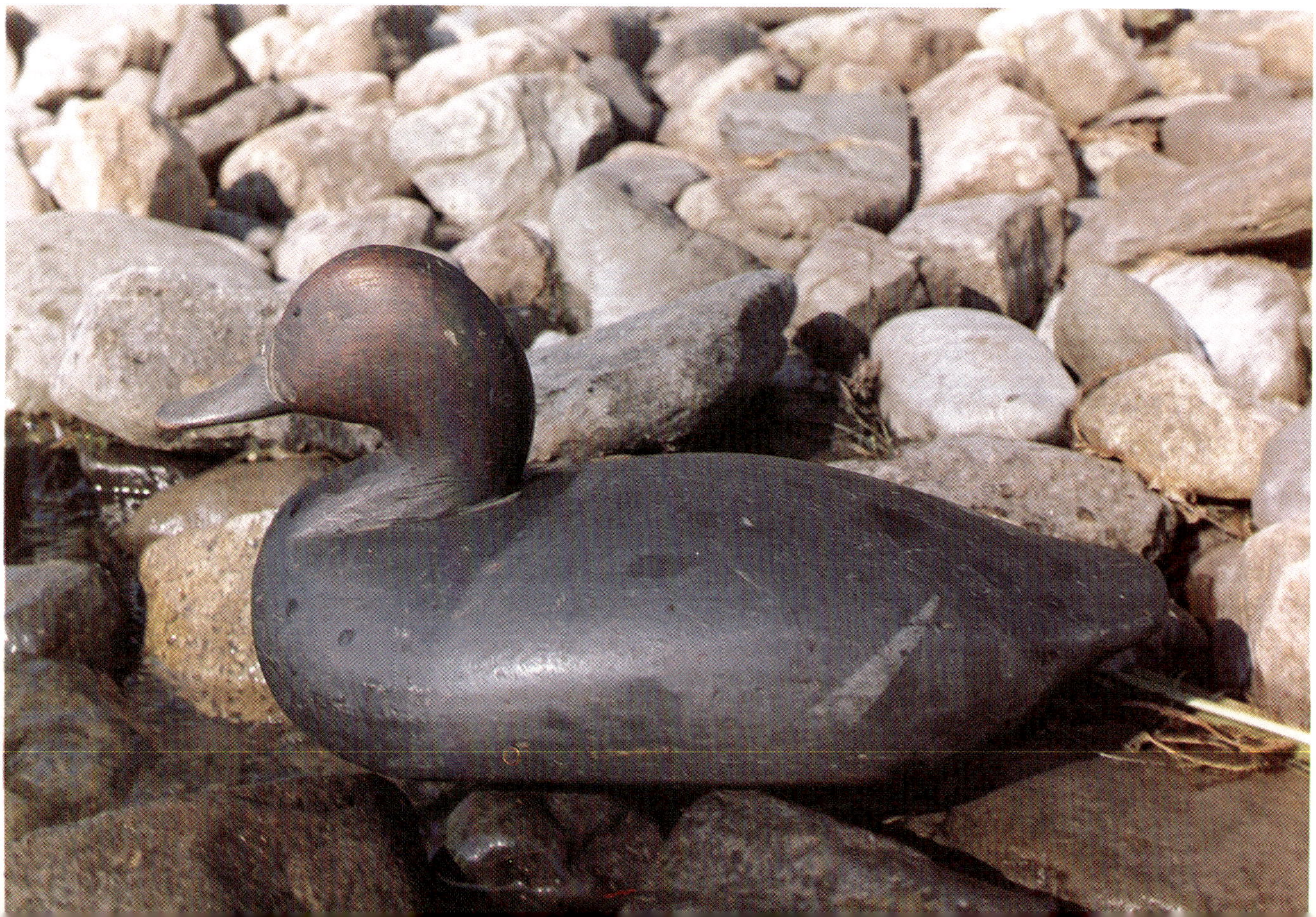

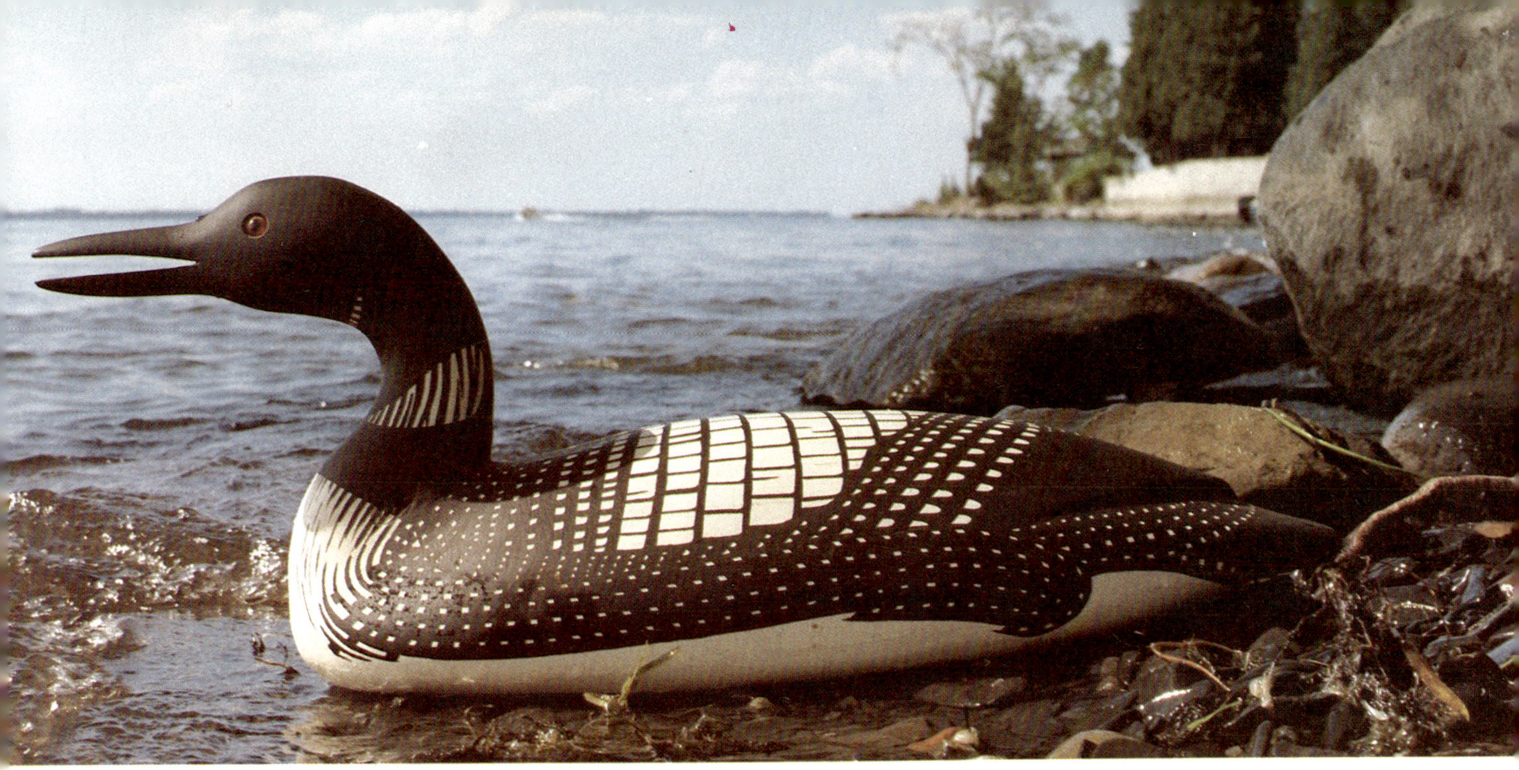

Loon confidence decoy by David Hoag. Original paint. Photographed at west edge of Grand Isle, Vermont.

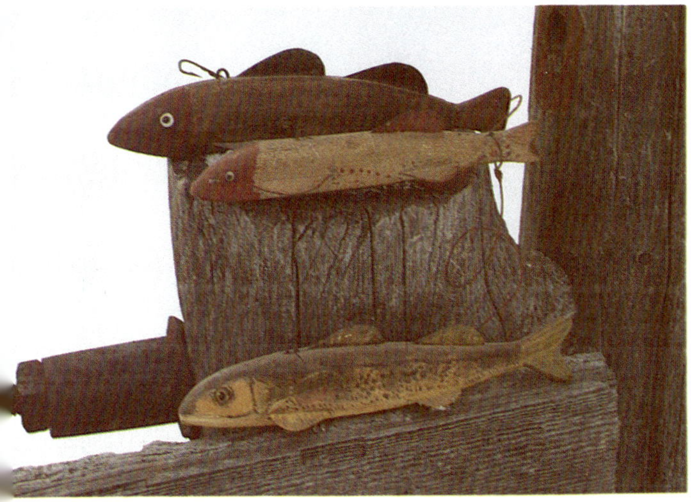

Fish decoys by J. Byron Hoag 1844-1965. Used in the islands between 1920-1935. Bottom decoy carved by David Hoag 1970.

Swimming black duck by David Hoag.

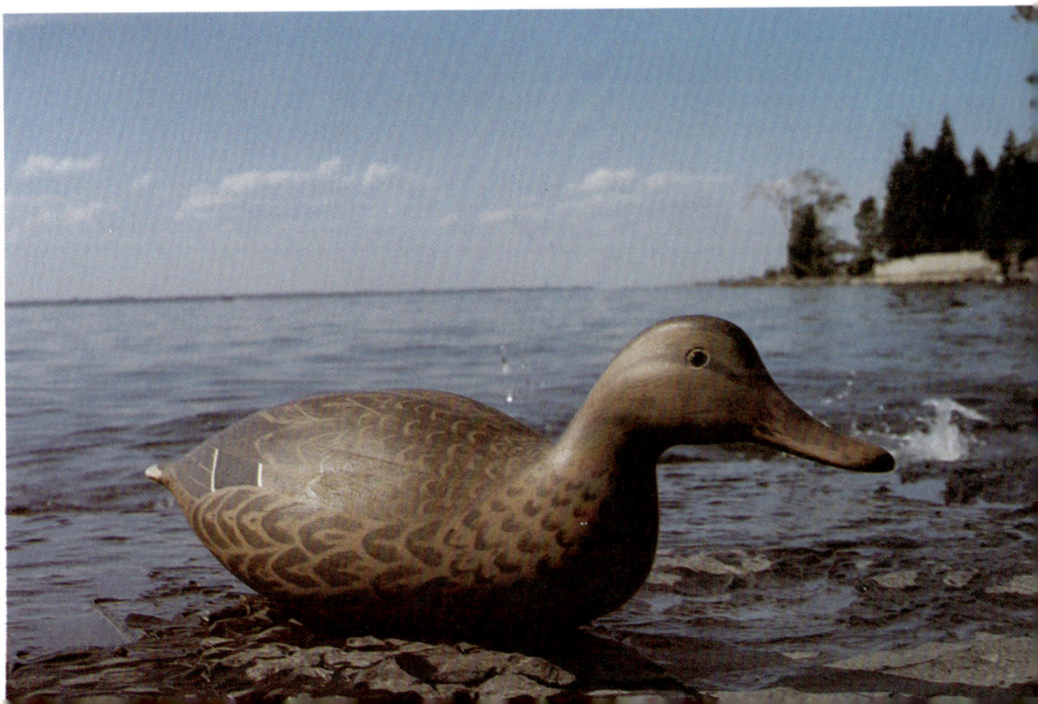

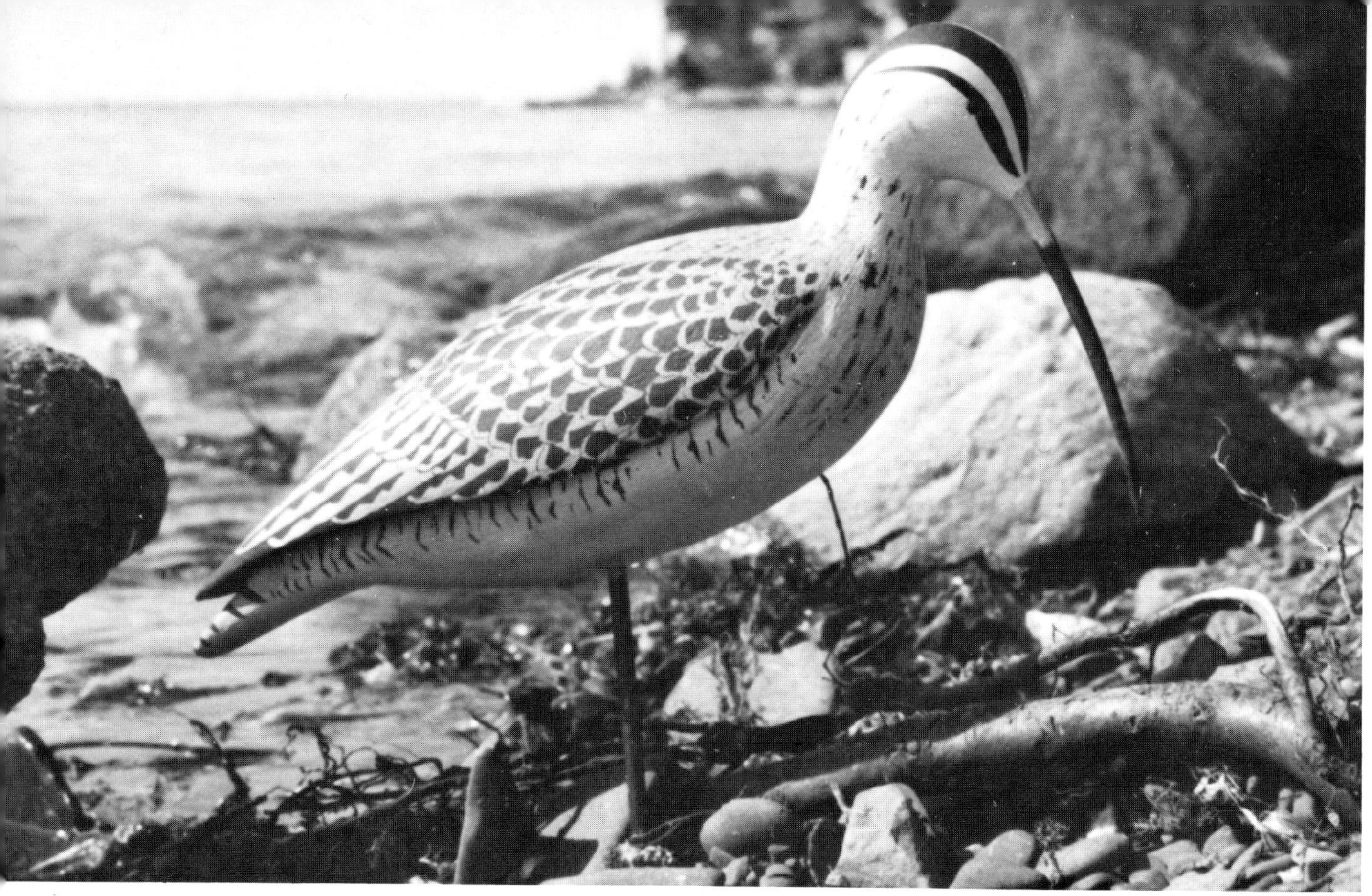

Curlew decoy by David Hoag. 1978.

David Hoag 1944- Grand Isle, Vermont. Hoag comes from a family who were early settlers on the island. They were traditionally farmers and fishermen. Today Hoag lives at the farm on the west shore of Grand Isle. His grandfather J. Byron Hoag carved decoys for duck hunting as well as fishing. It follows that David has become a carver for the same reasons. His working decoys, (forty-five in number) are superbly carved and painted. He also carves miniatures which he sells to various gift shops. Incidently, Hoag has one of the top collections of Orel Laboeuf decoys in the country.

Gadwall drake by David Hoag ca. 1975. Original paint.

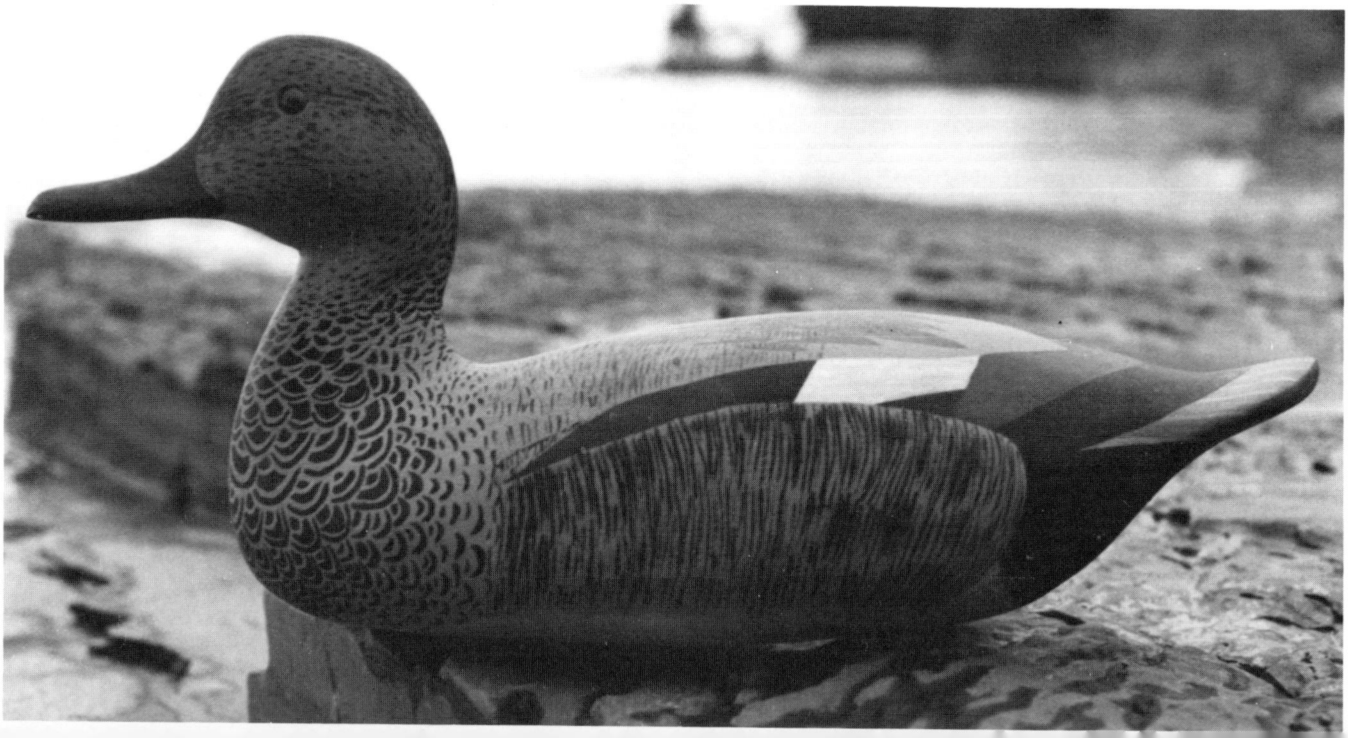

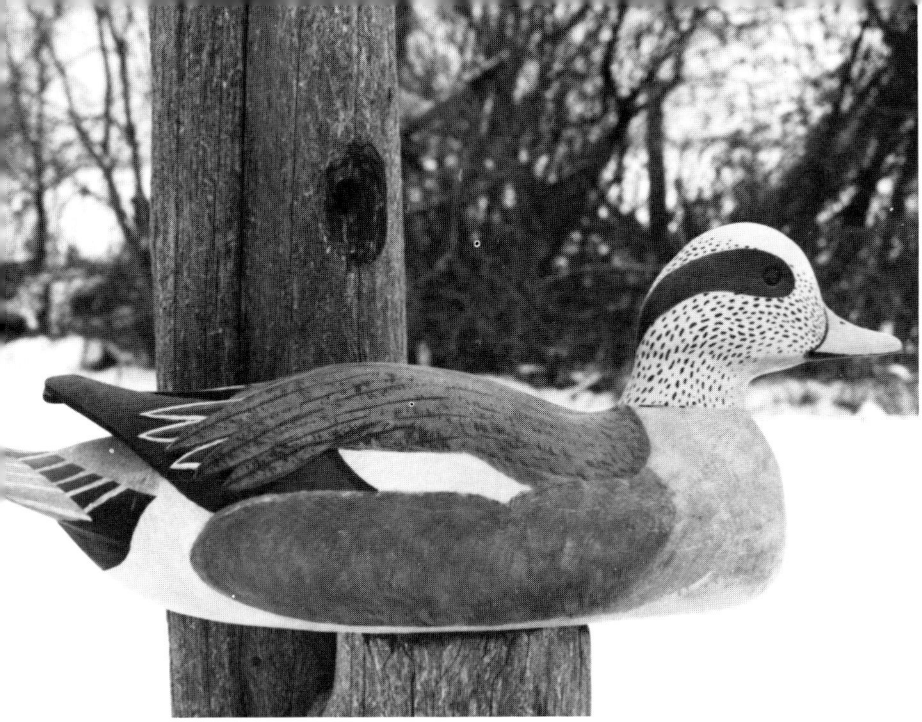

Widgeon drake by David Hoag. Original paint, working decoy.

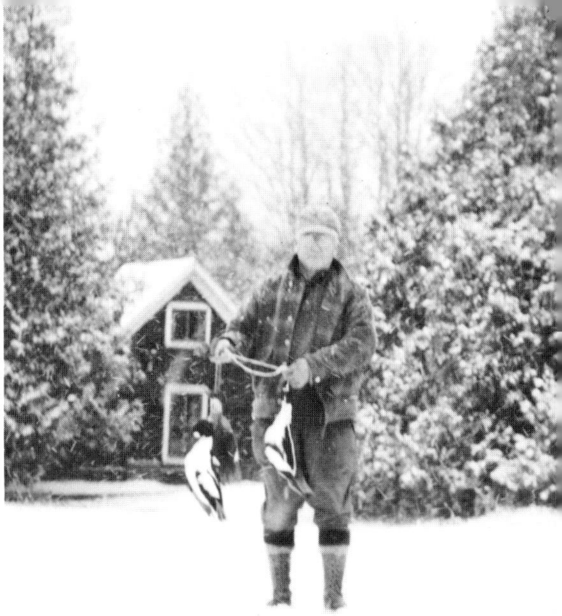

Photograph of William Hill ca. 1925 — "The Morning Bag".

William Austin Hill 1873-1951. Isle La Motte, Vermont. Hill, a descendant of early 18th century settlers on Isle La Motte, was minister of the Methodist Church on the island. His church, built in 1843 of black marble from the Ira Hill Quarry, still stands. Isle La Motte was named after the captain of the regiment sent from France to build Fort St. Anne, the first white settlement in Vermont in 1666 A.D. The island was discovered by Samuel De Champlain in 1609, which he described as "having the most beautiful pines I have ever seen". One can imagine duck hunting in the 18th and 19th century when the sky was literally filled with migratory wildfowl. Hill followed the great tradition of the pioneers of Isle La Motte as hunters and fishermen. He did both! Both his fish and duck decoys are functional and simplistic. A truly fine addition to any collection.

Drake goldeneye by William A. Hill ca. 1910. Original paint with wood platform floater. Hill family home in background.

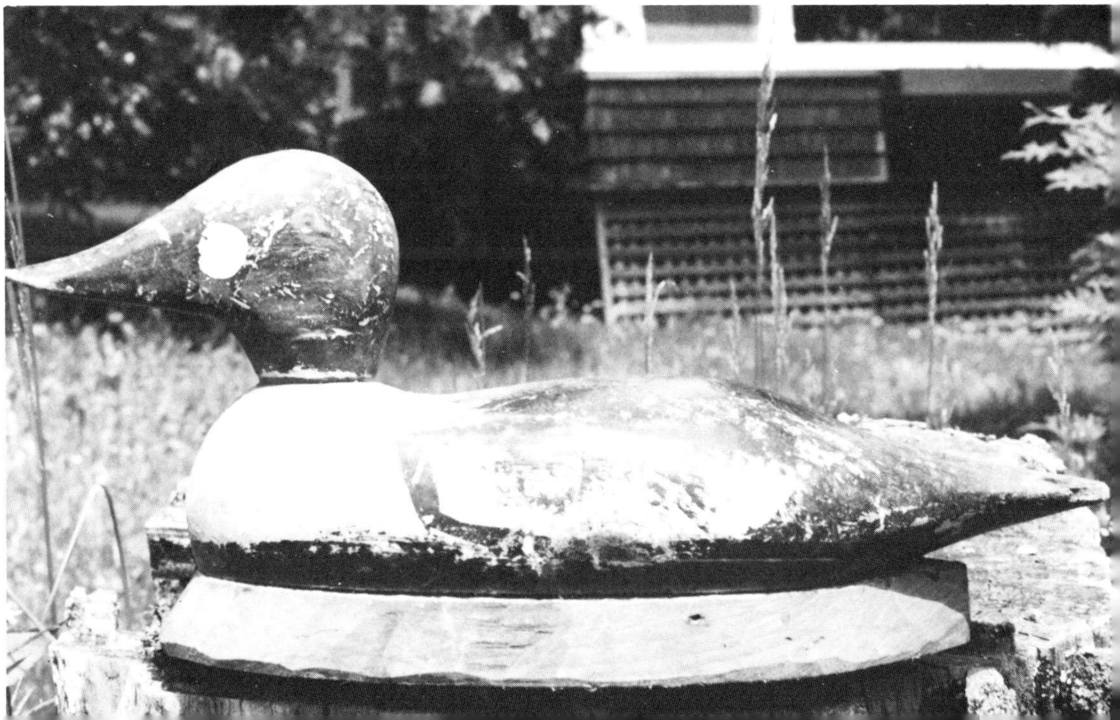

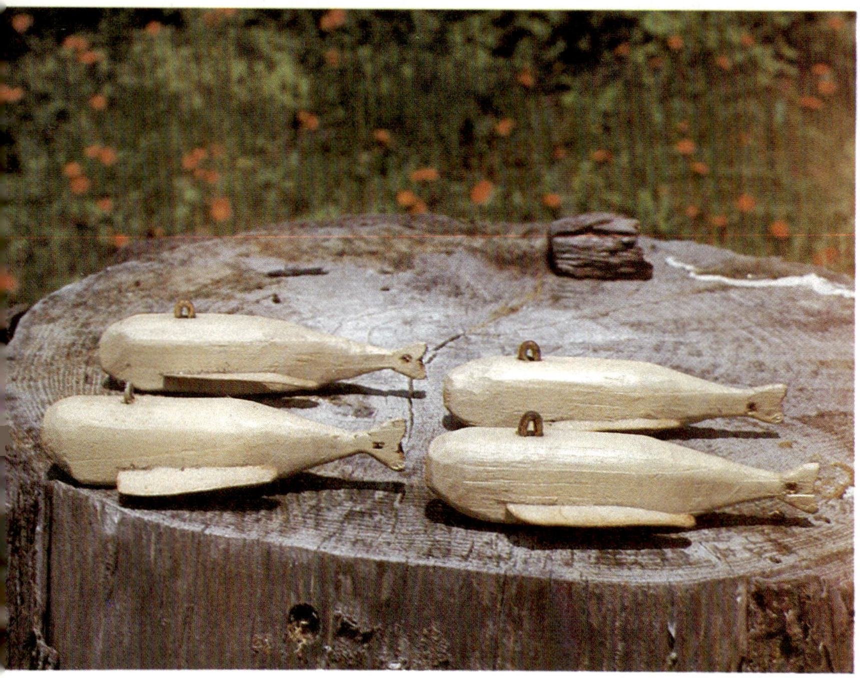

Ice fishing decoys by William A. Hill ca. 1920. Simplistic styling to lure in the "Big Ones". Collection of Ruth Hill McGregor.

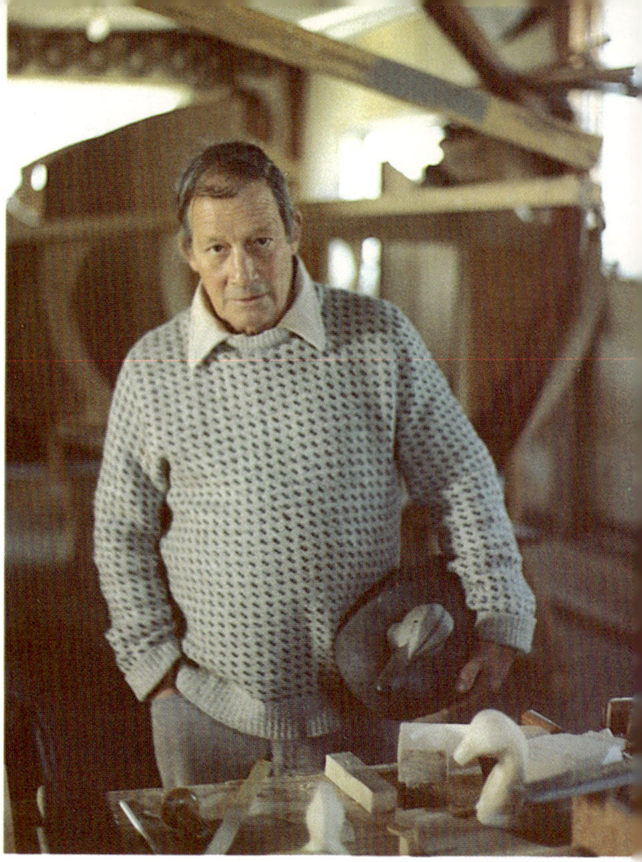

Charles Holloway in his Monkton workshop.

Charles "Tom" Holloway 1920 — Monkton, Vermont. Formerly a jockey and race horse trainer, Holloway spent much of his spare time on the waters of Chesepeake Bay and Cape Cod. There he learned the craft of wooden boat construction. In 1970, after moving to Vermont, Holloway, along with his artist wife, Betty, commercially made over four thousand mallard, whistler and black duck decoys. All were constructed from cork and pine. They were sold throughout the country to specialty stores and hunters. He also carved many decoratives using basswood construction. Today, Holloway still carves and repairs boats at his Monkton shop.

Mallard drake by Charles "Tom" Holloway. Cork body, pine head, original paint.

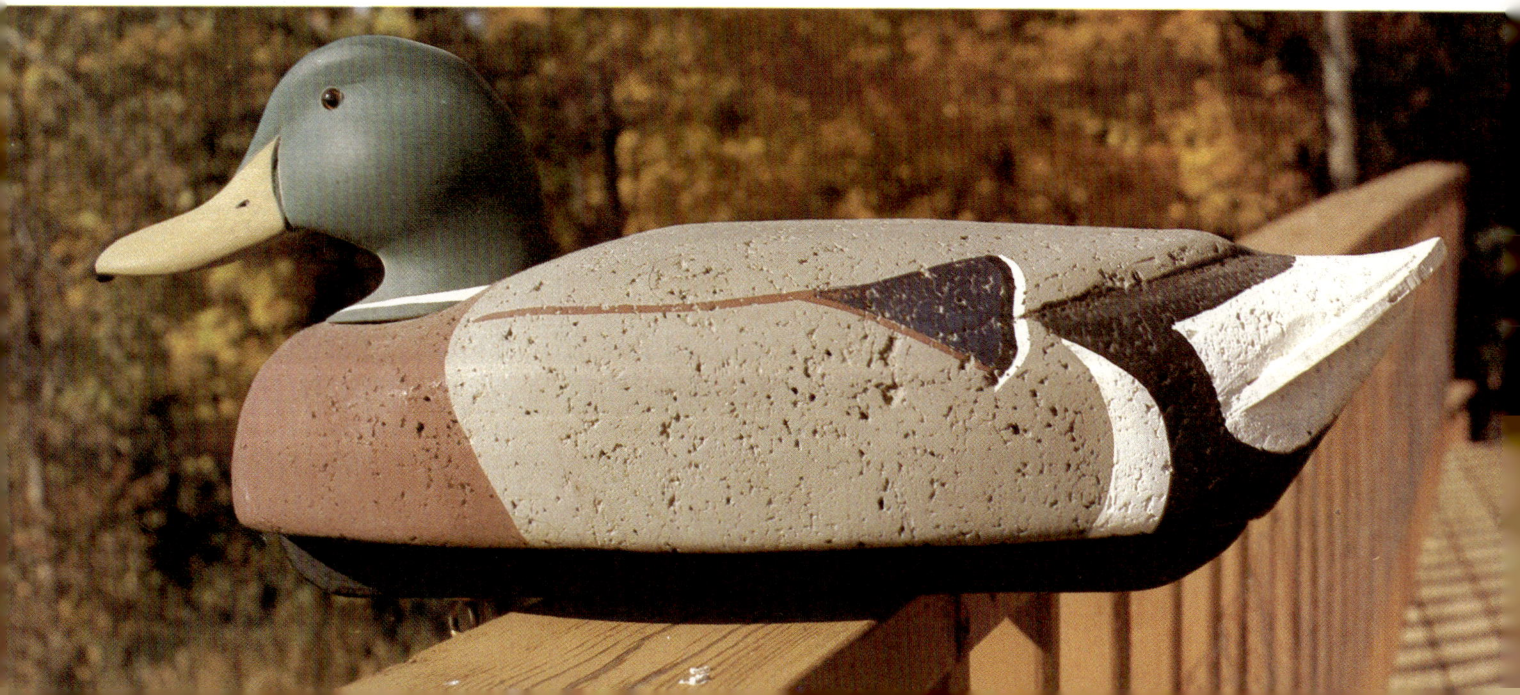

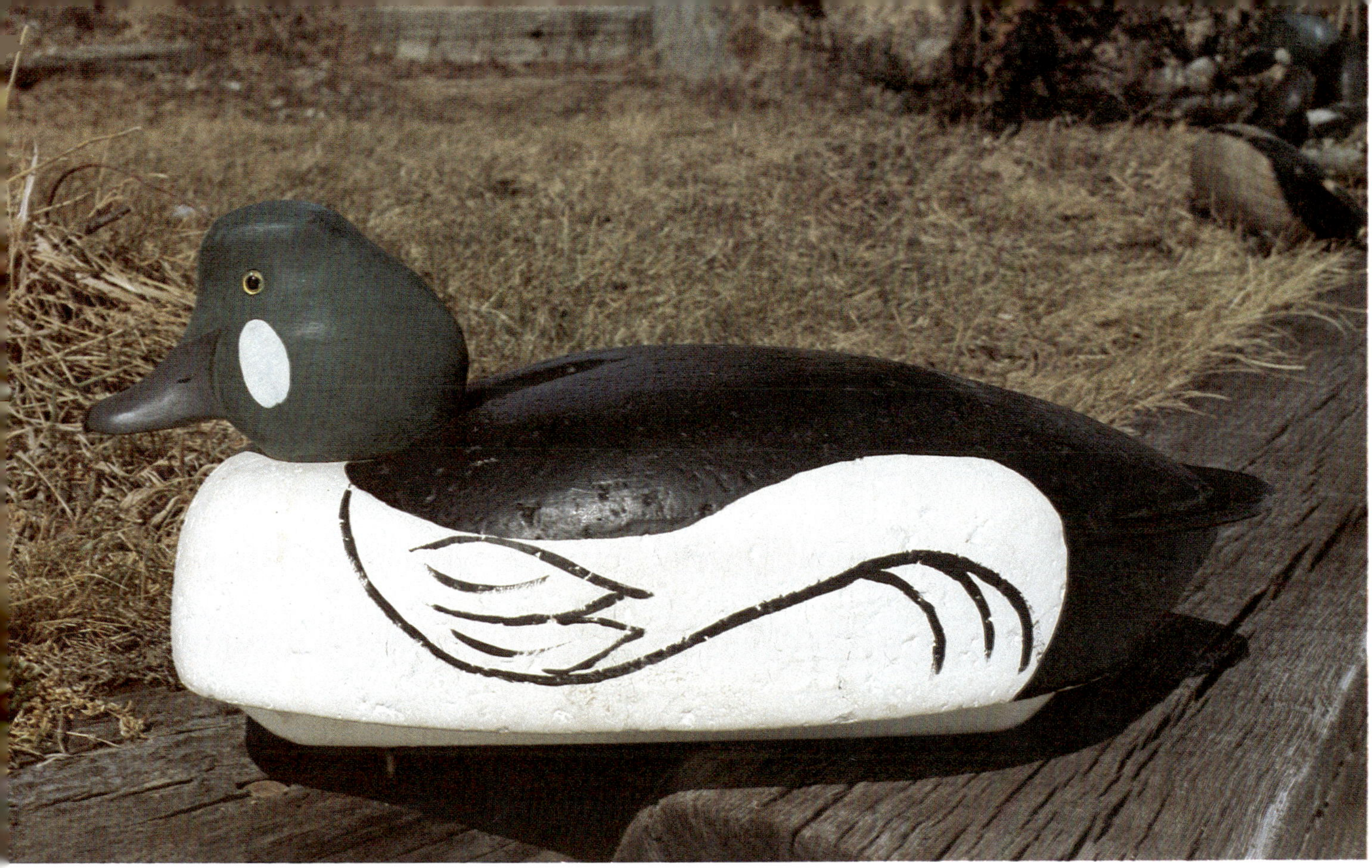

Goldeneye drake by Charles Holloway, painted by Betty Holloway ca. 1978.

Black duck by Charles Holloway. Original paint.

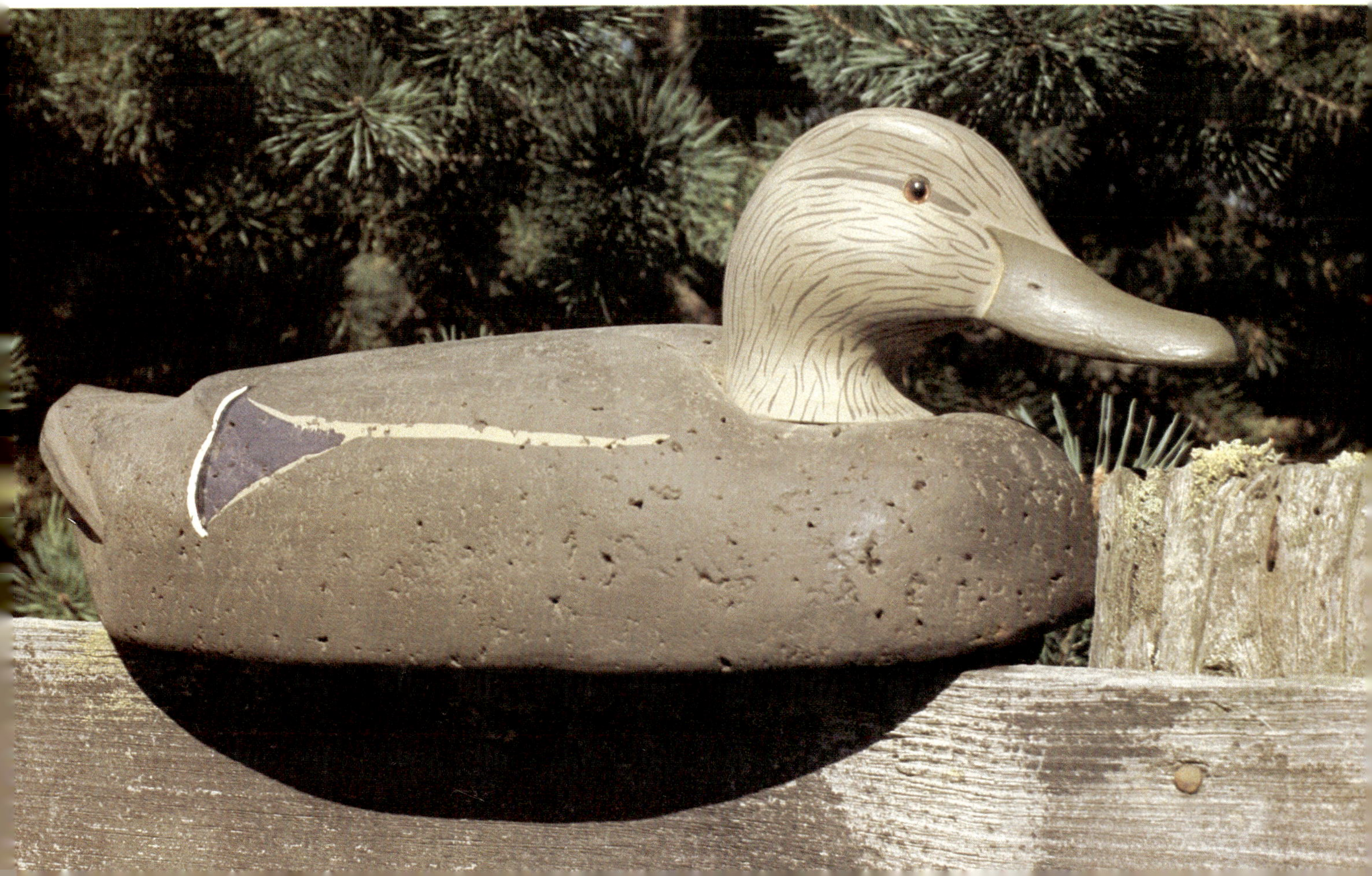

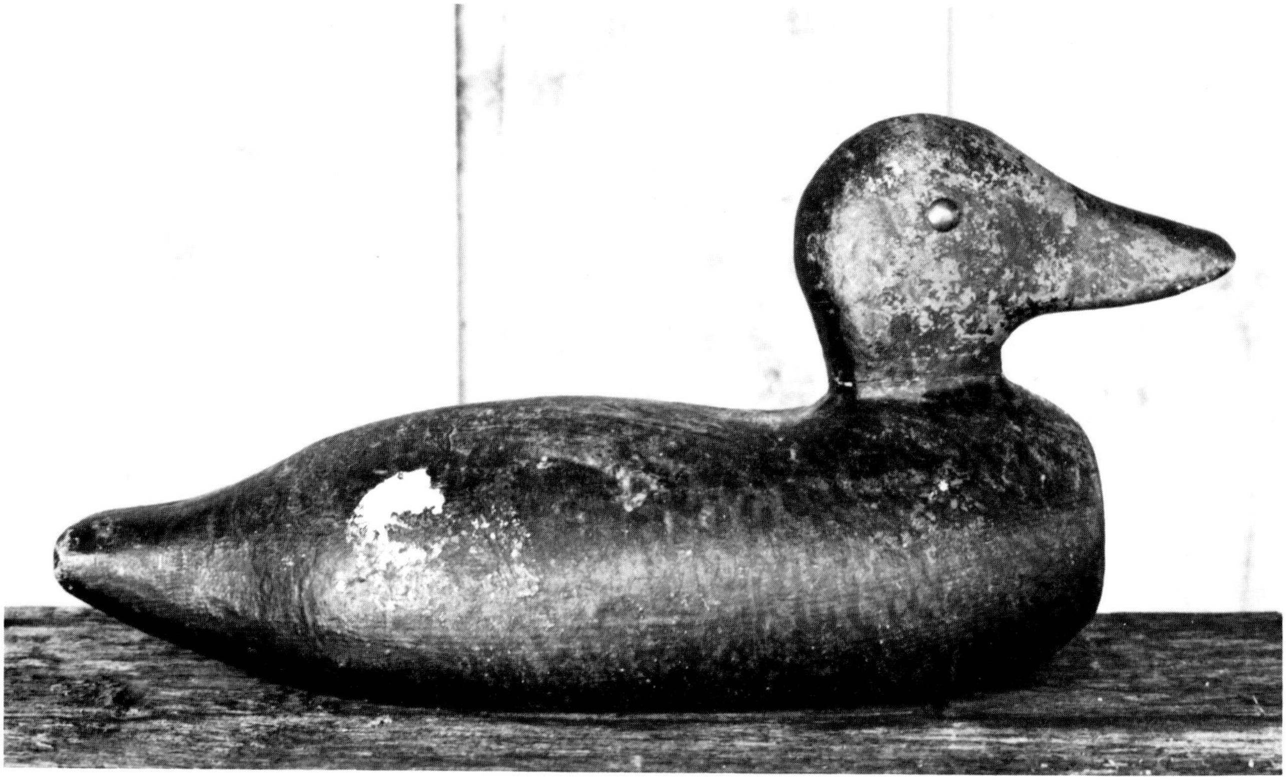

Black duck by Albert F. Jacques. Original paint and signed by the carver. Collection of Loy S. Harrell.

Albert F. Jacques 1908-1962. St. Albans, Vermont. Jacques was a construction worker by trade and was known for his workmanship and skill. He made both fish and duck decoys for use on Missisquoi and Campbell's Bay. Via the breast, he would drill a hole through the body and plug the opening. This was to lighten the decoy. The heads were dowelled and tack eyes used. Jacques carved over one hundred whistler and black decoys.

Goldeneye hen by Albert F. Jacques. Old repaint, tack eyes, collection of Bernard Jacques.

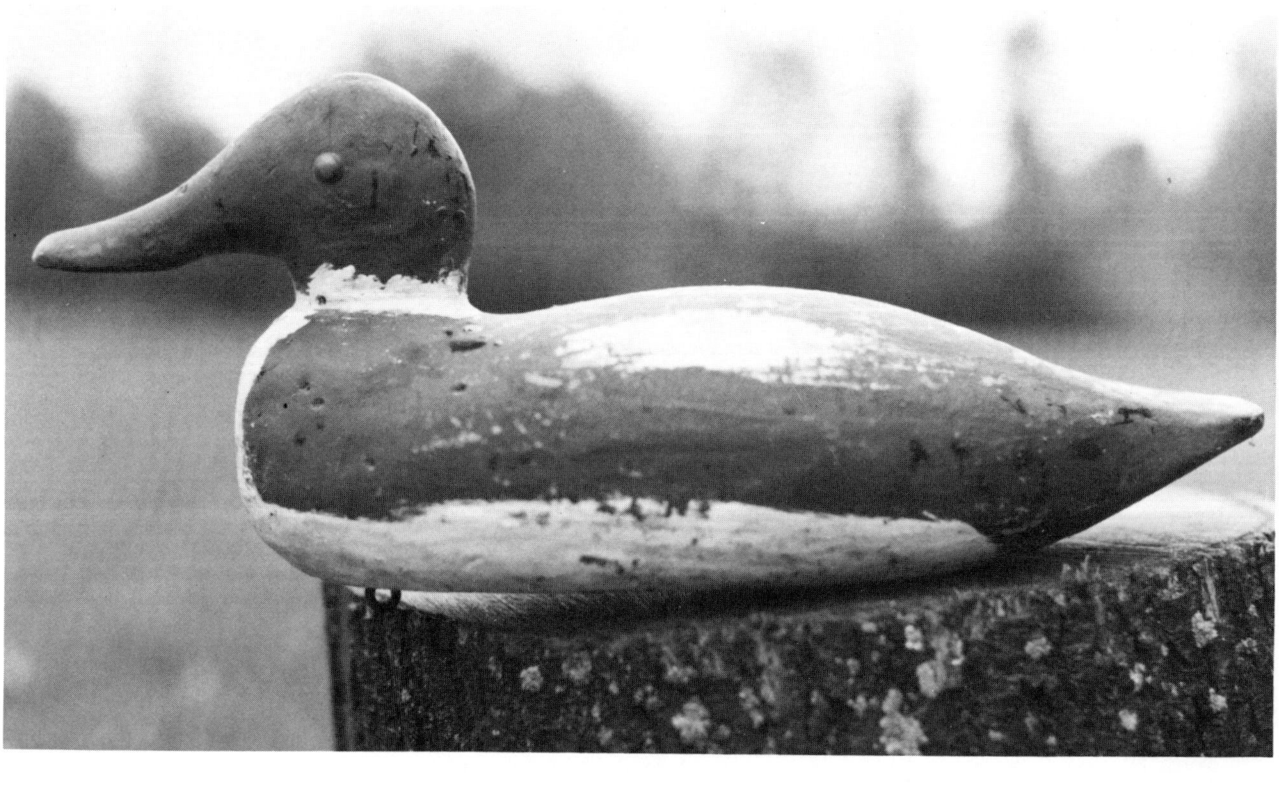

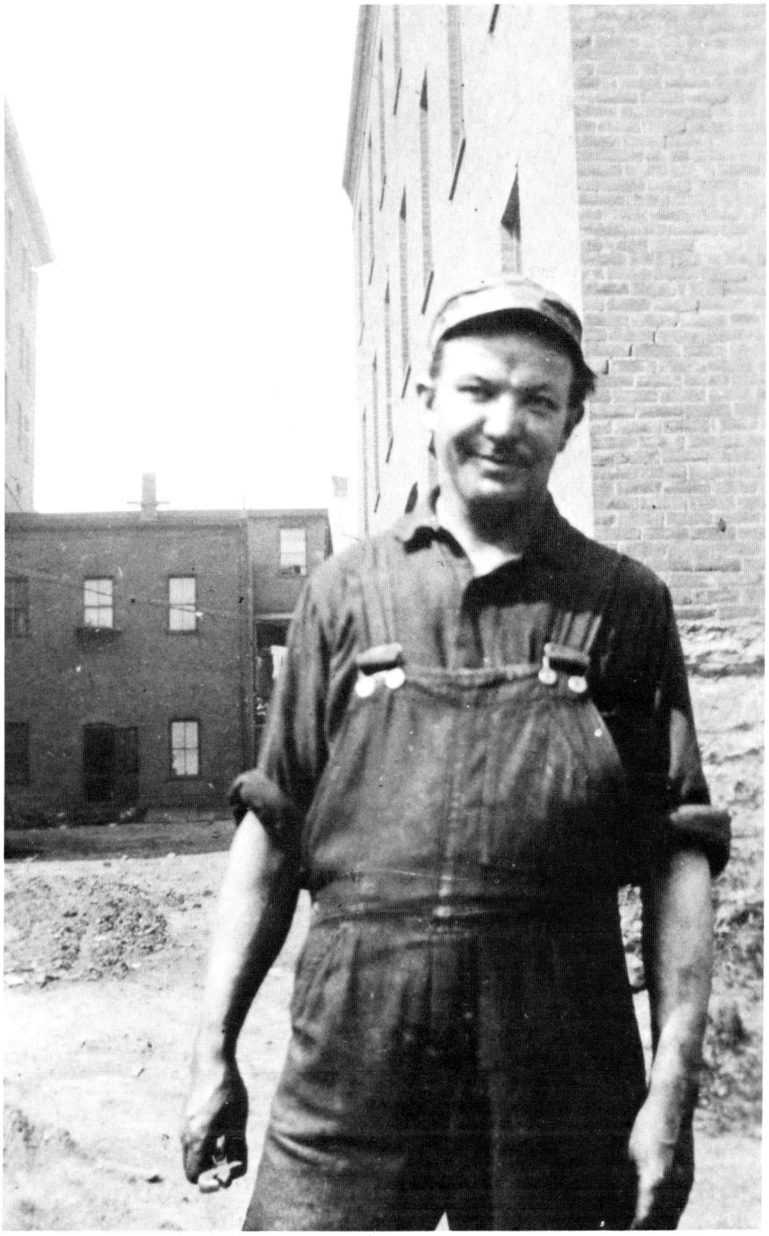

Charles Kirby, 1919 on lower Pearl Street, Burlington, Vermont.

Charles W. Kirby 1879-1958 Burlington, Vermont. Kirby, a member of the "Modern Woodmen of America", was a boat builder by trade. He made over three hundred for use on Lake Champlain; primarily for fishing. Before this endeavor, Kirby was an auto mechanic in Burlington, working with his brother, Arthur (1893-1973). Arthur continued to work with his brother constructing boats and later, decoys. Kirby's decoys took a wide variety of forms, from cork to hollowed cedar. All the heads were pine. His paint and form varied also with time. Therefore head form is the most identifiable aspect of his work. Kirby's original shop is where Bove's Restaurant is now located. He later moved to the foot of Colchester Avenue where he worked carving and selling decoys to area hunters. His boats can still be found on the lake and his decoys are being used today.

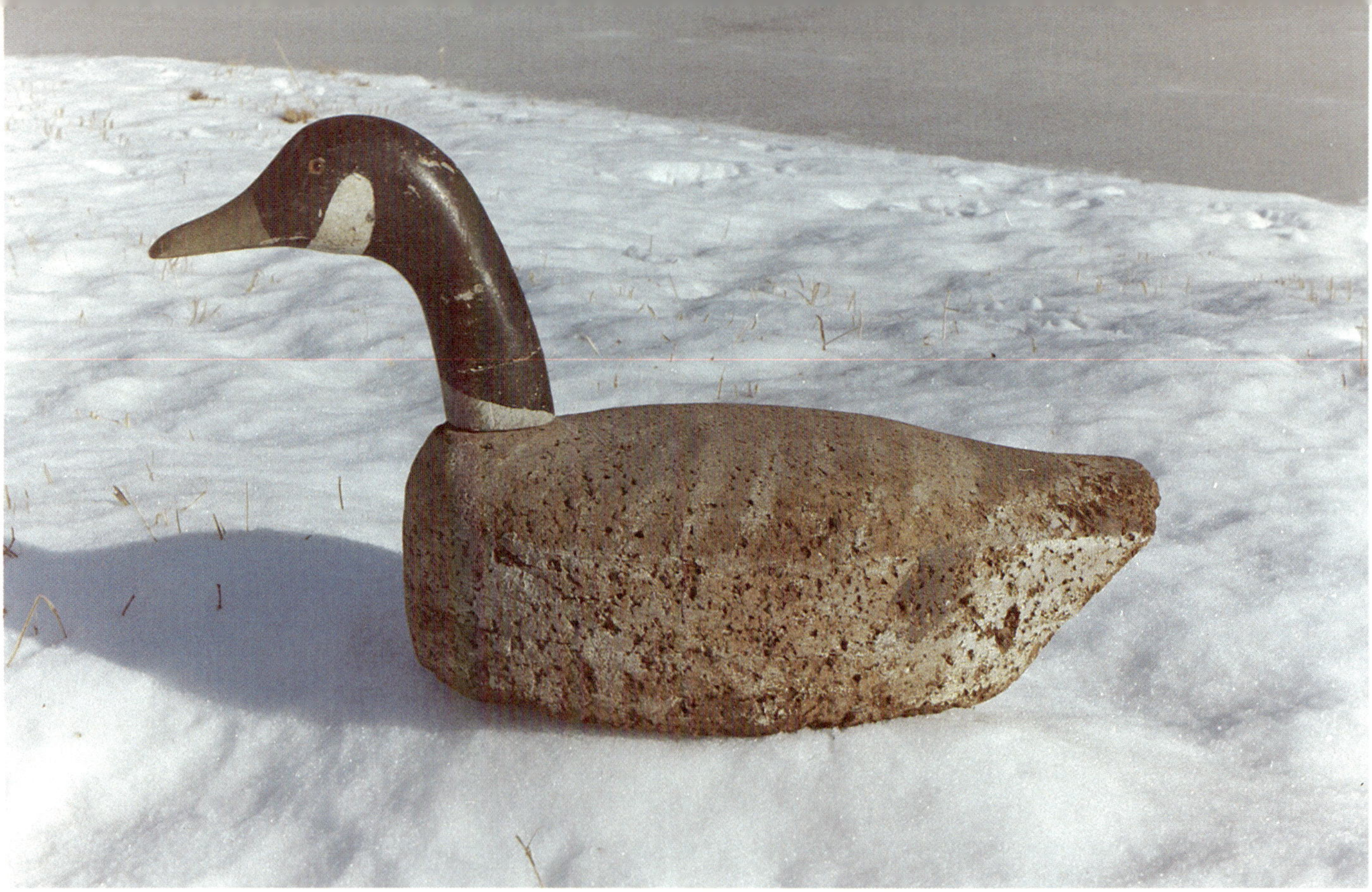

Canada goose by Charles Kirby ca. 1940. Original form and paint, cork body, pine head has "Kirby look".

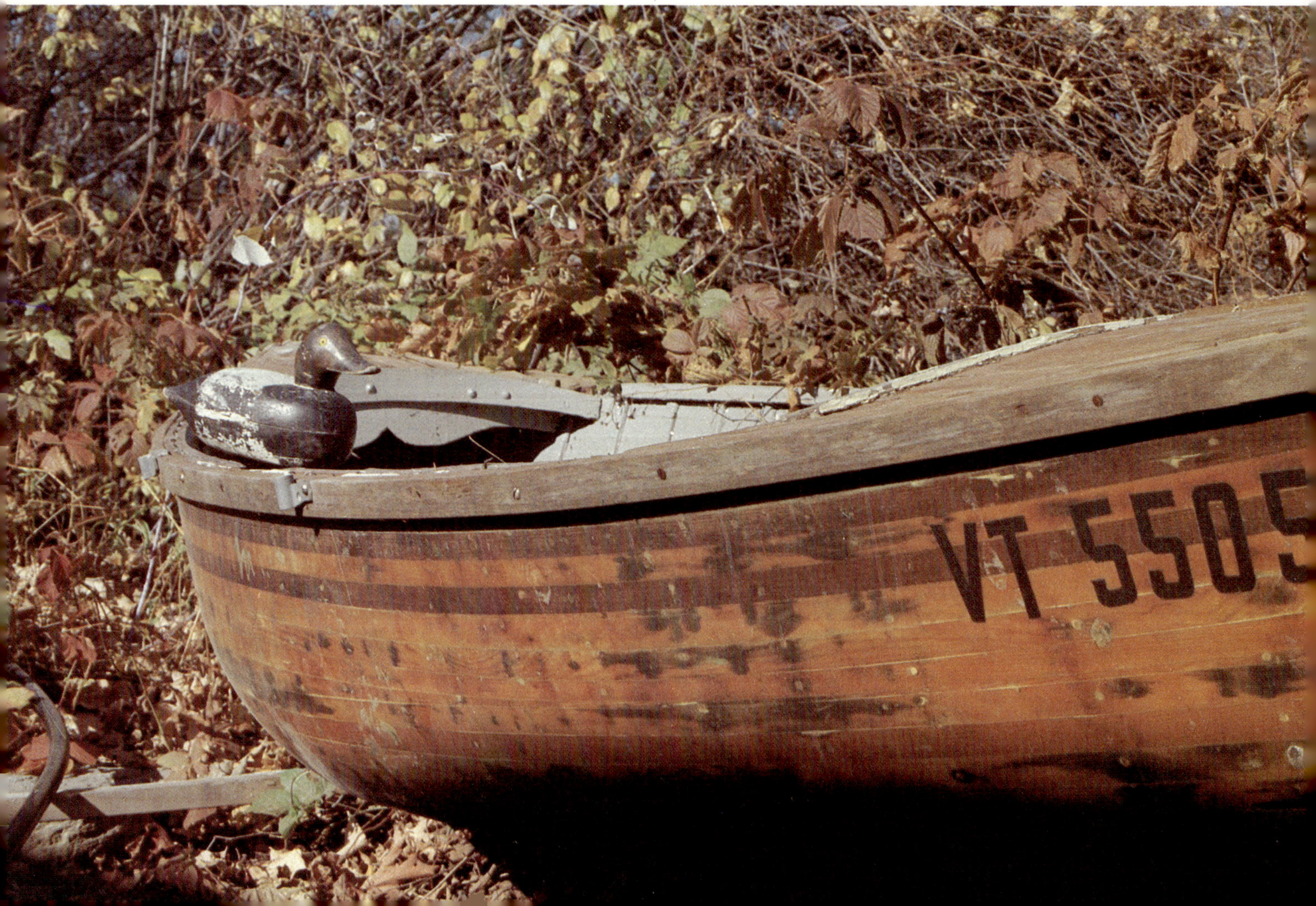

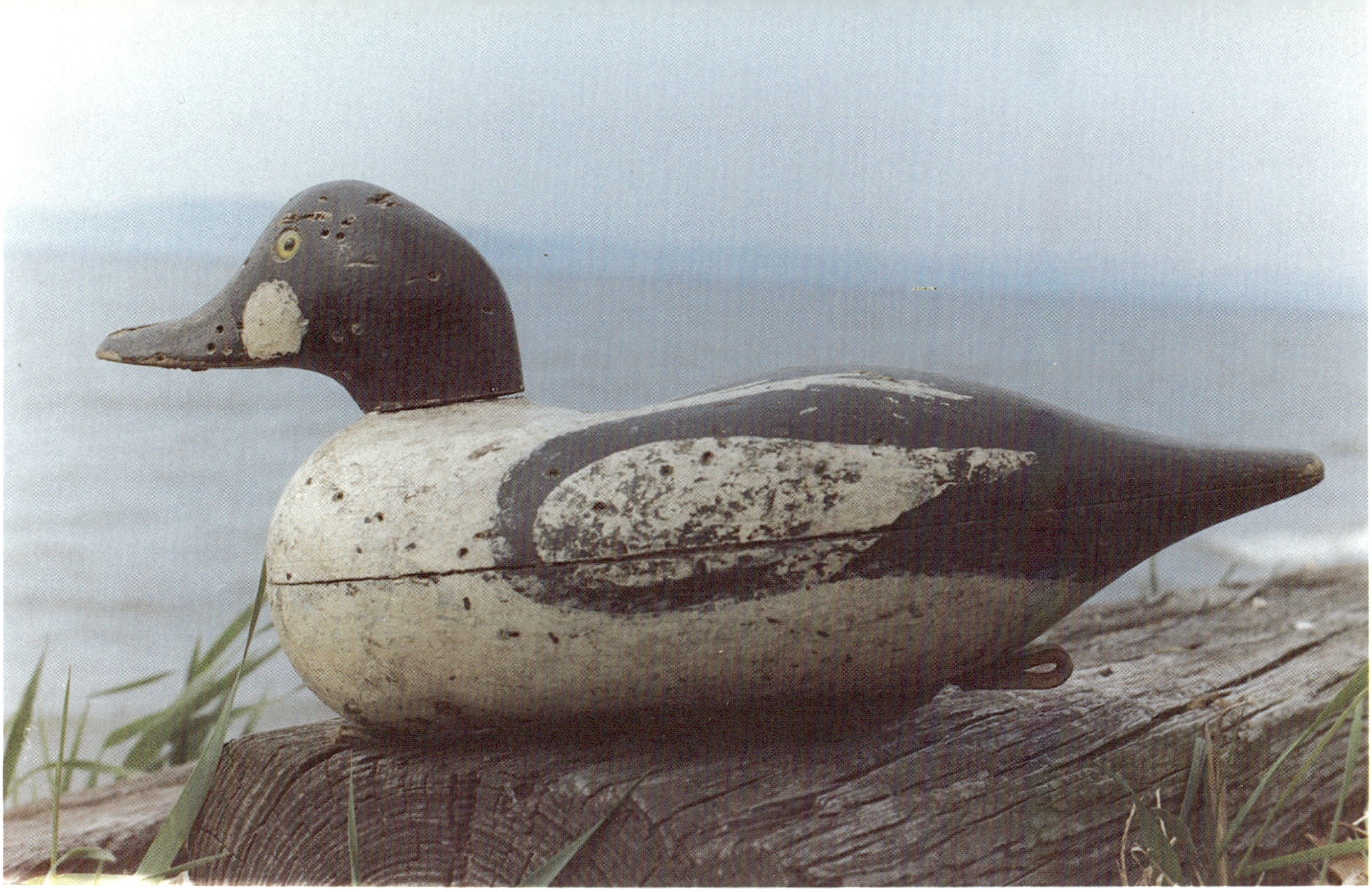

Whistler drake by Charles Kirby, original paint, hollow cedar, ca. 1920. Collection of Joseph Duggan.

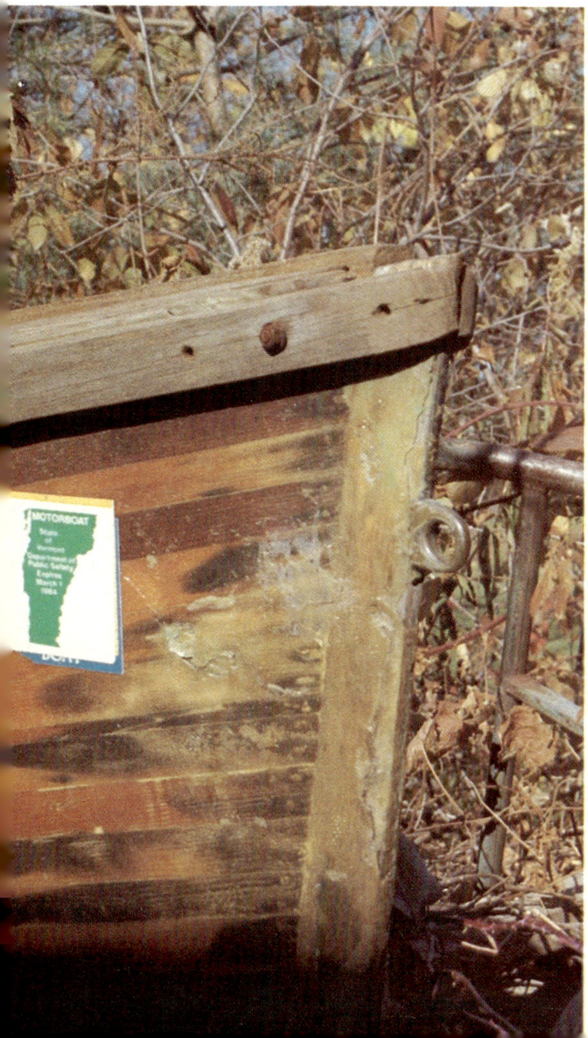

Pike or Adirondack skiff ca. 1953. Built by Charles Kirby. Hollow whistler hen by Kirby on gunnel, collection of Robert Bushey.

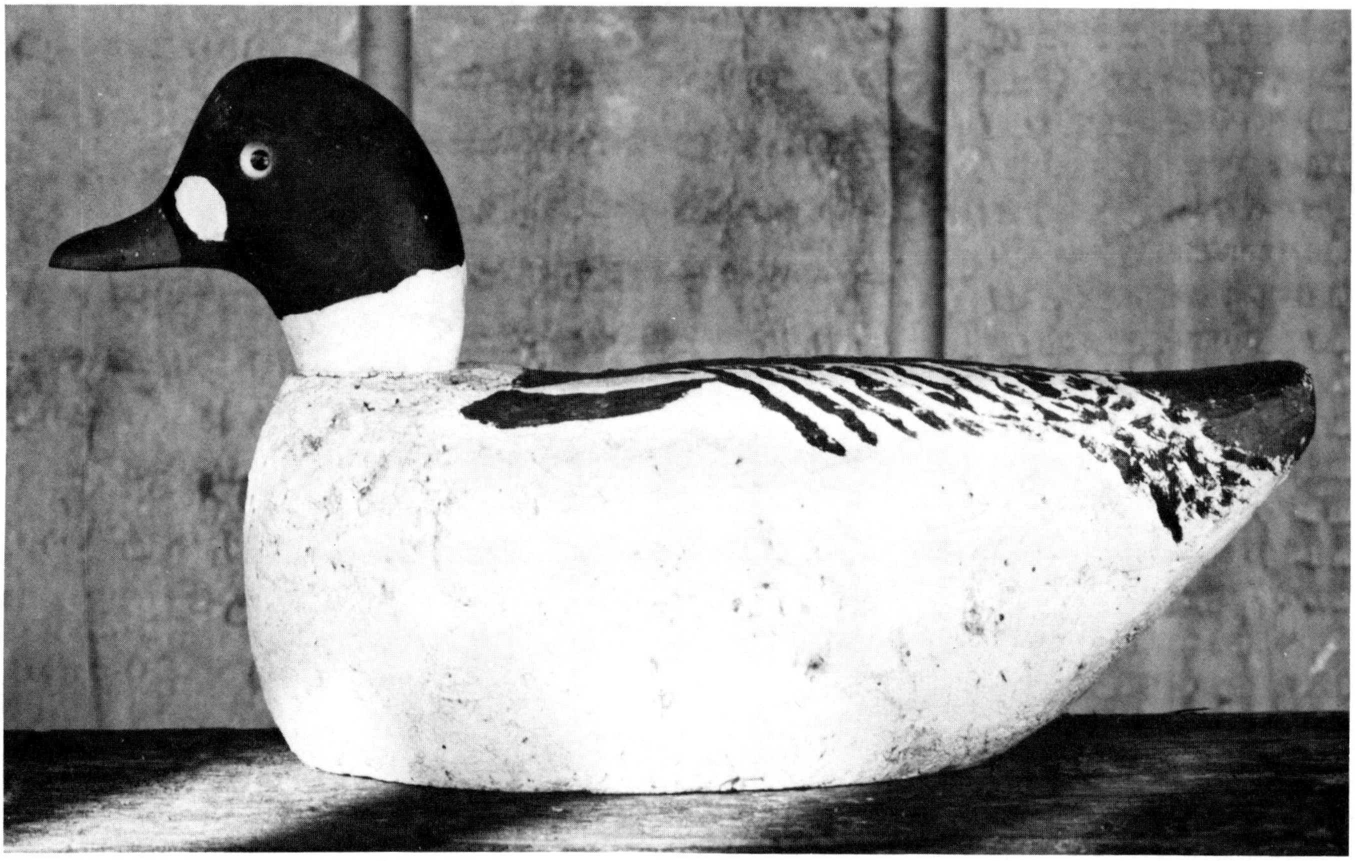

Whistler drake by Charles Kirby ca. 1945. Cork body, original paint from the collection of Dr. A.J. Crandall.

Middle period whistler by Charles Kirby. Note change in paint pattern. From A.J. Crandall collection.

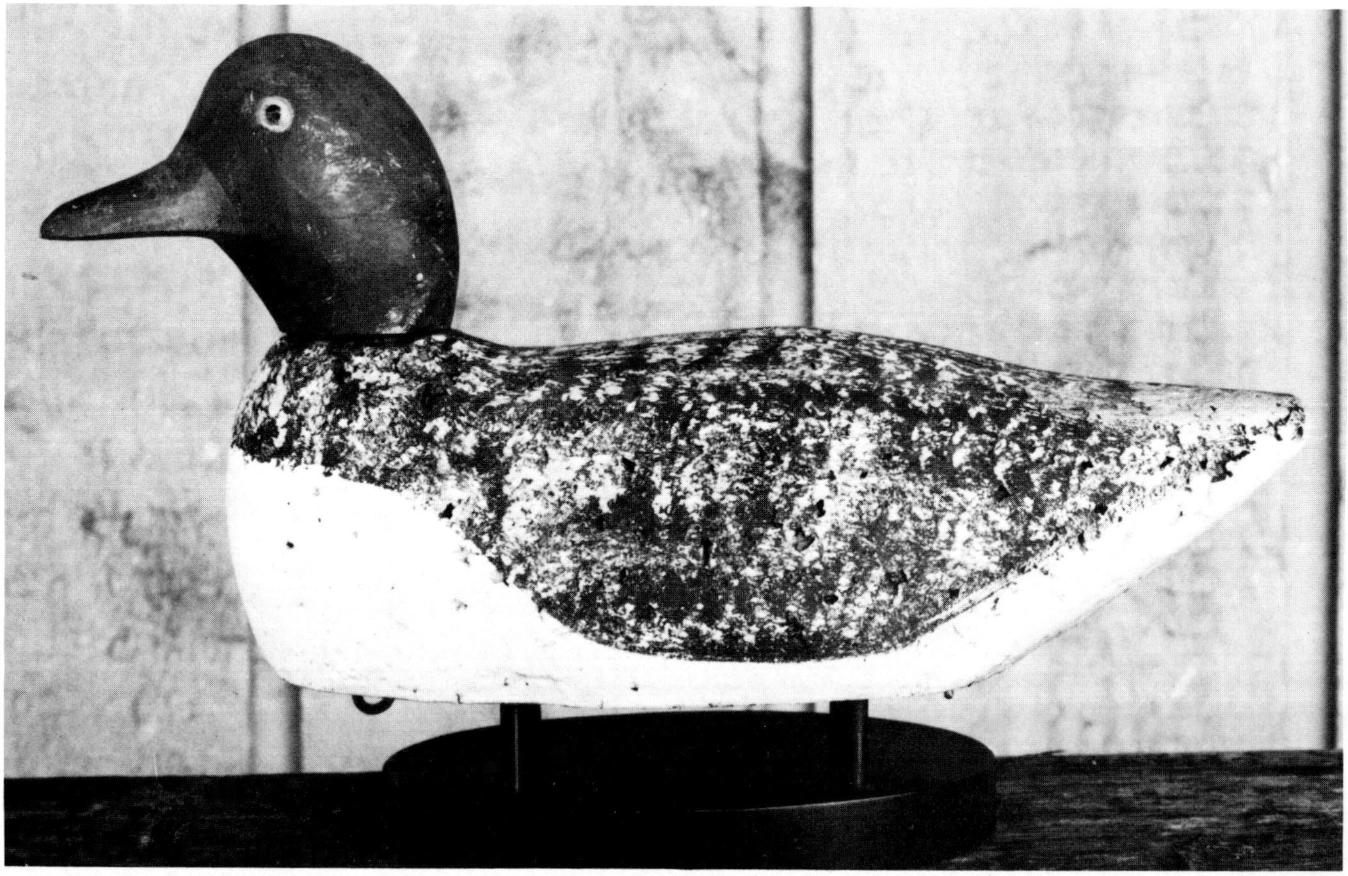

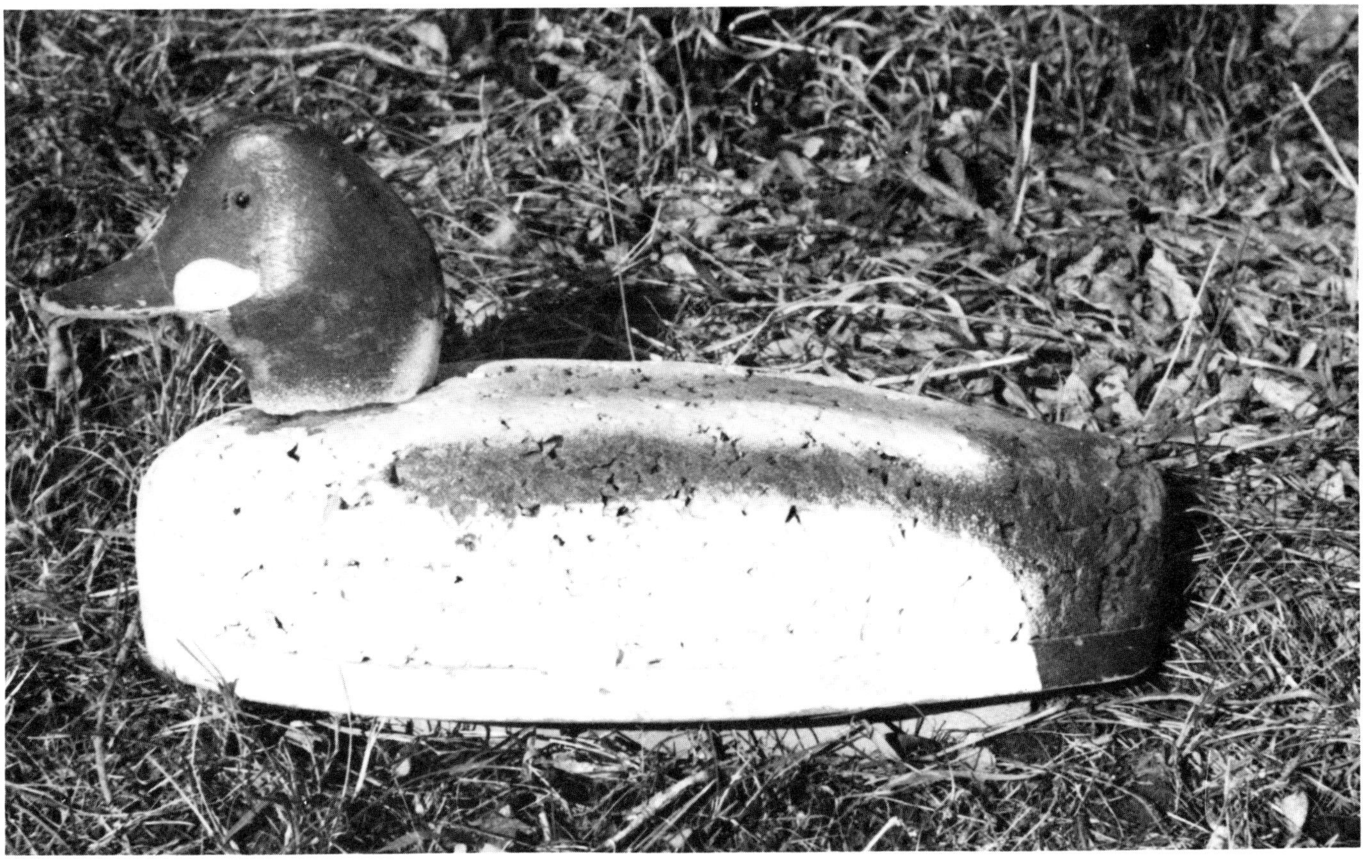

Whistler drake by Charles Kirby ca. 1952. Collection of William Coates. Note style change.

Whistler hen by Charles Kirby ca. 1920. Cedar, hollow construction. Collection of Loy S. Harrell.

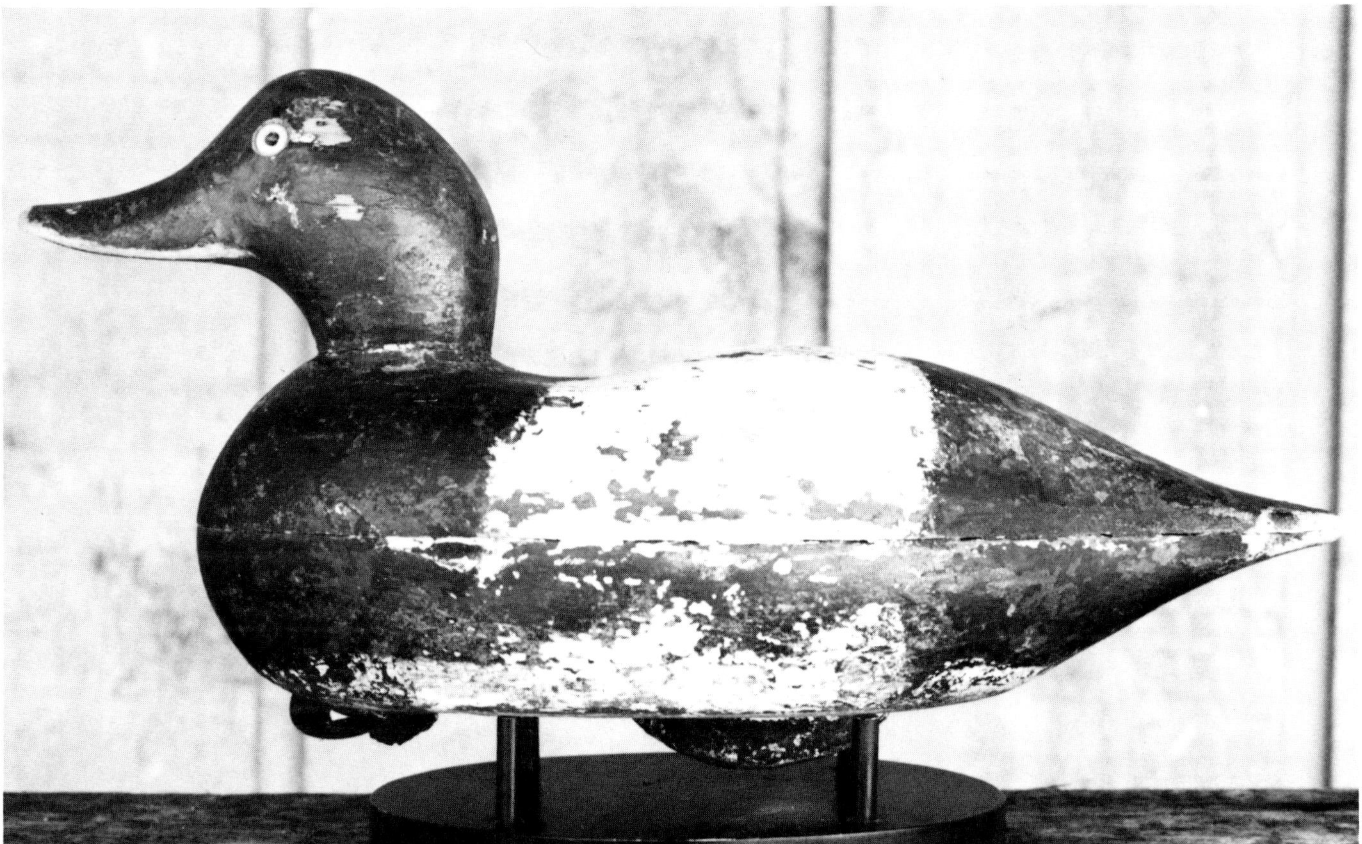

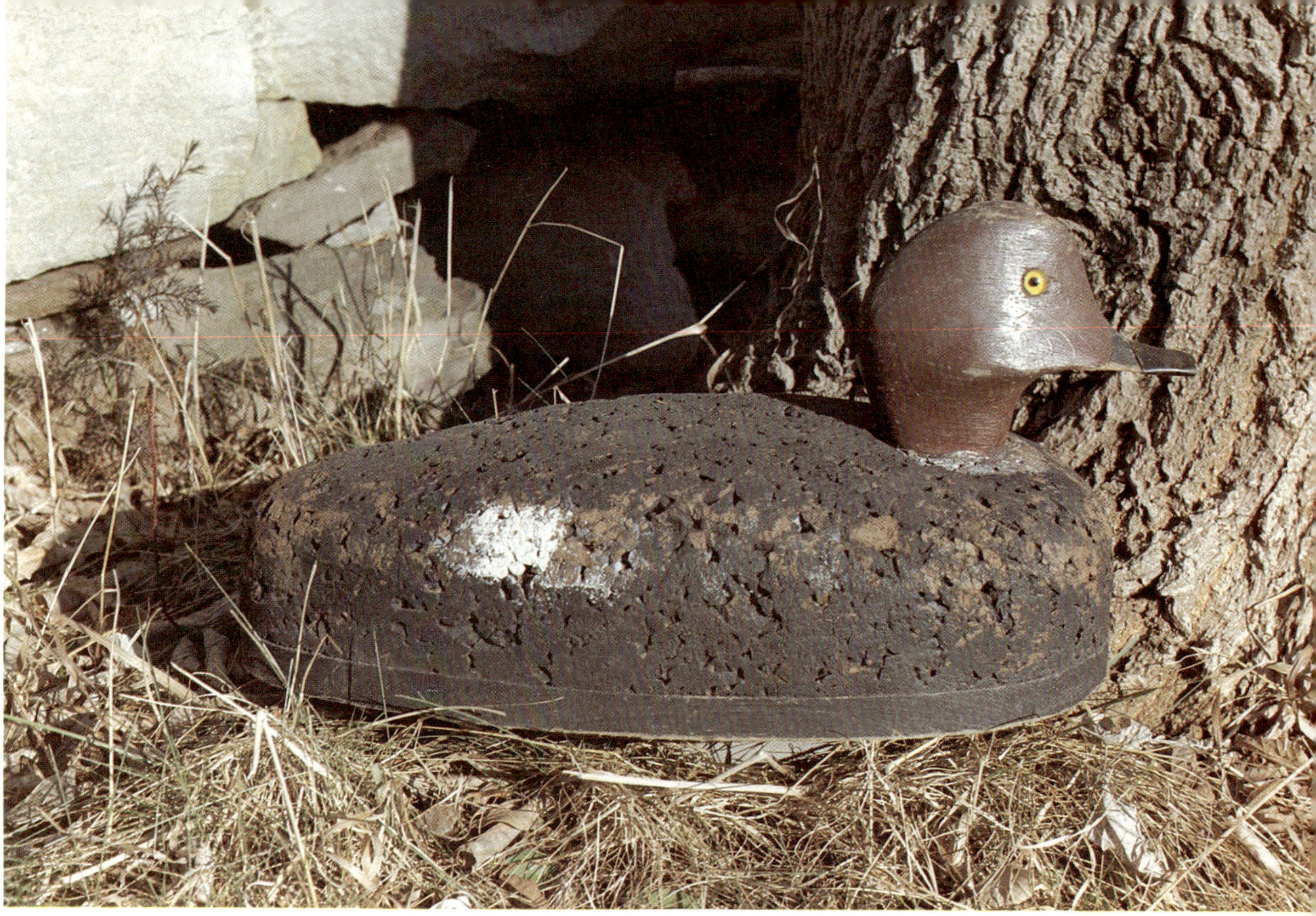

Whistler hen by Charles Kirby. Collection of William Coates.

Bluebill hen by Rupert King ca. 1950.

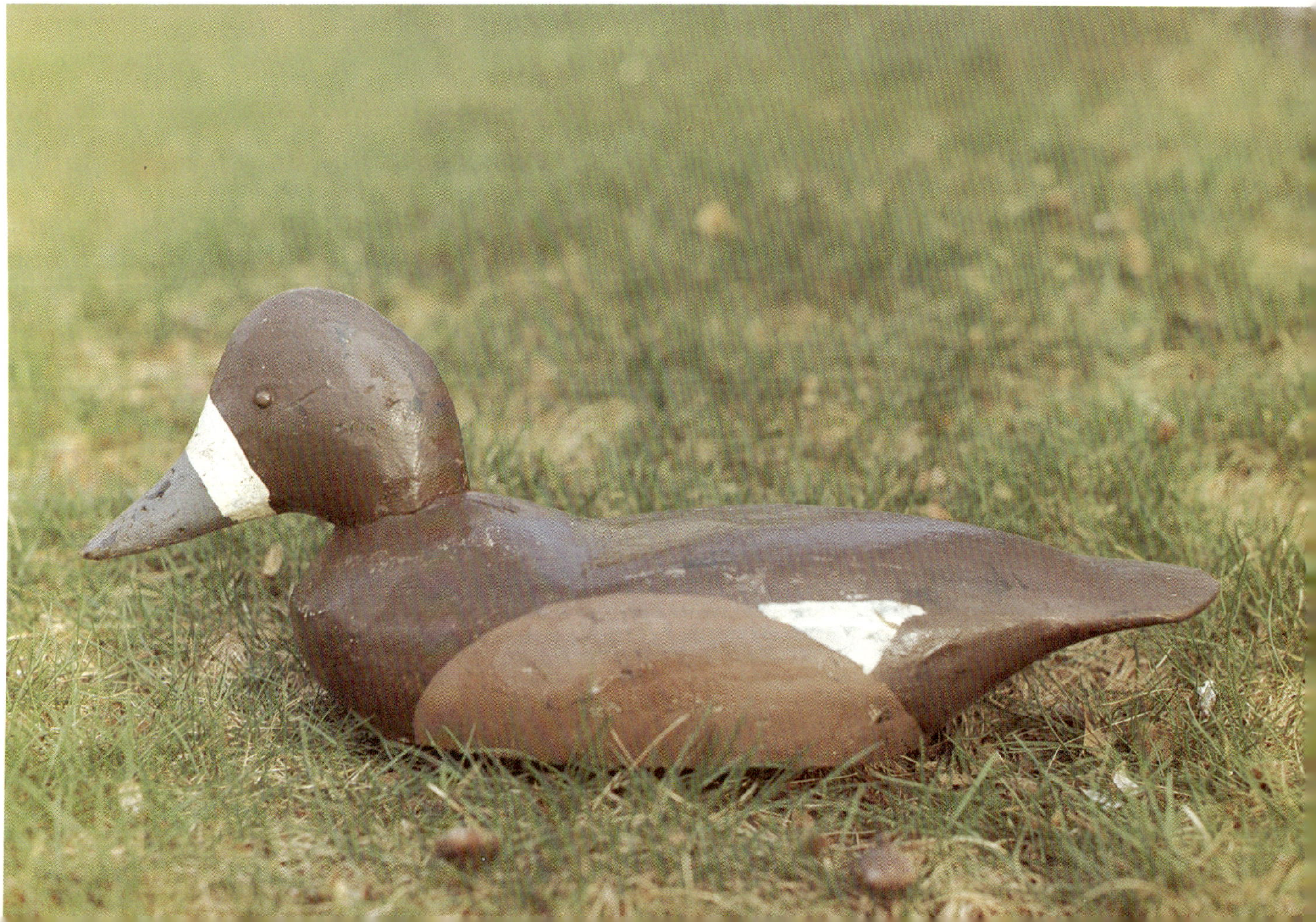

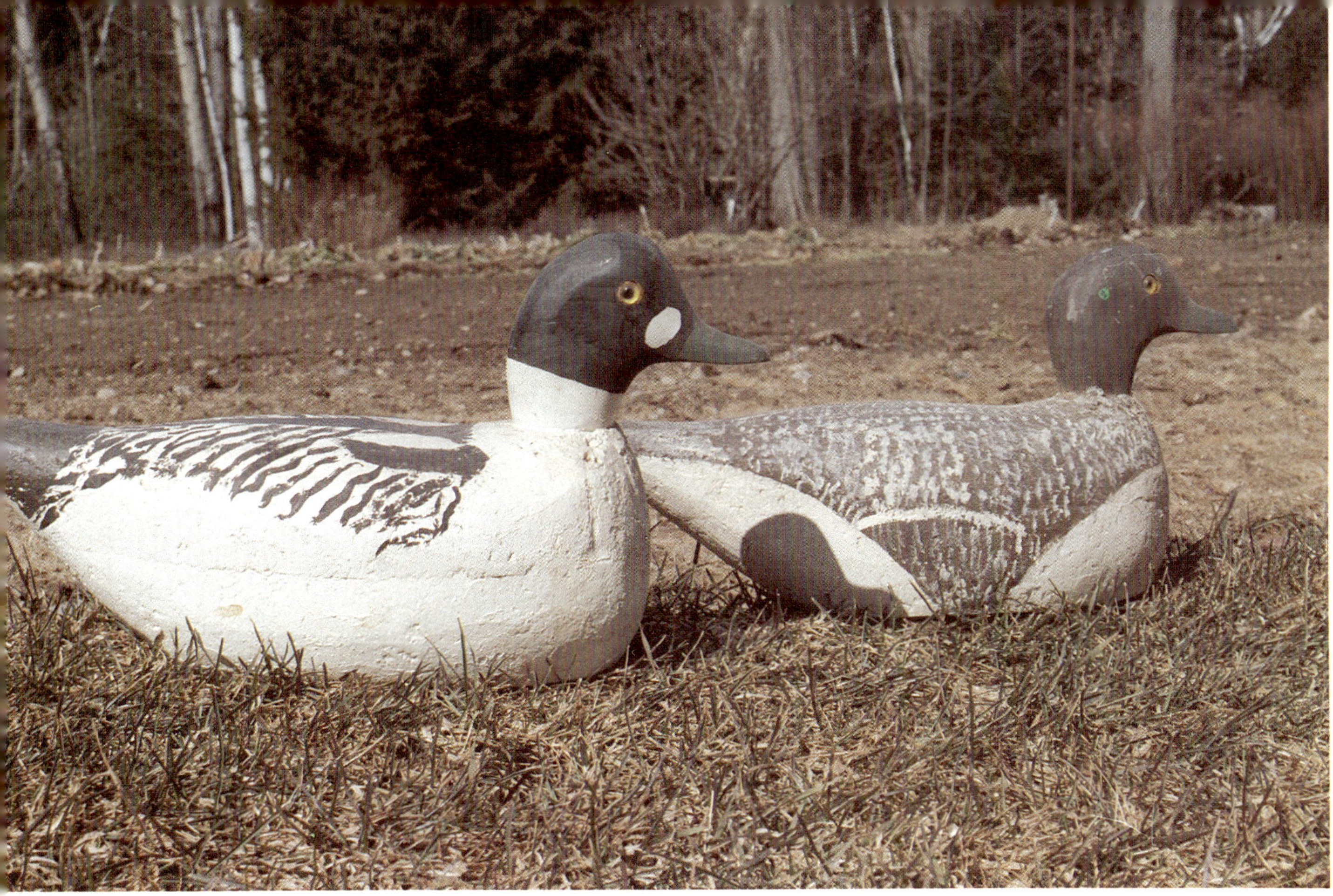

Pair of Kirby whistlers ca. 1945. Note paint patterns.

Black duck by Rupert King ca. 1935. Hollow cedar, original paint with relief carving. Collection of Rupert King Jr.

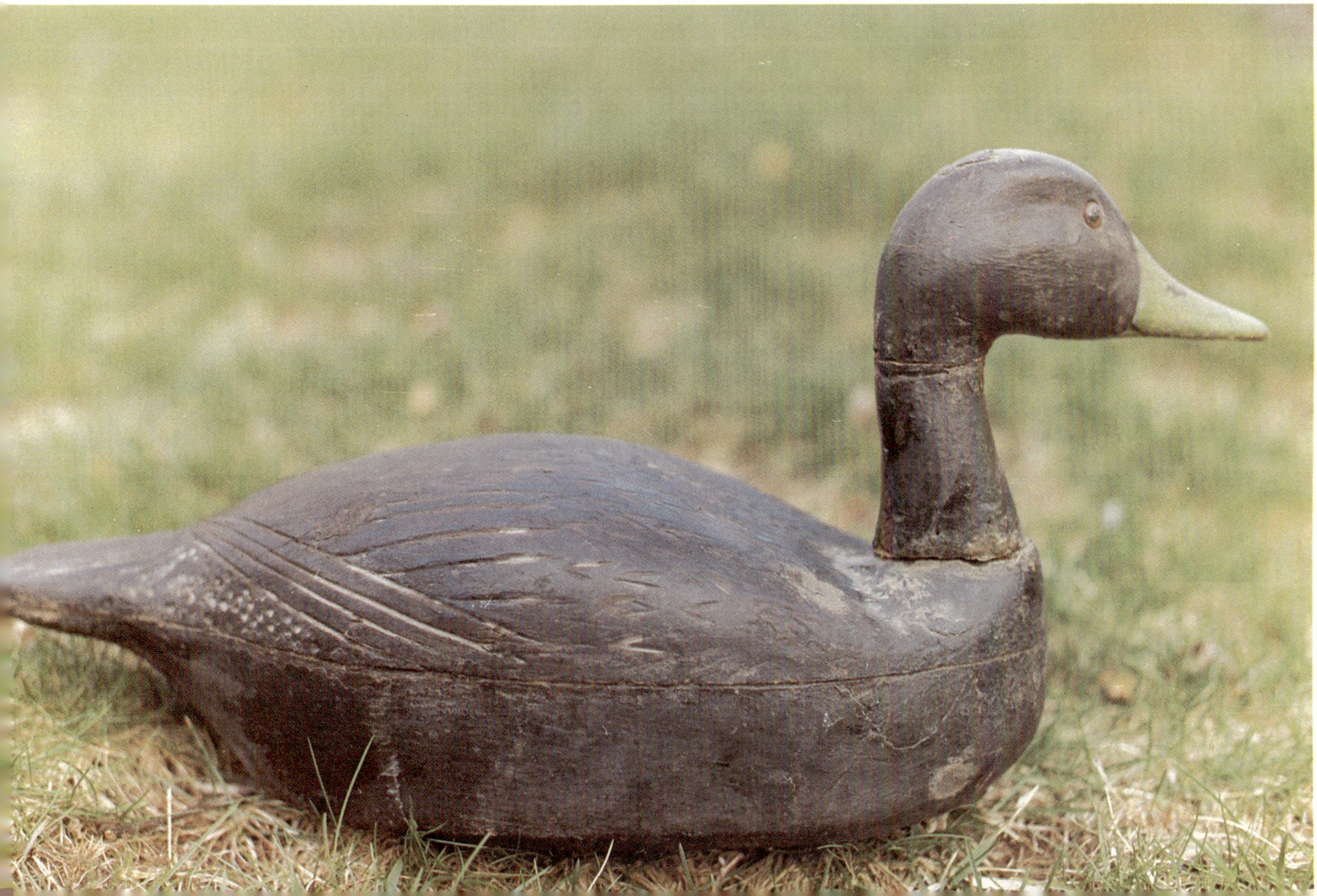

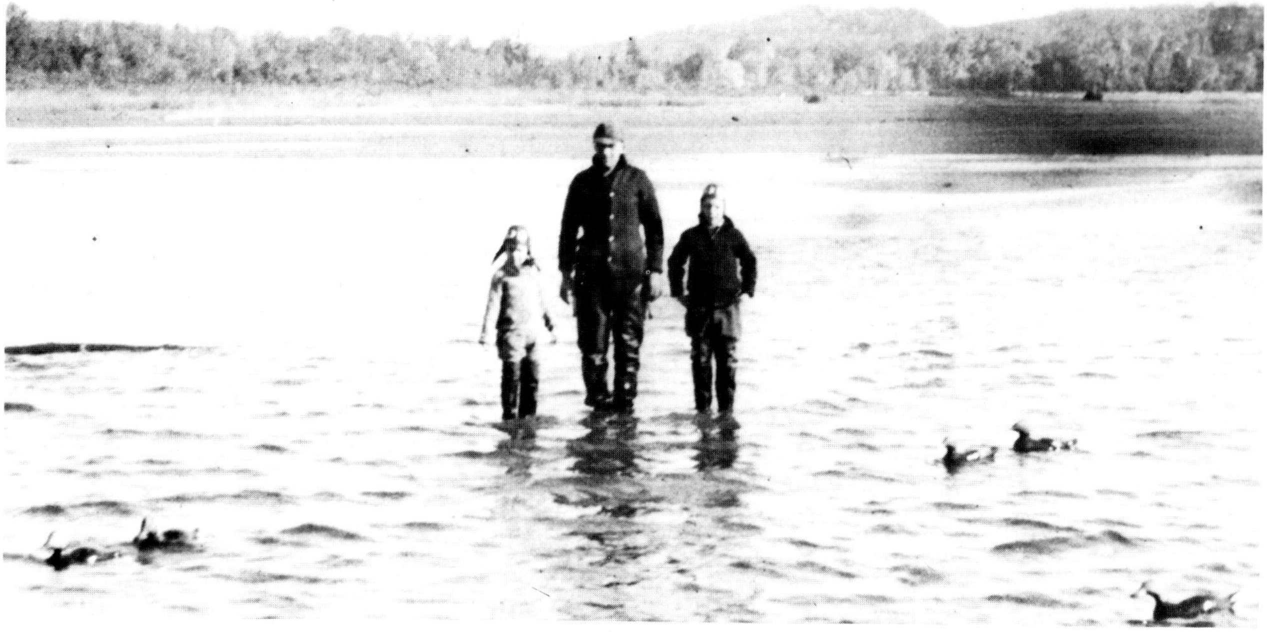

Rupert King with his sons Frederick (left) and Rupert Jr. 1935 on McNall Bay, Lake Champlain. Background is house blind with two bunks, stove and shooting deck. Note King decoys.

Rupert King 1892-1972, Burlington, Vermont, was at home on the water especially when duck hunting. As a close friend of Russell Merriman and Phil Gregory, King spent time carving decoys, hunting, and talking "ducks". His decoys were hollow, cedar construction with relief carving. This was characteristic of his blacks and earlier work. His later birds, especially whistlers and bluebills, are solid cedar. King carved over fifty decoys.

Pictured left to right: Rupert King, Phillip Gregory and Russell Merriman at the Sand Bar, Lake Champlain, Vermont, 1940. "The Day's Bag". With Merriman labrador retriever.

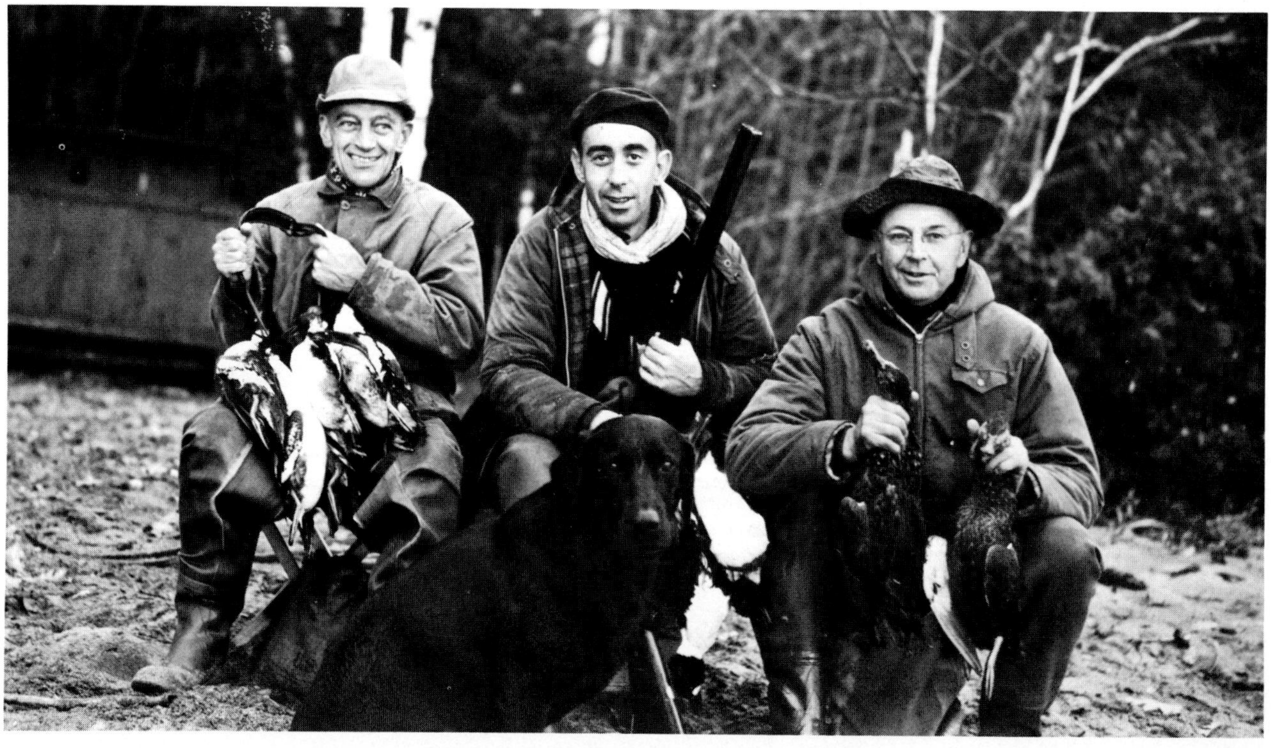

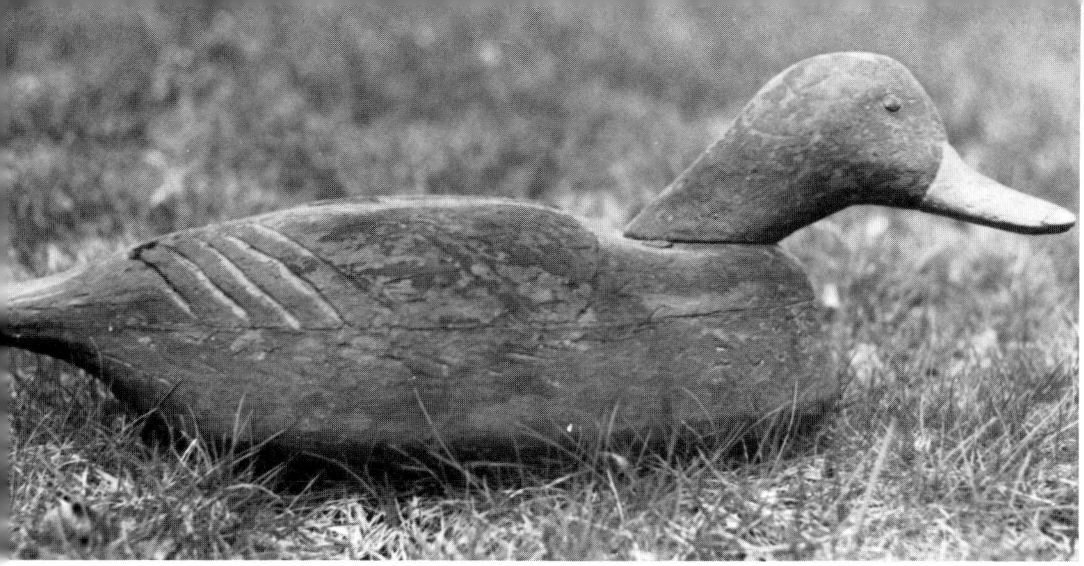

Black duck by Rupert King ca. 1935. Swimming position.

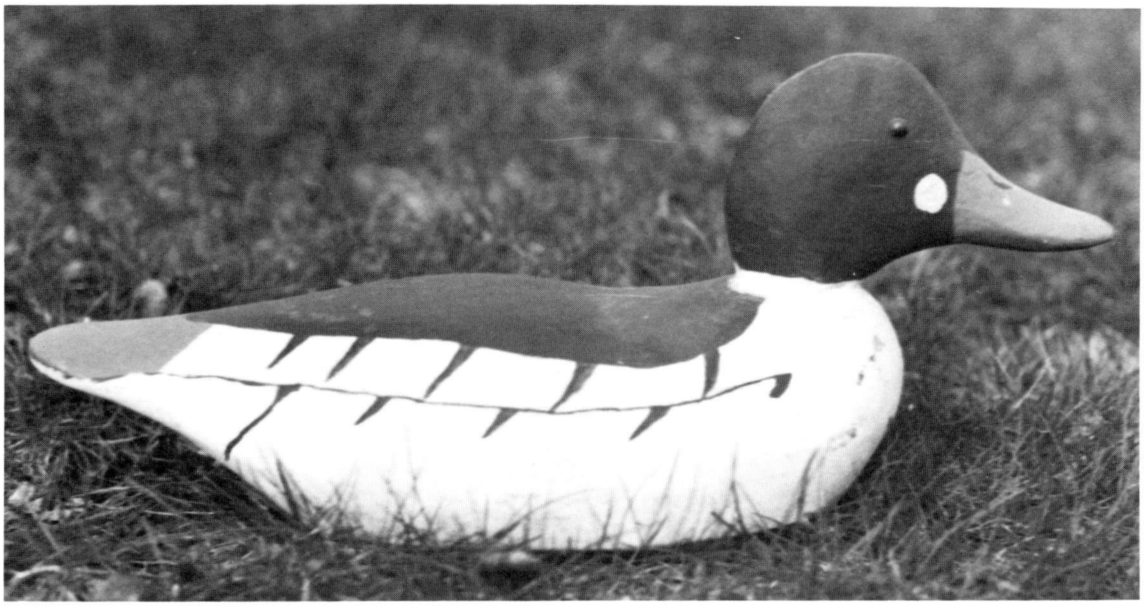

Whistler drake by Rupert King ca. 1950. Solid cedar construction.

Goldeneye drake by Elmer Lang. Original paint, cedar construction.

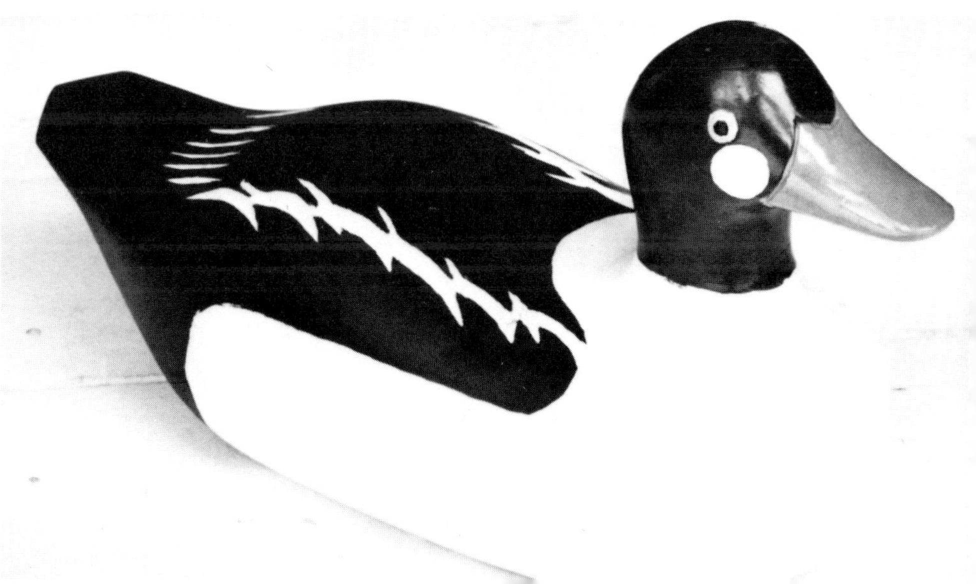

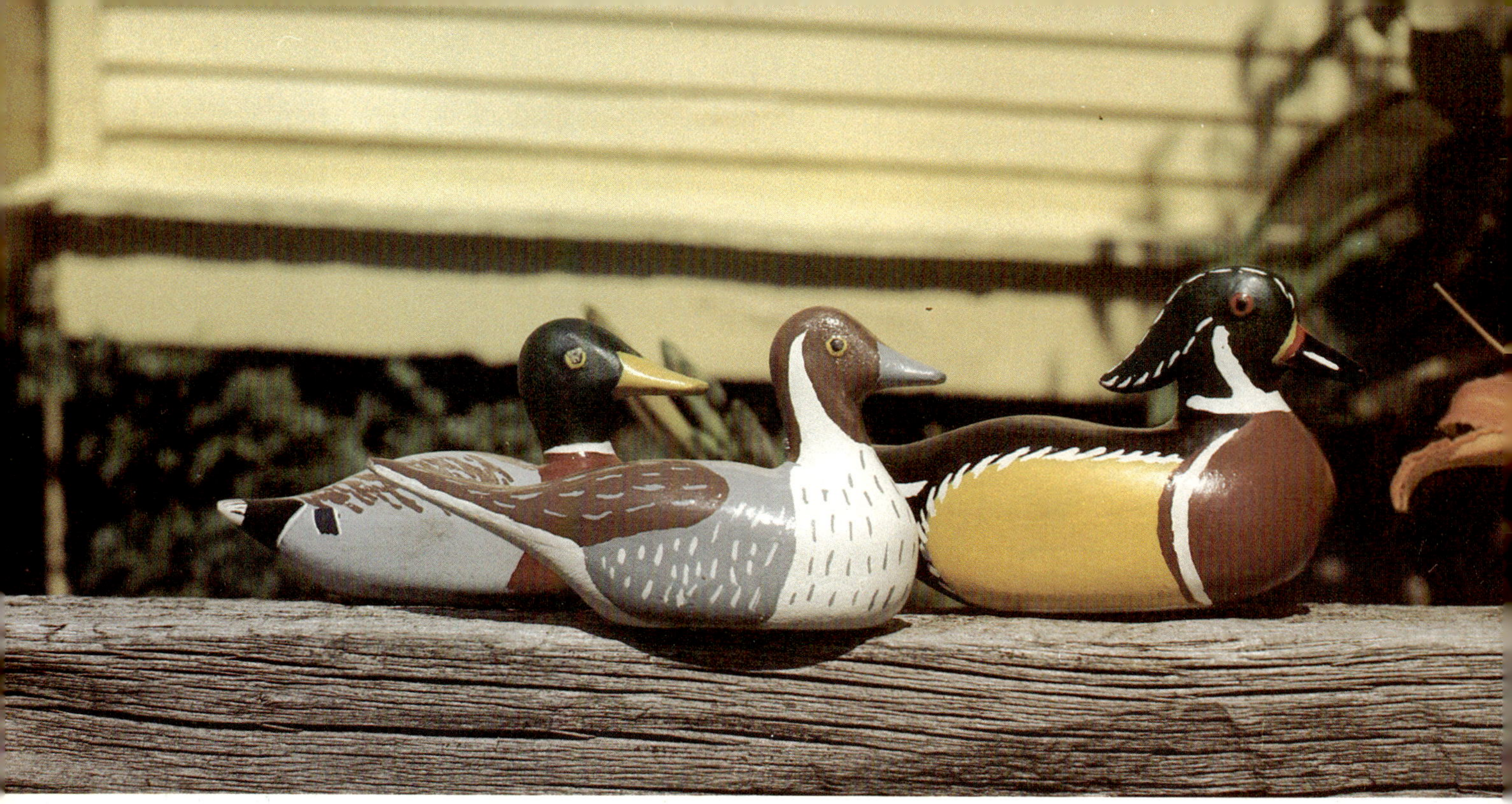

Mallard, pintail and woodduck miniatures by Elmer Lang. Ca. 1984. Collection of the author.

Elmer Lang 1920- Port Henry, New York. Lang, who lives on Bulwagga Bay, Lake Champlain, New York is a boat builder and mechanic by trade. He has had a "lifelong love affair" with the lake and made almost a hundred boats including many flat bottomed duck boats. He has carved over one-hundred decoys with many of his earlier ones "lost in a storm". Lang now sells turkey decoys and miniature duck carvings commercially.

Turkey hen decoys by Elmer Lang. Used along Lake Champlain, Port Henry, New York.

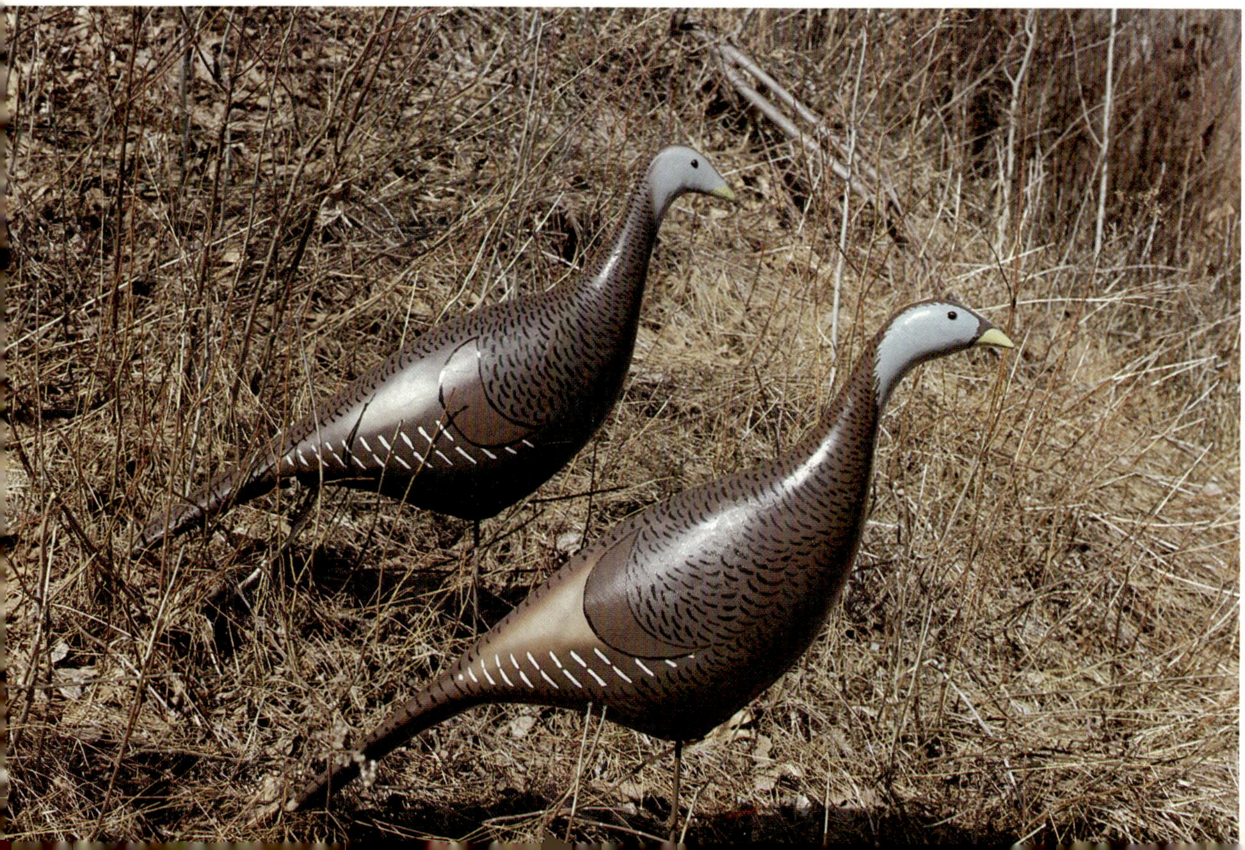

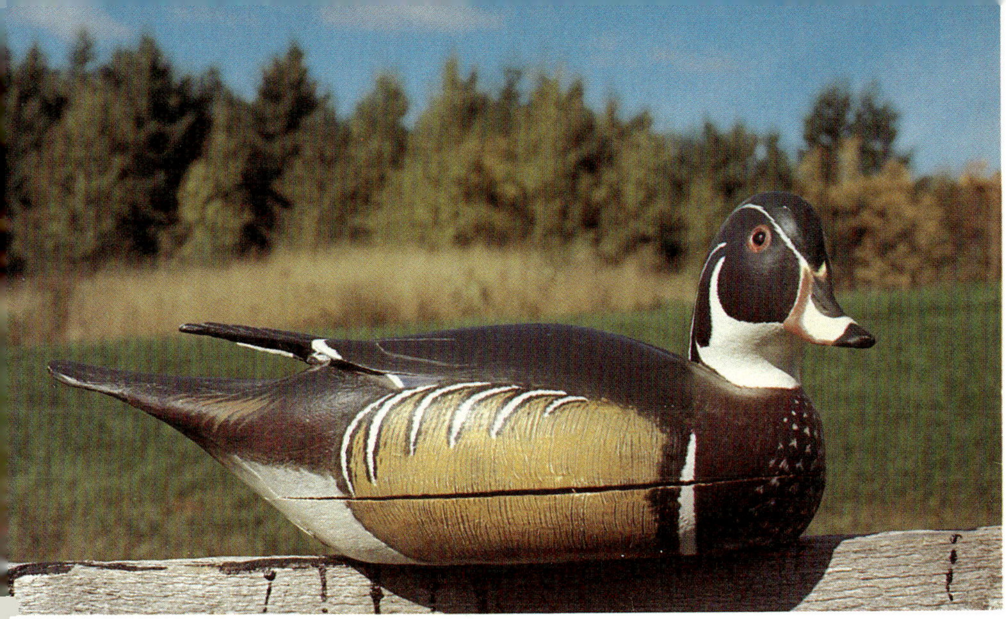

Woodduck drake by Robert Lasher ca. 1970. One of six to ten decoratives made.

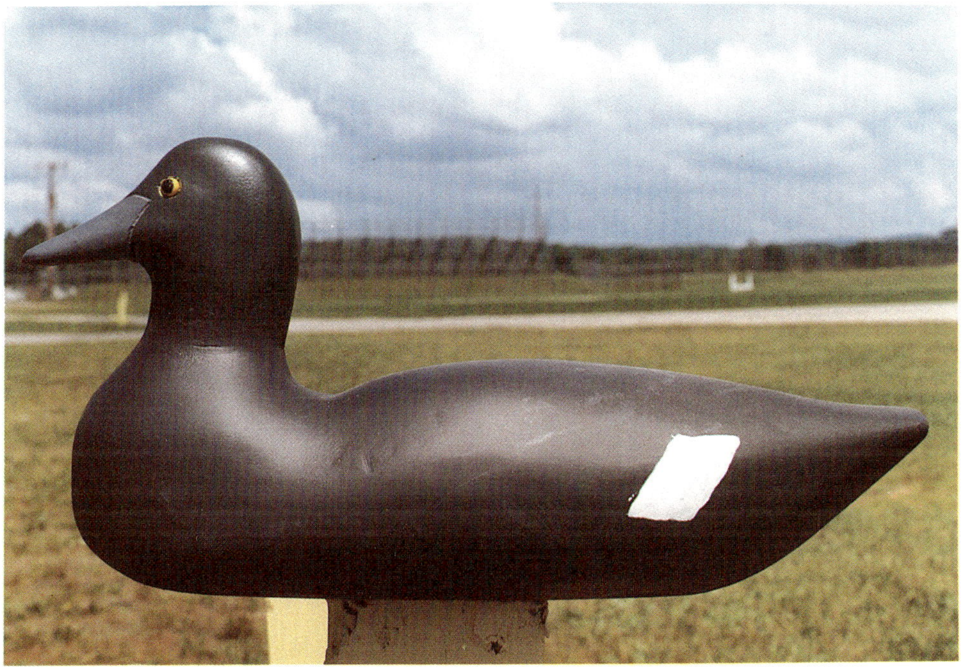

Bluebill drake by Elmer Lang.

Mallard drake miniature by Robert Lasher ca. 1981.

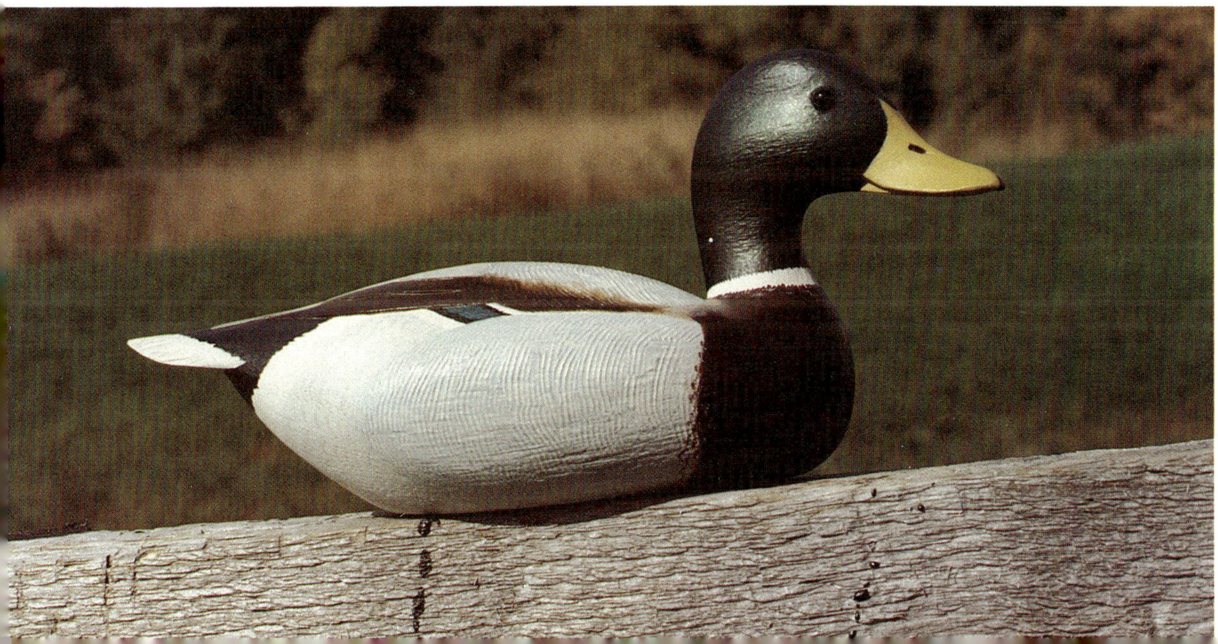

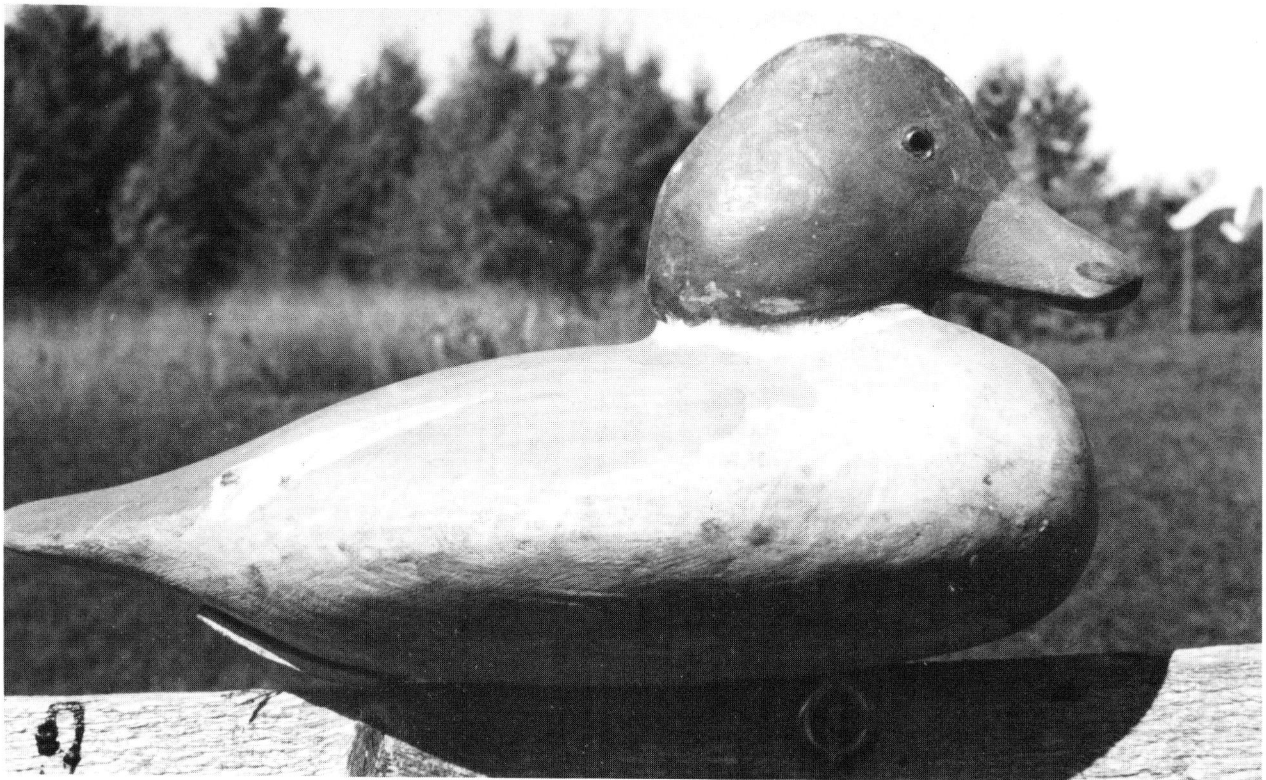

Goldeneye hen by Robert Lasher ca. 1968.

Robert M. Lasher 1951- Bakersfield, Vermont, was influenced by his association with David Harrington, to carve decoys. Beginning in 1967 Lasher carved working birds for his own use, including whistlers, bluebills and mallards. These decoys were used in the Vermont "islands". In 1970 he began carving commercially, mostly miniatures, and sold them to shops throughout New England. Made of sugar pine, Lasher's miniatures include twenty-six different species and total almost three hundred.

Mallard drake by Robert Lasher ca. 1967—Made fifteen to twenty. Rasped surface, original paint.

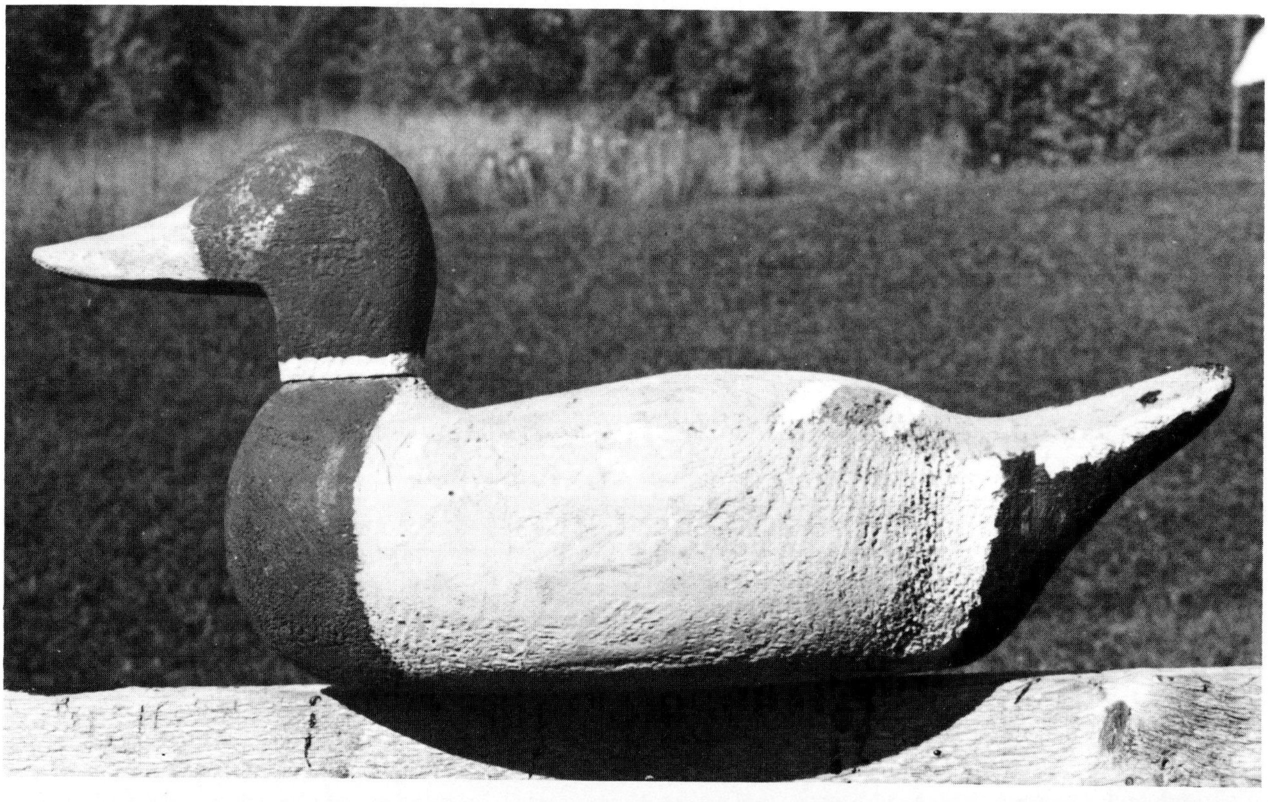

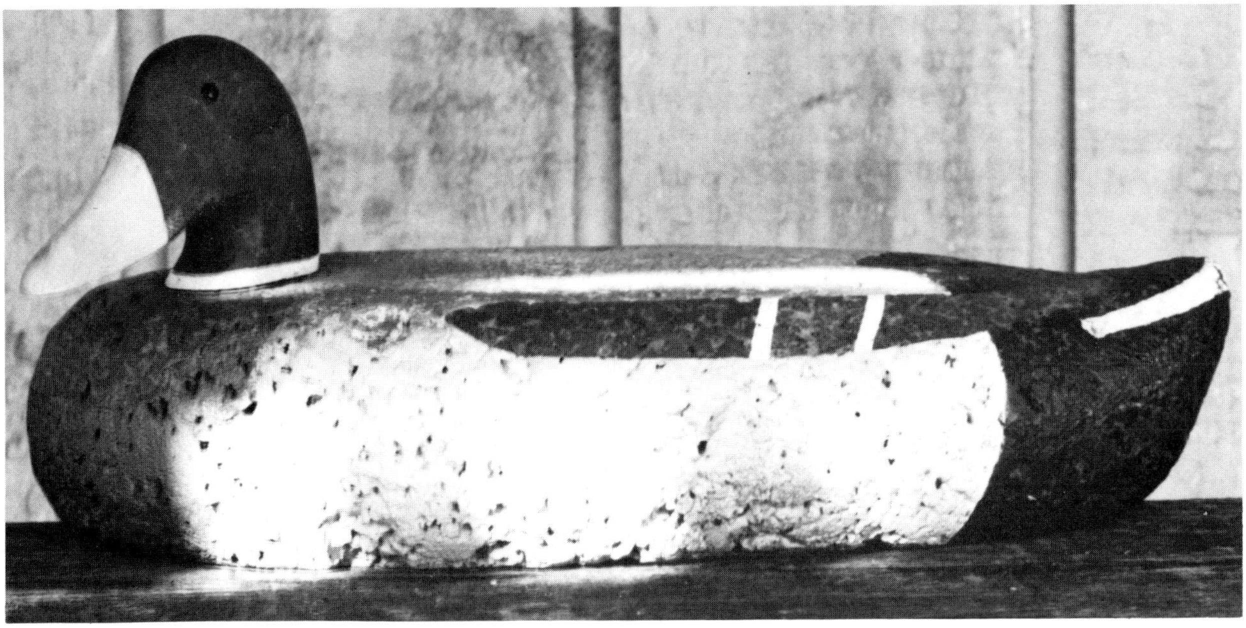

Mallard drake by James "Jess" Lyman. Ca. 1955. Cork body, pine head. Collection of Loy S. Harrell.

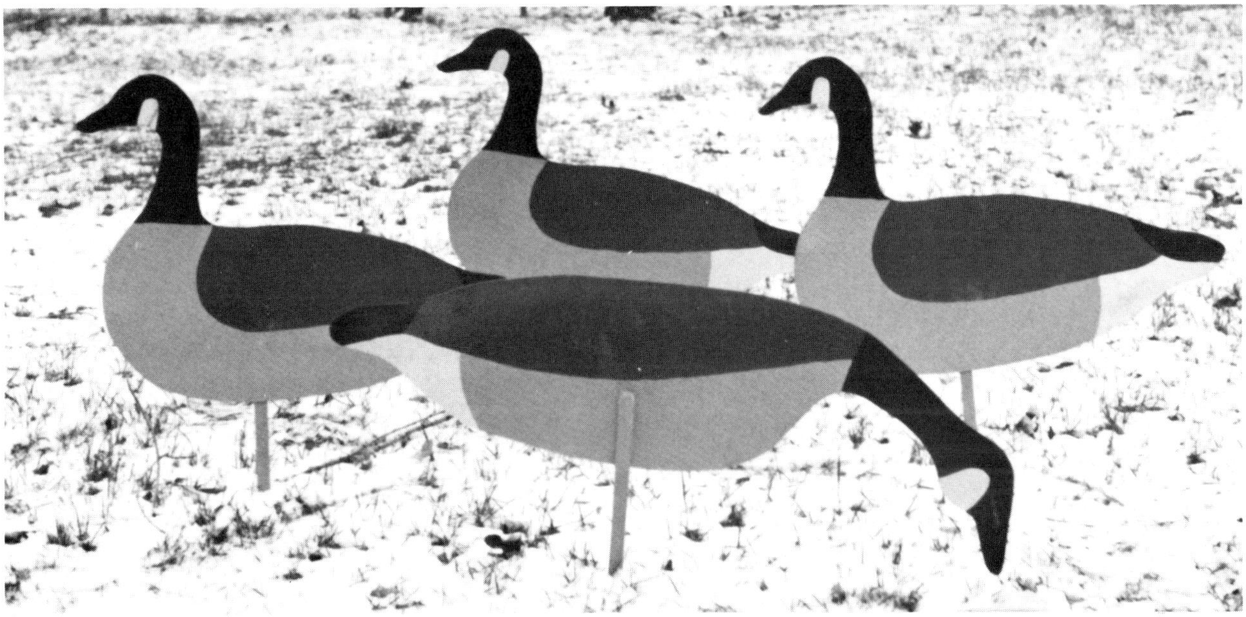

Canada goose profile stickups by Jess Lyman, wood veneer construction. How could these decoys miss?

Mallard hen by Jess Lyman. Rig mate to above drake. Both are magnums.

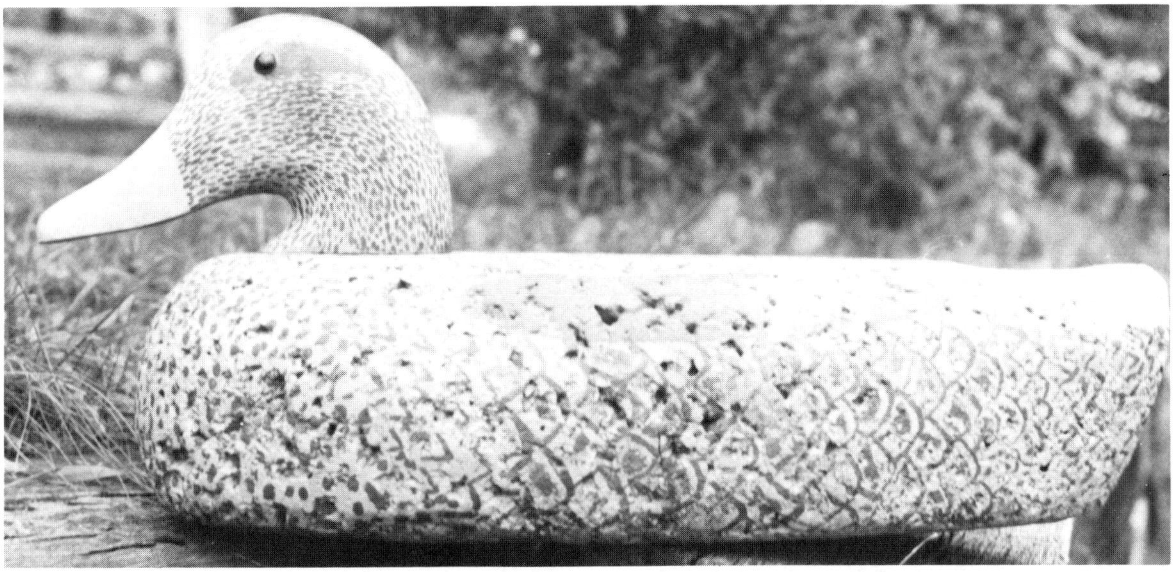

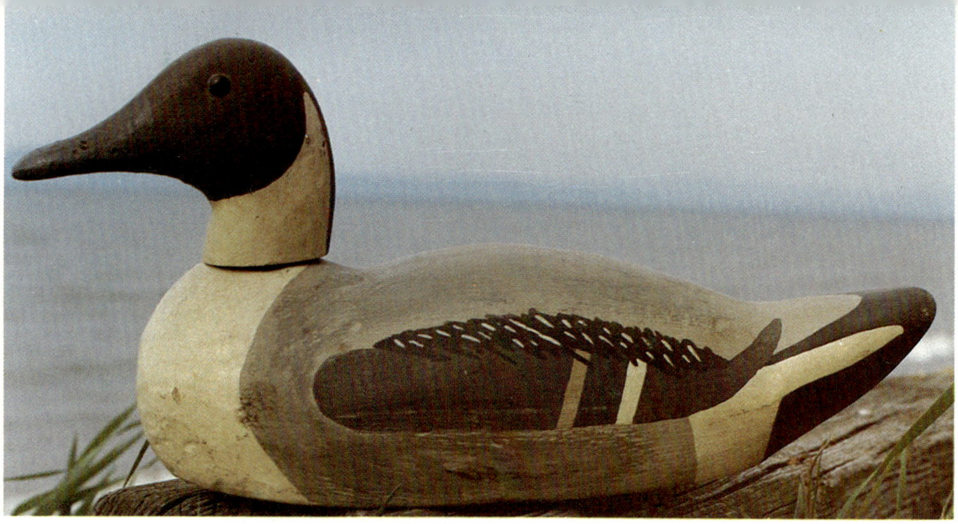

Pintail drake by Jess Lyman. Original paint, cedar construction ca. 1950. Collection of Joseph Duggan.

James "Jess" Lyman 1925, Burlington, Vermont was a carpenter by trade and in the construction business. His natural talent lent itself to his decoy carving. Lyman carved many mallards, blacks, bluebills, goldeneyes and Canadian geese. Most were of cork construction he obtained "from the old Sealtest plant on Winooski Avenue", and a number were of cedar. He used an undercoat of Herter's paint and four coats of linseed oil as a preservative. All pine heads are removable and carried separately. Lyman is also noted for his fly fishing expertise and he is considered one of Lake Champlain's top fishermen.

Canada goose decoy by Jess Lyman ca. 1953. Original paint with detachable pine head. This decoy is a fine floater.

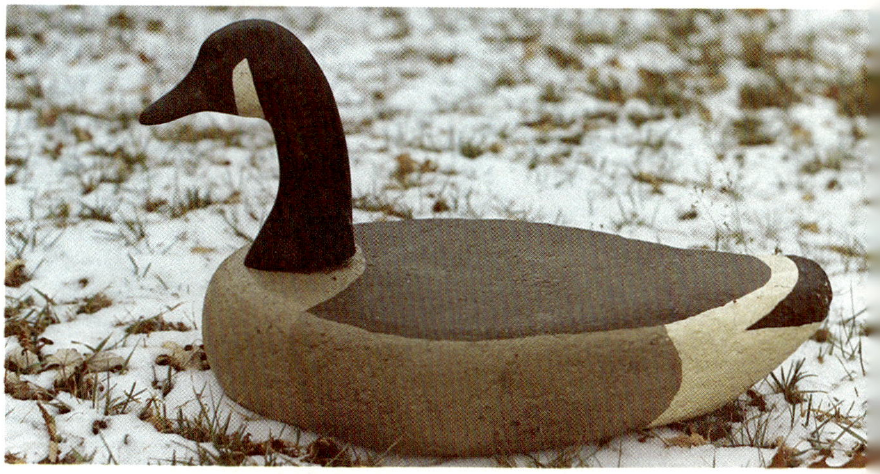

Goldeneyes by Jess Lyman. Cork body, pine heads, built to scale.

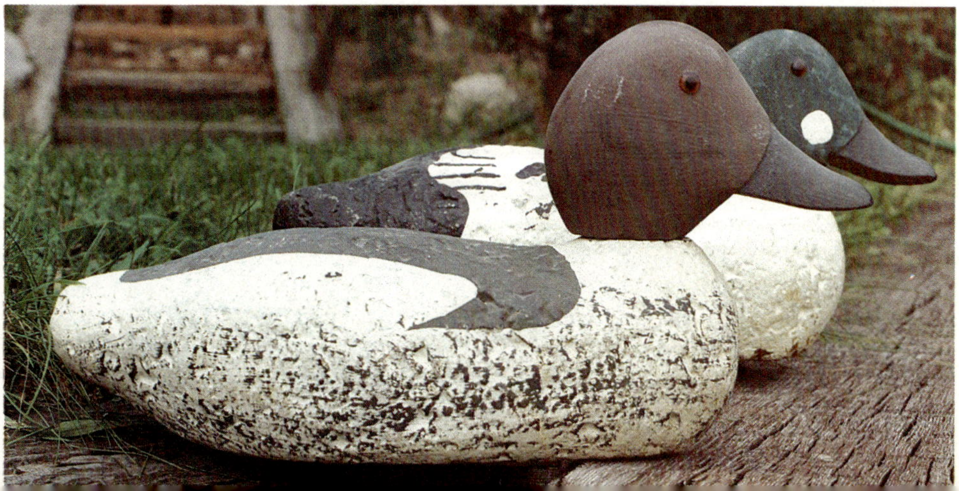

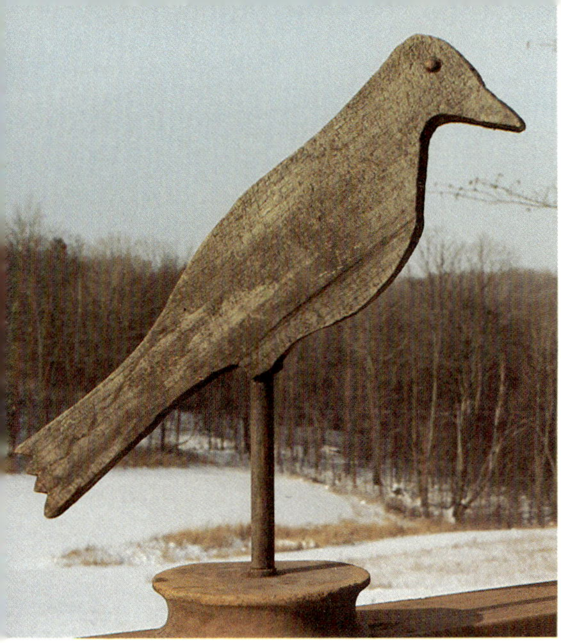

Crow decoy by William Maxfield ca. 1935. Found in the Maxfield "back shed" in 1984. Collection of Rae Harrell.

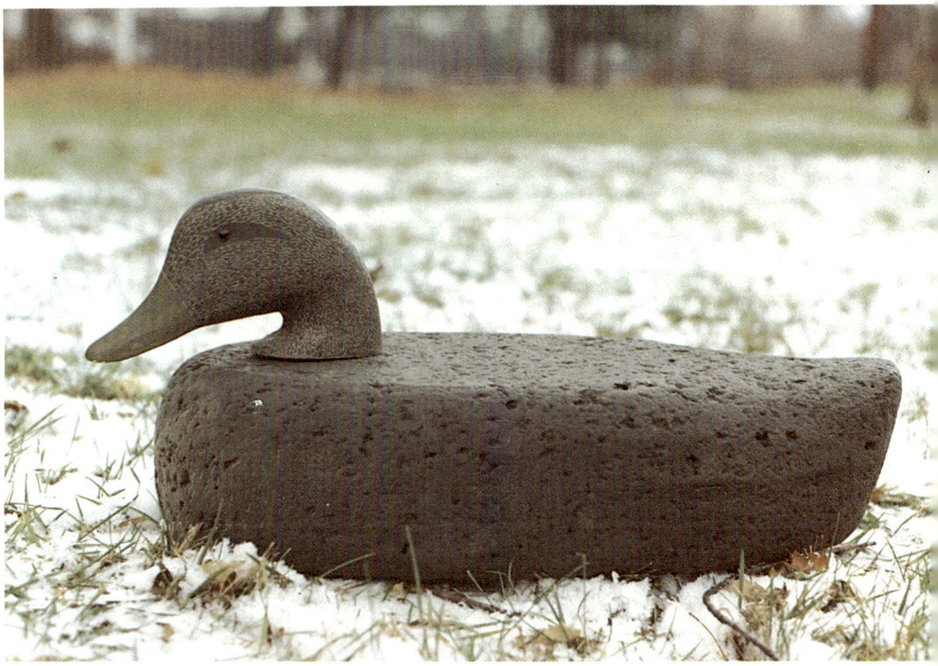

Black duck by Jess Lyman, cork magnum body.

William Maxfield 1881-1950, Georgia, Vermont, was raised in the hills of Georgia and was known as a hunter, fisherman and craftsman. He trapped along the Lamoille River and made boats, decoys and furniture. His cedar decoys were primitive but functional and were hunted over at Beaver Meadow Brook and the Lamoille River. Through time and disregard his decoys have disappeared although some have been attributed to Maxfield but not documented.

Black ducks by Arthur Maxwell, ca. 1920. Original paint, cedar bodies. Collectin of John Farnham.

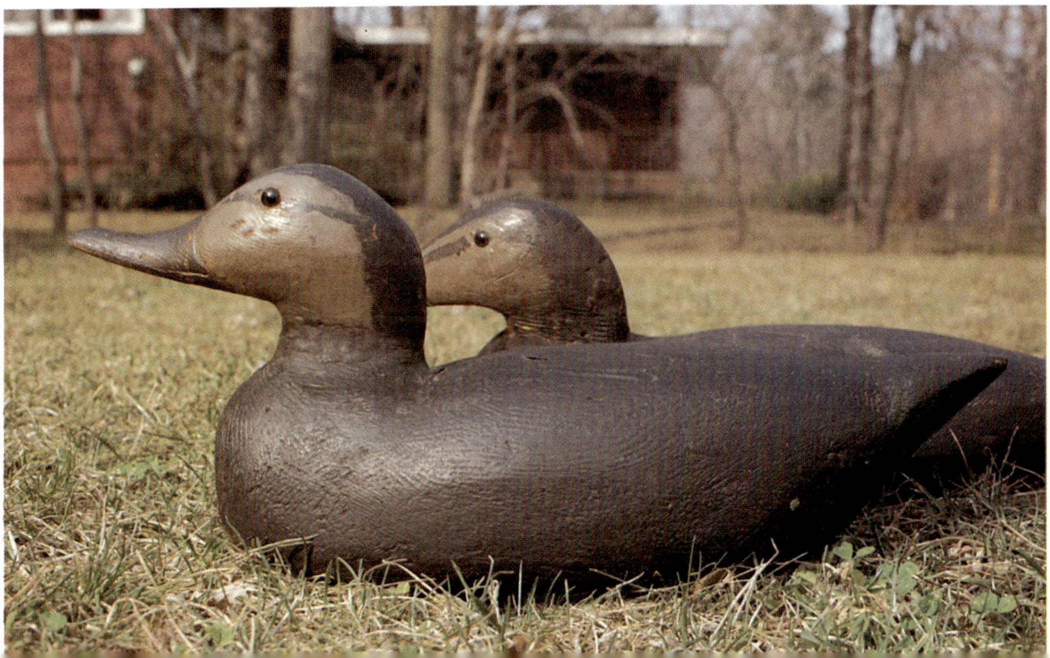

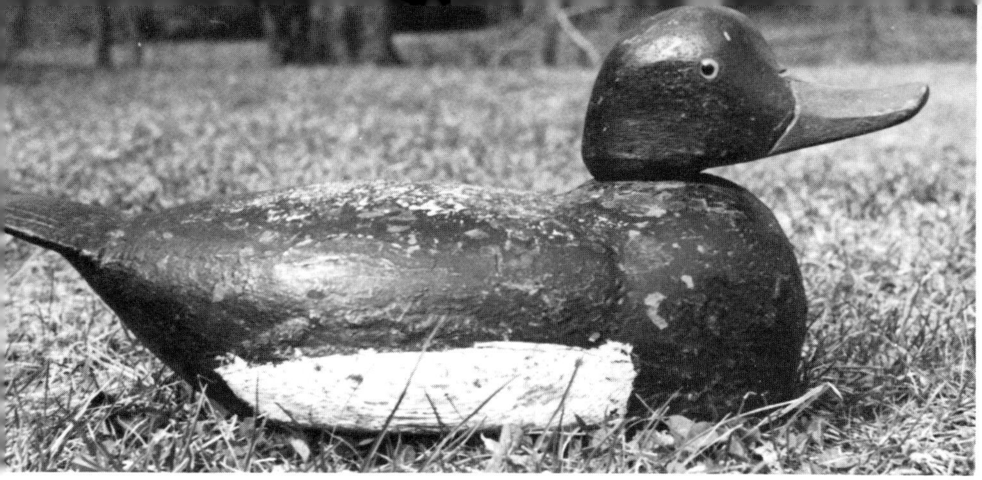

Bluebill drake by Arthur Maxwell ca. 1920. Collection of Daniel Farnham.

Arthur Maxwell 1884-1970. Salisbury, Vermont. From 1932 to 1953 Maxwell was director of the Vermont State Fish Hatchery in Salisbury. He was well familiar with the lake and hunted most of the Vermont shore. Besides carving decoys, Maxwell made fish profiles for mounting. He carved forty-five cedar working decoys.

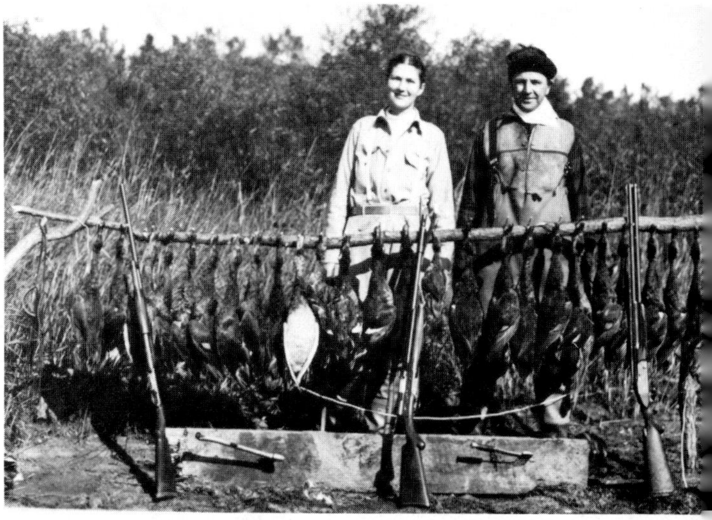

Charlotte and Russell Merriman of Montpelier, Vermont. Taken "Opening Day", 1942, at Merriman Bay, Colchester, Vermont. The Merrimans were noted hunters and Charlotte a "great shot". They raised many champion labrador retrievers that "cut their teeth" on Lake Champlain. Photo courtesy of Jane Gregory.

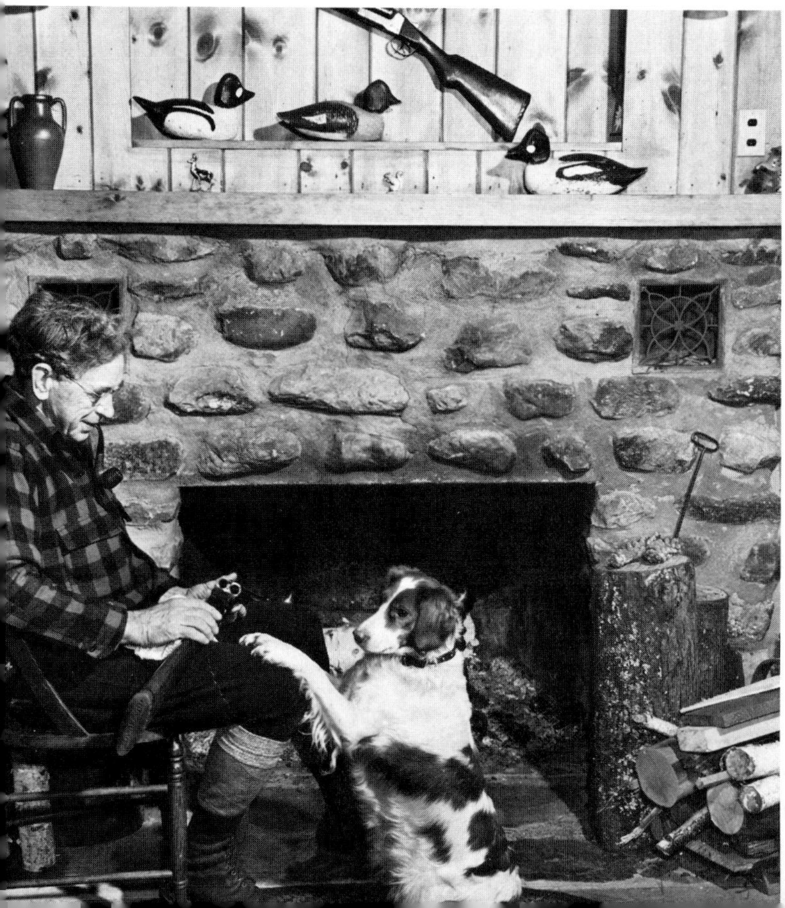

Arthur Maxwell, ca. 1945 in his camp with "Lady". Note Maxwell decoys on the mantel.

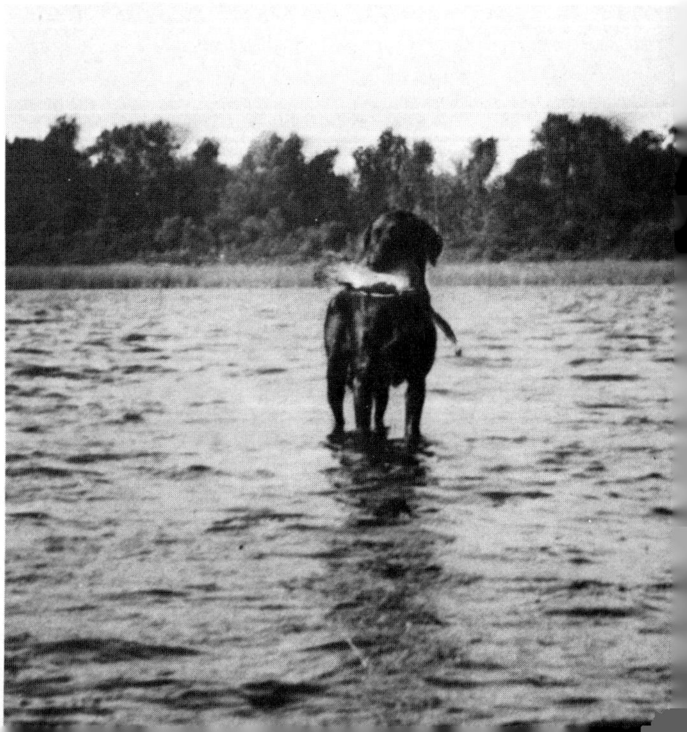

Hand-tinted photograph of Russell Merriman labrador, retrieving a pintail duck on Lake Champlain ca. 1942.

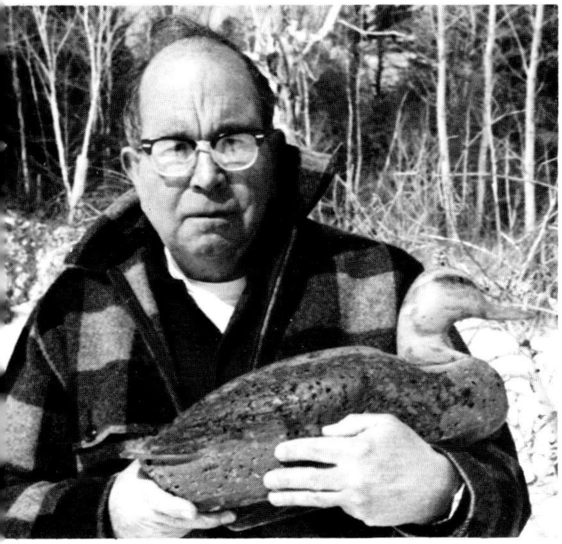

Simeon McIntyre 1923- Crown Point, New York, in his vineyard holding a black duck decoy. Photograph taken 1984.

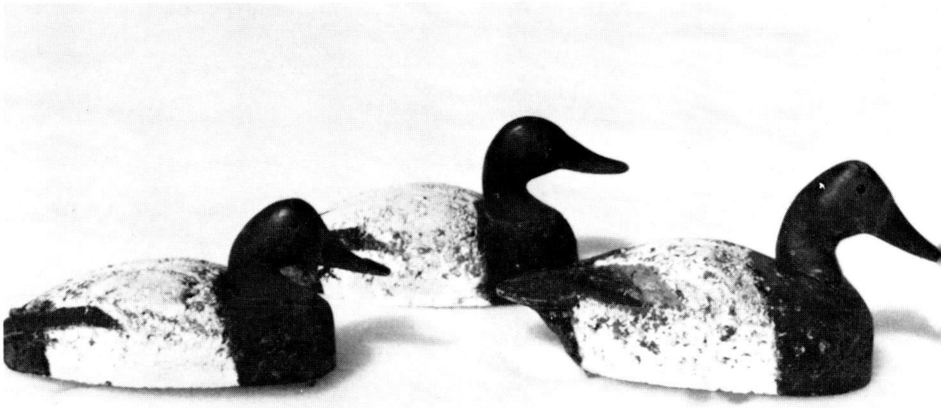

Canvasback decoys by Simeon McIntyre ca. 1960. Cork body style.

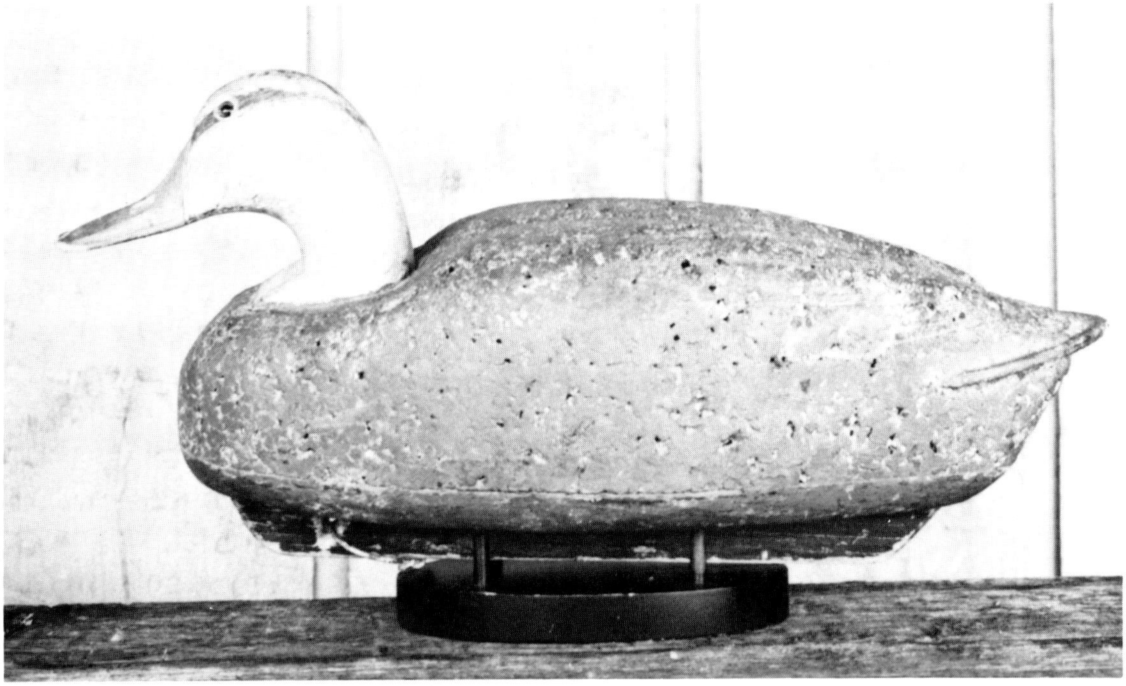

Black duck by Simeon McIntyre ca. 1950. Cork body, pine head and base.

Simeon McIntyre 1923- Crown Point, New York, is one of the true old time lake hunters. He and his brother, Donald, had a blind south of the Crown Point Bridge at Ticonderoga and used one hundred and twenty-five plus decoys in their rig. Many were Ken Harris whistlers, Wildfowlers, Herters and even two Ben Schmidt canvasbacks. However the majority were made by McIntyre. He constructed most from cork but also made wood (cedar) decoys. He states that he made almost one hundred canvasbacks, bluebills and blacks.

McIntyre, who was superintendent of area schools, is also noted for his grape vineyards and his wine, "Woodhedge". He and his wife, Margaret, grew the perfect Adirondack grape and were featured in *Adirondack Life* in 1976. Margaret died recently but Simeon still maintains his vineyard.

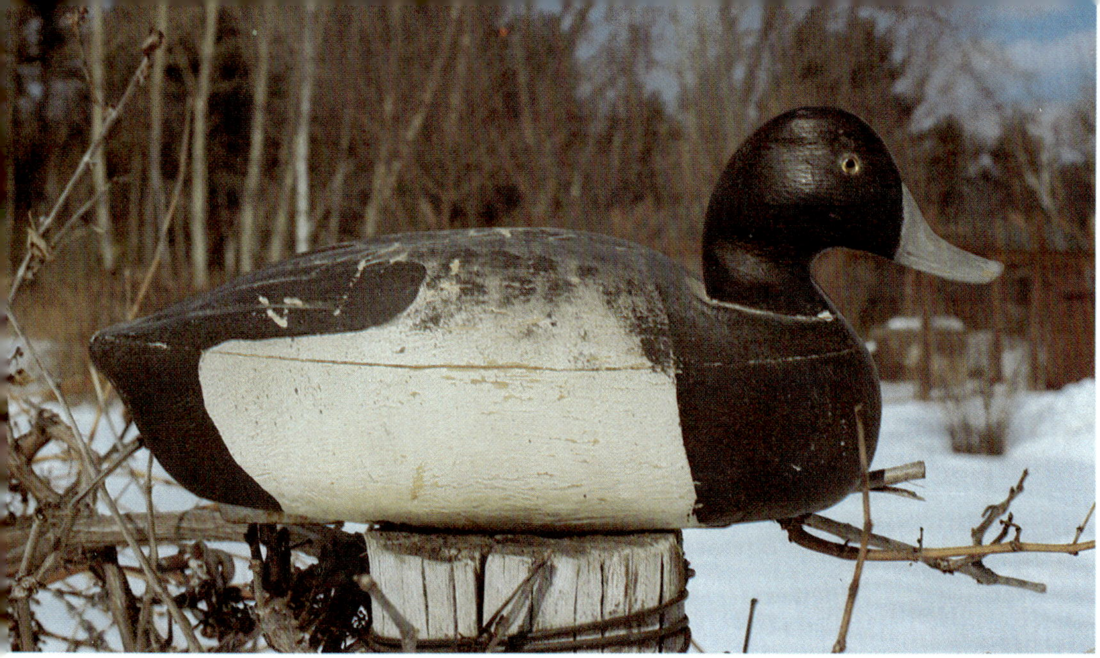

Bluebill drake by Simeon McIntyre ca. 1955. Hollow cedar construction, original paint. Collection of Simeon McIntyre.

Daniel McNally 1913- Swanton, Vermont, carved close to two hundred decoys between 1930-1975. His bluebills are cedar construction and "folky" to say the least. Earlier birds were made of cork. He retired from the Central Vermont Railroad and spends every fall hunting on Lake Champlain.

Black duck by Daniel McNally ca. 1933. Cork and pine construction.

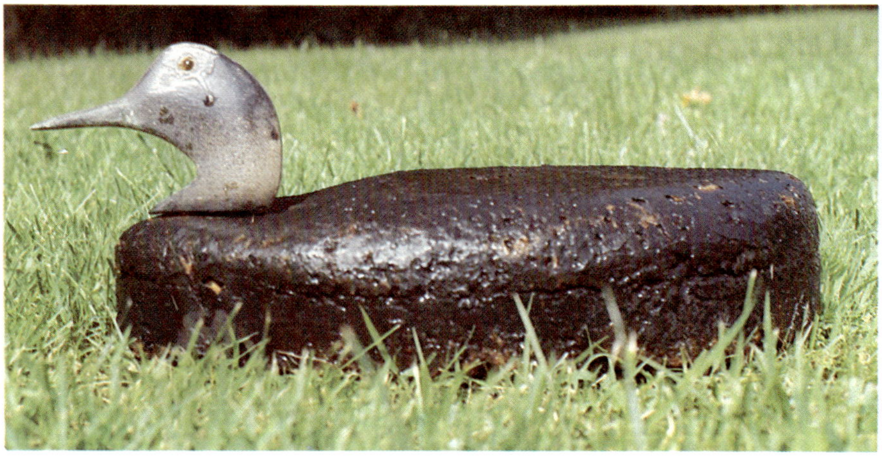

Bluebills by Daniel McNally. Solid cedar, tack eyes. Ca. 1970.

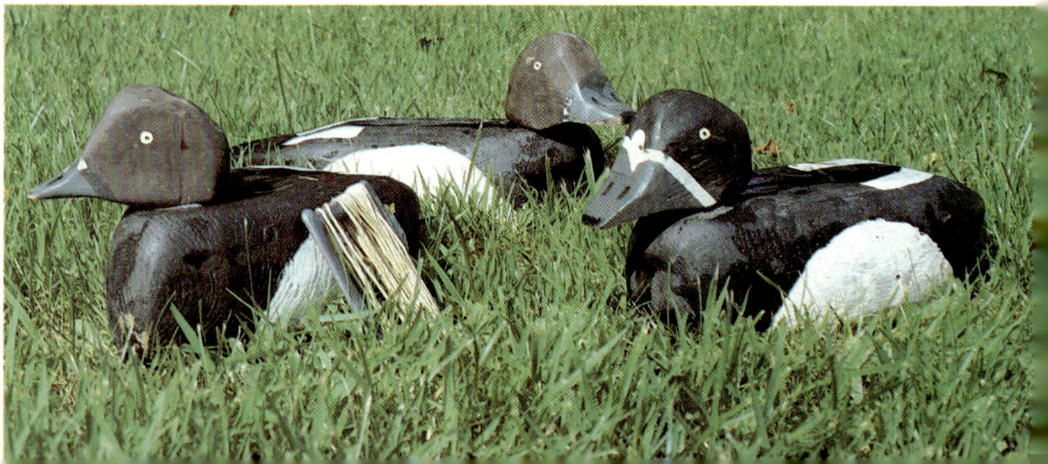

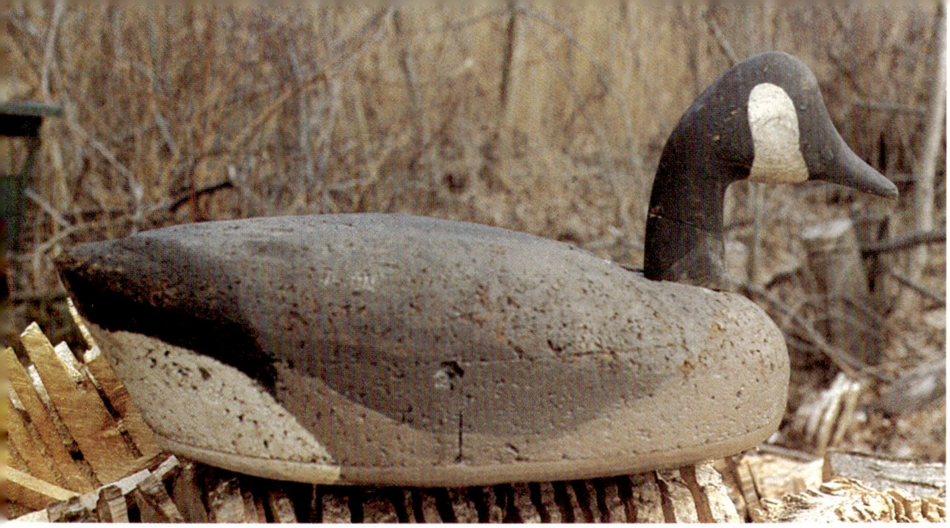

Canada goose by Irving Melendy ca. 1957. Cork and pine construction.

Irving "Lum" Melendy 1926- Burlington, Vermont. Carved seventy-five to one hundred working decoys. Most are of cork construction with wood bases and pine heads. He also carved several dozen cedar decoys. Melendy, who was born the year after George Bacon died, was always conscious of Bacon's tradition as a carver and hunted with many friends of Bacon. Melendy presently owns a chainsaw and engine repair store.

Goldeneyes by Irving Melendy, ca. 1958. Paddle tail style with "Bacon" heads.

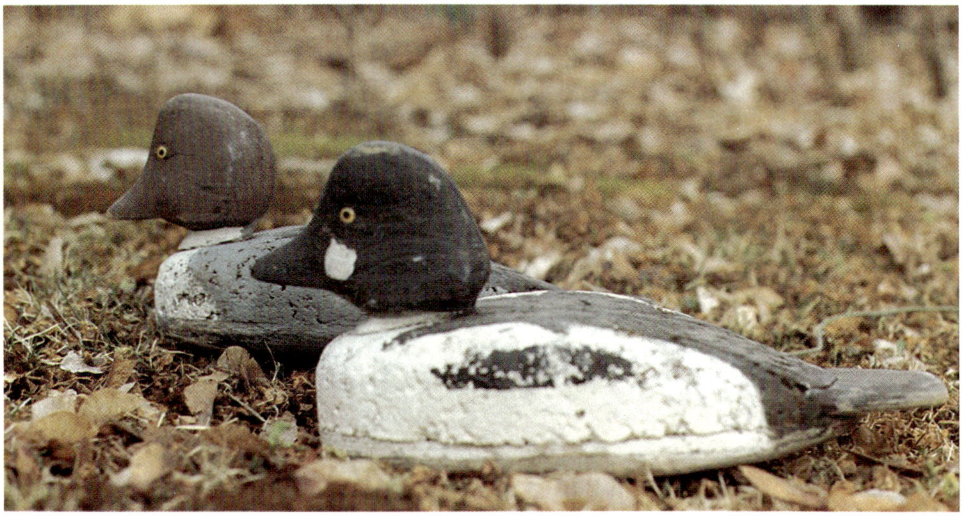

Black duck by Irving Melendy, ca. 1955. Cork body, pine head and base.

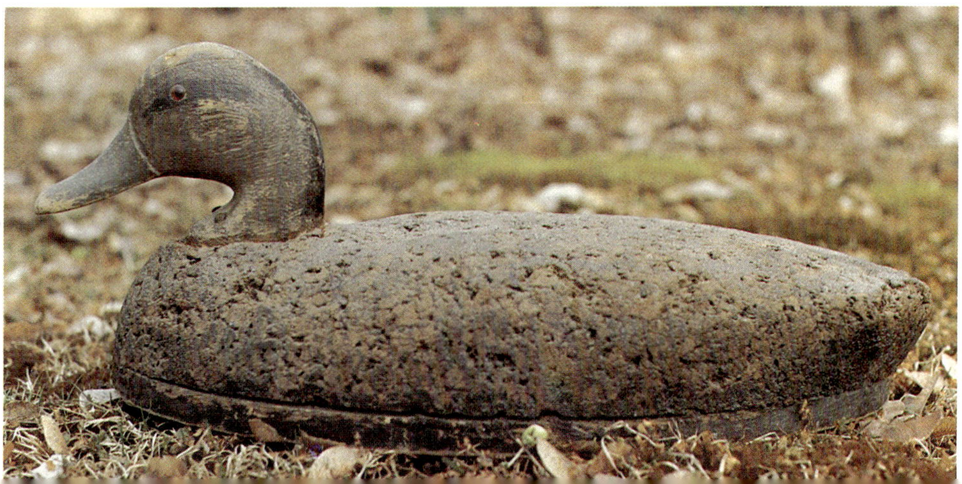

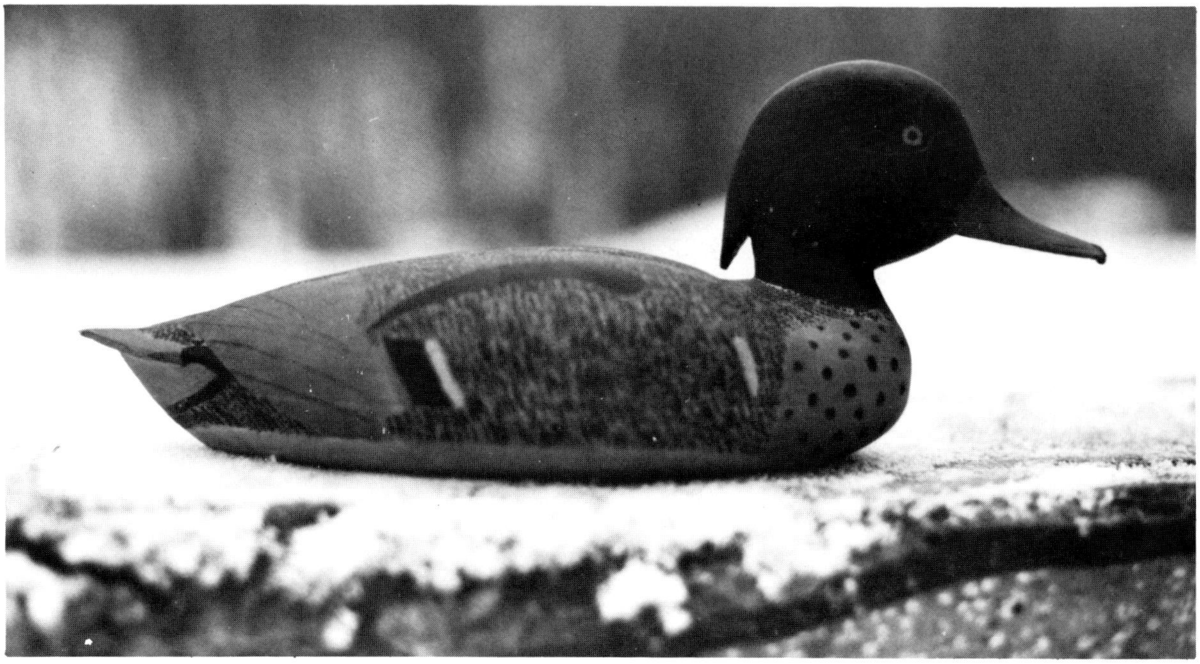

Green wing teal by Irving Melendy, solid cedar, original paint.

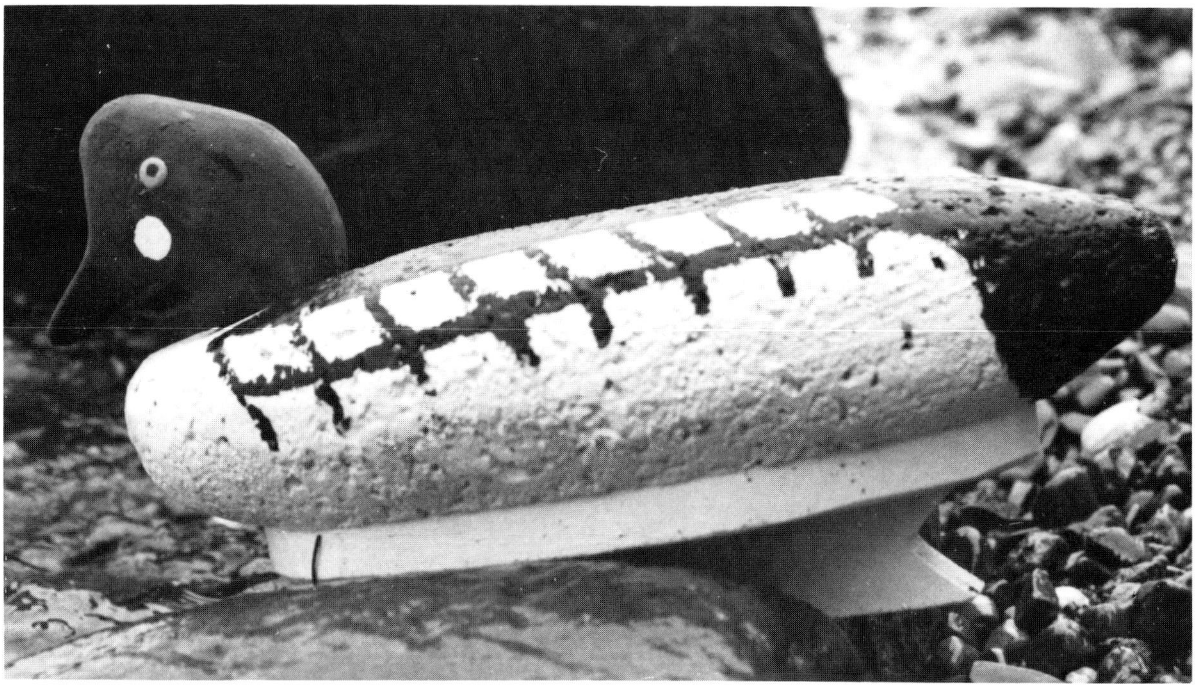

Goldeneye drake by **Stanley Mitchell** 1909- Isle La Motte, Vermont, carved over one hundred decoys to use on Alburg Bay.

Omer Moreau 1906- Burlington, Vermont. Decoys were all carved with a "shoemakers" knife after shaping with a hand axe. He carved five dozen goldeneyes in 1942, using cedar construction with tack eyes. Unfortunately, most were lost in a 1955 boat house fire. Moreau, a retired Burlington lawyer, hunted primarily at the "Sand Bar" and made black ducks on platforms "for the marshes".

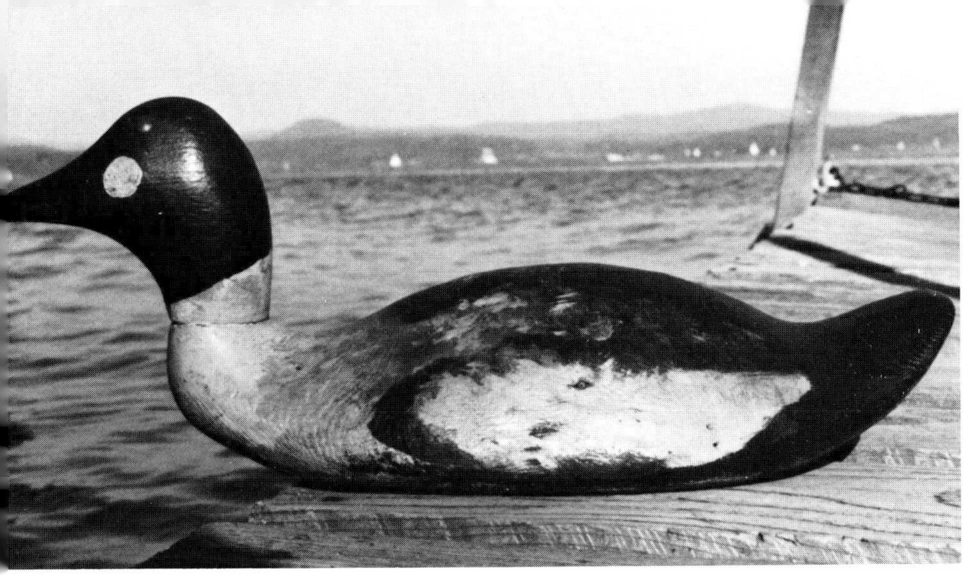

Whistler drake by Omer Moreau. Original paint, cedar with tack eyes. One of five dozen made. Photographed on Mallets Bay, Vermont.

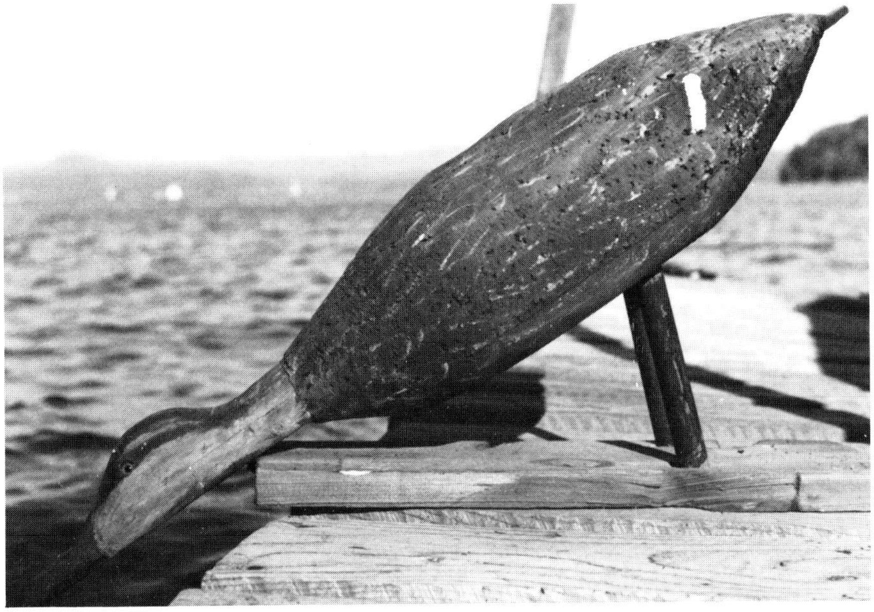

Black duck by Omer Moreau. Ca. 1945. Cork and pine construction. Used to "Marsh Hunt" near the Sand Bar Bridge.

Three platform black duck decoys by Omer Moreau, cork, pine construction ca. 1945.

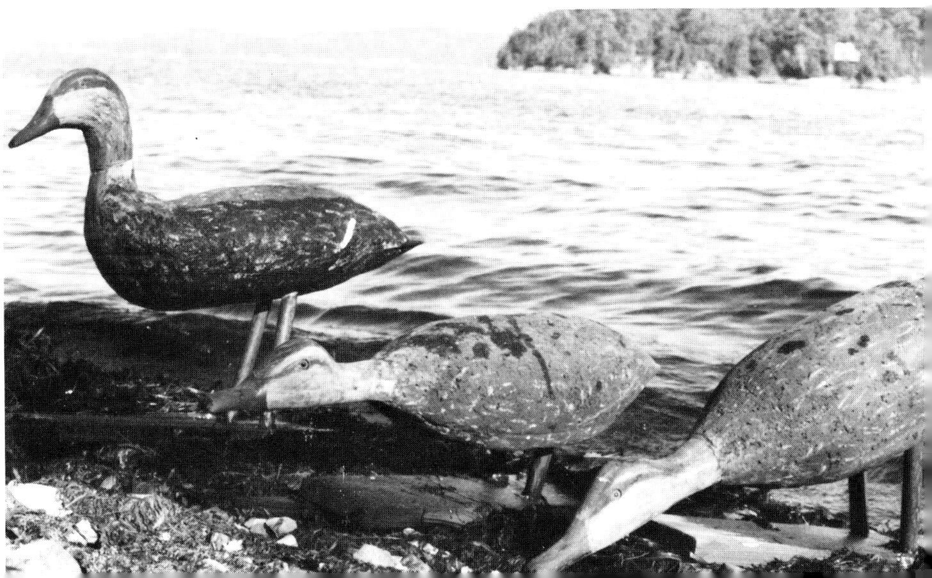

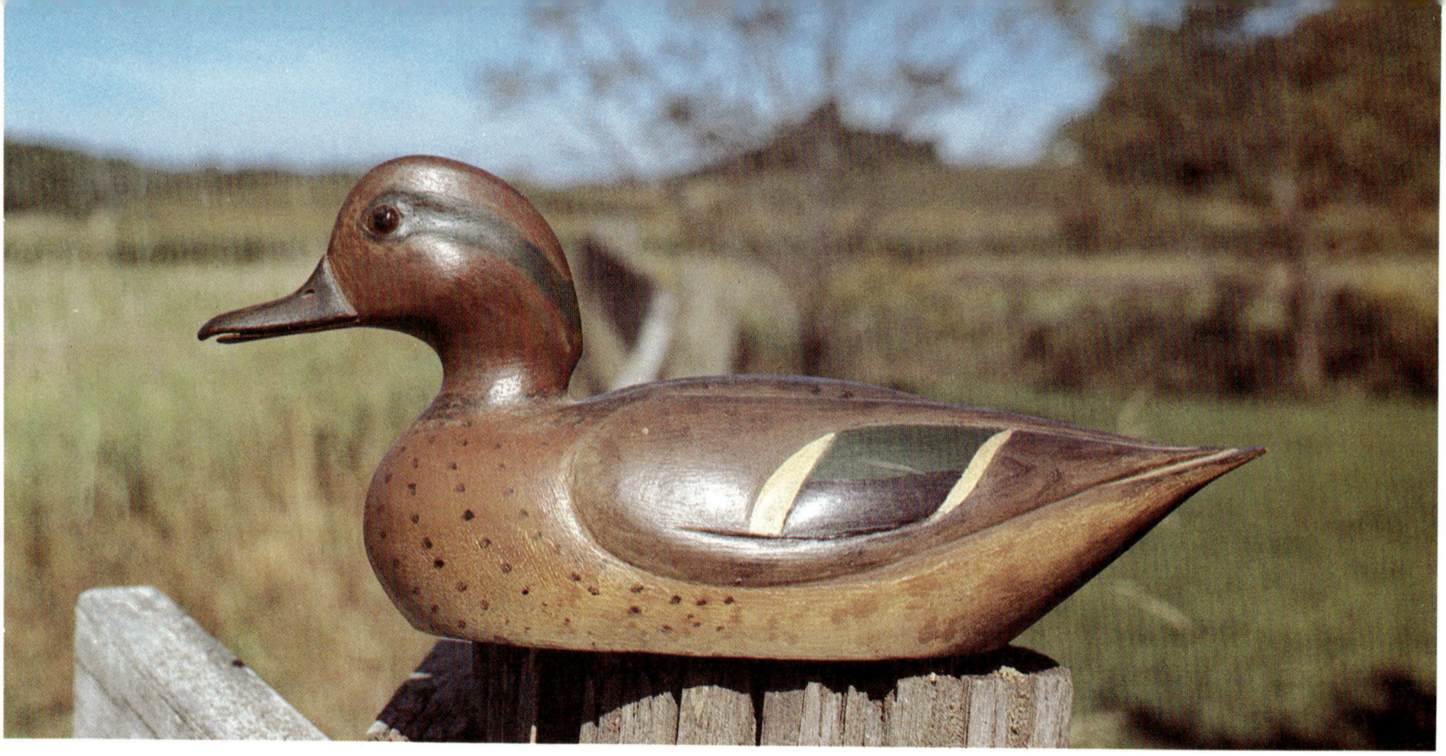

Green wing teal drake by Einars Menges ca. 1963.
Collection of Tom Holloway.

Einars J. Menges 1932-1974. Burlington, Vermont. Menges was born in Latvia and after World War II, he and his parents came to the United States as displaced persons. After a short stay in Orwell, Vermont they moved onto the grounds of the Shelburne Museum, Shelburne, Vermont. Menges was hired as staff photographer and his parents, repairing dolls, quilts and general maintenance. Menges was the photographer for over twenty years and took all the photographs for the museums' *Decoys at Shelburne Museum,* published by the Shelburne Museum, 1961. Besides carving decoys, Menges was a trained jeweler and furniture maker. His decoys are pine construction with raised wing carving.

Mallard drake by Einars Menges ca. 1960. Original paint.
Collection of Loy S. Harrell.

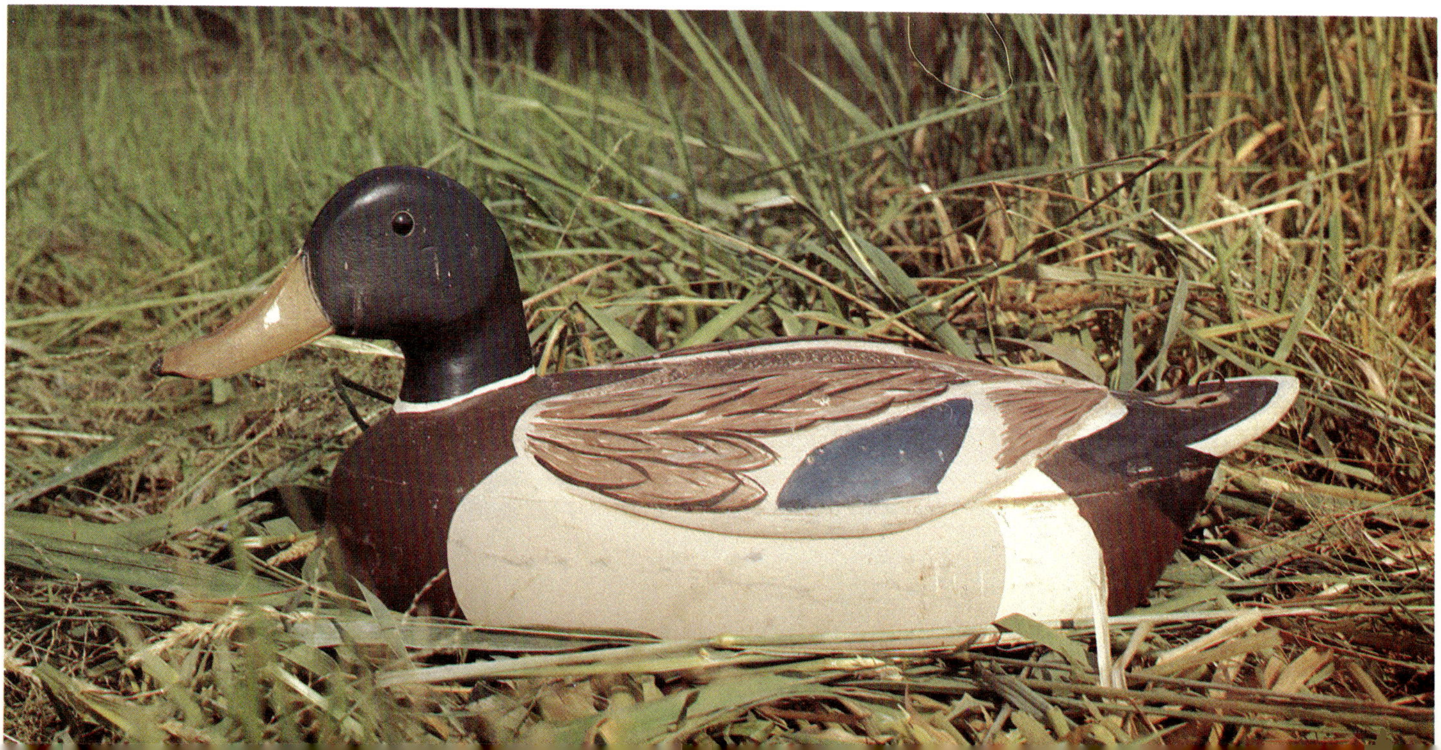

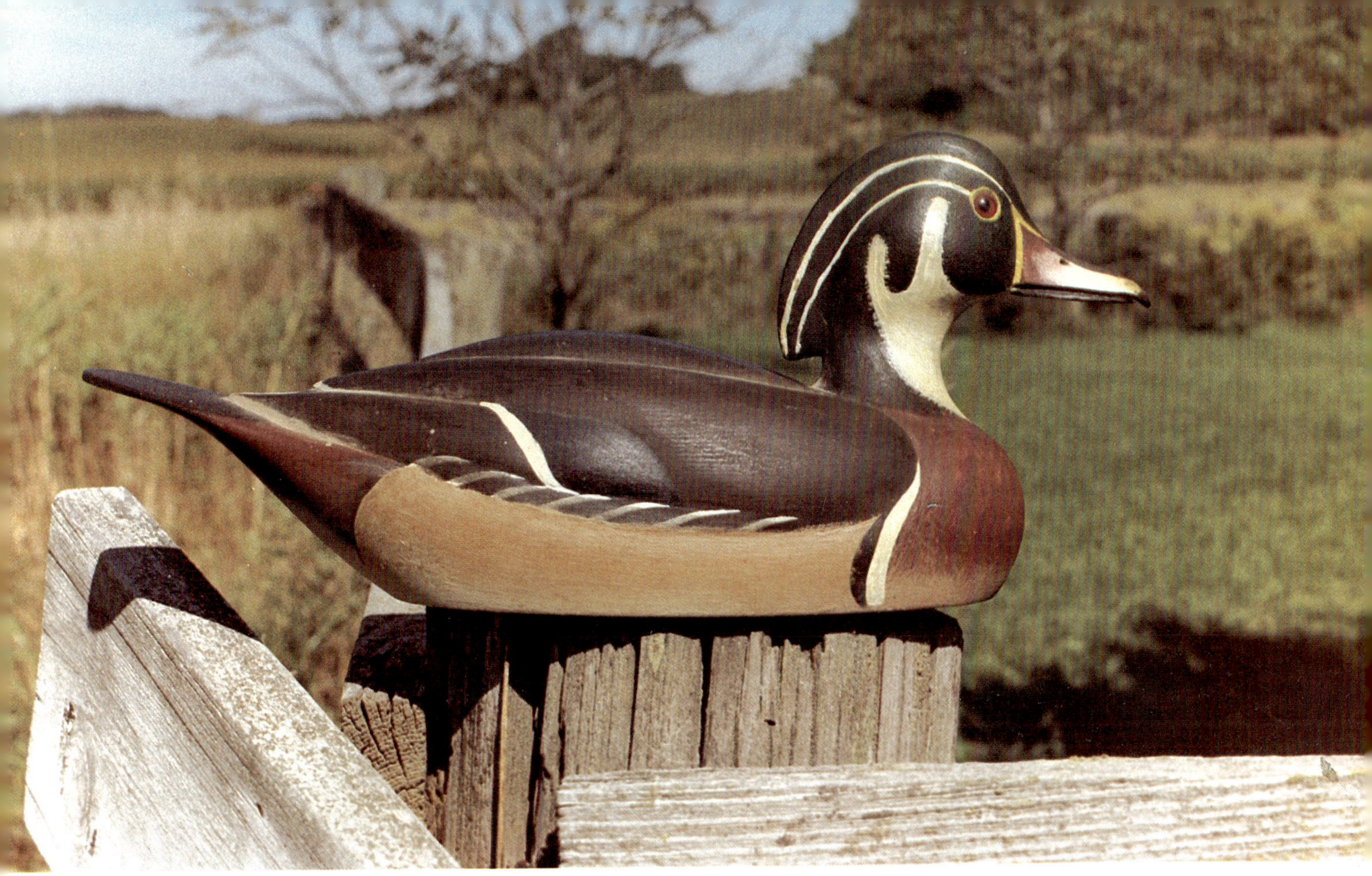

Woodduck drake by Einars J. Menges ca. 1960. Collection of Tom Holloway.

Fan-tailed bluebill by William Nautel. Ca. 1928. "Designed to carry in my back pack for a miles hike".

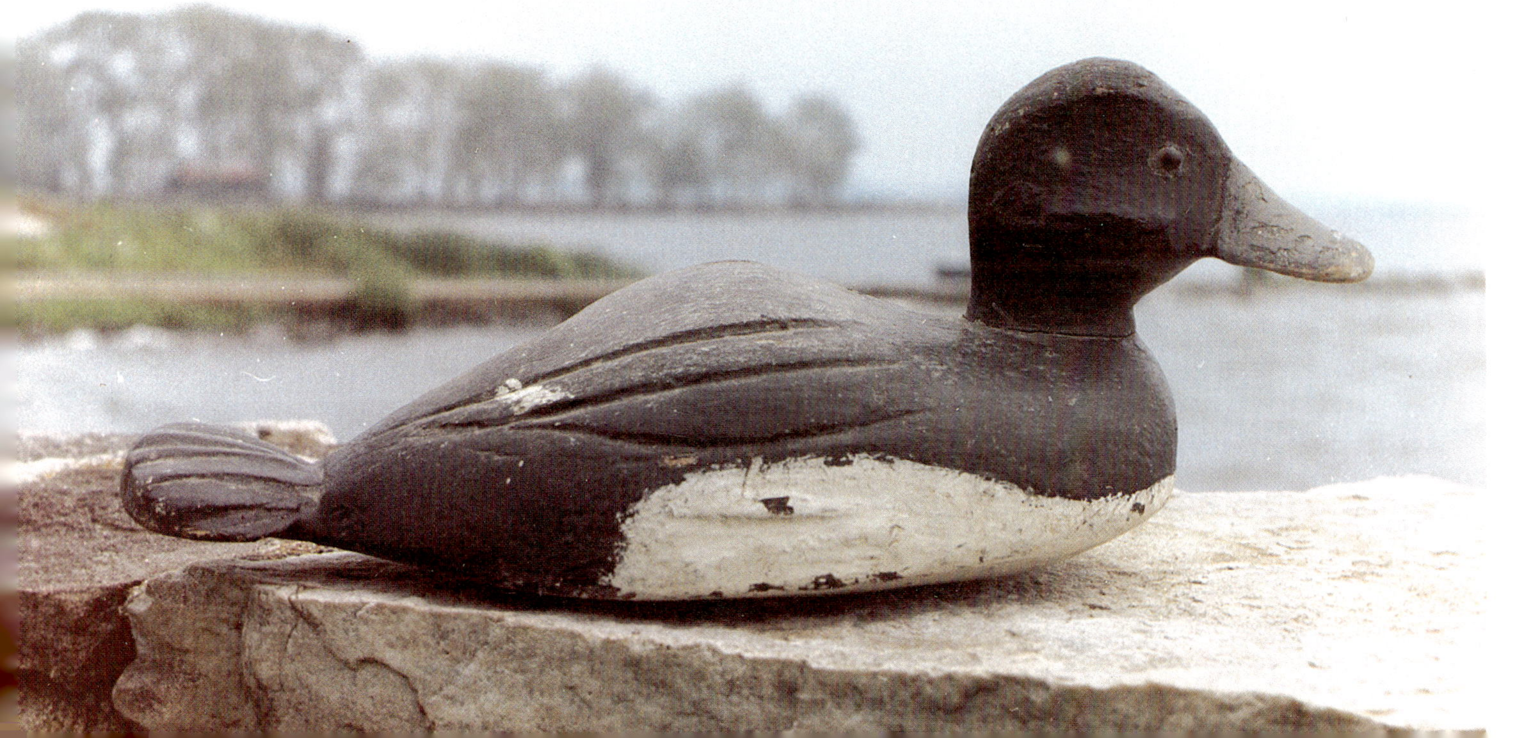

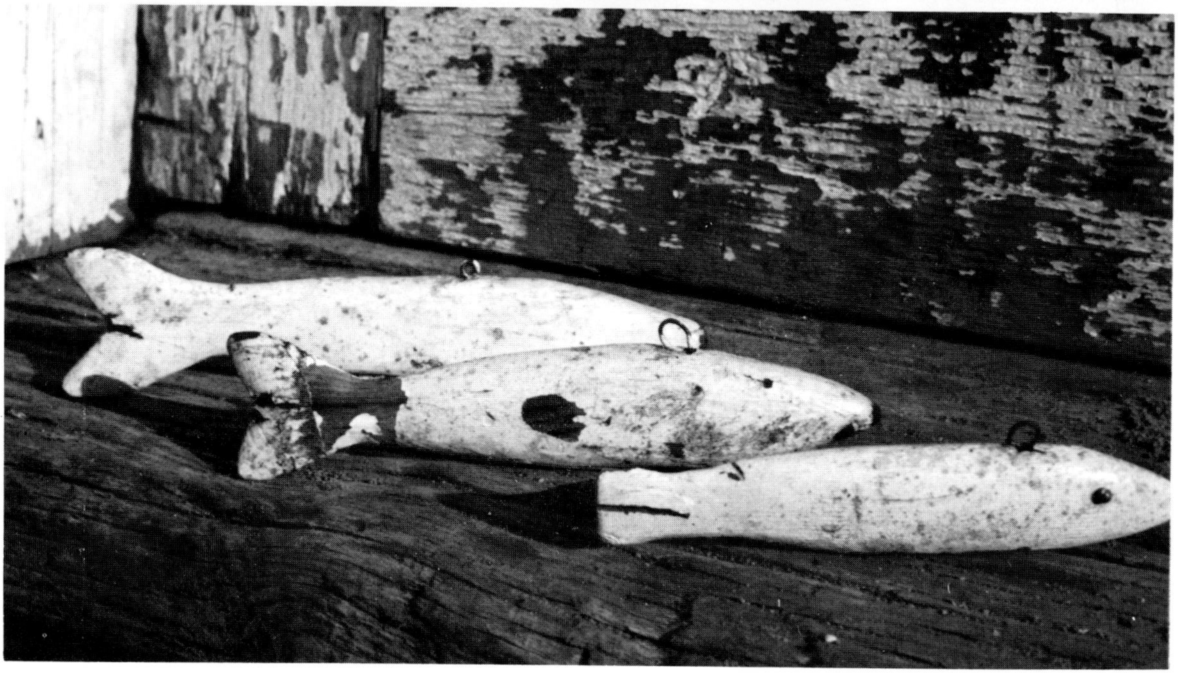

Fish decoys by William Nautel ca. 1930. Used for ice fishing on the St. Lawrence River and Lake Champlain. Collection of Peter Lafountain.

William Hilan Nautel 1901- Rouses Point, New York, is one of the foremost historians of wildfowl and decoys alive today. He was a close friend of Robert McGaw, Havre De Grace, Maryland, the first person to commercially use a lathe to make decoys in 1922. Nautel was also a friend of the late Joel Barber, who sought out Nautel when he lived at Waddington, New York on the St. Lawrence River. One of Nautel's decoys became part of Barber's famous collection.

Nautel carved over three hundred birds but unfortunately many were lost in a boat house fire in 1937. He moved to Lake Champlain in 1944 where he hunted on Alburg, Kings and Kelly Bays. Nautel still welcomes visitors to his home in Rouses Point to discuss "history".

William Nautel at the "Red Barn", 1952, with sixteen bluebills.

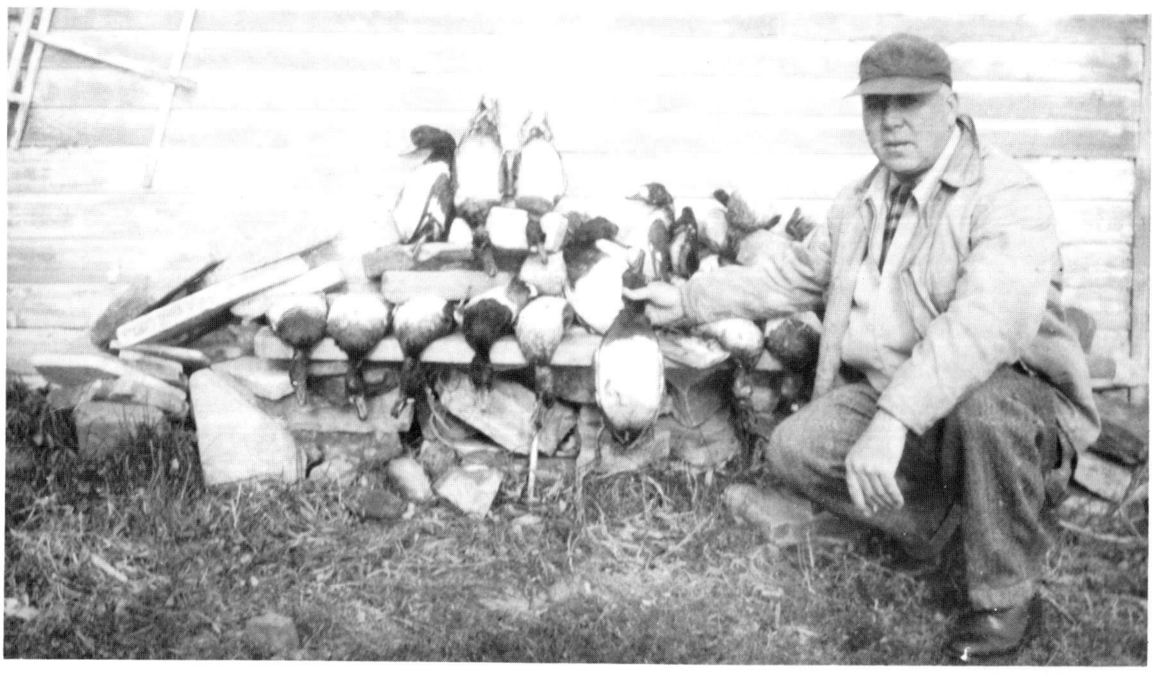

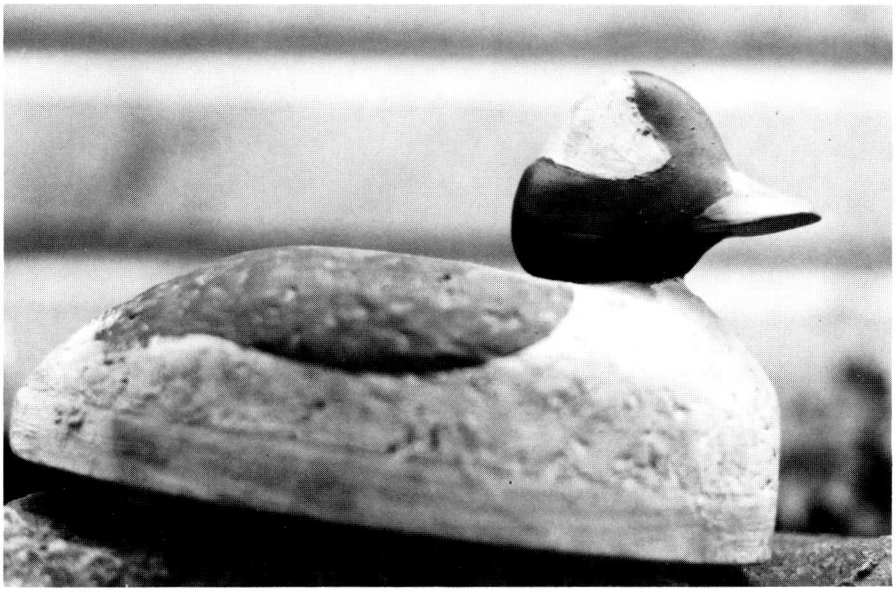

Bufflehead decoy by Charles Novotny ca. 1950. Cork with pine base. Original paint.

Charles P. Novotny 1936- Burlington, Vermont, was raised on Long Island Sound, New York, where he learned decoy carving from a "bayman" at the age of fourteen. His early birds were made of cork he got from WWII life preservers. Novotny's later decoys are constructed of basswood, have leaded keels and are numbered with Roman numerals and branded "N". He states he designed them after the style of Joel Barber. Novotny, a professor at the University of Vermont, has carved almost three hundred decoys which he uses at Jackson Point, South Hero, Vermont.

Black duck by Charles Novotny. Basswood construction.

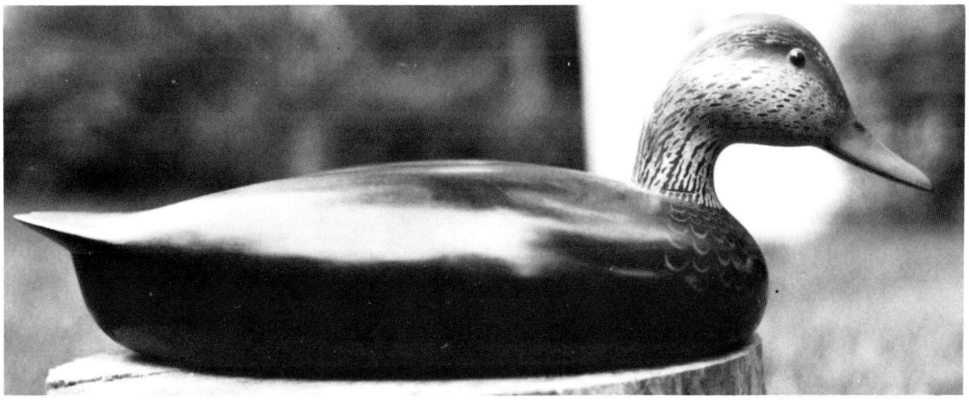

Goldeneye drake by Charles Novotny.

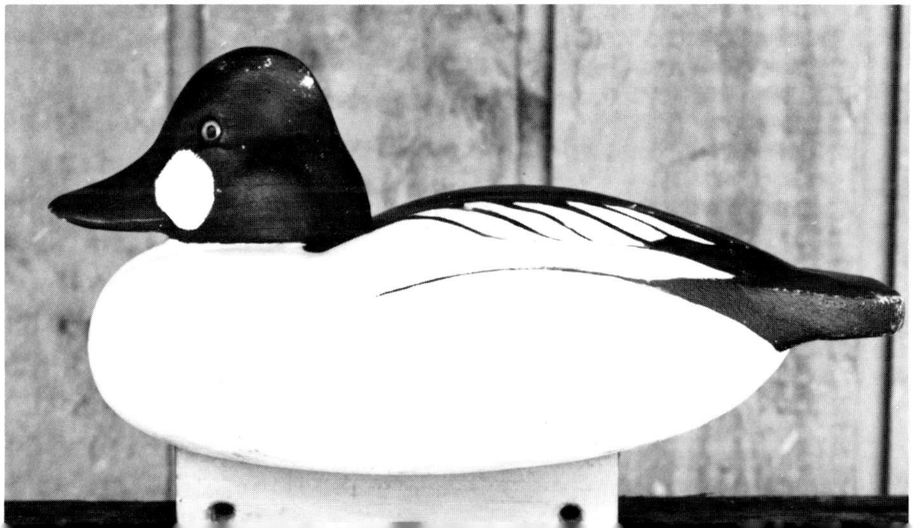

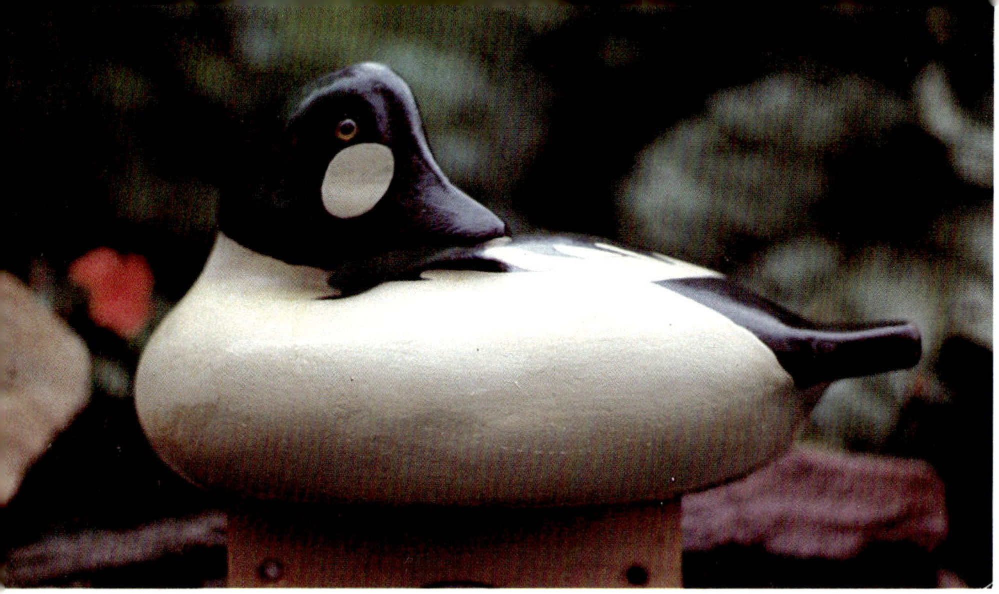

Preening goldeneye by Charles Novotny ca. 1975. Basswood with leaded keel. Branded "N".

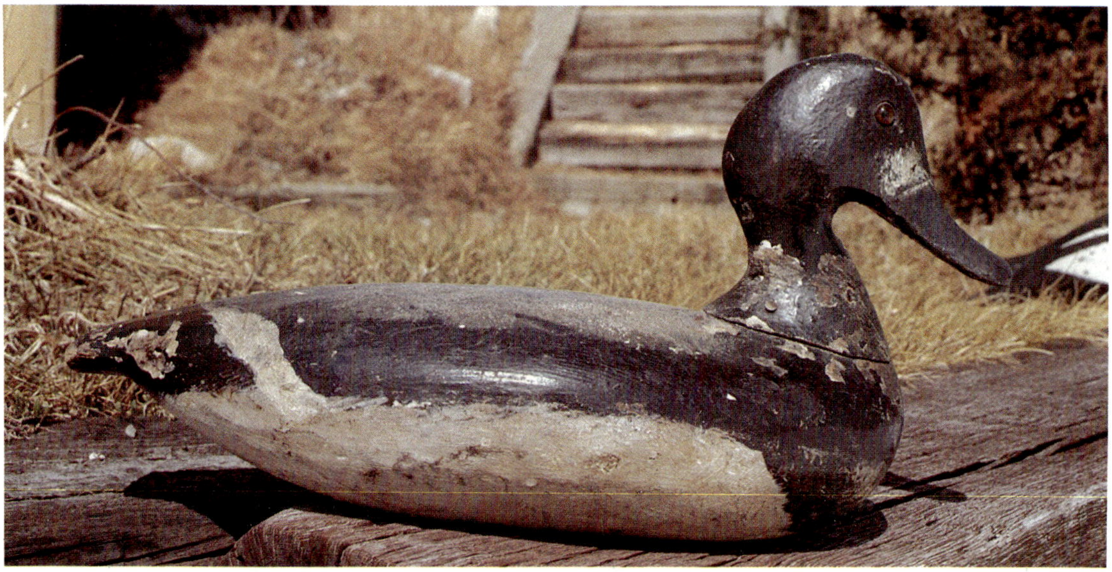

Bluebill hen by Frank Owen ca. 1840. Original paint. From the collection of Dr. P.K. French whose home was built by Abel Owen in 1806.

Frank Owen goldeneye hen ca. 1840. Original paint. From the Frank Gage rig. Collection of Loy S. Harrell.

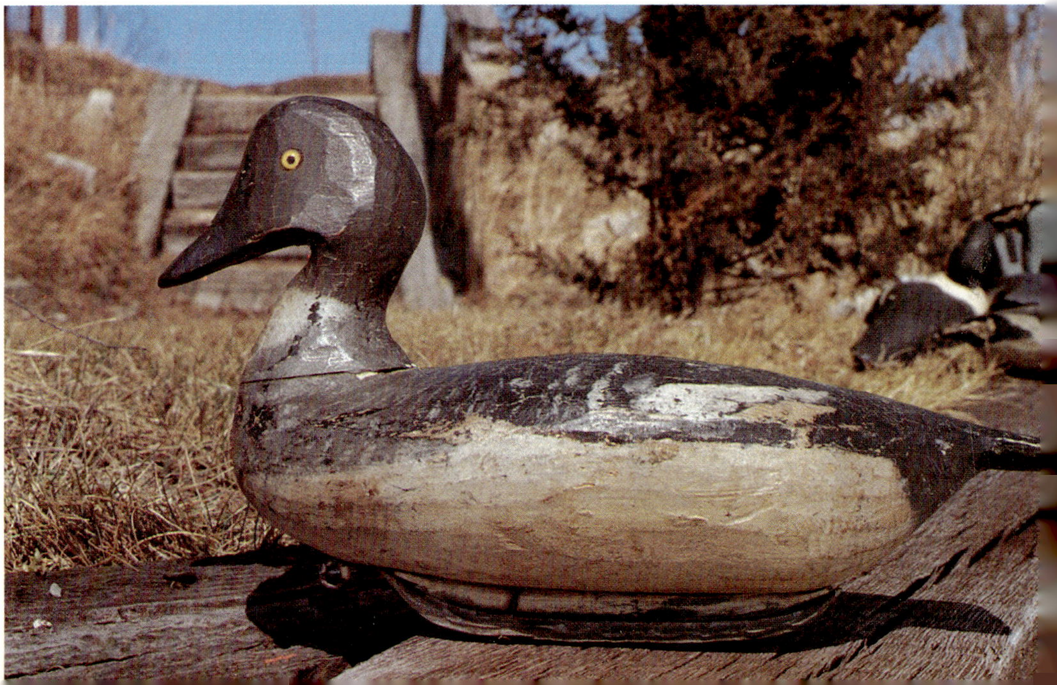

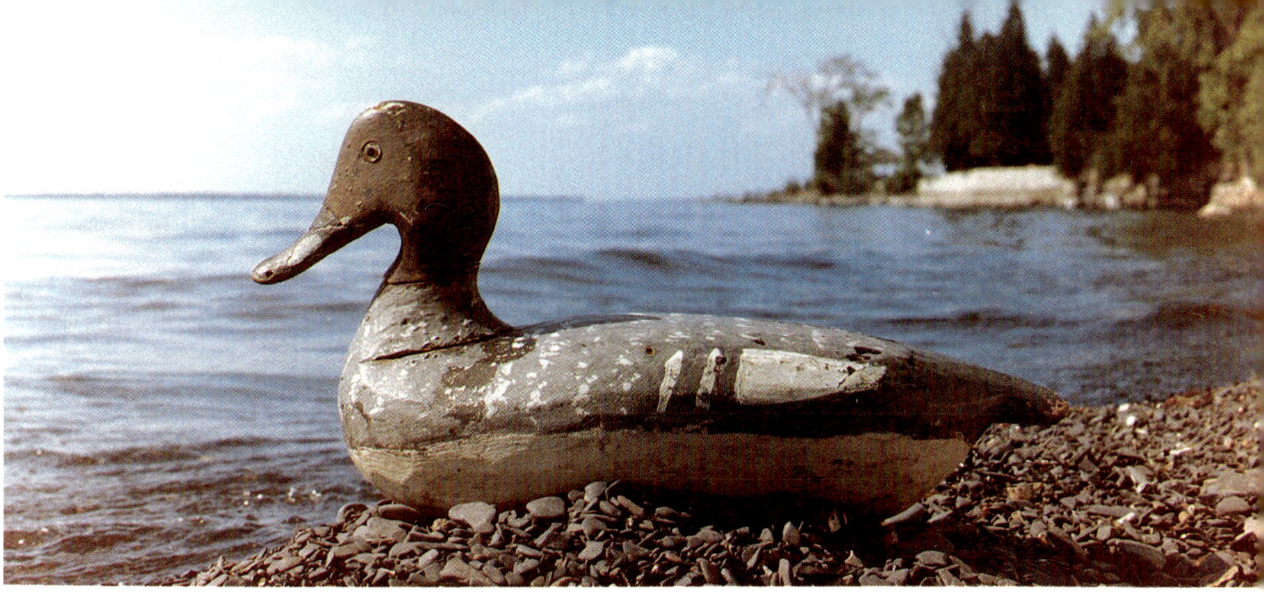

Goldeneye hen by Frank Owen ca. 1835. Old repaint. Branded C.E. IRVING. Collection of David Hoag.

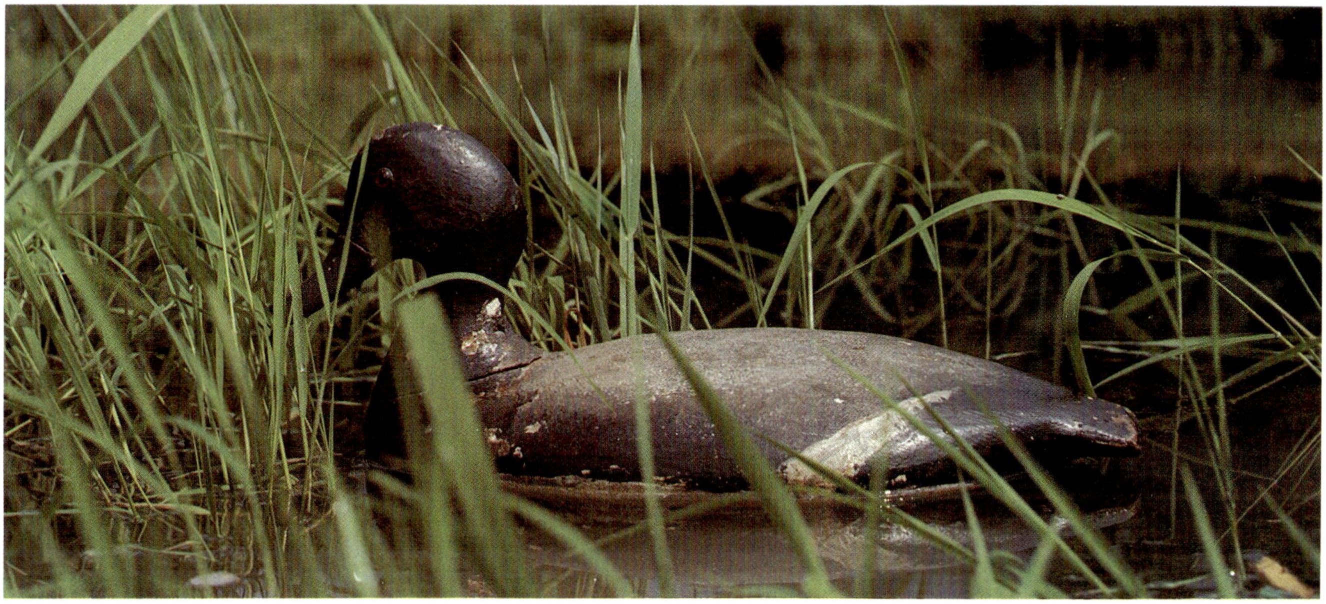

Frank Owen bluebill "In the Marsh" Hinesburg, Vermont.

A great twosome. Left, George Bacon goldeneye and right, Frank Owen goldeneye. Collection of David Hoag.

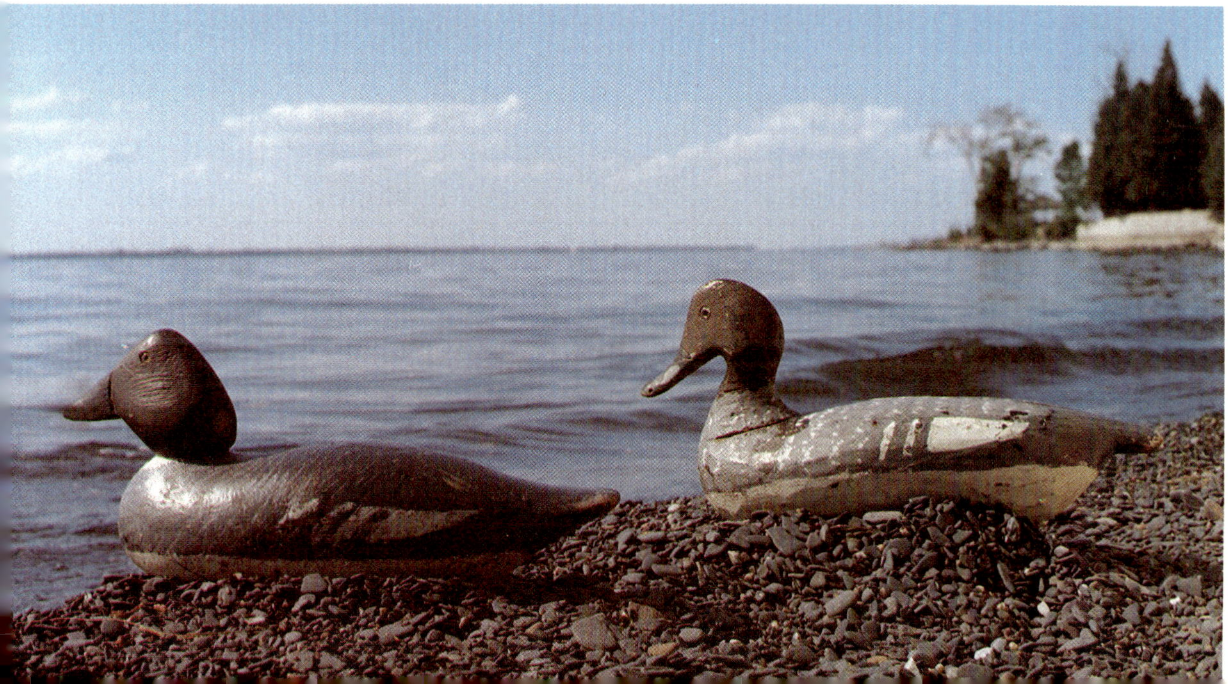

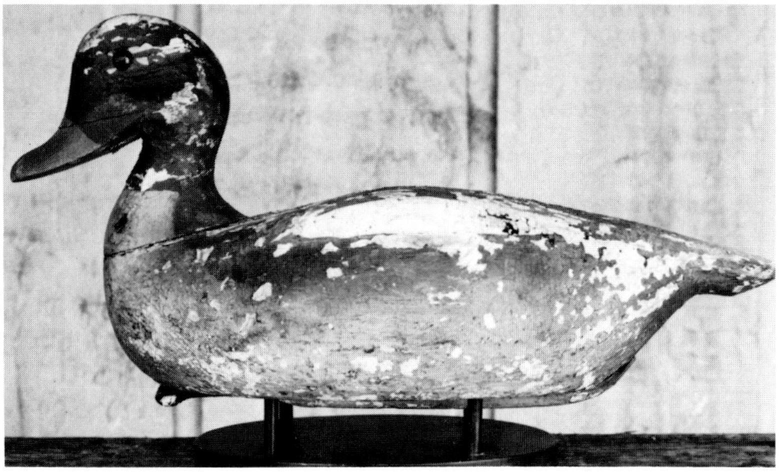

Bluebill by Frank Owen ca. 1835. Old repaint. Branded "C.E. IRVING" from the F. Gage rig.

Frank Owen, South Burlington, Vermont, is thought to have been a stonemason living in Vermont during the mid-19th century. He was a descendant of Abel Owen 1772-1850, who originally settled in Milton, Vermont. It was Abel's great grandson who sold the stone house built by Abel to Dr. Paul French, South Burlington, and in which the Owen bluebill hen was found. Only five of Owen's decoys are known to still exist. One, a redhead was in the collection of Joel Barber and is now in the Dorset House, Shelburne Museum. (It is pictured on page 46 of *Decoys at Shelburne Museum,* 1961). A "Stone House" at the Shelburne Museum is attributed to Owen but many historians date the house to 1800 and claim it was built by Asa R. Slocum, an early settler of Shelburne, Vermont. (Based on information from Betty Bandel and Fred Leduc). Owen decoys are no doubt the oldest documented carvings known.

Goldeneye drake, attributed to **Jack Phillips,** St. Albans, Vermont. A rig of these whistlers were bought in 1935 from Phillips by Jack Biggie of St. Albans. They have original paint and a strong resemblance to George Bacons work. Photograph taken at the author's "duck pond" in Vermont.

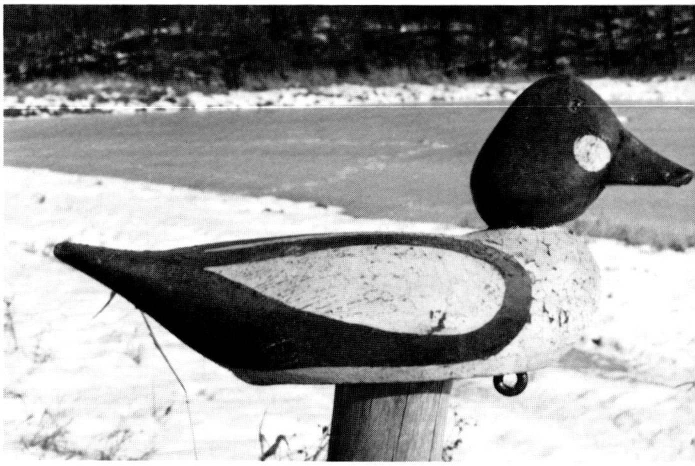

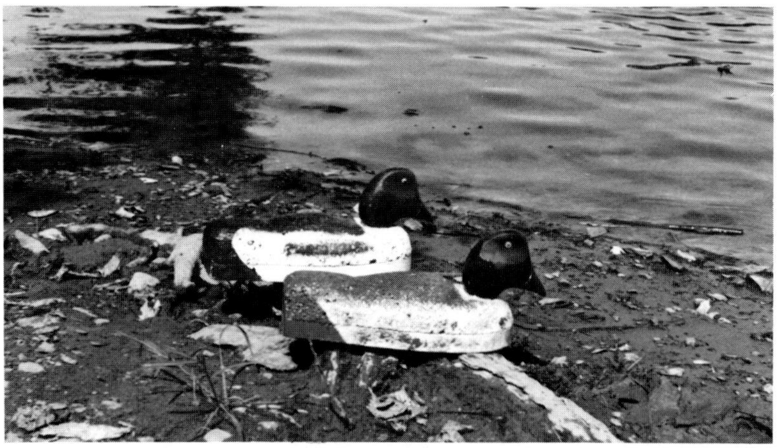

Pair of goldeneyes by Leo J. Papineau, Swanton, Vermont. Ca. 1940- cork and wood construction. Photographed on shore of Missisquoi River. Collection of Warren Fournier.

Whistler drake by Ford Patno. Original paint. Ca. 1980.

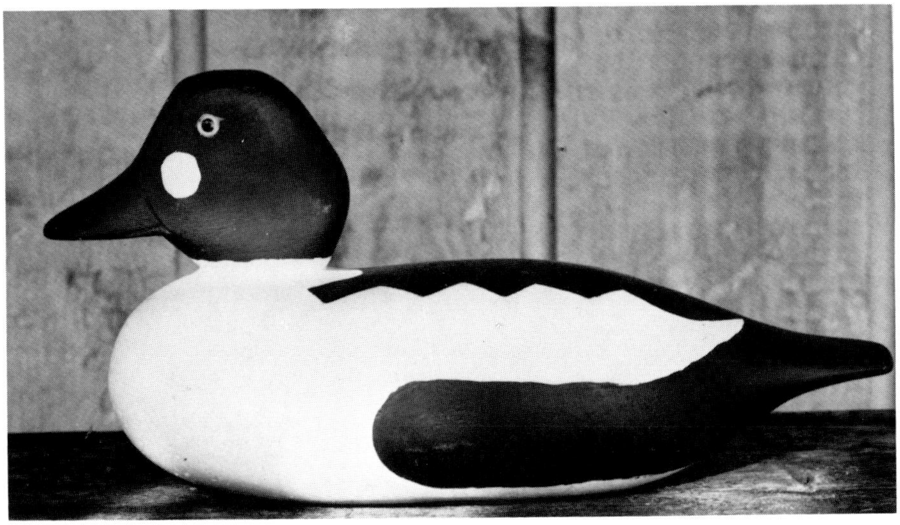

Ford Patno 1905- Burlington, Vermont, is truly one of the area "old timers". He began carving decoys in 1930 and hunted in the islands, Shelburne Bay and later at the Sand Dunes, Colchester, Vermont. Patno claims he used a Winchester pump that held ten shells and getting "fifteen birds a day was no problem". Patno made eighty to one hundred whistlers and bluebills. He never made made mallards or blacks claiming that they would decoy into the whistlers. He now spends his retirement carving working decoys and miniatures.

Bluebill drake by Ford Patno ca. 1965. Cyprus body, pine head marked "Sand Dunes".

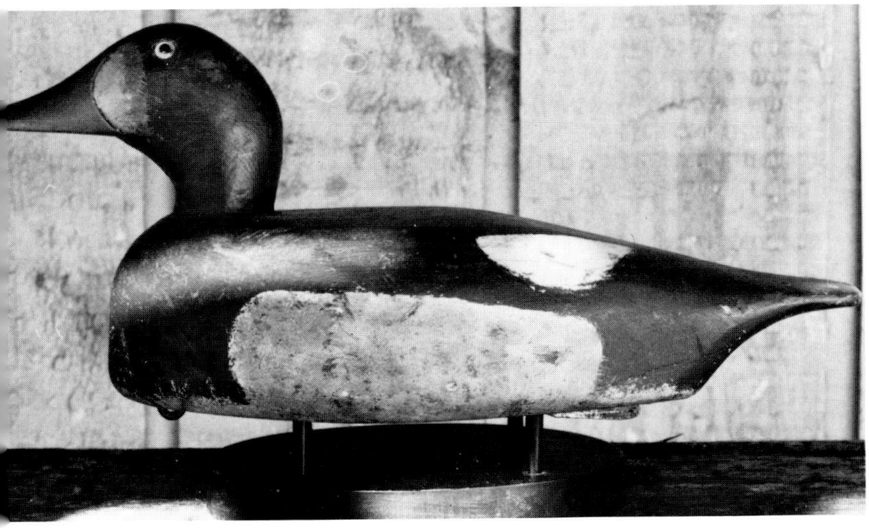

Goldeneye hen by Ford Patno. Original paint, cedar construction, ca. 1940.

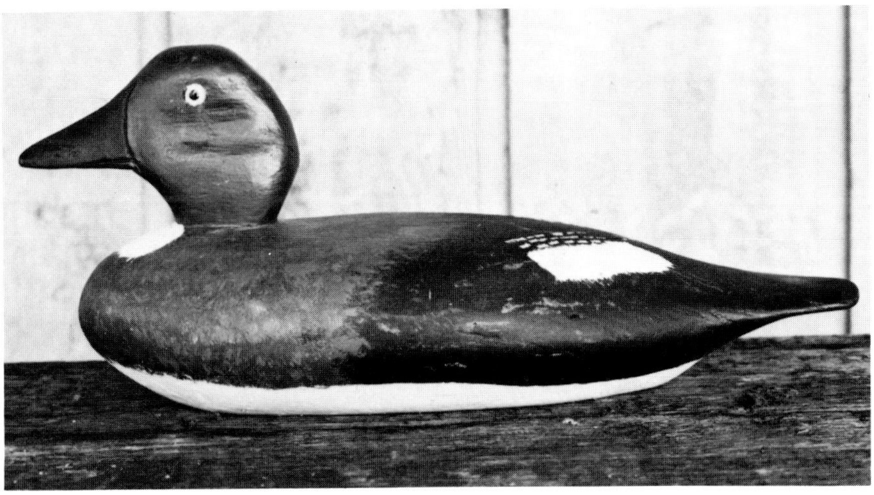

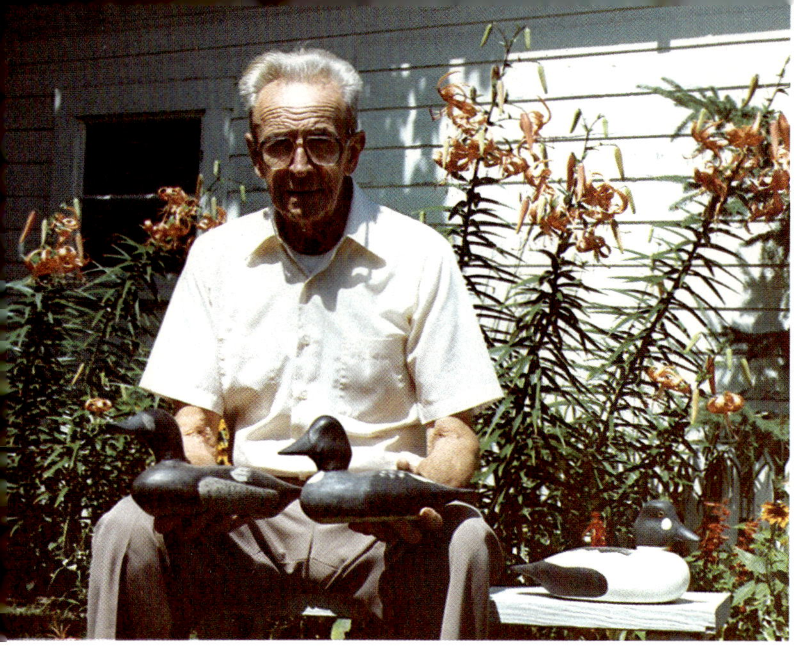

Photograph of Ford Patno taken at his home in Burlington, Vermont, 1984. Surrounded by his flock.

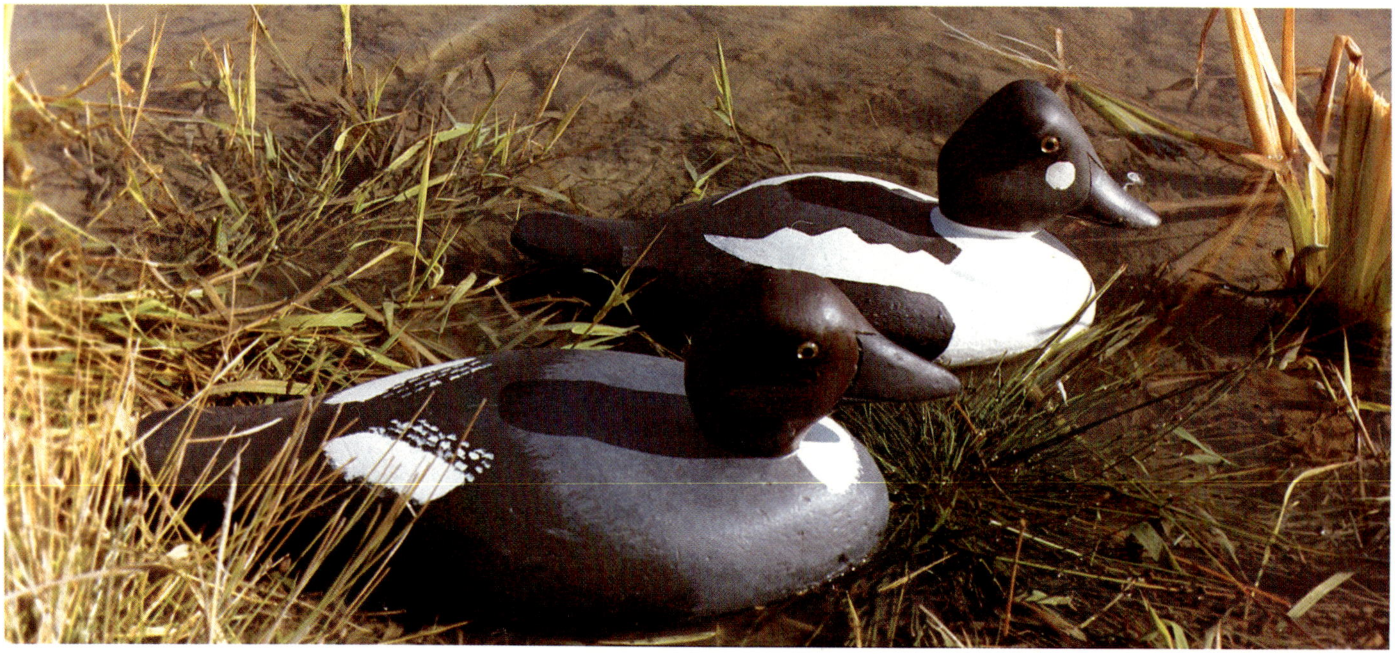

Pair of Patno Goldeneyes, "stopping over".

Bluebill hen by Ford Patno ca. 1965. Signed by Patno. Collection of Loy S. Harrell.

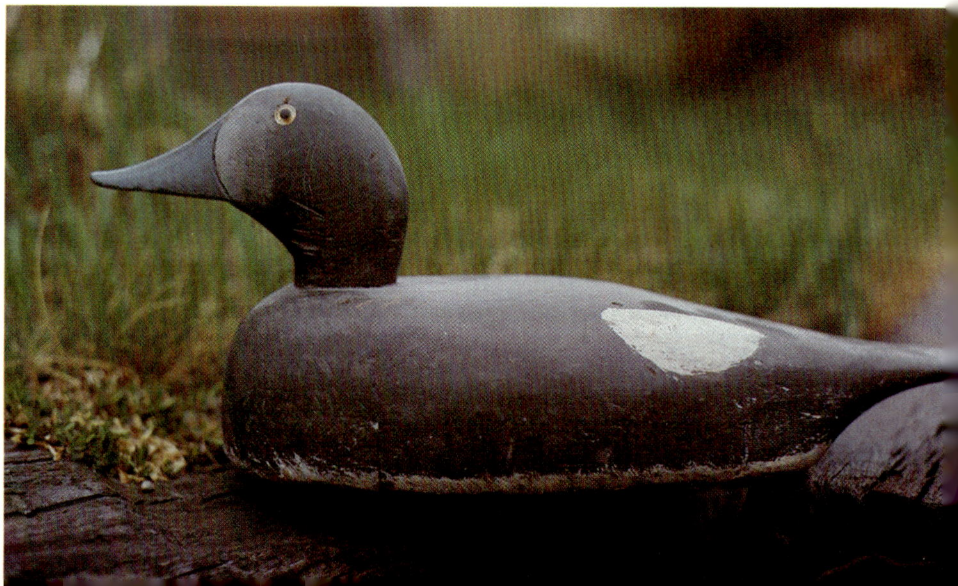

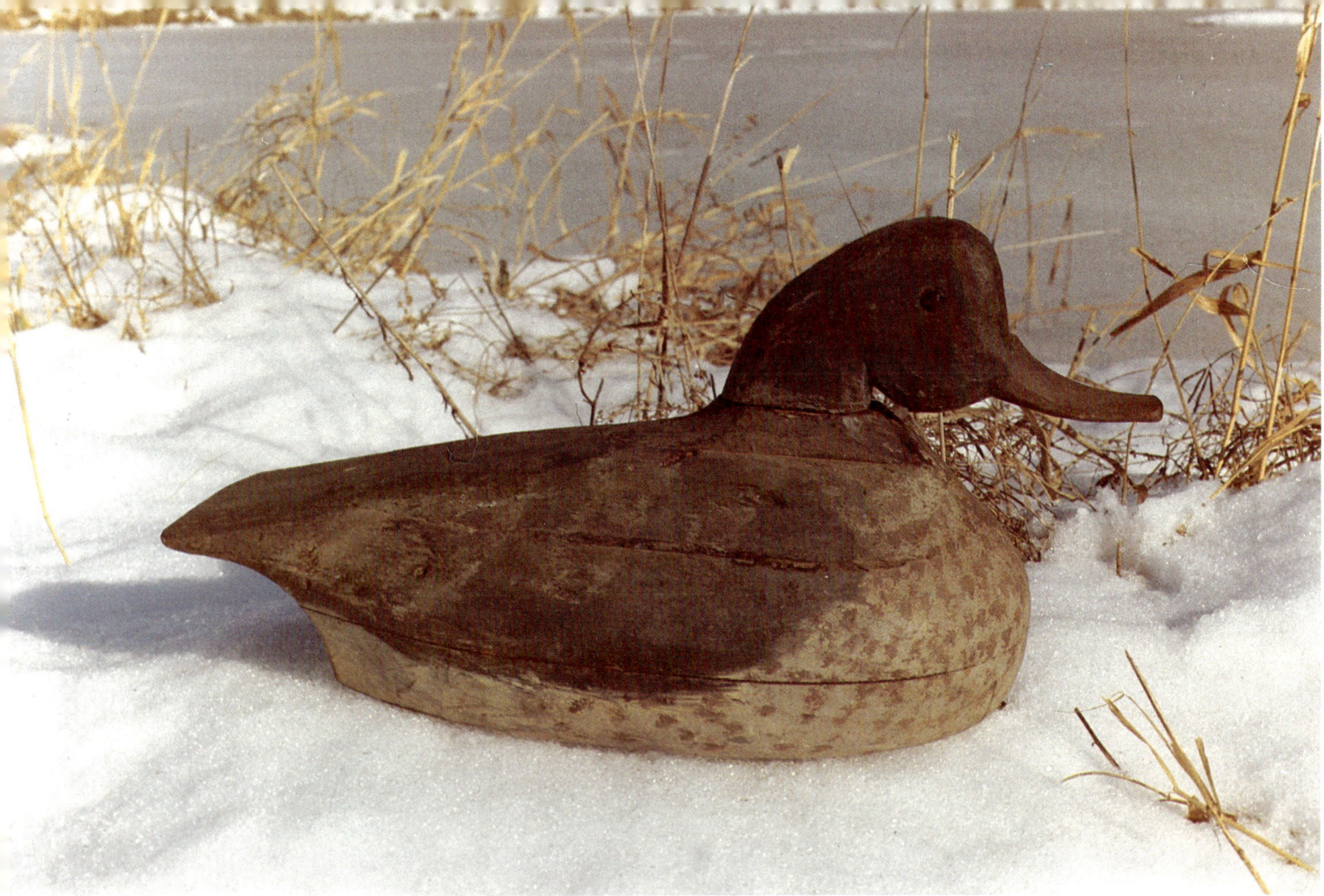

Mallard drake from the rig of Peveril Peake, Bristol, Vermont. Carved by his grandfather Royal Whitman Peake (1808-1893). Hunted over at Fort Casson Rod and Gun Club, Ferrisburg, Vermont. Ca. 1865. Original paint.

Canada goose floater by Thornton Penrose ca. 1940. Cork with pine head and base. One of two dozen made. Collection of James Dickerson.

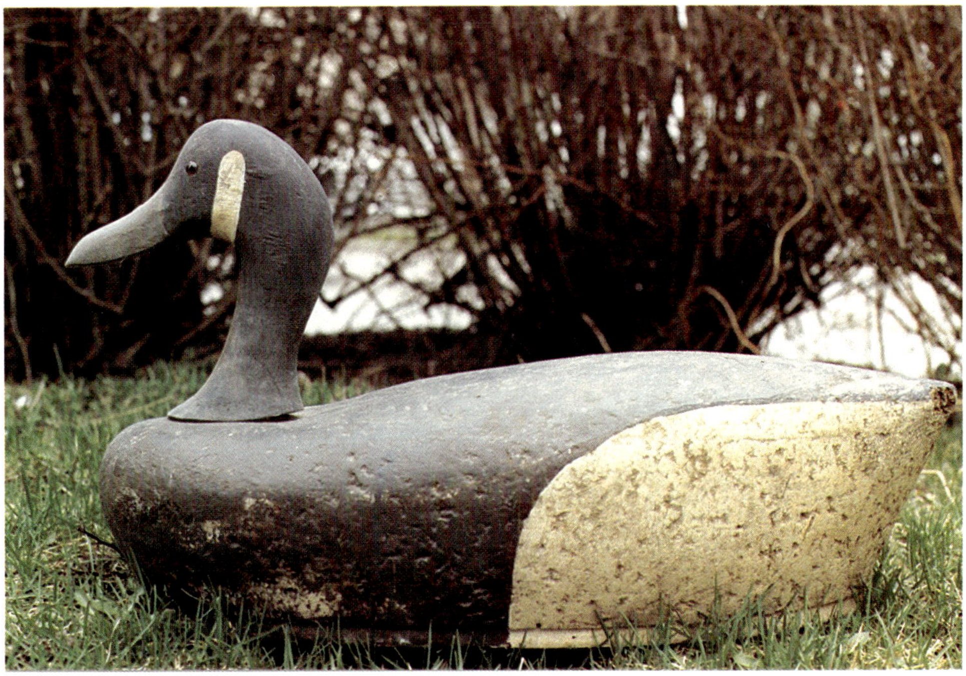

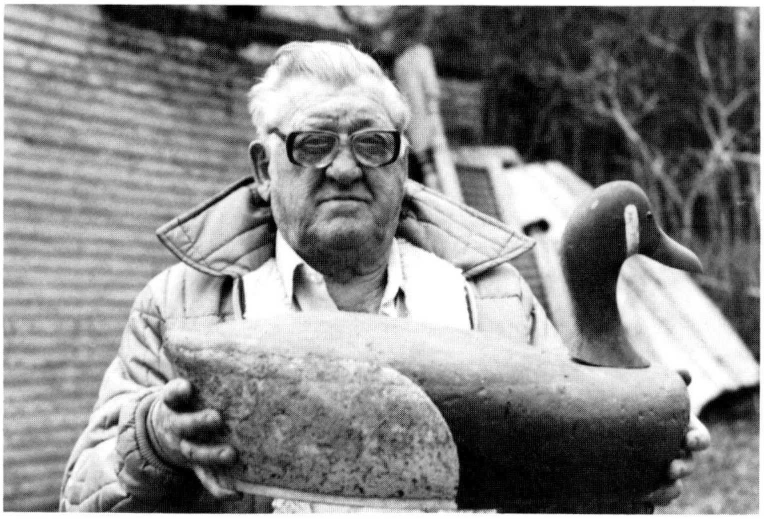

Photograph of Thornton Penrose, Sr., taken at his home in Burlington, Vermont, 1984.

Thornton Penrose, Jr. 1913- Burlington, Vermont, started carving decoys in 1930 as a teenager. His first birds were of wood and cork and later ones of pine and cedar. He was a prolific maker and is known to have carved almost four hundred birds. Most were whistlers and bluebills although he carved several dozen blacks and geese. Penrose's decoys show precise workmanship and diversity. To combat ice buildup, he designed his bluebills after decoys used on the Hoosetonic River, Connecticut. His whistlers have the "Bacon" look and have a round inleaded weight. Many Penrose decoys can still be found.

Black duck decoy by Thornton Penrose, Jr. Ca. 1935. Cork and pine construction.

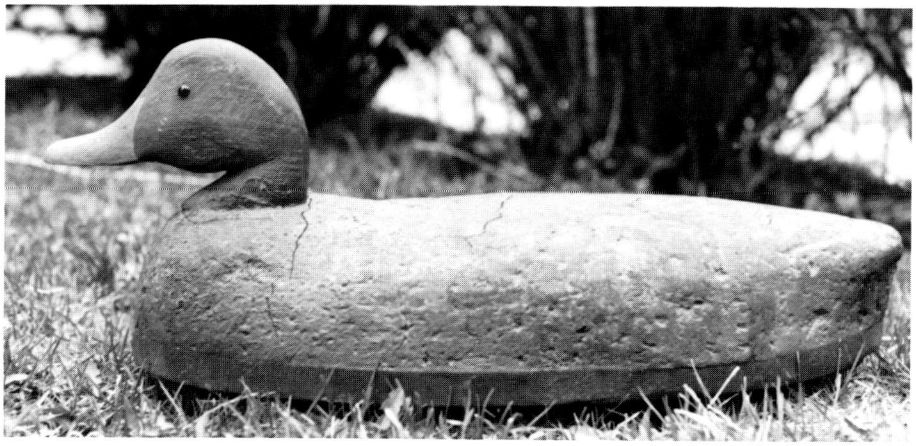

Bluebill drake by Thornton Penrose, Jr. Ca. 1945.

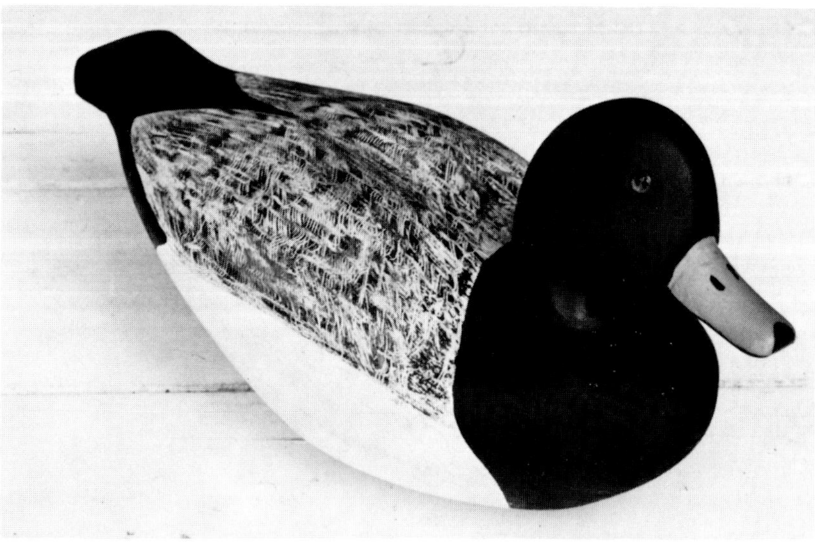

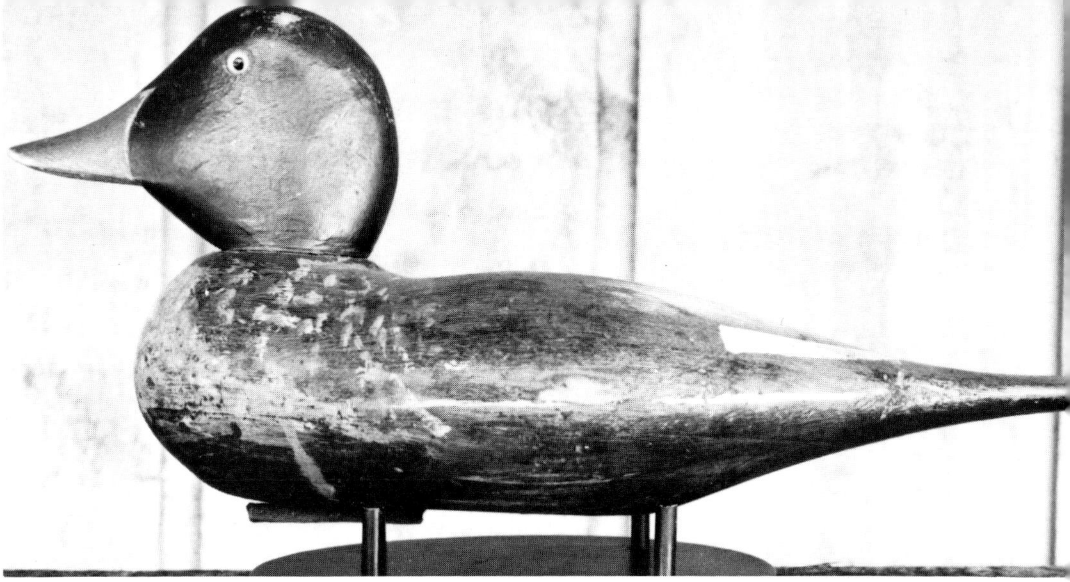

Whistler hen by Thornton Penrose, Jr. Ca. 1940. Original paint with "Penrose tail". Collection of Loy S. Harrell.

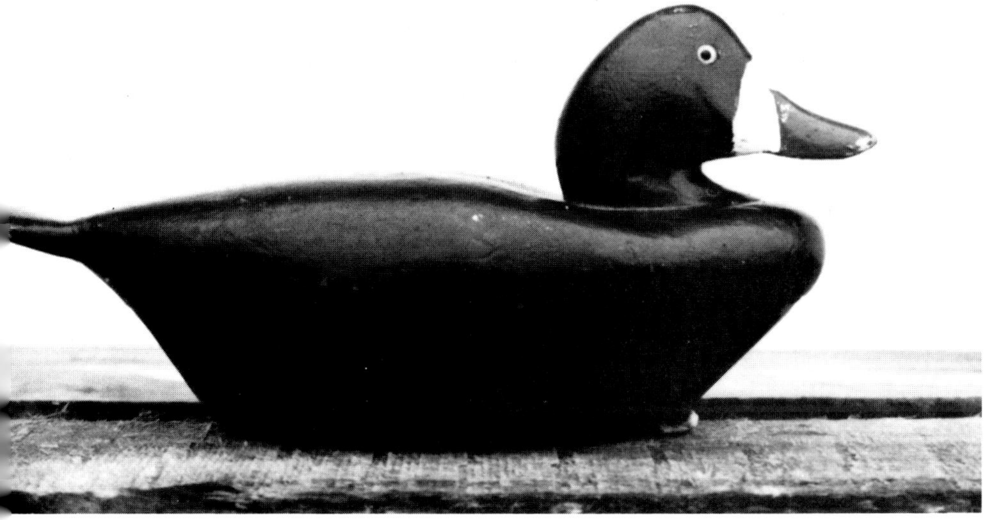

Bluebill hen by Thornton Penrose, Jr. Ca. 1945. Laminated cedar. Note "Connecticut look", constructed to prevent ice buildup.

Whistler hen by Thornton Penrose, Jr. Ca. 1935. His early carving. Collection of Holly Harrell.

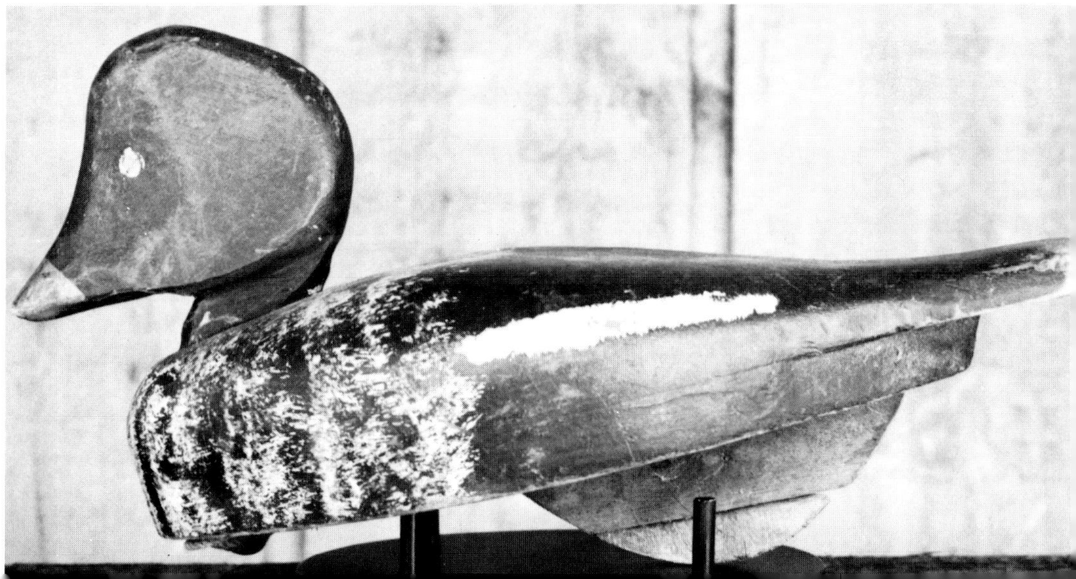

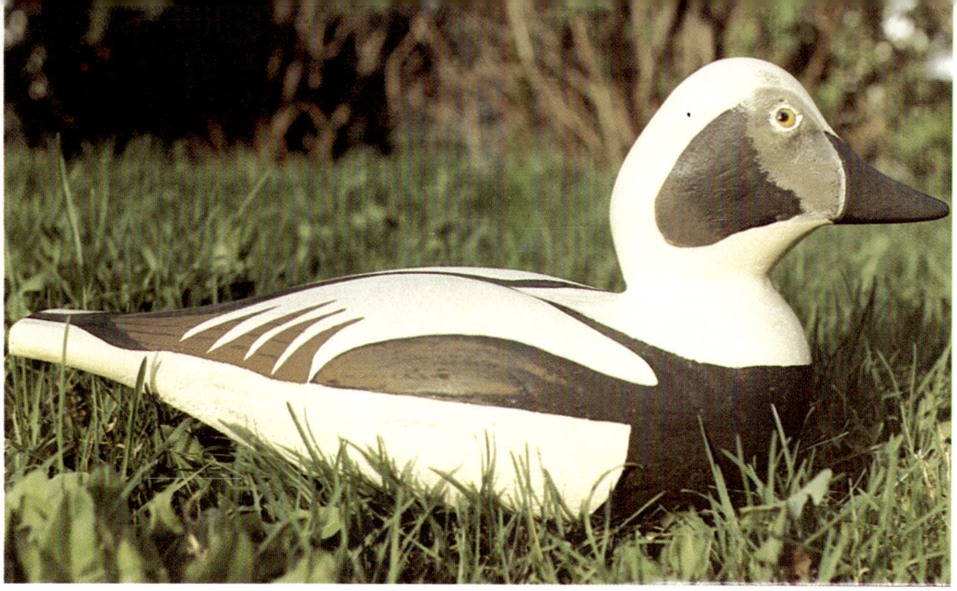

Old squaw decoy by Thornton Penrose, Jr. Ca. 1970. Painted by David Harrington.

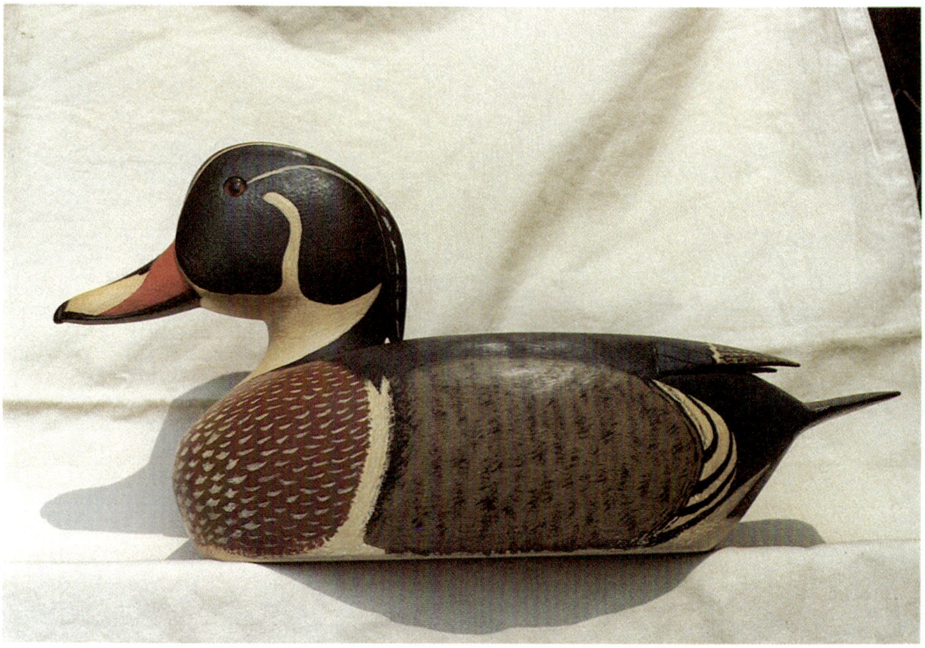

Woodduck decoy by Royal Perry ca. 1950. Cedar, original paint.

Black duck by Royal Perry. Cork body, pine head with keel.

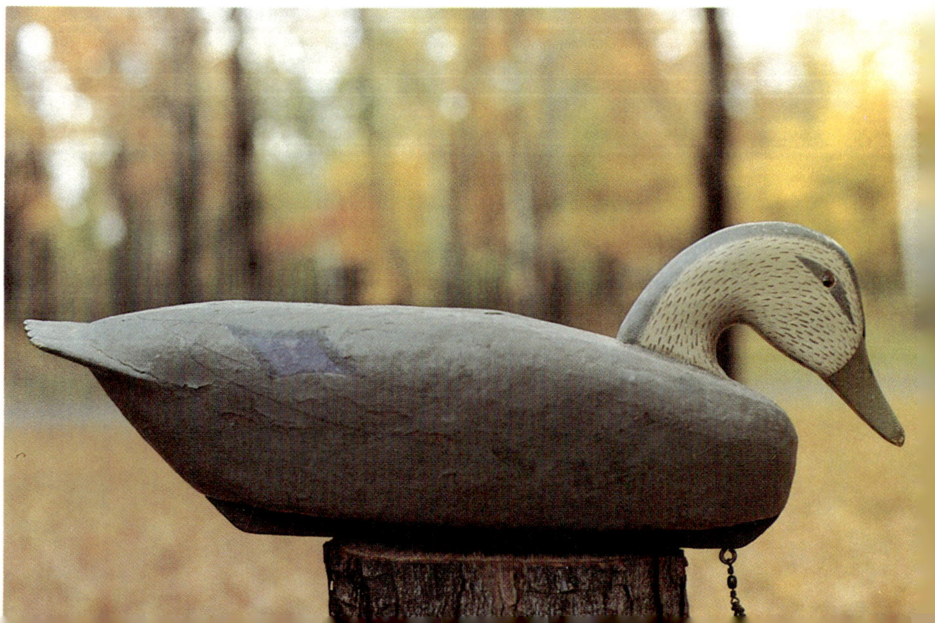

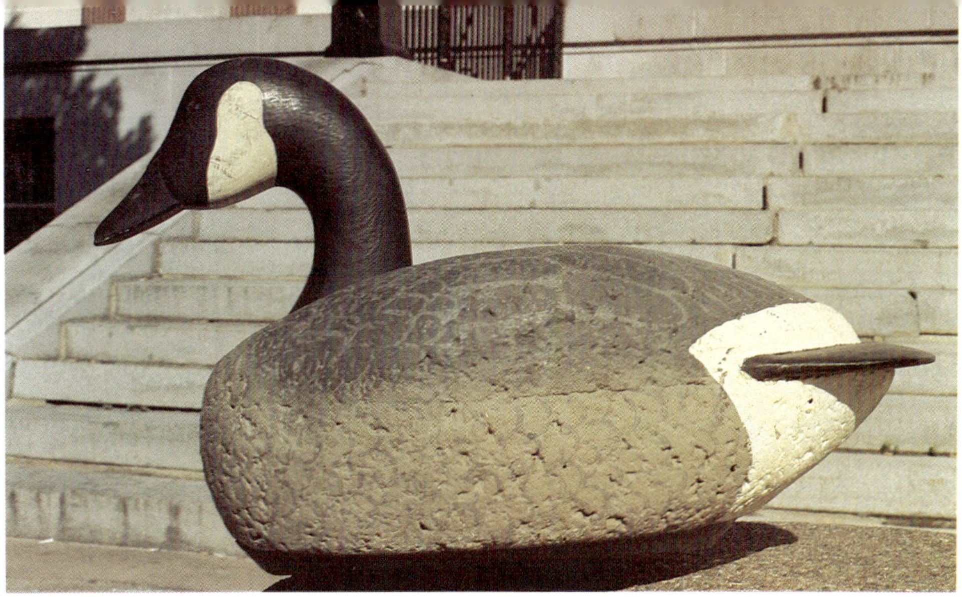

Canada goose decoy by Royal Perry. Ca. 1945. Pine head and tail. Used as a floater.

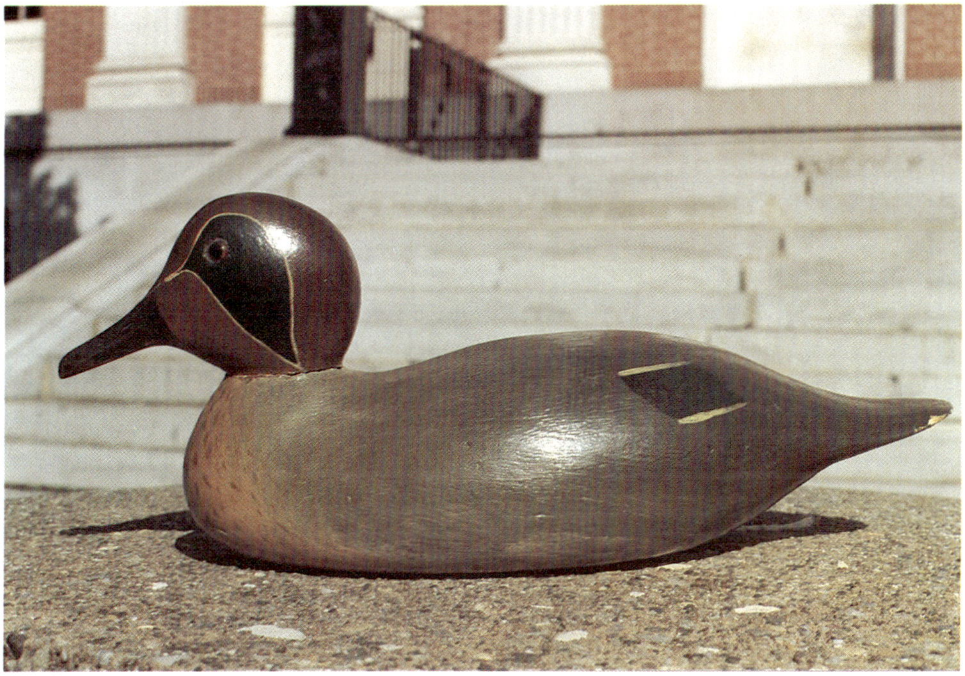

Greenwing teal by Royal Perry. Collection of Michael Goldblatt.

Whistler hen by Royal Perry ca. 1970. Cedar construction, original paint. Collection of Loy S. Harrell.

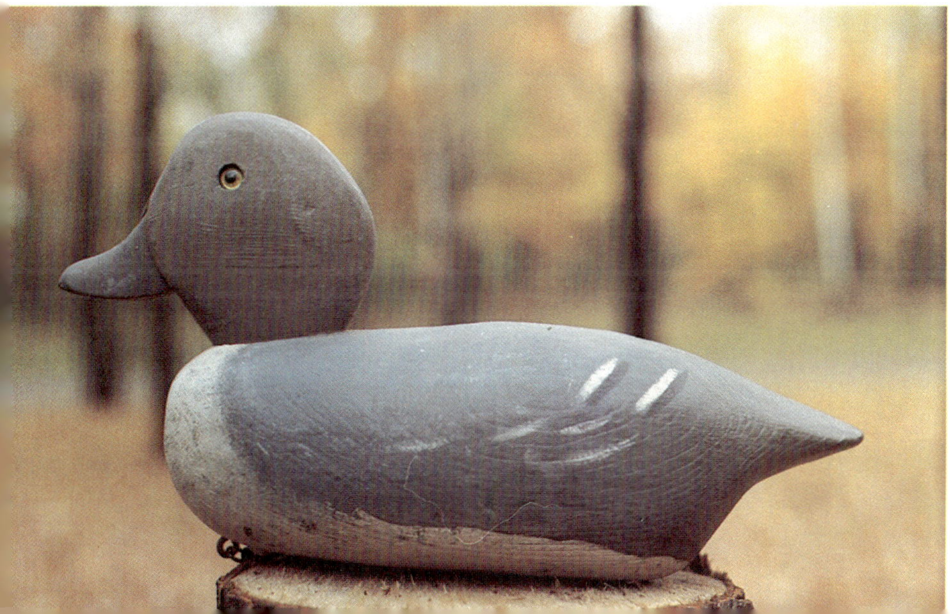

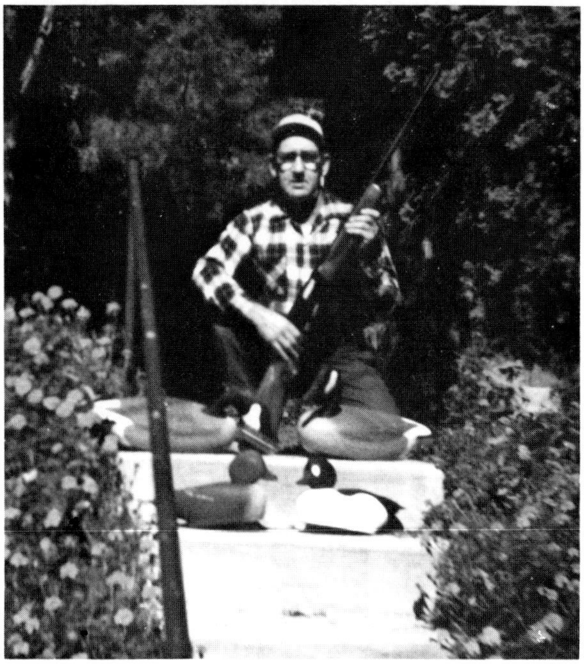

Royal Perry with a goose and a whistler decoy. 1981.

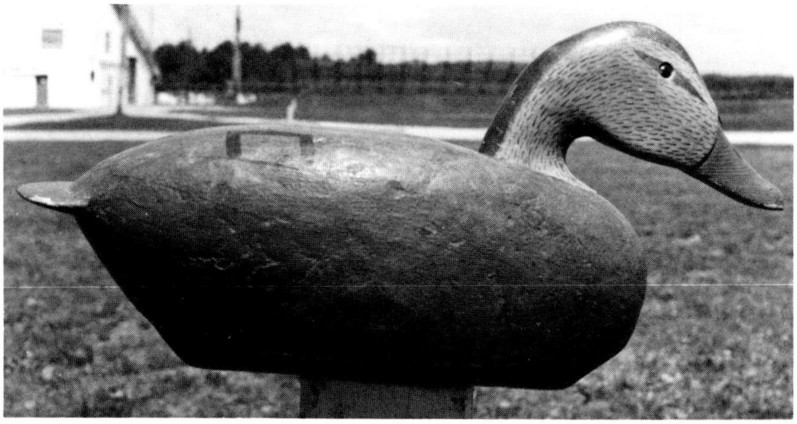

Black duck by Royal Perry. Ca. 1940. His earlier style. Collection of Phillip DeLaricheliere.

Royal F. Perry 1916-1983. Burlington, Vermont, was always known among his peers as an outstanding hunter. His avid duckhunting lead him to begin carving as a young man. The evolution of his work is evident. Earlier birds were bulky and rode the water in an unrealistic way. Later his decoys became both more efficient and clean in their design. Perry carved cork and cedar rigs together with more elaborate decoys. His experience in the construction business and his artistic talent lent themselves to making "the perfect decoy". Smooth, simple heads with deep recessed glass eyes are characteristic of Perry's work.

Whistler hen, rigmate to above drake.

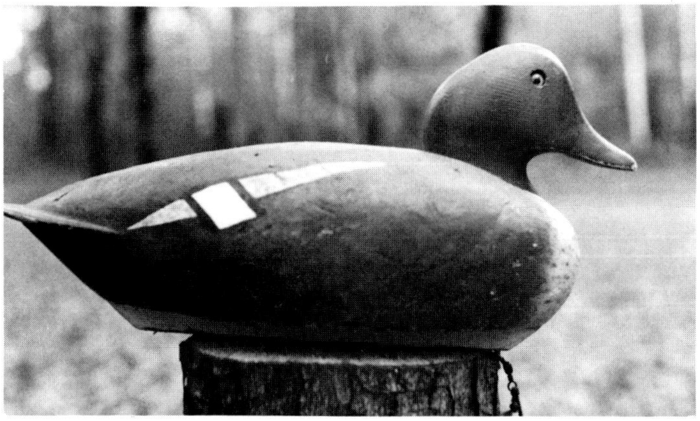

Goldeneye drake by Royal Perry. Cork body, pine head and keel. Original paint. Collection of Janet Lapan.

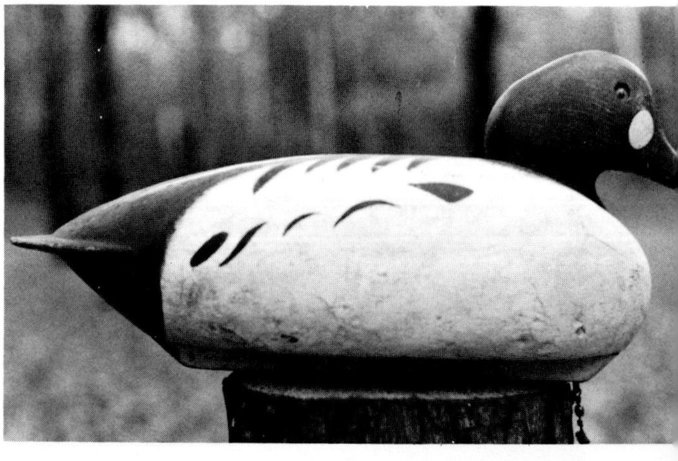

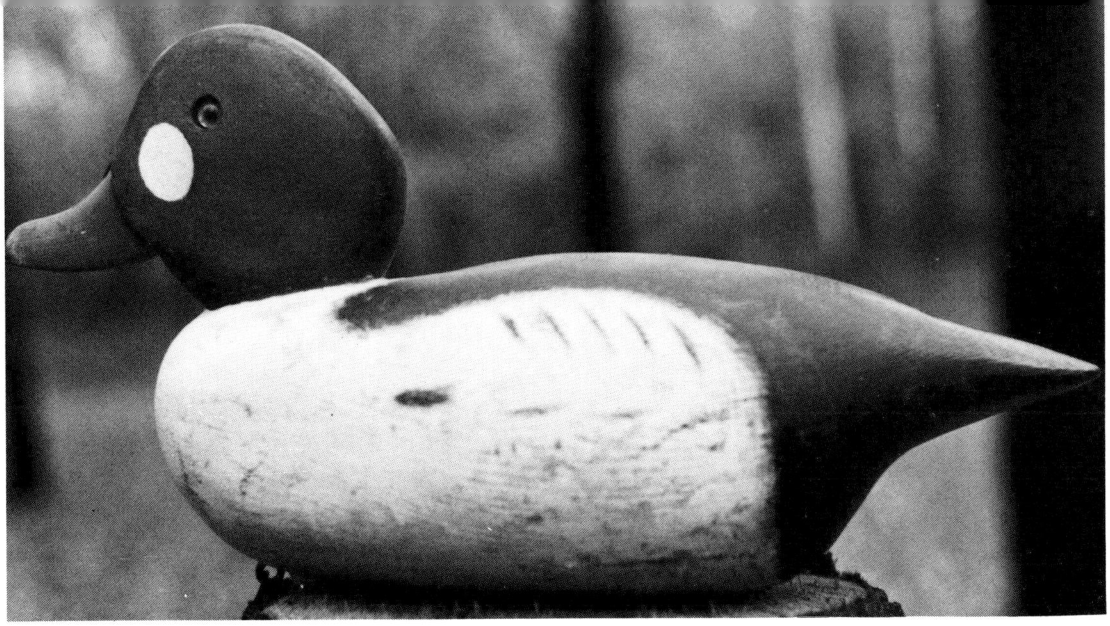

Whistler drake by Royal Perry. Solid cedar.

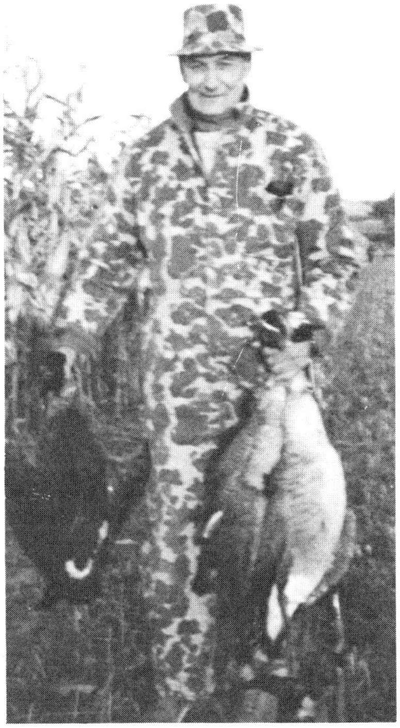

Raymond Poquette, October, 1973. After goose hunting Vermont cornfield.

Raymond Poquette 1905-1981, Alburg, Vermont, was a duck hunting guide from 1941 until his death. He began to carve decoys in 1943 to supply the needs of his guests and himself. Although Poquette never carved commercially, he always made decoys to sell to the persons he either guided or stayed at his home in Alburg. There he and his wife, Linnie, ran a hunting camp. Poquette was a multi-faceted man. He was the area representative to the Vermont State House 1968-1981 and served twelve years as Grand Isle County State Attorney. But he was especially known for his great love of the outdoors. He raised Chesapeake Bay retrievers (his favorite was Fury), carved over four hundred decoys, and contributed articles to *Field and Stream*. Truly a historical figure in the lore of Lake Champlain folk art.

Canada goose decoys by Raymond Poquette. Used as floaters or field rigs. Cork body, pine heads with wood base. Collection of Peter Bergh.

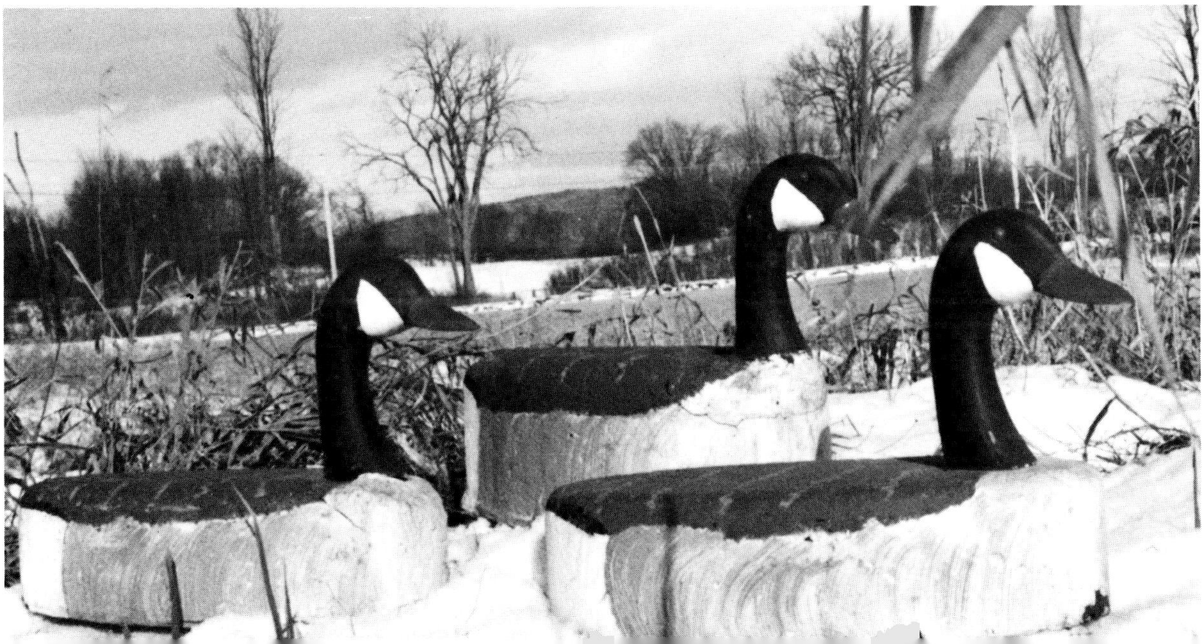

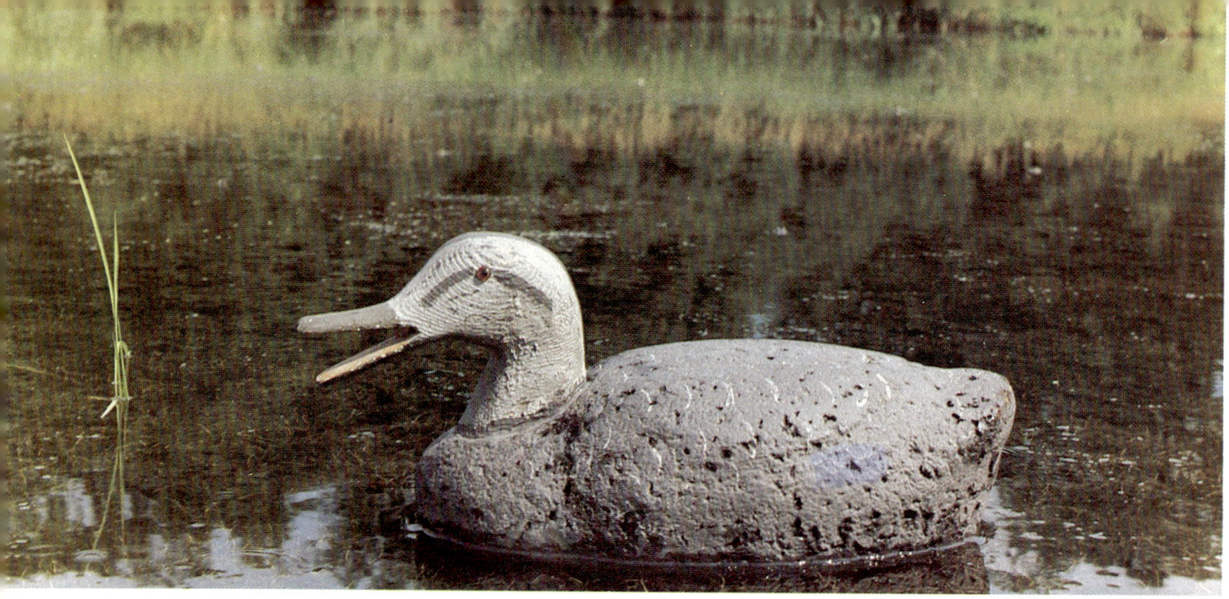

Black duck by Raymond Poquette. Ca. 1945. Collection of Loy S. Harrell.

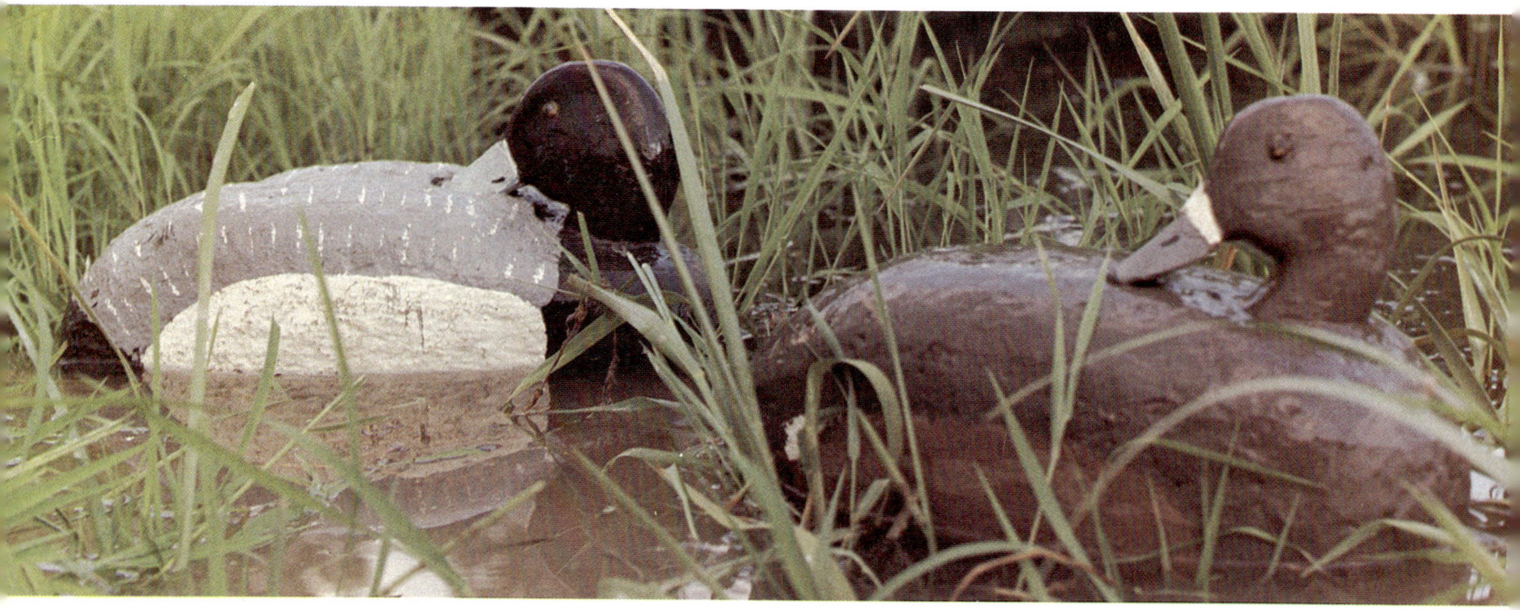

Pair of Poquette sleeping bluebills ca. 1950.

Black ducks by Raymond Poquette. Cork bodies, pine heads. All original paint.

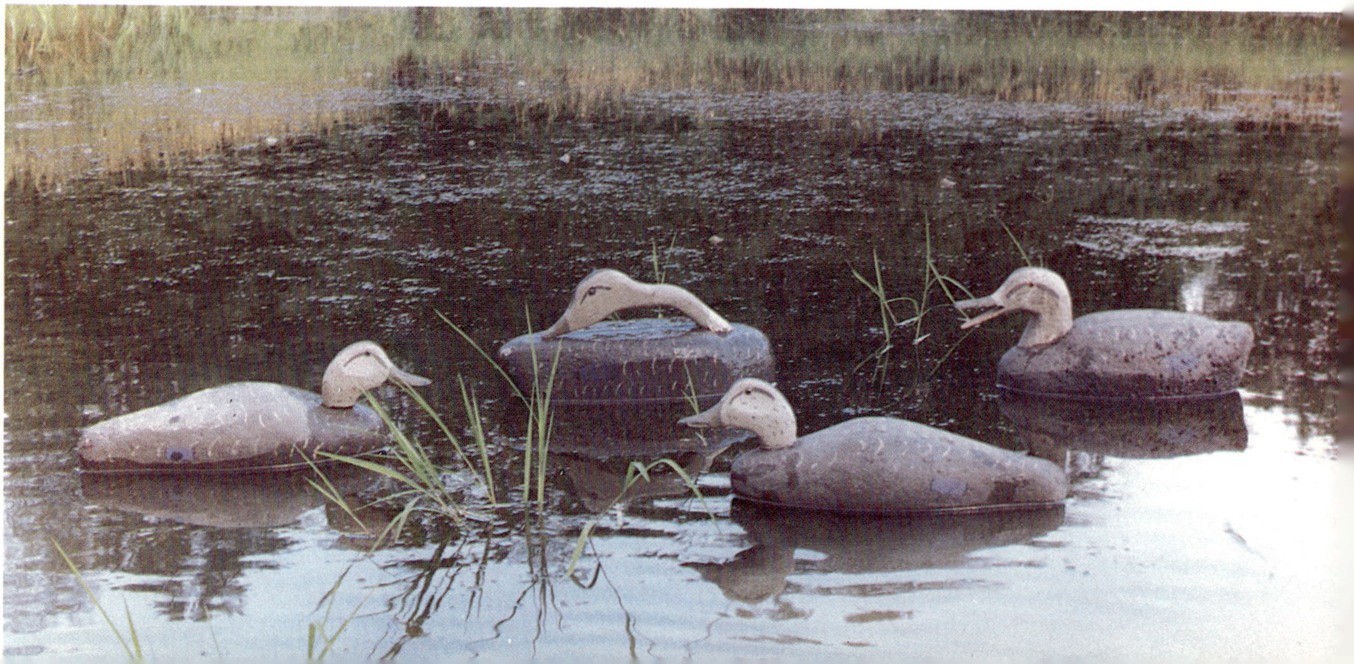

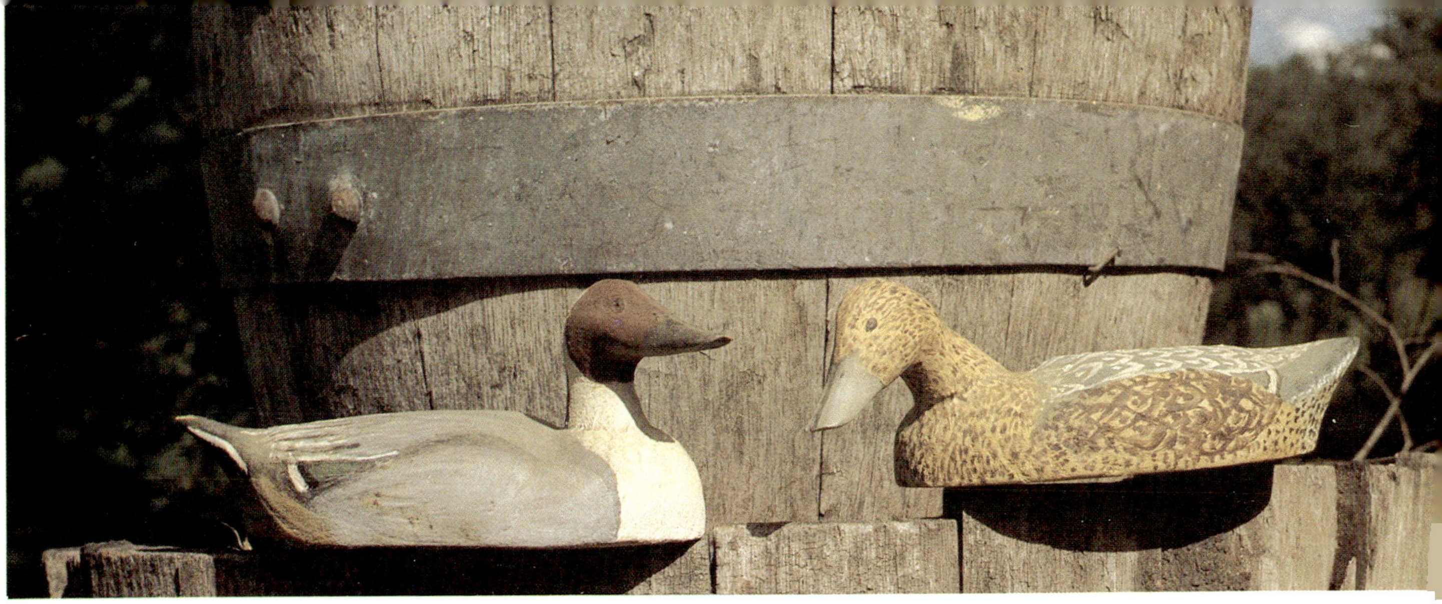

Pair of miniature pintails by Charles Porter.

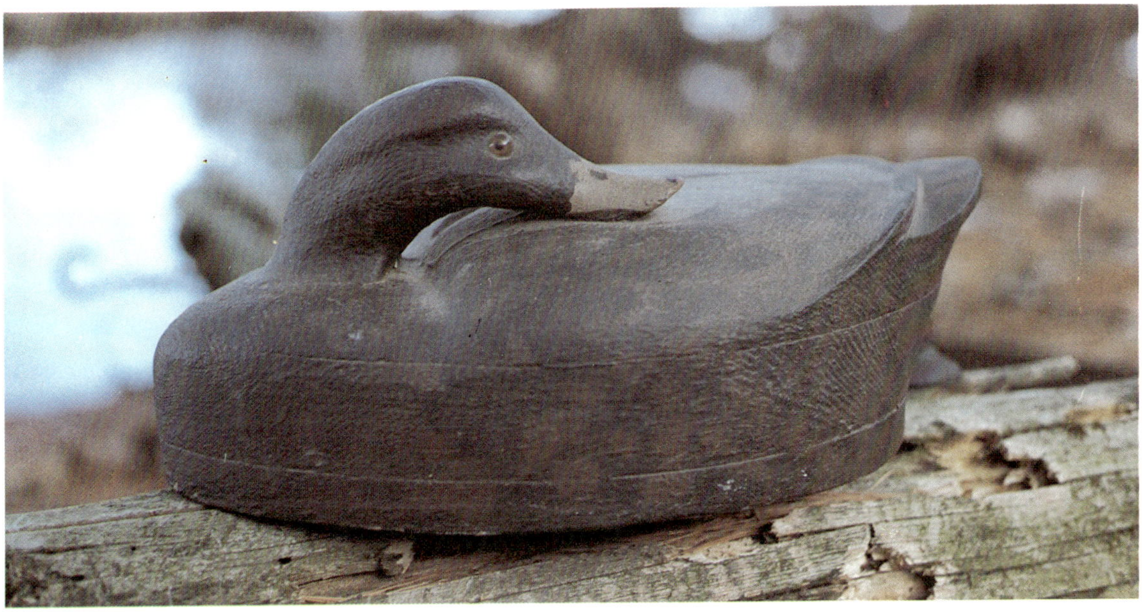

Black duck decoy by Charles Porter ca. 1965. Hollow and laminated. Original paint. Collection of Loy S. Harrell.

Swimming black duck by Charles Porter. Hollow, laminated.

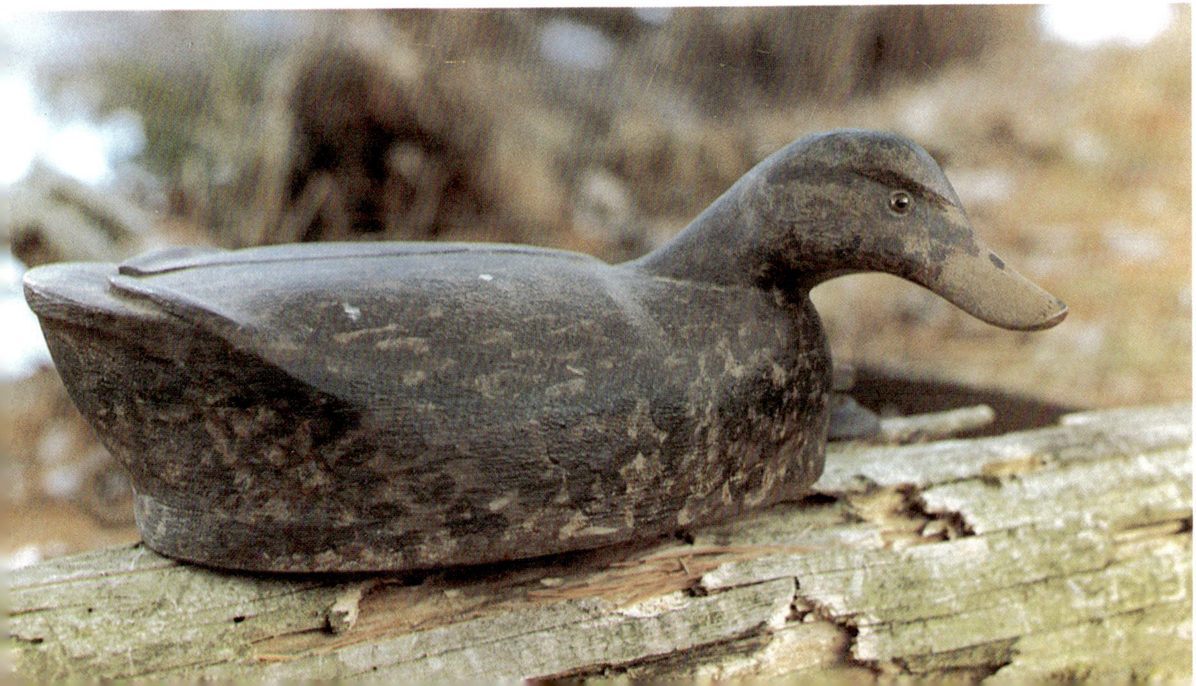

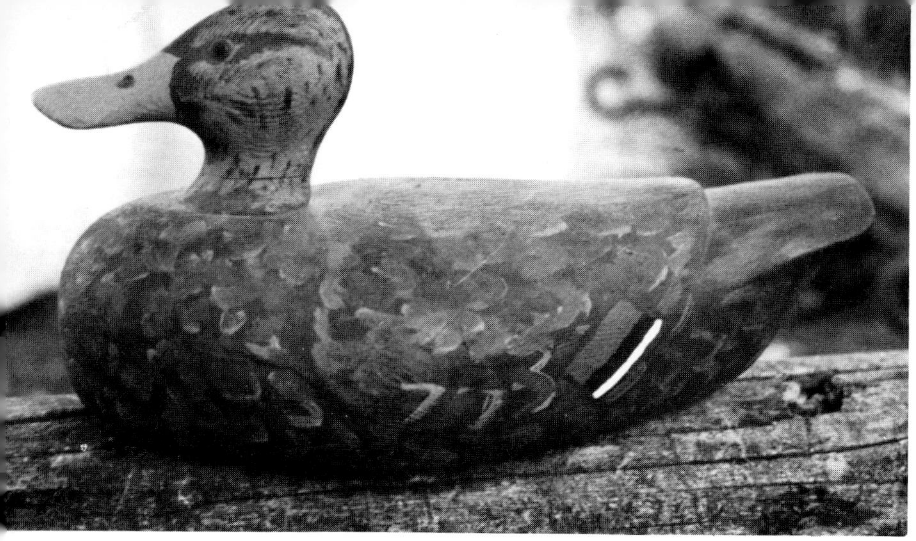

Working black duck by Charles Porter. Solid pine and cedar construction.

Charles Porter 1930- Port Henry, New York, has carved over eighty decoys, including blacks, goldeneyes and bluebills. Many are hollow, laminated and constructed of cedar with pine heads. Porter's decoys are considered the "folkiest on the lake", and are sought after by folk art collectors. He has hunted over most of them along the west shores of Lake Champlain.

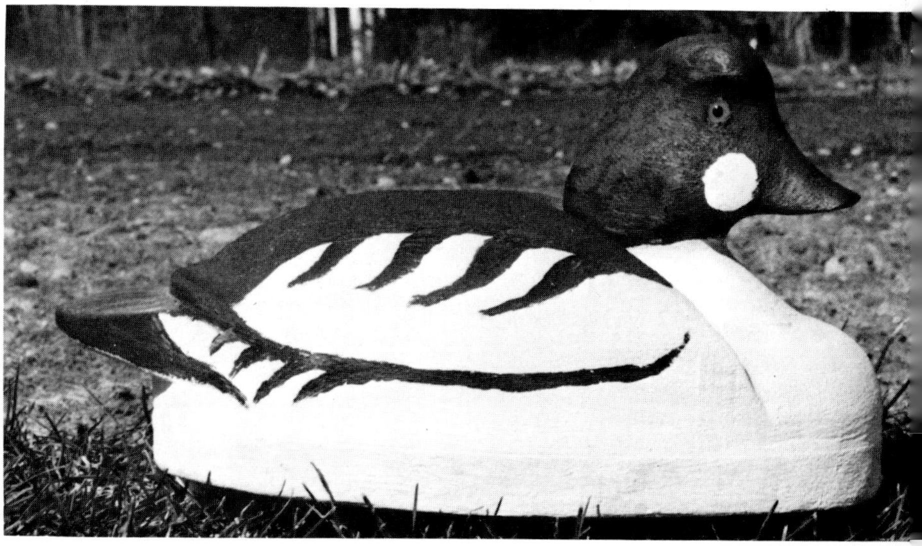

Whistler (goldeneye) decoy by Charles Porter. Working decoy in rig of Simeon McIntyre.

Bluebill hen by Charles Porter. Shot over on Miller Marsh, Lake Champlain.

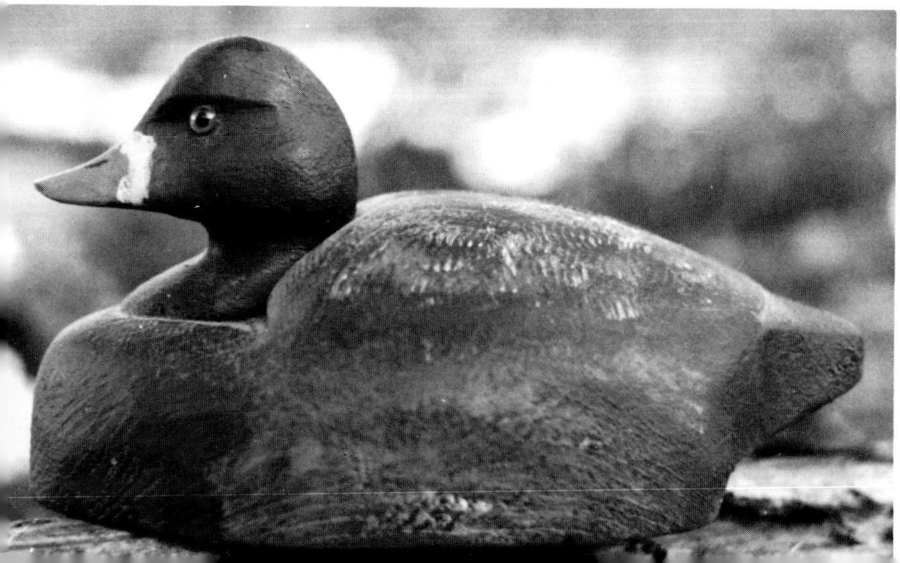

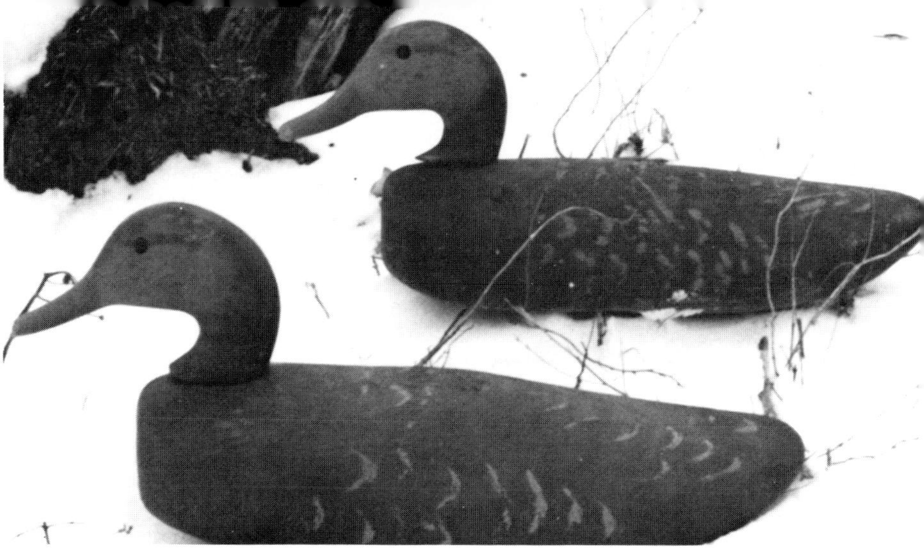

Black duck decoys by Herbert Prakelt. Westford, Vermont ca. 1960. Original paint. Collection of David Lavallee.

Casius Alexander Putnam 1908-1978. Ticonderoga, New York. Always known as a prodigious hunter and fisherman, Putnam could be found either in the woods or on the water. He spent his spare time carving decoys with his companion, Donald Hanson from Crown Point. They rough-hewn blocks of pine with a wood hasp and hatchet. They were crudely painted and tack eyes were later applied. Putnam used these decoys on Bulwagga Bay, south of Port Henry, New York.

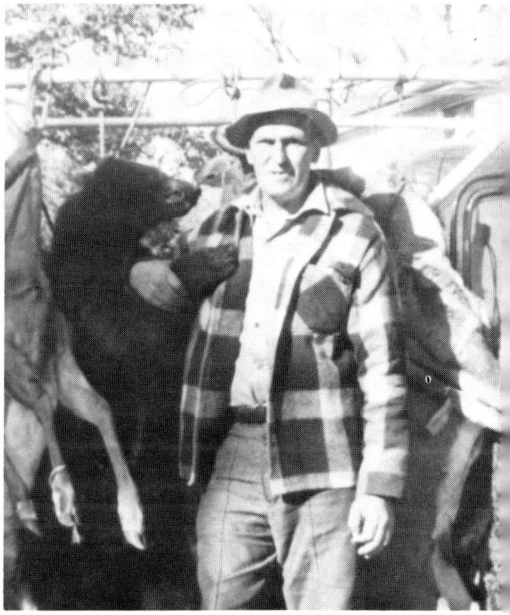

Photograph of Casius A. Putnam, 1945. After a hunt in the Adirondacks west of Lake Champlain.

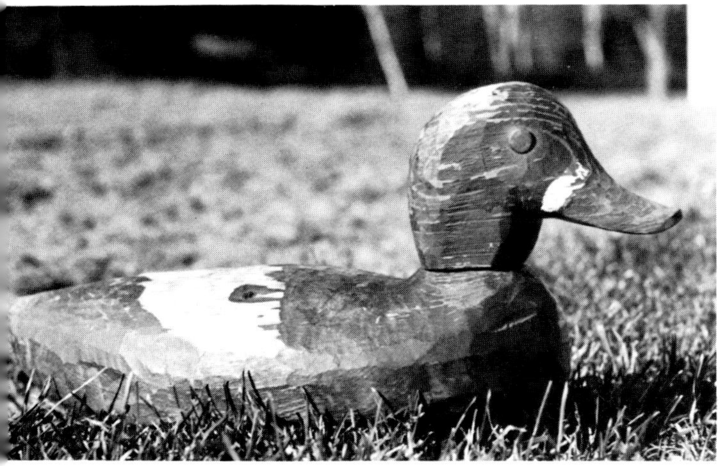

Bluebill by Casius Putnam. Ca. 1948. Tack eyes. Collection of Donald Hanson.

Canada goose decoy by Casius Putnam. Solid cedar, two piece neck, head with tack eyes. Collection of John Smart.

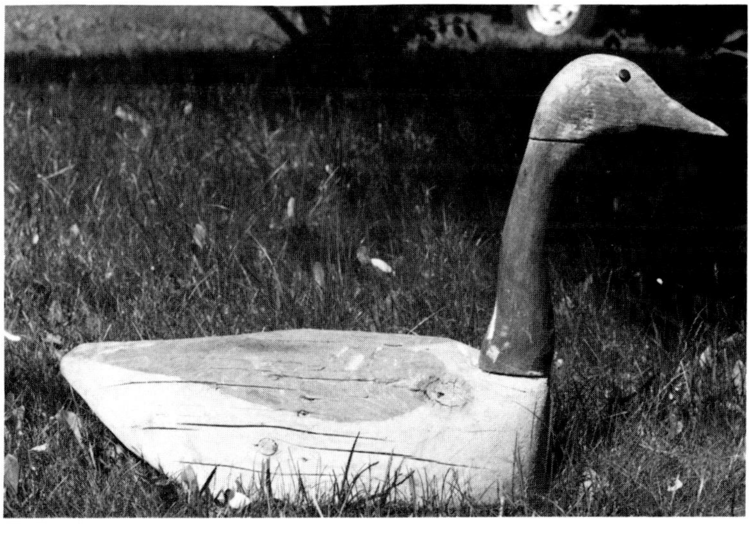

Reginald Pudvar 1904- St. Albans, Vermont, was a professional butcher most of his life but found time to carve almost a hundred decoys. He made mallards, blacks and bluebills from cedar and cork goose decoys. Most of his birds were made between 1945-1960. Pudvar's birds are shaped with a jackknife, giving them a characteristic finish. He used both glass and tack eyes. Pudvar hunted at Shanty Point and Campbells Bay between St. Albans and Swanton. He is also one of the few fish decoy carvers on the lake.

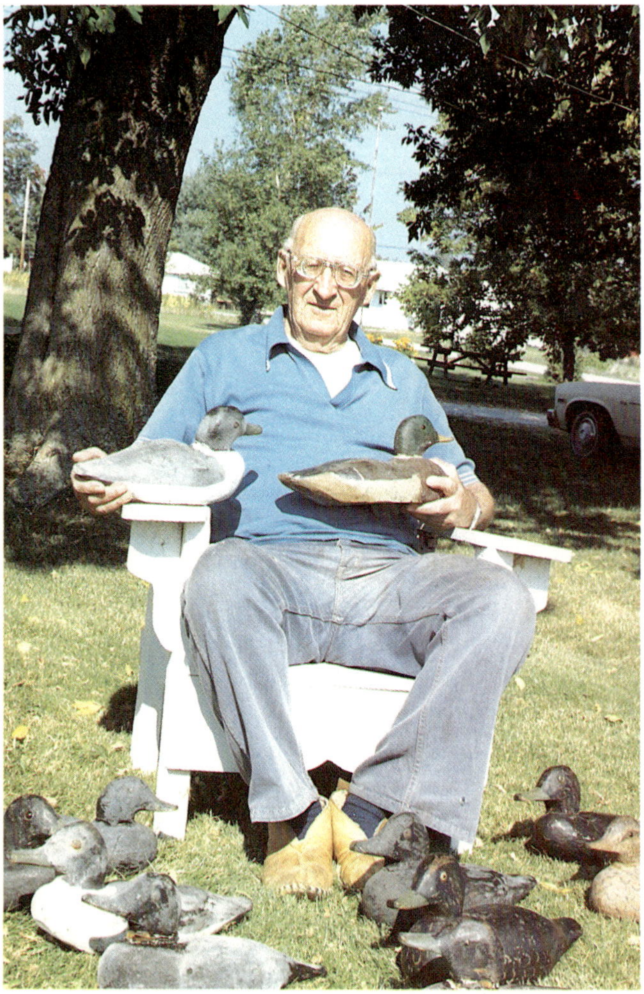

Reginald Pudvar at his St. Albans home, 1985. Surrounded by his working rig.

Black duck by Reginald Pudvar. Ca. 1950. Tack eyes.

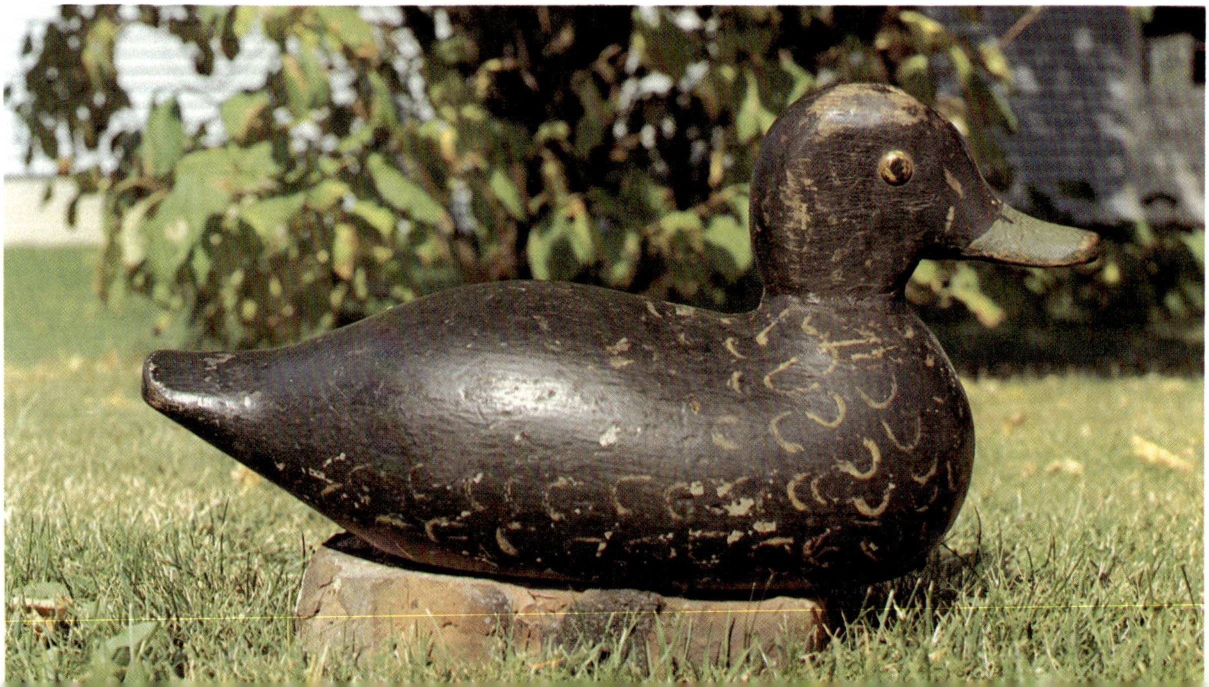

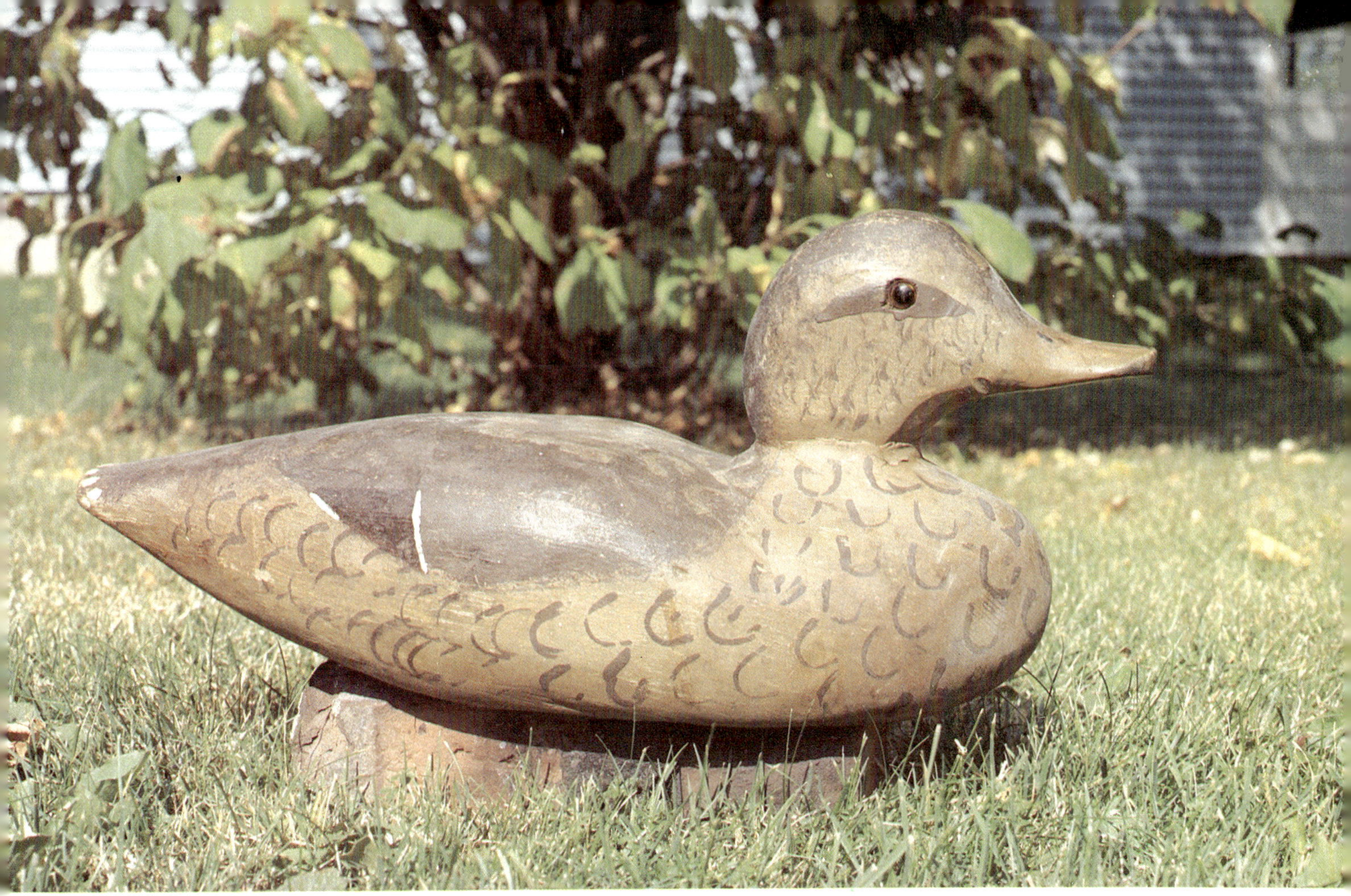

Mallard hen by Reginald Pudvar. Cedar construction. Original paint.

Mallard drake by Reginald Pudvar. Ca. 1945. Original paint. Collection of Loy S. Harrell.

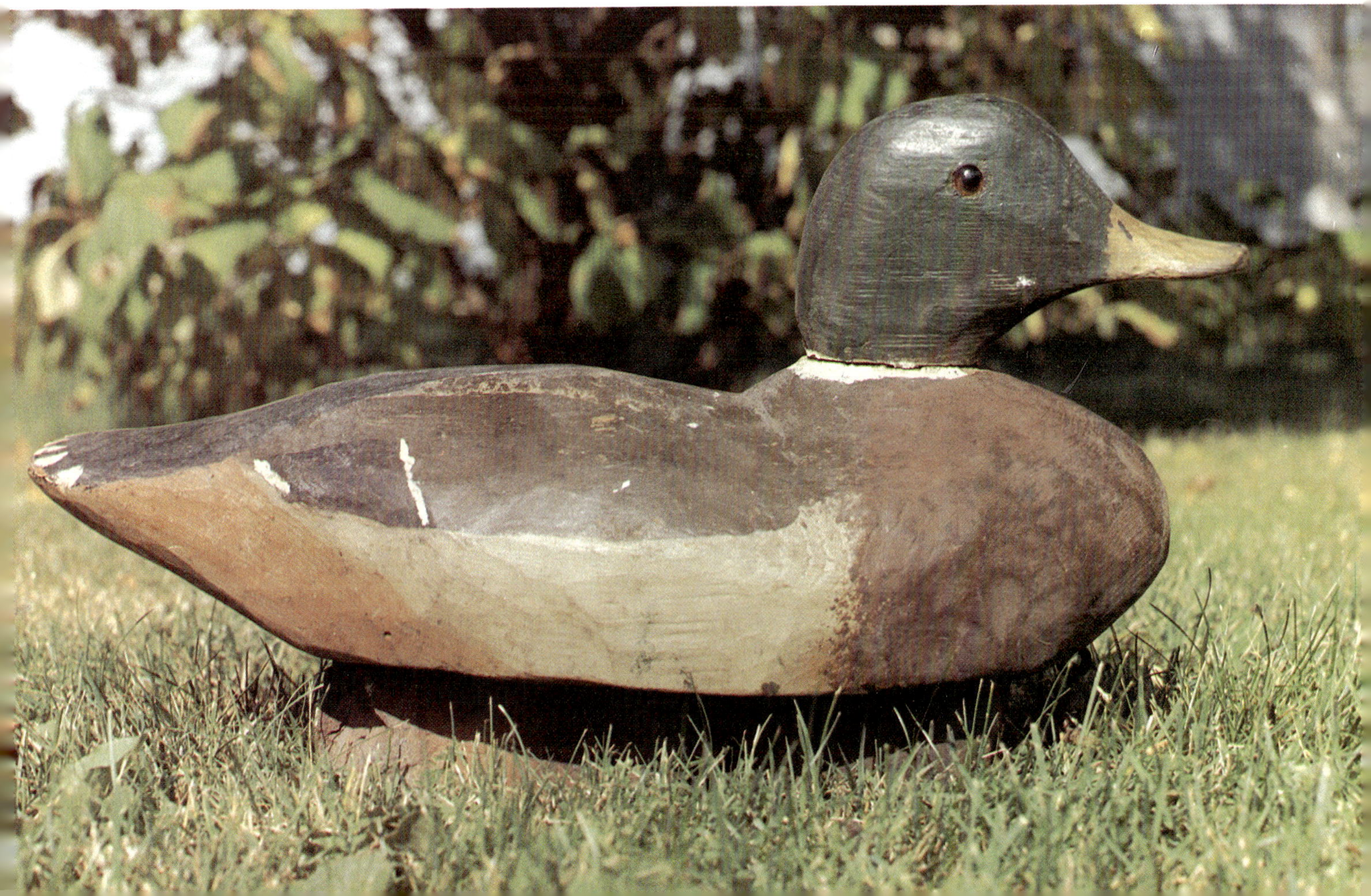

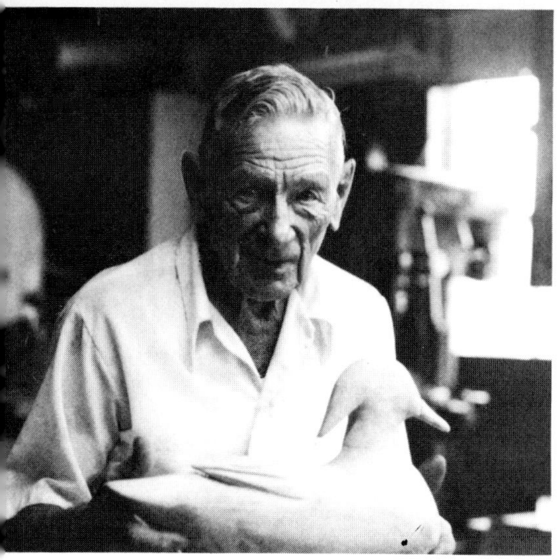

Alphonse Rocheleau 1906- Bedford, Quebec, Canada, is the only documented carver on the Canadian side of Lake Champlain. He hunted on the Pike River, Black Creek, Hog Island near the Vermont border and at Jamieson Point, a rocky prominance halfway between Phillipsburg and Venice in Missisquoi Bay (where many ducks would pass between Black Creek and the National Wildlife Refuge west of Swanton, Vermont). Rocheleau was also a noted trapper and fisherman who began carving in 1930. He used cedar blocks and shaped them with a hatchet and draw shave, finishing them with a rasp and sandpaper. His first one hundred decoys had tack eyes and later ones glass. He also cast and moulded his own weights and anchors. Rocheleau carved over five hundred decoys between 1930-1950, including blackducks, canvasbacks, whistlers and bluebills.

Photograph of Alphonse Rocheleau taken at his workshop, Bedford, Quebec. July, 1985.

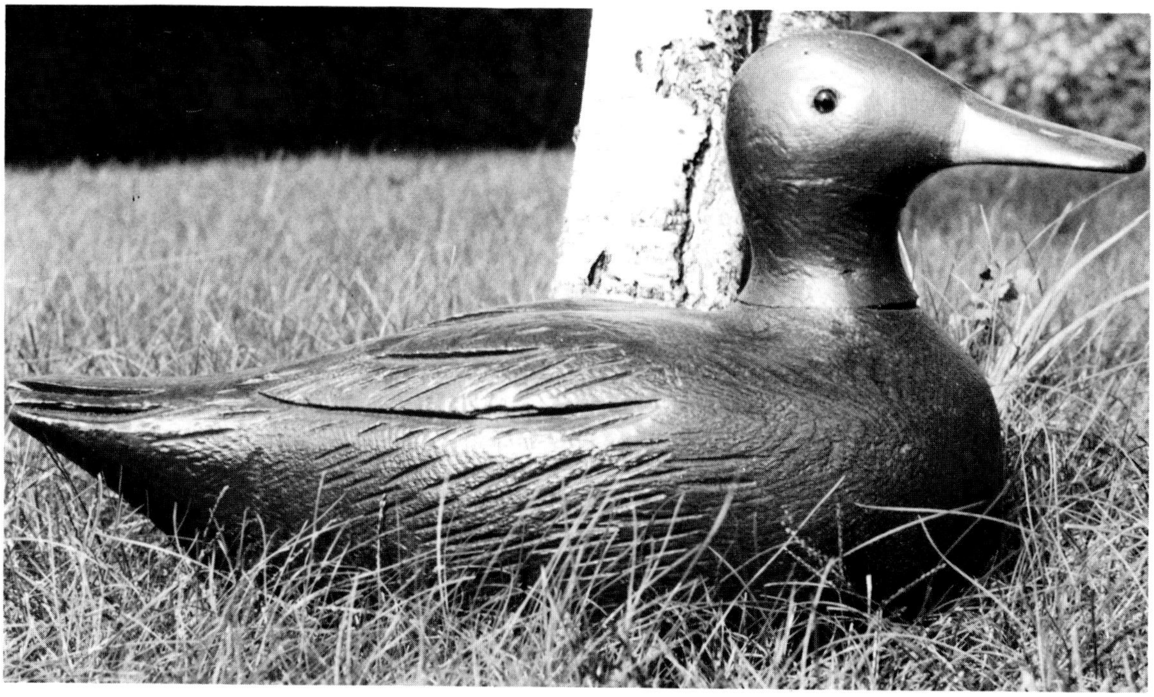

Working black duck by Alphonse Rocheleau ca. 1935. Collection of Laurent Larocque.

Goldeneye drake by Alphonse Rocheleau ca. 1950. Original paint.

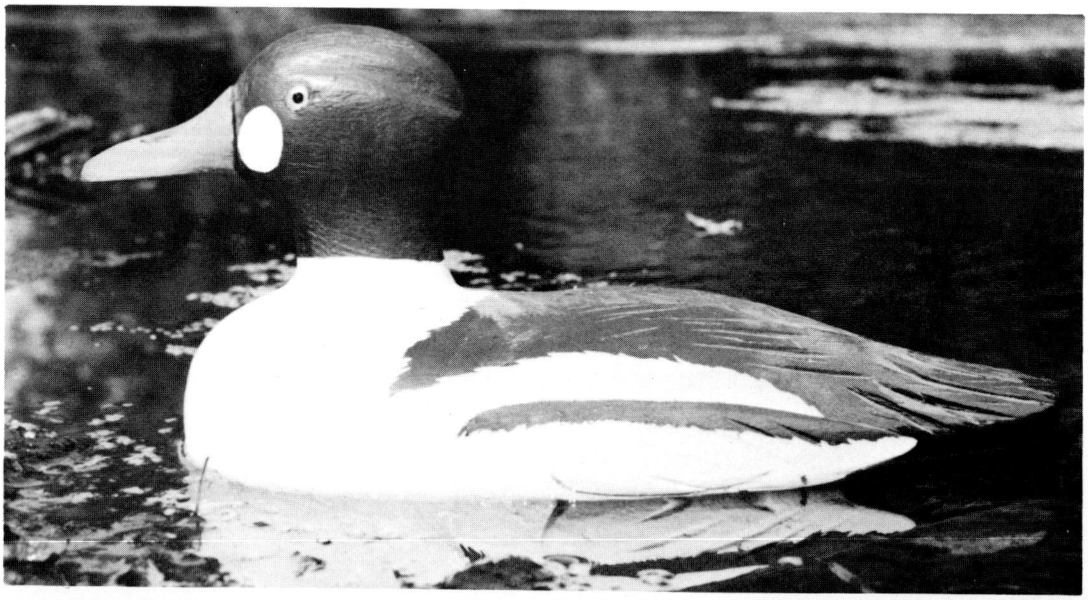

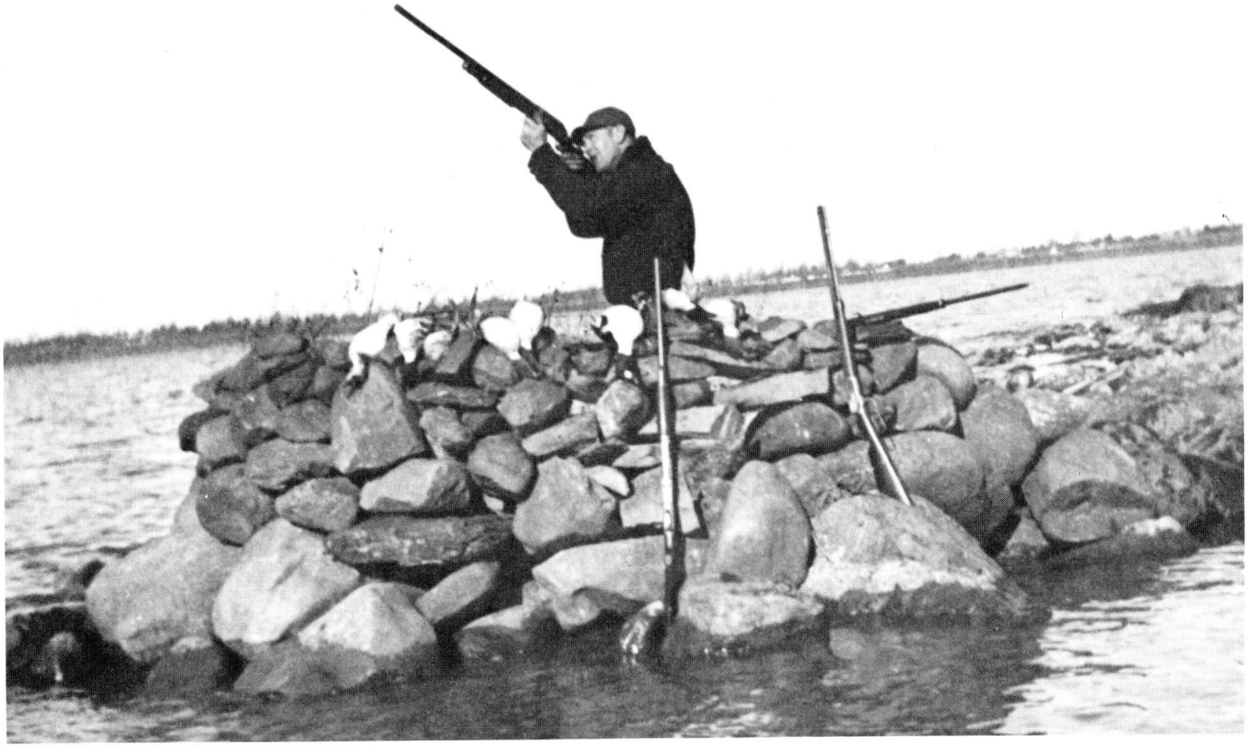

Alphonse Rocheleau in rock blind, Jamieson Point, 1935. Missisquoi Bay, Lake Champlain, Quebec, Canada. Note kill of goldeneyes. Photograph courtesy of A.R.

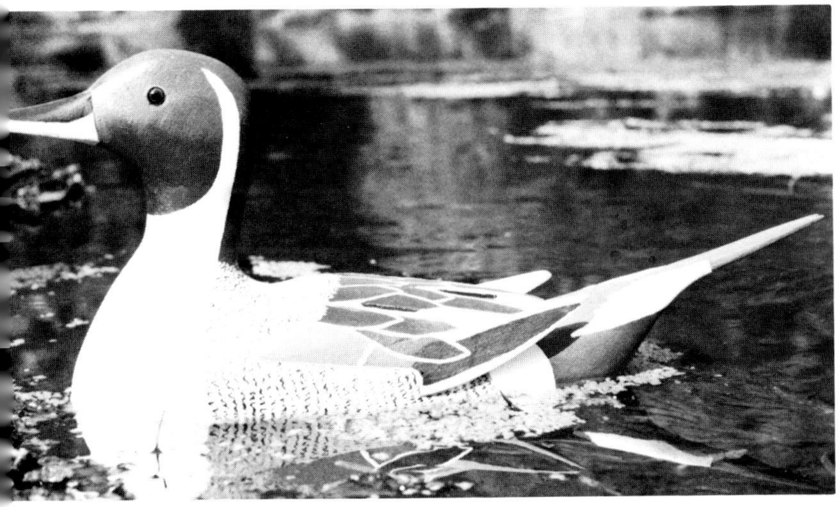

Pintail drake by Alphonse Rocheleau. Raised wing carving. Decorative.

Bluebill hen by Alphonse Rocheleau. Working decoy in original paint. Ca. 1948.

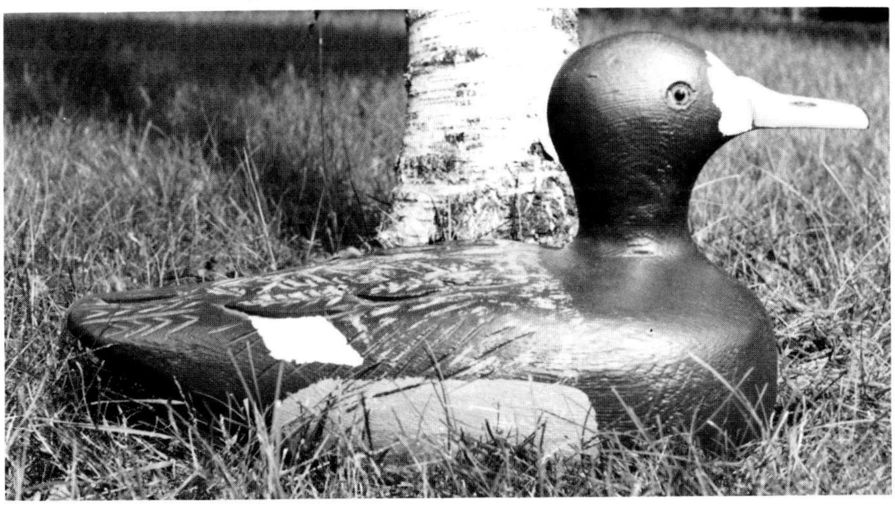

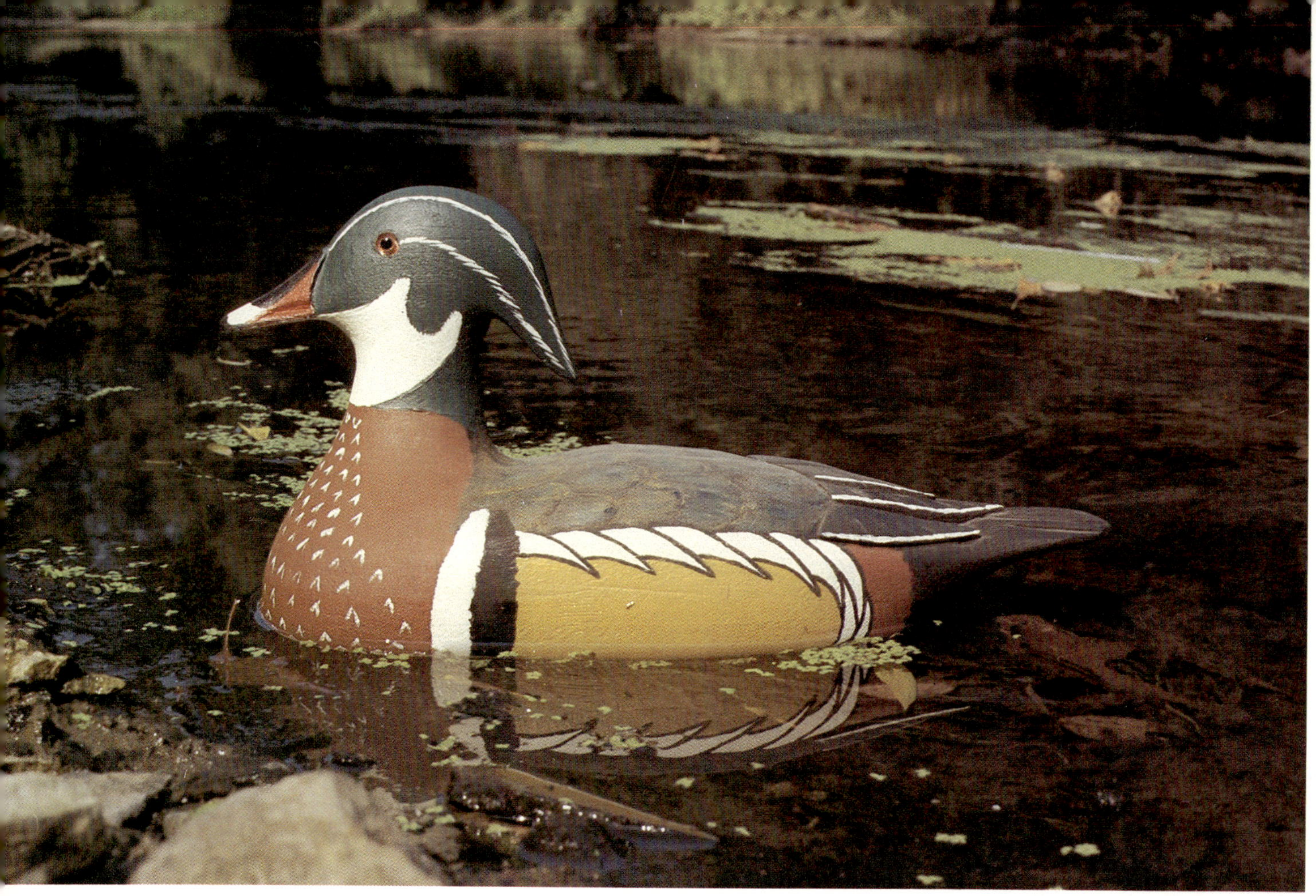

Woodduck drake by Alphonse Rocheleau. Ca. 1950. Collection of Theodore Hirt.

Preening blackduck by Alphonse Rocheleau. Photograph taken on Pike River, Quebec.

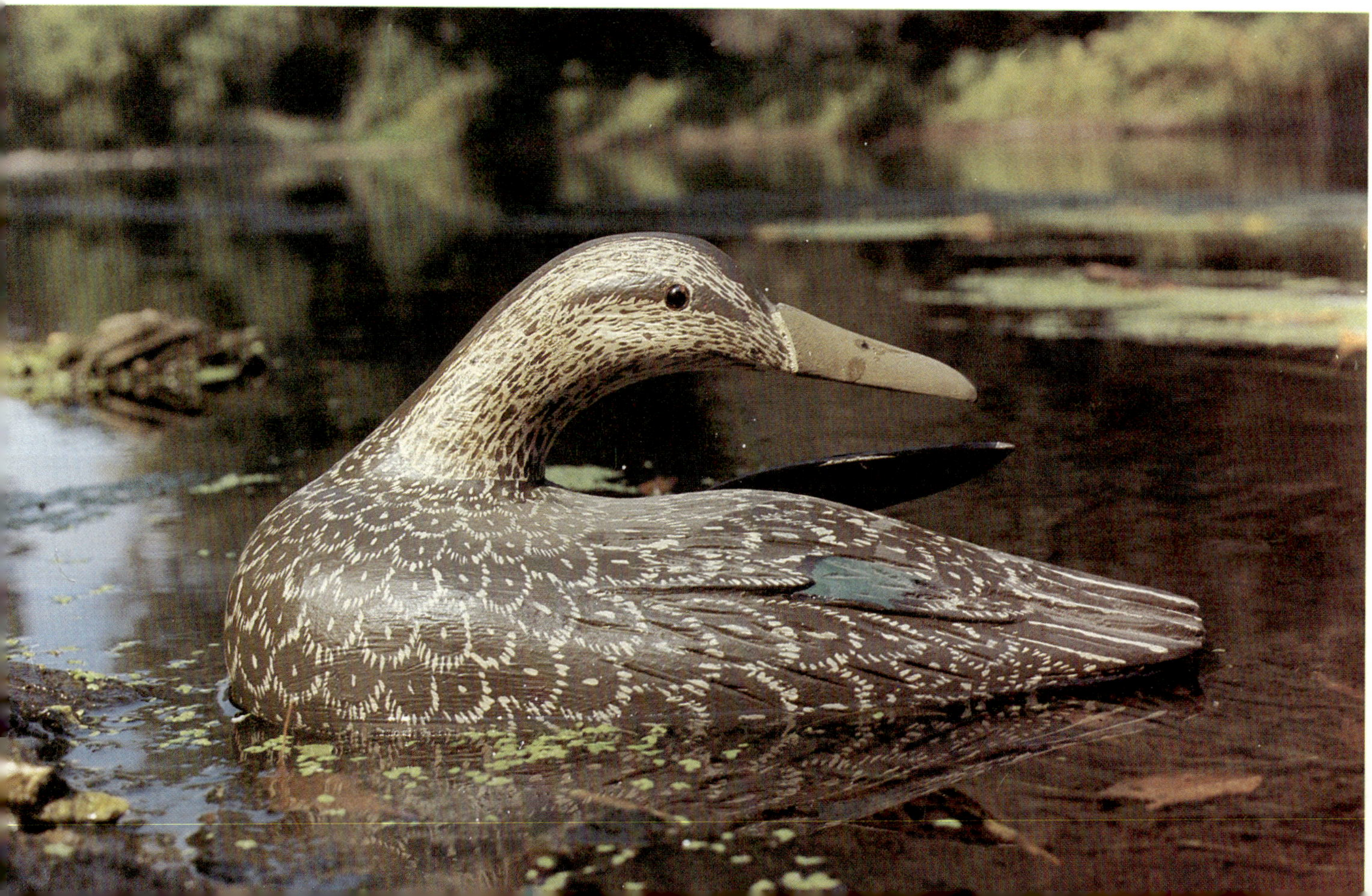

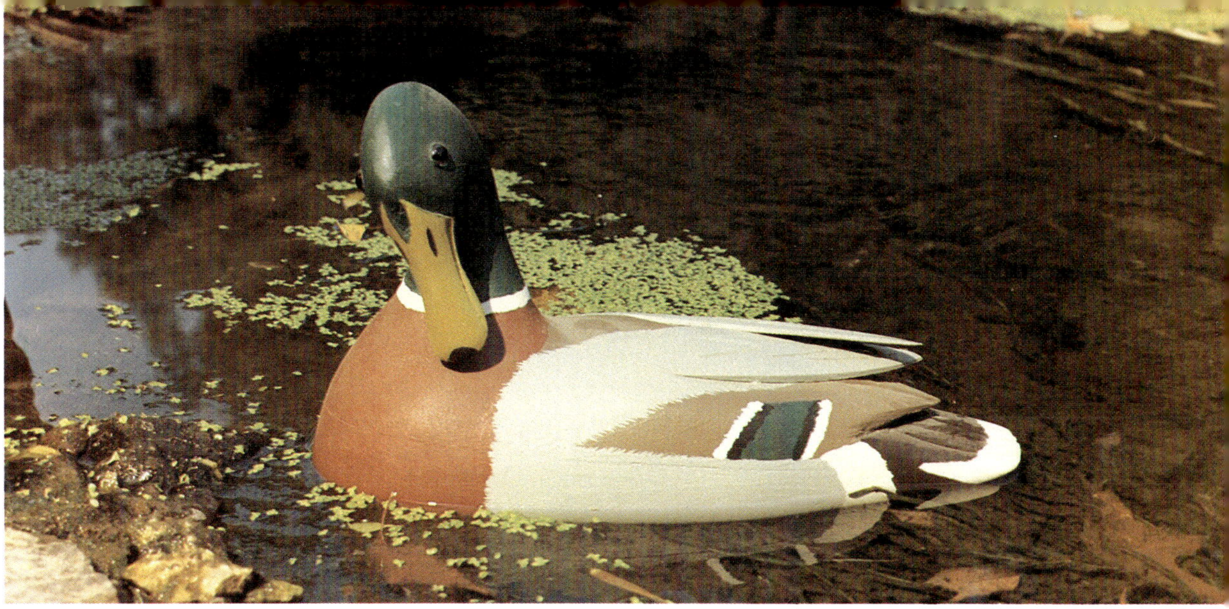

Preening mallard drake by Alphonse Rocheleau. Raised wing carving, glass eyes. (A beautiful decoy).

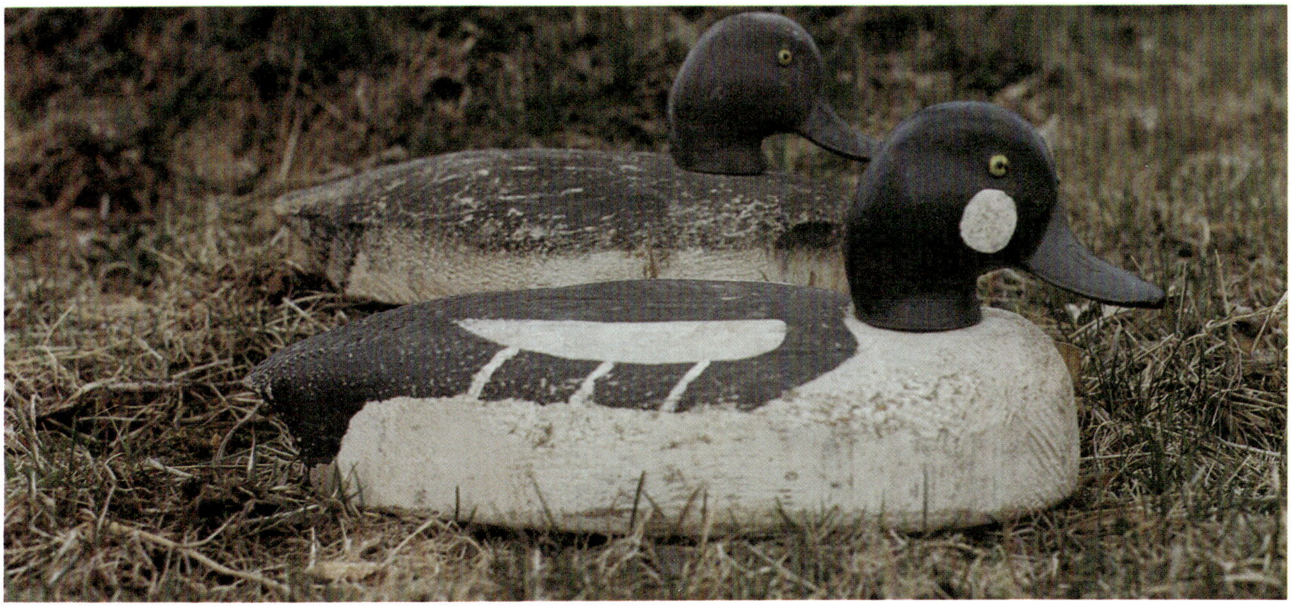

Bluebill by Hiram Rochester ca. 1930. Collection of James Reynolds.

Pair of goldeneyes by Hiram Rochester ca. 1940. Cork body, pine heads, old repaint. Collection of James F.. Rochester.

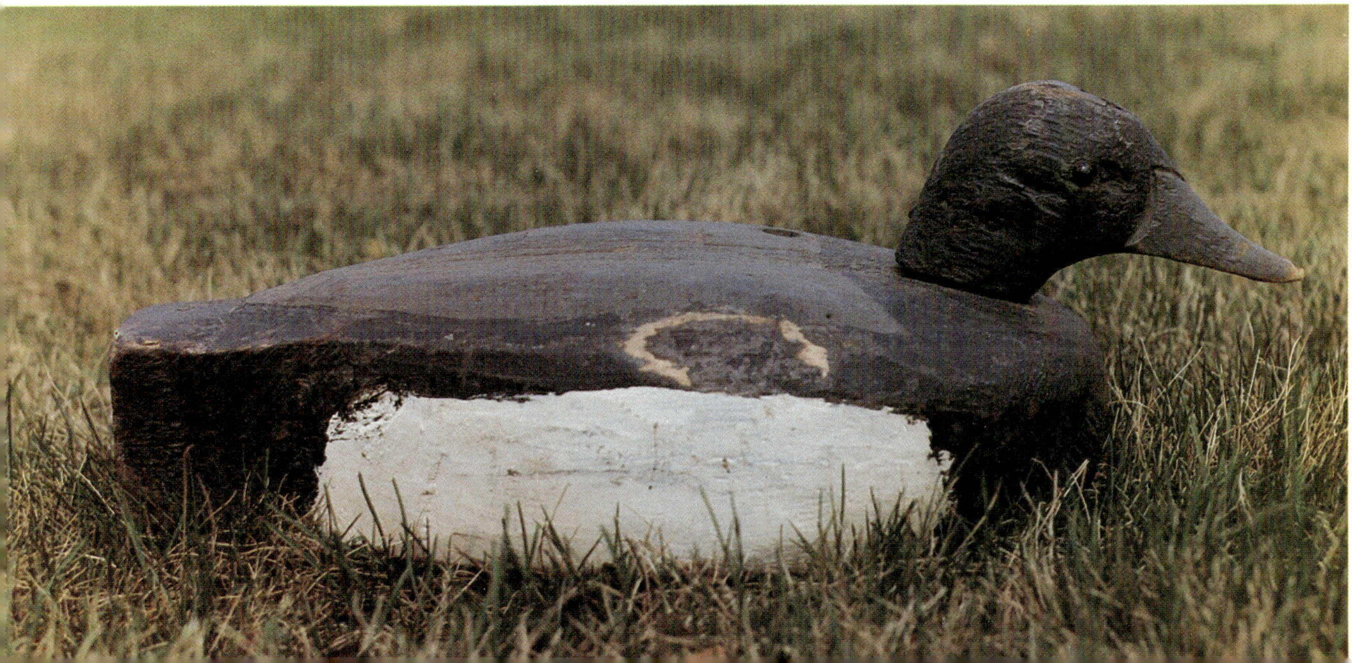

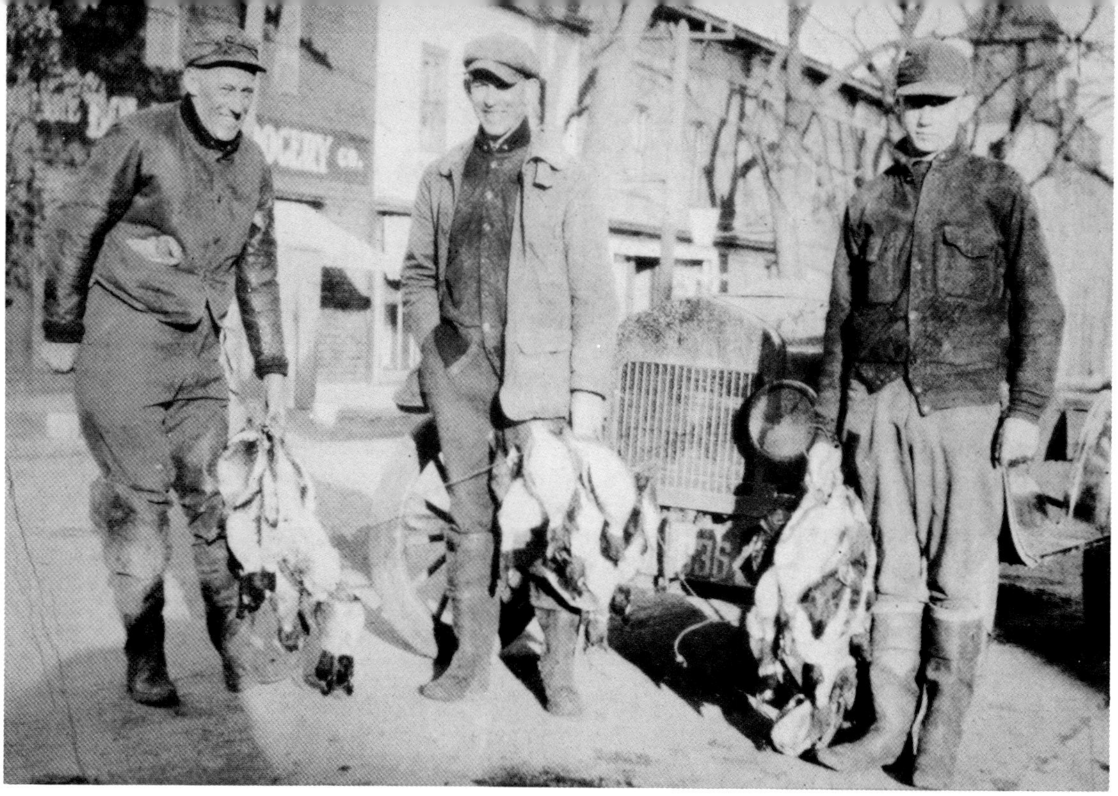

Left to right; Earl Thurston, Hiram Rochester and Dewey Sequin taken in 1925, Main Street, Rouses Point, New York. (You can imagine the duck population in 1925 from their bag of goldeneyes.). Shot at the Rochester Blind, Rochester Point on Kings Bay.

Hiram Rochester 1897-1973, Rouses Point, New York, was a railroad engineer for the Naperville Railroad. He also fired steamboats on Lake Champlain which ran from Rouses Point to Whitehall, New York. Rochester was a descendant of a family that settled on Point Au Fer in the early 1700's. It was natural for him to use the lake both for a source of employment and recreation. He carved almost five hundred cork or cedar decoys; mostly whistlers, many have raised wing carving but most are plain in their lines.

Hiram Rochester on Lake Champlain with his decoys and days bag. Ca. 1968.

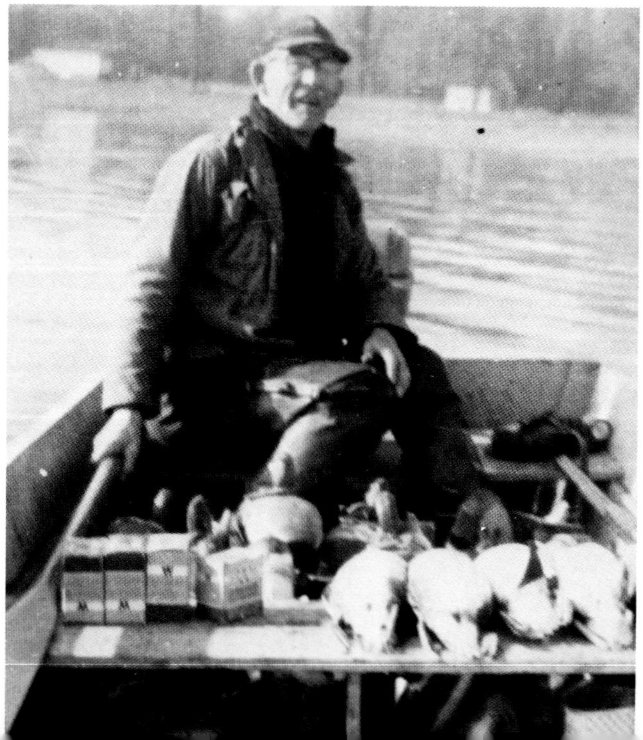

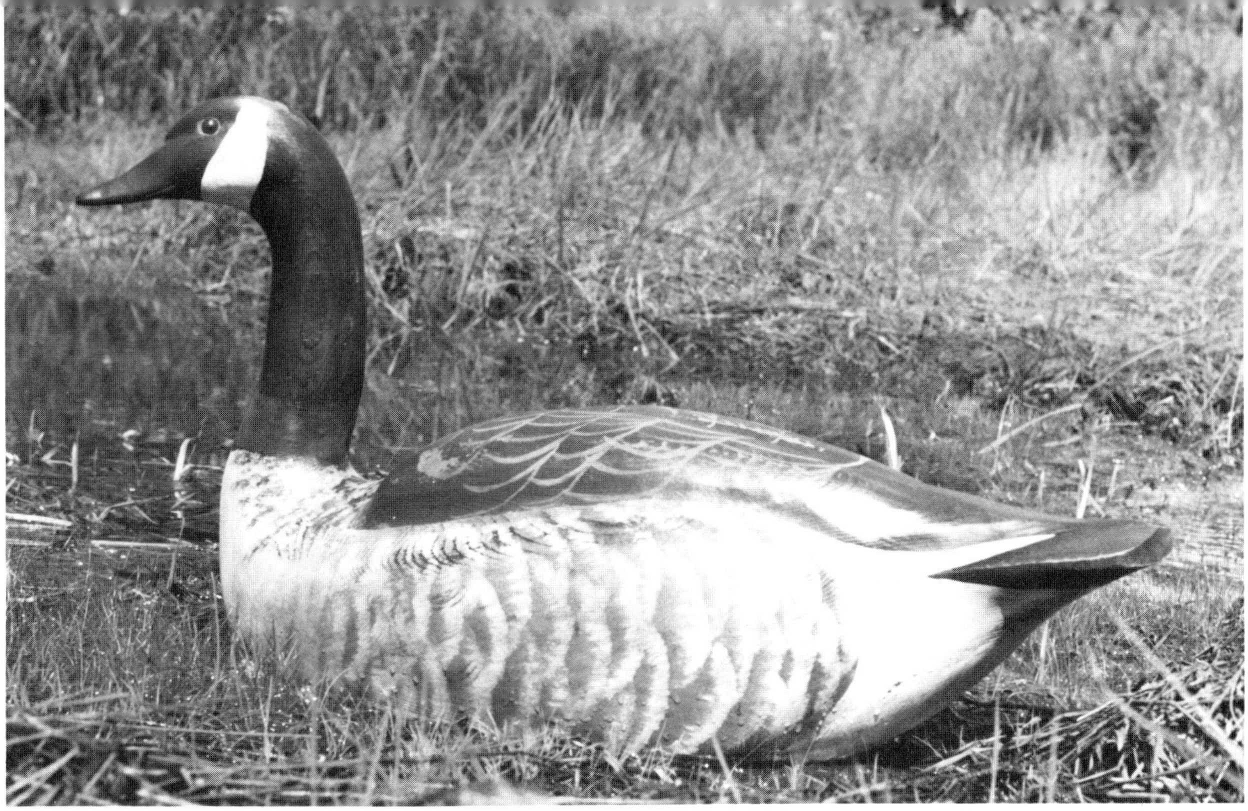

Canada goose by Frank Russell. Working floater ca. 1981.

Frank C. Russell 1937- Fairfax, Vermont, is a full time carver of wildfowl. His carvings are commercially sold under the logo of *Stonegate Studios*. Russell, a former industrial arts teacher, decided in 1981 to devote his energy to his "love of the outdoors" and to being creative. Since then he has won various awards in both national and international contests and his carvings are sold throughout the country. Naturally, this all began by making his own gunning decoys. Russell made forty-five geese, six dozen whistlers and sixty-seventy blacks and mallards. Construction was of basswood, cork or pine.

Whistler drake by Frank Russell ca. 1970. Cork body, pine head.

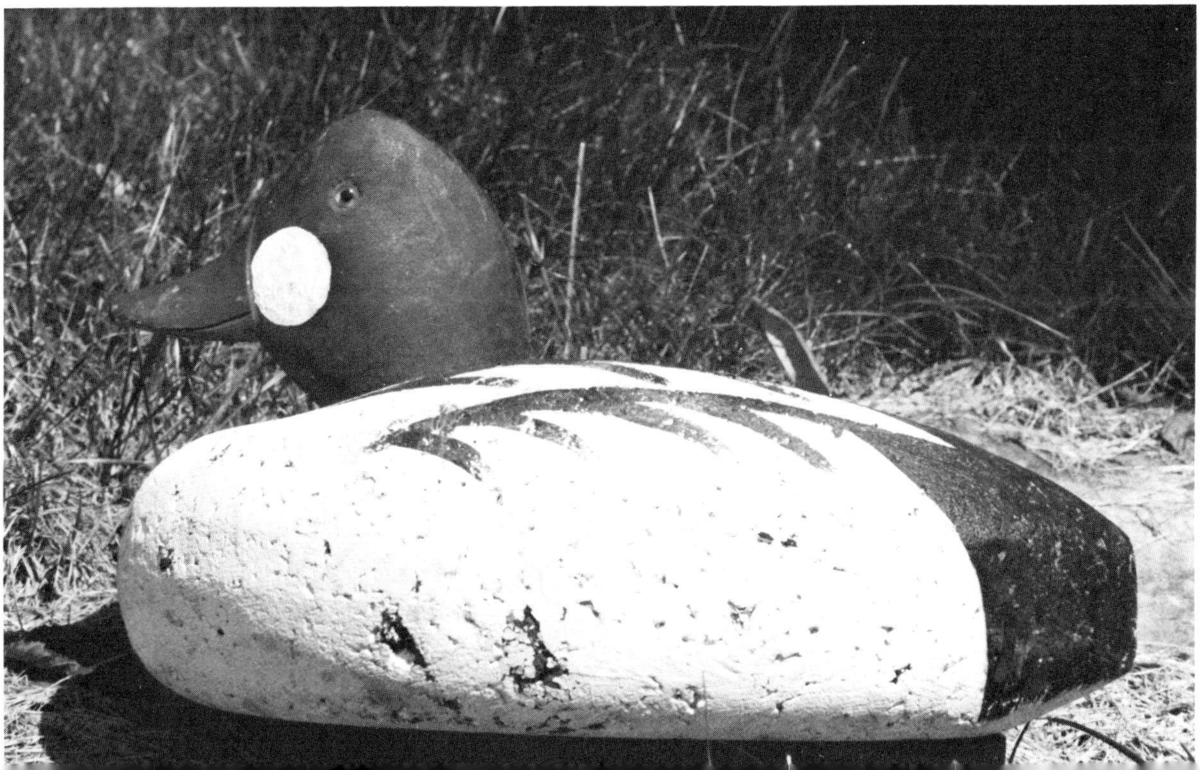

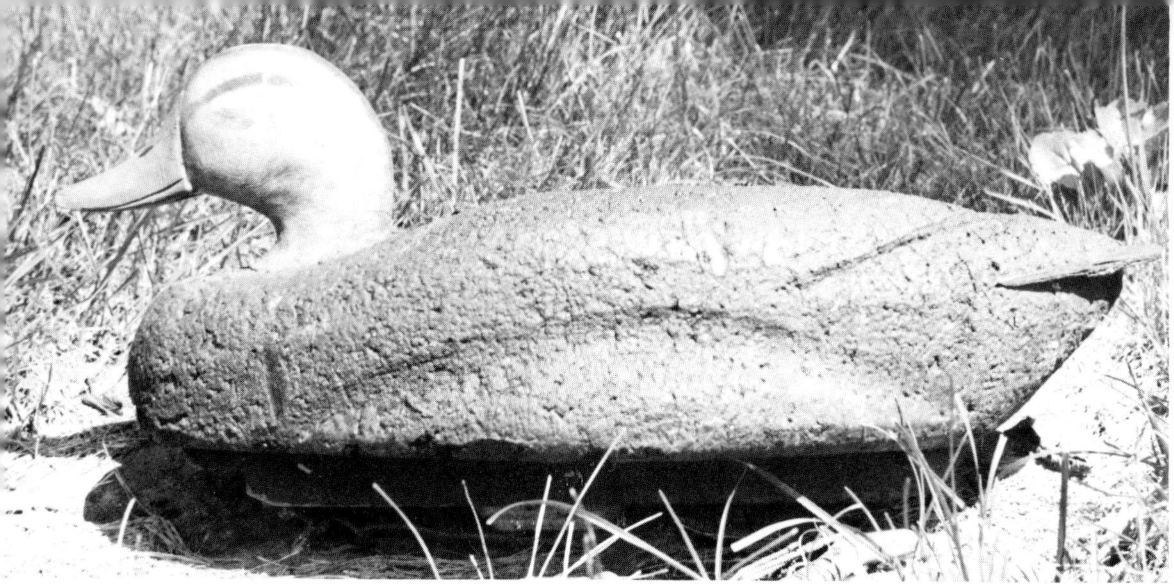

Black duck by Frank Russell, ca. 1972. Cork body, original paint.

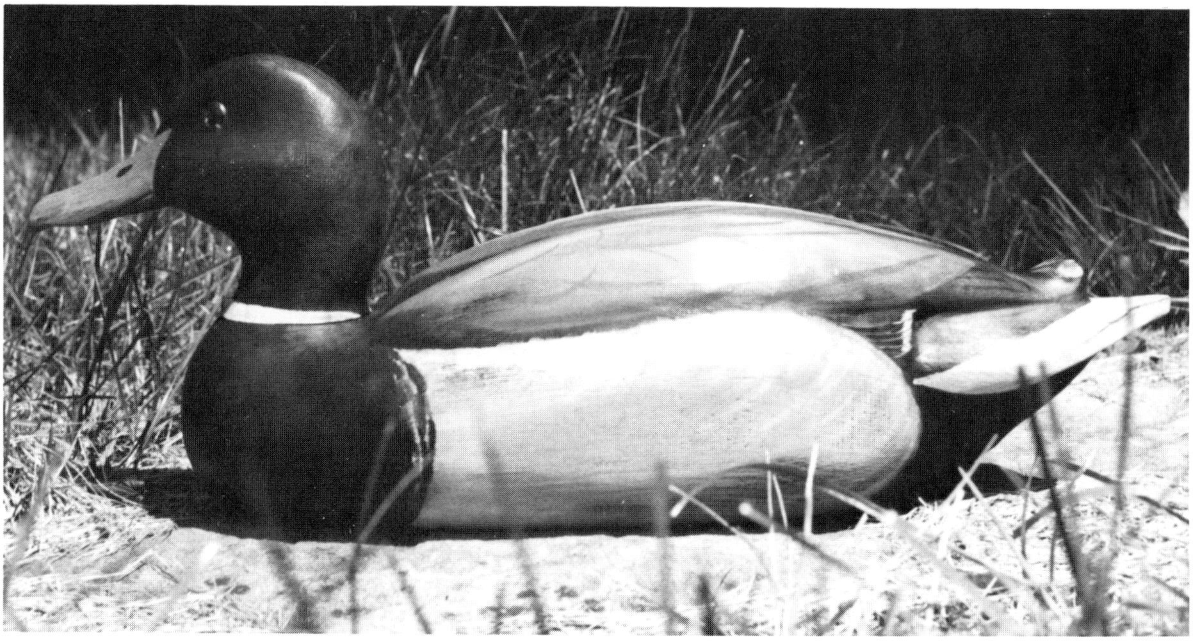

Photograph taken on remains of old Scales boat blind at Point Au Fer; the site of a British military post during the revolutionary war.

Mallard drake by Frank Russell ca. 1980. Original paint.

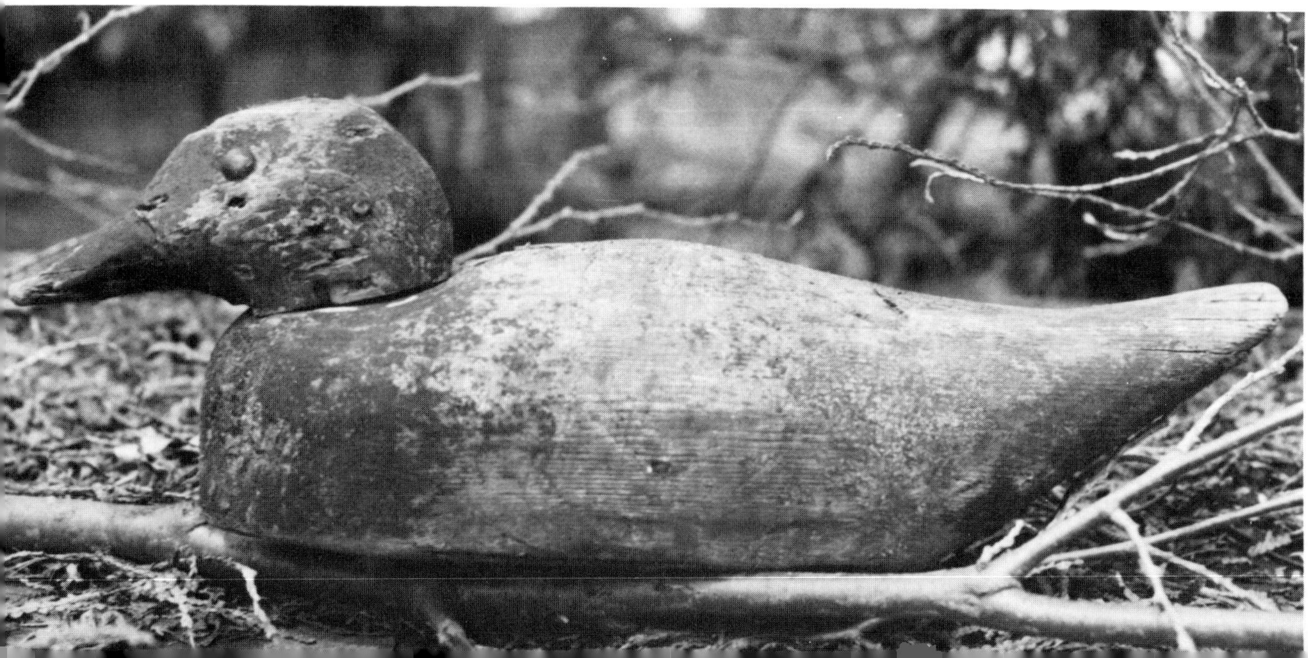

Arnold "Buck" Scales 1895-1966. Point Au Fer, New York, ws a guide and commercial hunter who developed a unique floating blind that was featured in a sporting magazine ca. 1930. He carved many functional decoys to hunt on Kings Bay, Lake Champlain.

James Senesak 1953- Isle La Motte, Vermont. Worked as a guide for Raymond Poquette. He carved several dozen goldeneyes.

Goldeneye drake by James Senesak.

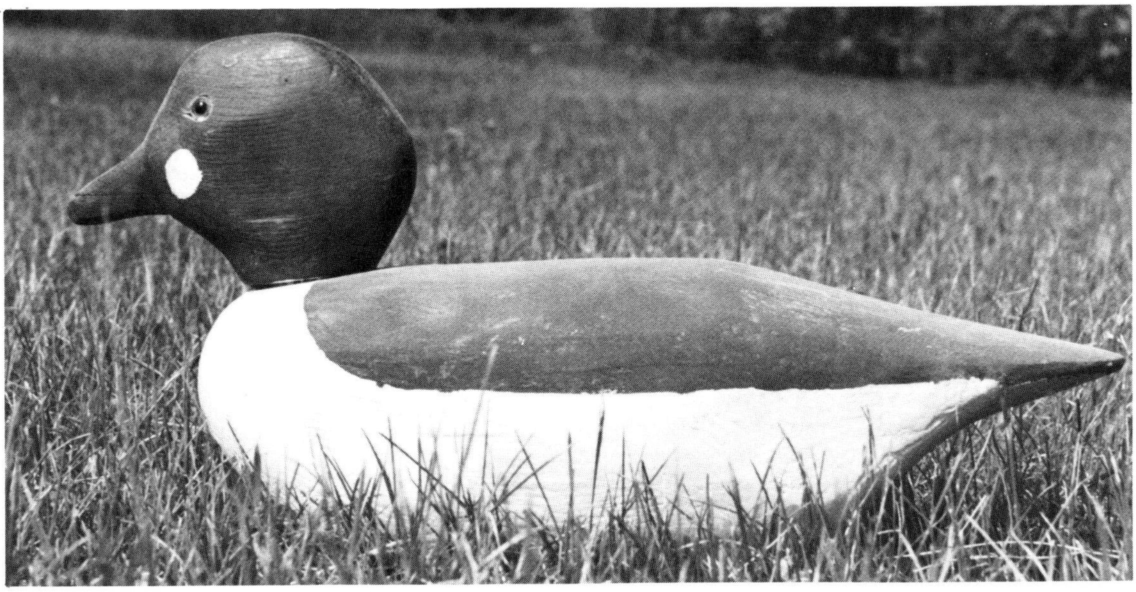

Bradley Sharrow 1927- Burlington, Vermont, now resides on Malletts Bay where he runs Calm Cove Cottages. He began making decoys in 1954 commercially and for his own use. Included were three hundred and fifty cork magnum whistlers with a 3/4" bottom board; one hundred and fifty blacks of cork, pine or spruce, and thirty mallards. Some of his more detailed carvings brought over one hundred dollars from collectors. Sharrow relates a hunting trip in 1968 to the "Colchester fill." A storm came up and he had to abandon his decoys. After the storm was over he could only find seven of his eighty decoys in the rig. His comment was "I guess a lot of people have lamps made from my decoys".

Bradley Sharrow in his workshop, on Malletts Bay, Vermont. 1984.

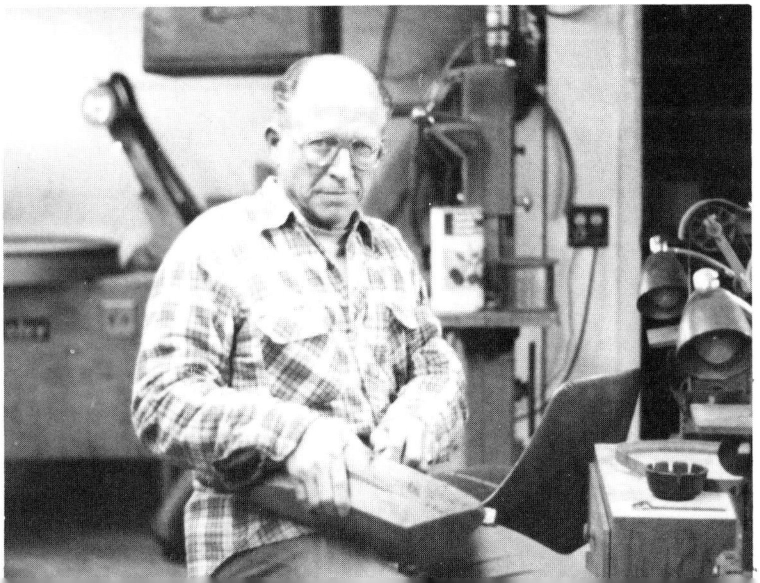

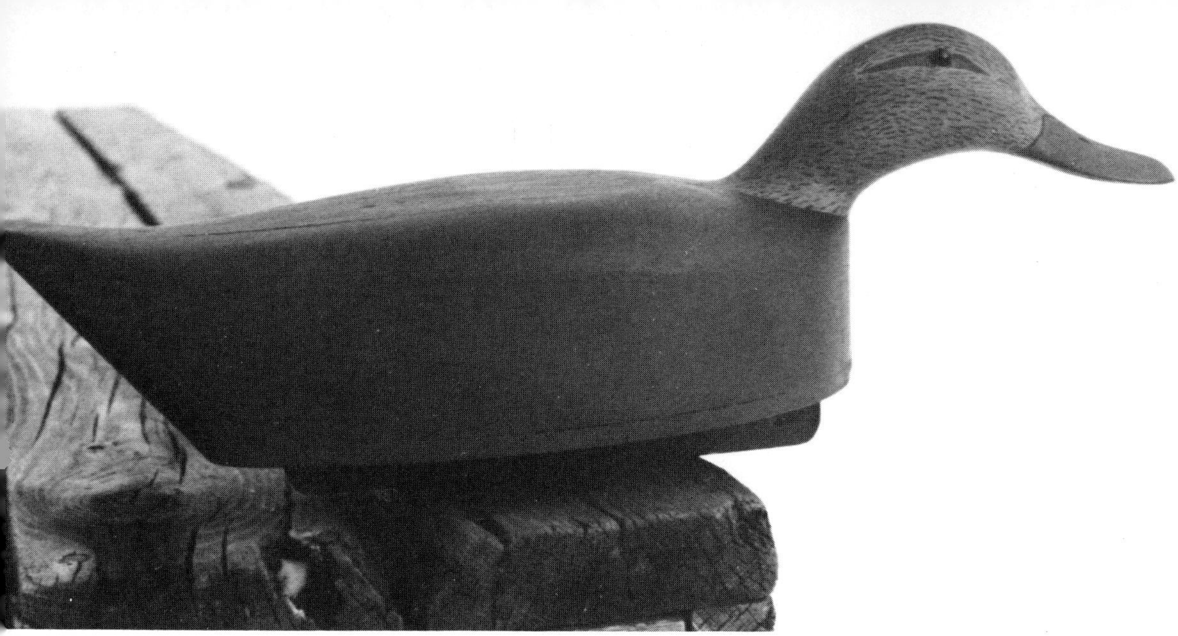

Black duck swimming by Bradley Sharrow ca. 1960. Pine head and body with a keel. Original paint.

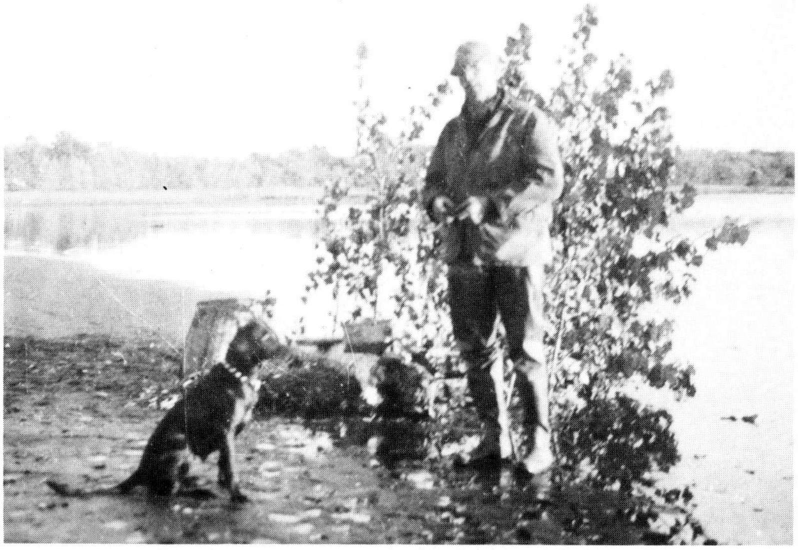

Ralph Thayer with his labrador, "Lady" on the edge of Malletts Bay, Vermont, ca. 1952.

Bluebill by Ralph Thayer ca. 1945. Photographed at Thayer Beach, Malletts Bay, Vermont.

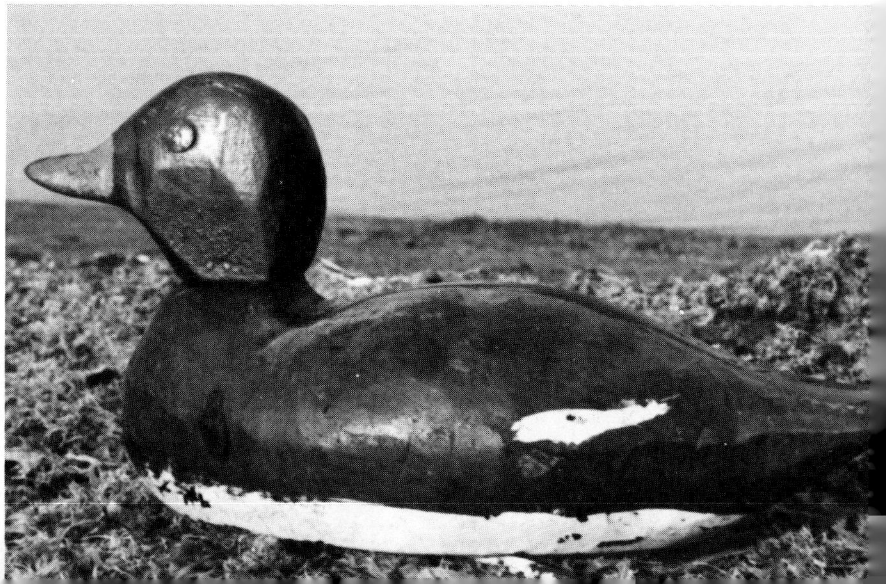

George Thompson Sr. 1921-. **George Thompson Jr.** 1945-. Charlotte, Vermont. This father and son team are well known and respected Vermont hunters. The senior member carved almost one hundred decoys, all whistlers which are very stylized. His son carved almost three hundred decoys, including blacks, whistlers, bluebills and geese. Most of their decoys are still used along Lake Champlain, especially in the Addison, Otter Creek area.

Ralph Thayer 1903-1970 Burlington, Vermont, was a carpenter and boat builder. He was a friend of Charles Kirby and often "compared notes" with him regarding boat and decoy making. Thayer made over fifty bluebills in the 1940's. He hunted at the mouth of the Lamoille River in Malletts Bay.

Black duck decoy by George Thompson Jr. Cork body, pine head. Ca. 1970.

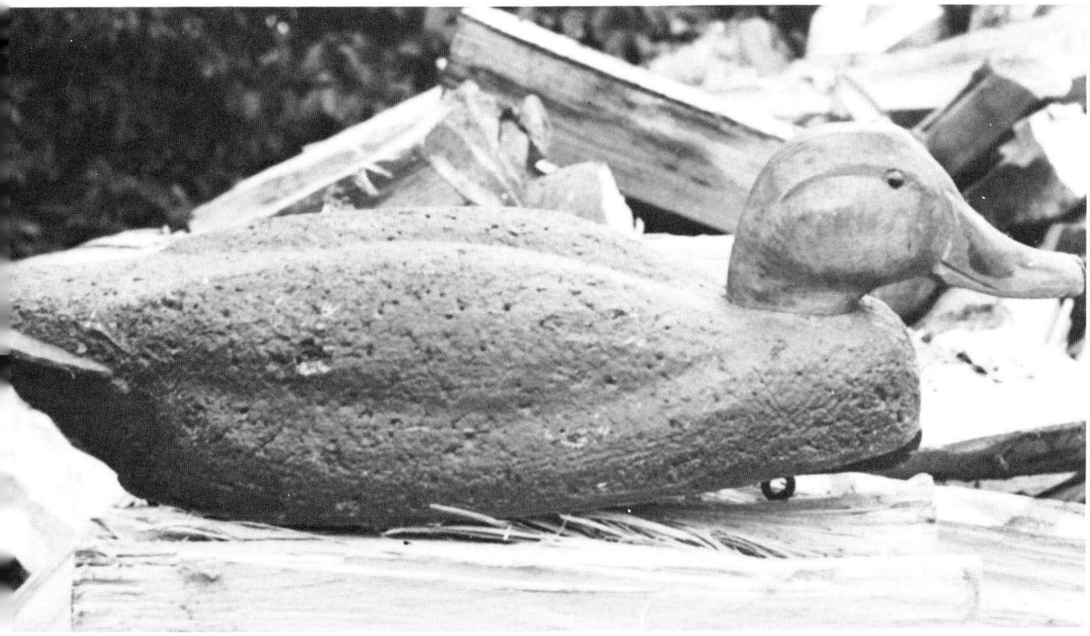

Whistler drake by George Thompson Sr. Cedar construction with relief wing and tail carving, carved and painted eyes.

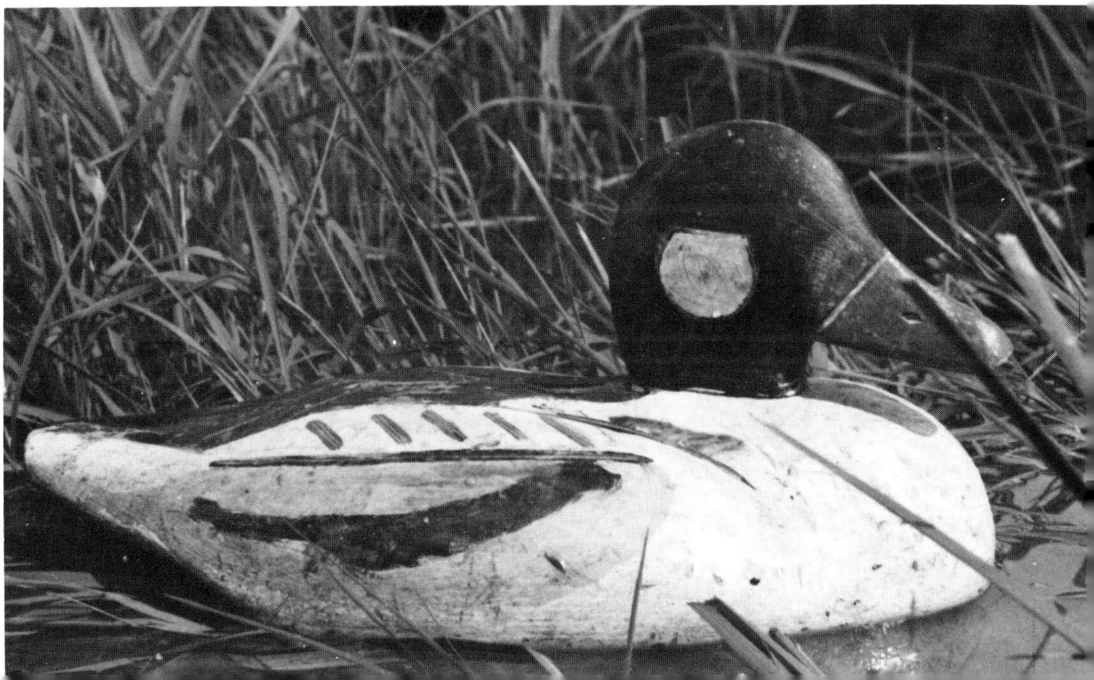

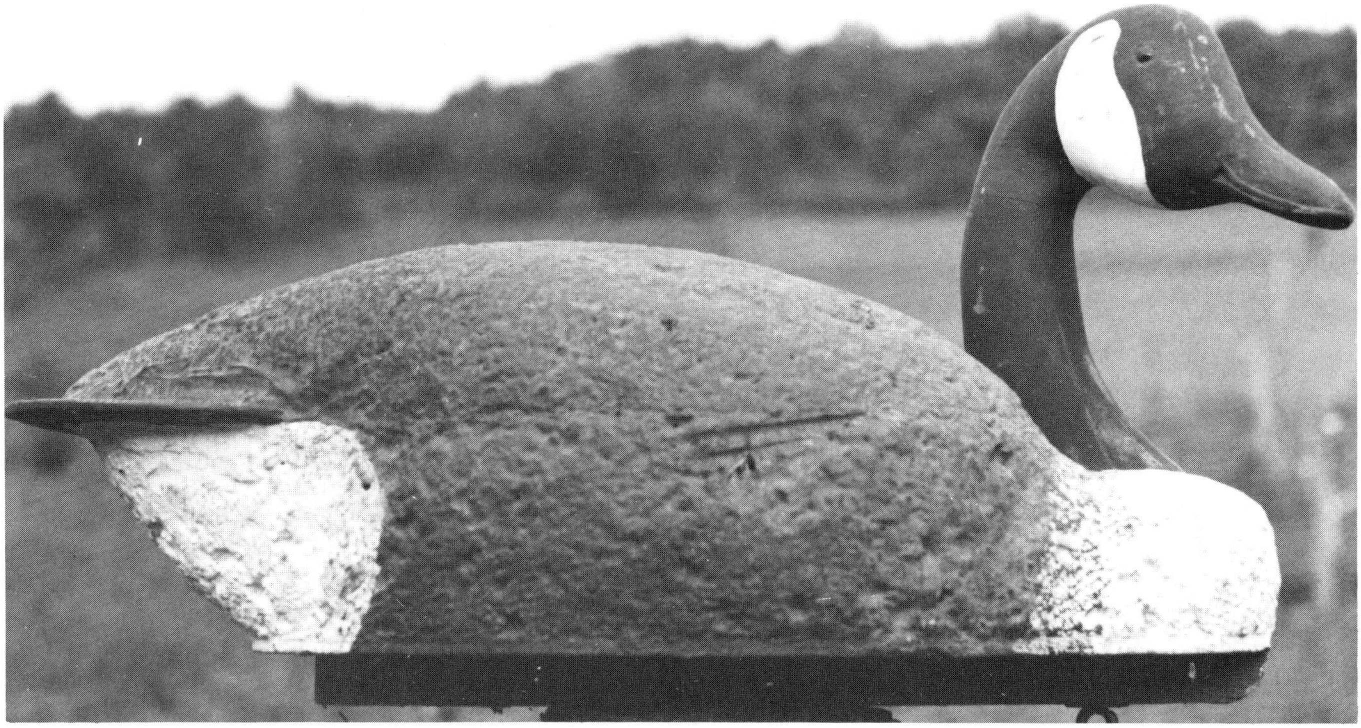

Canada goose decoy by George Thompson Jr. Cork body, pine head, leaded keel. Used as a floater.

Arthur Toutant 1929- South Burlington, Vermont. Is one of the "Old time carvers and collectors". He has hunted with all the name gunners in Vermont and used his decoys for almost thirty years. Toutant carved on a semi-commercial basis, selling rigs of whistlers and blacks to local hunters. He and Brad Sharrow also experimented with molded decoys. Toutant has an extensive collection of decoys by local carvers.

Whistler decoy by Arthur Toutant ca. 1955. Cork body, pine head with tack eyes. Background is view of Mt. Mansfield, Vermont.

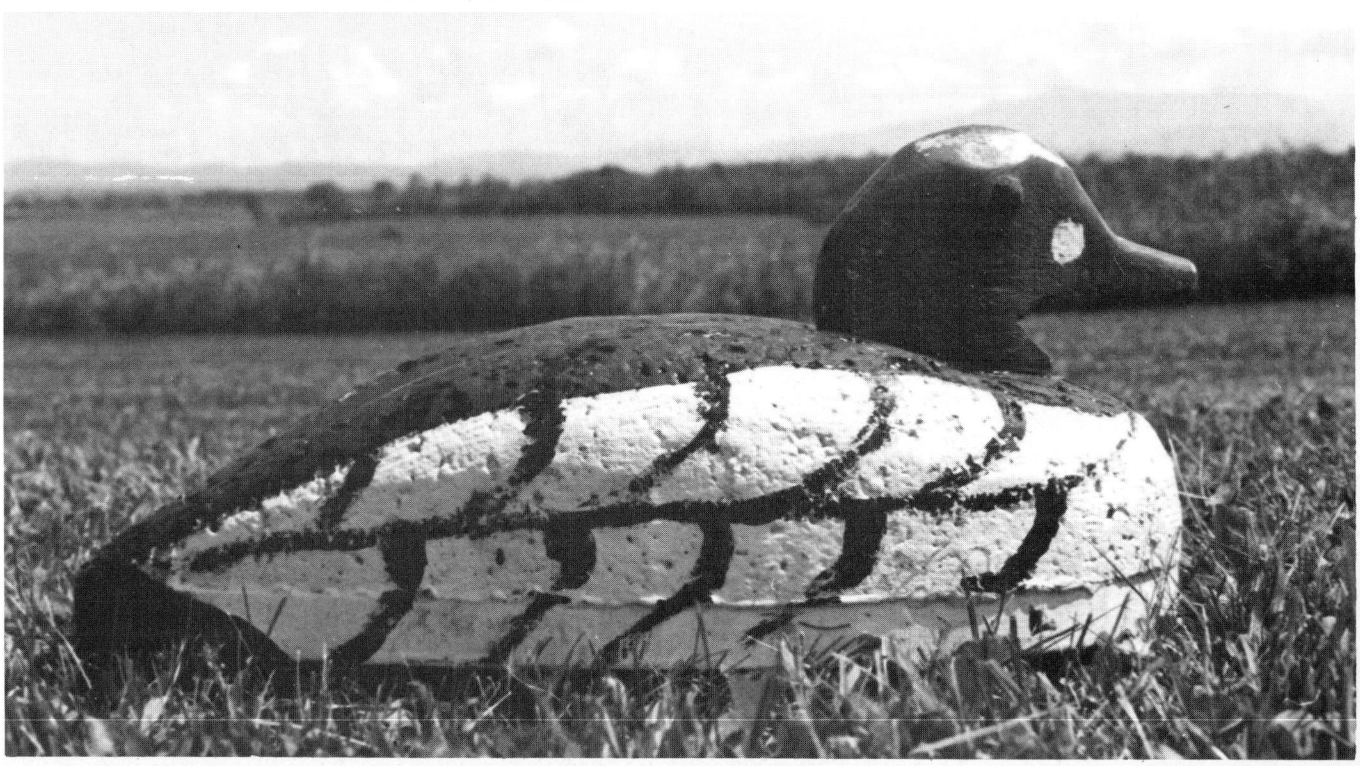

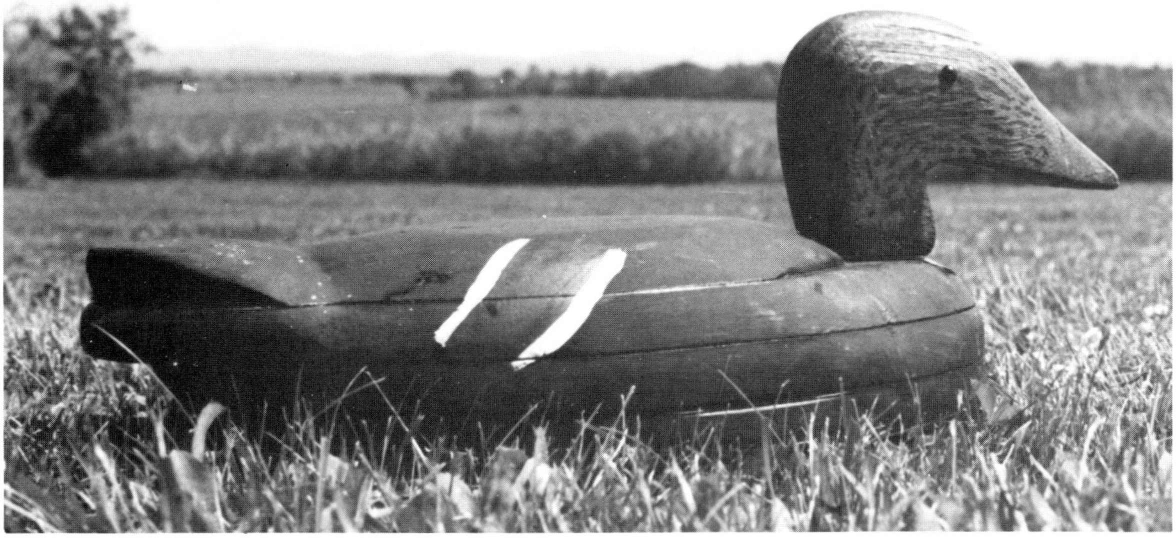

Black duck by Arthur Toutant ca. 1950. Laminated pine construction.

Gerald Tremblay 1918- Alburg Springs, Vermont, was no doubt the most prolific decoy carver on Lake Champlain. He claims to have made "five thousand plus or minus one or two". He states he has carved "every duck that flew through Vermont i.e. seventeen different varieties". Tremblays earlier birds were narrow with pinched breast-form. He later changed, especially the diving ducks, to give them a wider, not so thick appearance. All his decoys are "chip carved to simulate feathers". Some decoys have relief wing carving and his miniatures are made in detail. Tremblay sold thousands of working decoys to hunters and miniatures to shops throughout the country, including Saks Fifth Avenue. His carving began in 1938 as the "mother of invention" after he had lost the use of his legs because of poliomyelitis at age three. Tremblay put away his carving tools in 1977.

Goldeneye hen by Gerald Tremblay ca. 1944. Three pairs of these goldeneyes were made for Gilbert Bohannon's birthday, 1944. They are branded "G.B." Original paint signed by Tremblay. Collection of Loy S. Harrell.

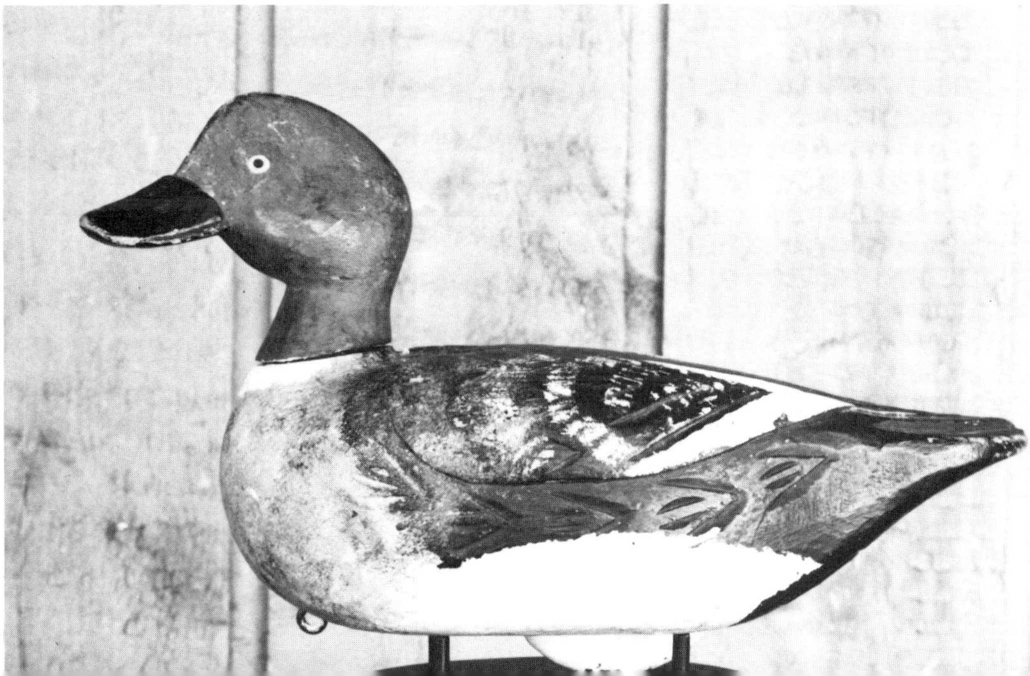

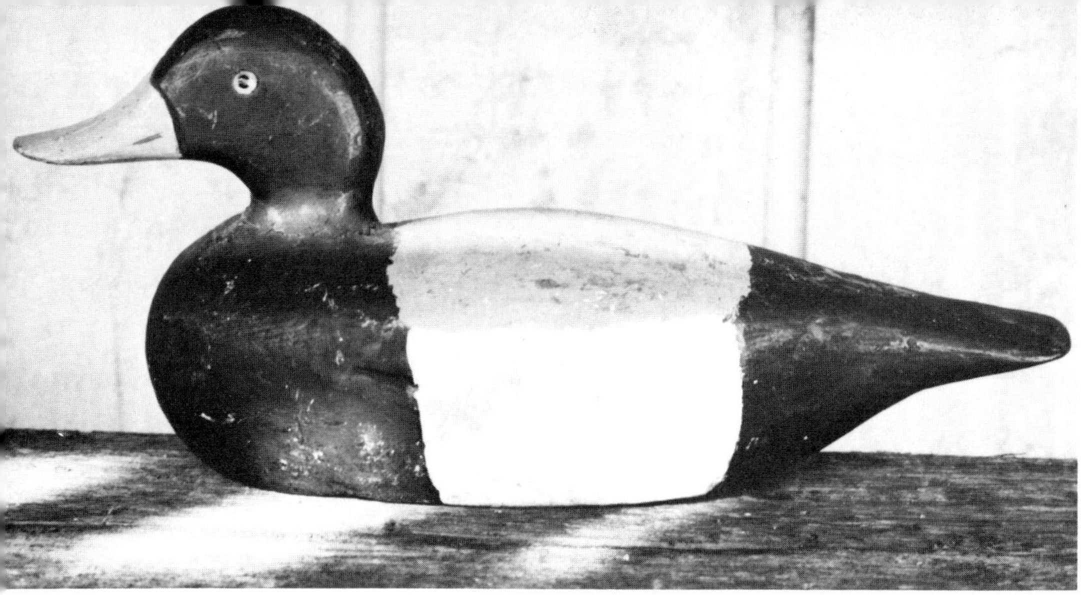

Bluebill by Gerald Tremblay ca. 1955. Glass eyes, chip carved. Old repaint.

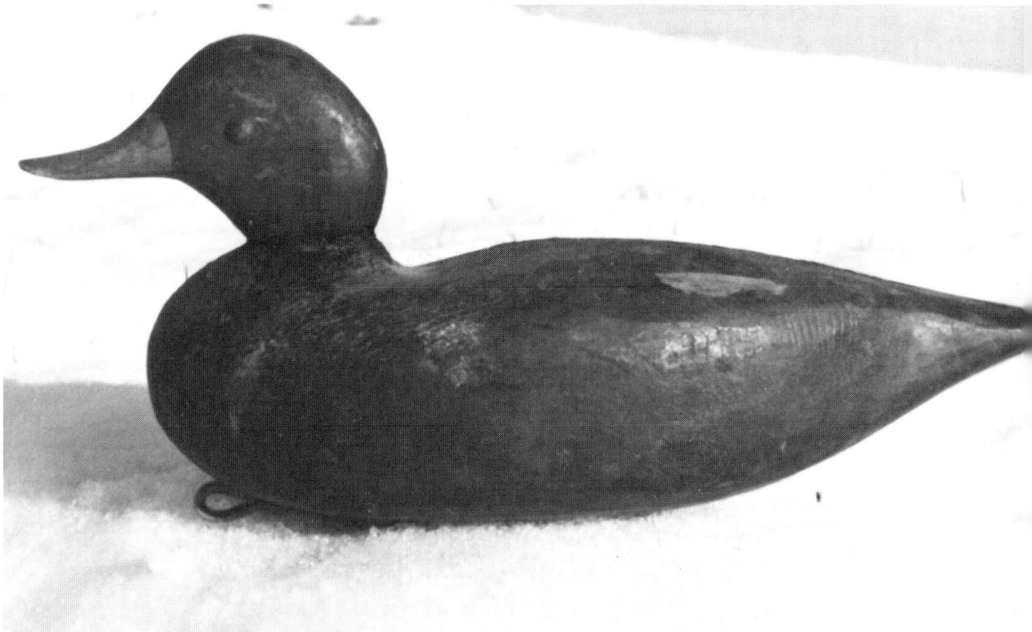

Bluebill by Gerald Tremblay ca. 1955. Collection of Daniel Beauregard.

Black duck decoy by Gerald Tremblay ca. 1940. From rig of Russell Merriman.

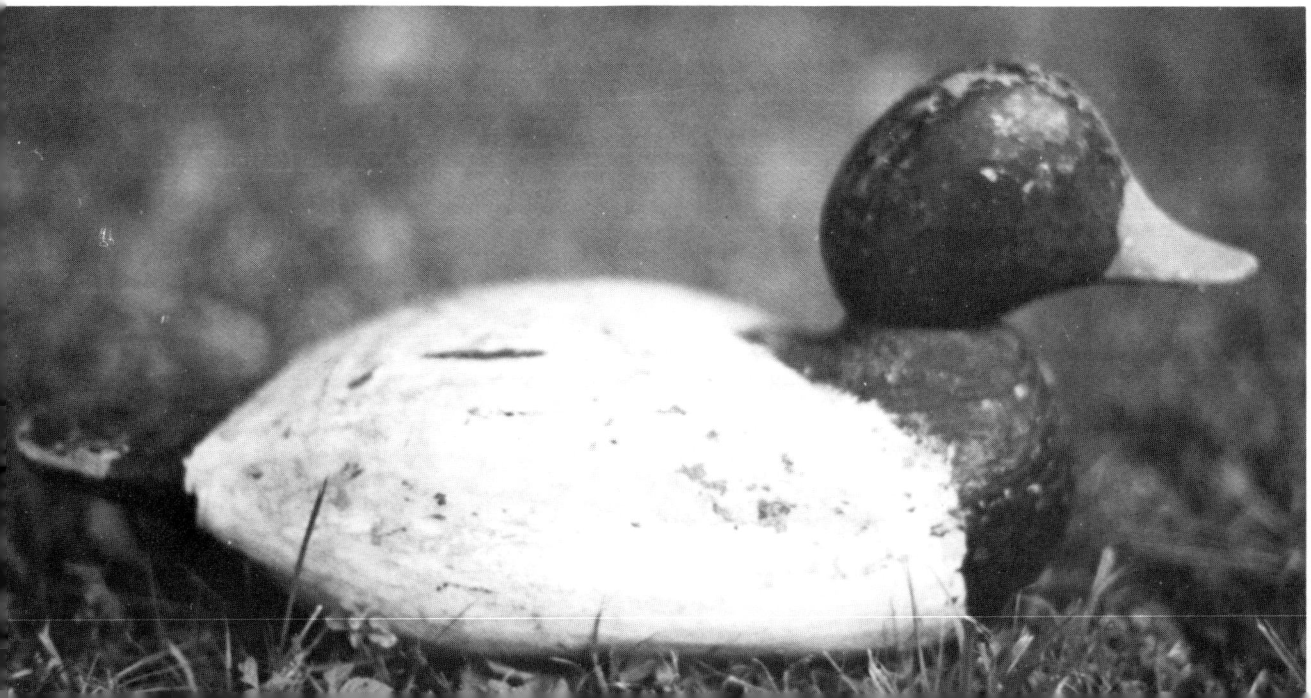

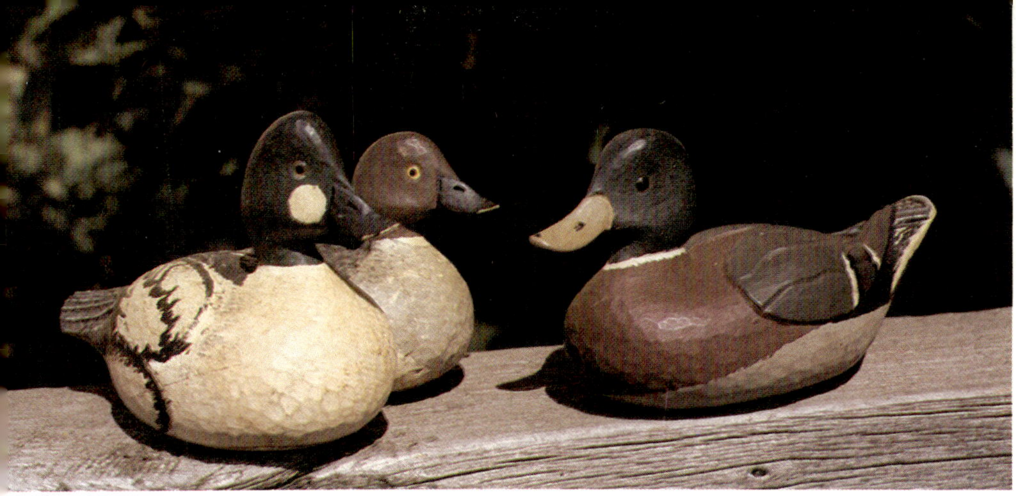

Mallard drake and pair of goldeneye miniatures by Gerald Tremblay. Ca. 1970. Both of these decoys along with others were auctioned by R. Oliver, Kennebunk, Maine in 1985. The mallard is labeled "G. Tremblay Carvings. Alburg Springs, Vermont." The goldeneyes are carved attached in a heart shape and were sent by Tremblay to "My valentine Dorothy 1972" and so marked on the bottom. Collection of Loy S. Harrell.

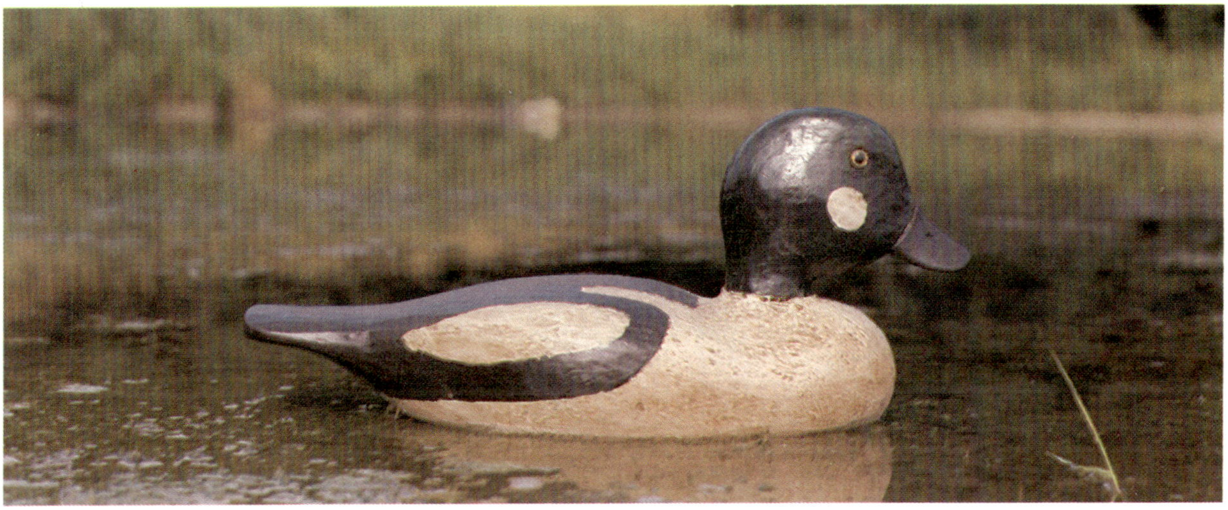

Goldeneye drake by Gerald Tremblay ca. 1942. Purchased unpainted from Tremblay by Raoul Beaulieu. Painted by his son, Richard Beaulieu, former chief of police, Burlington, Vermont.

Green wing teal by Gerald Tremblay. Original paint and signed by Tremblay. Collection of David Hoag.

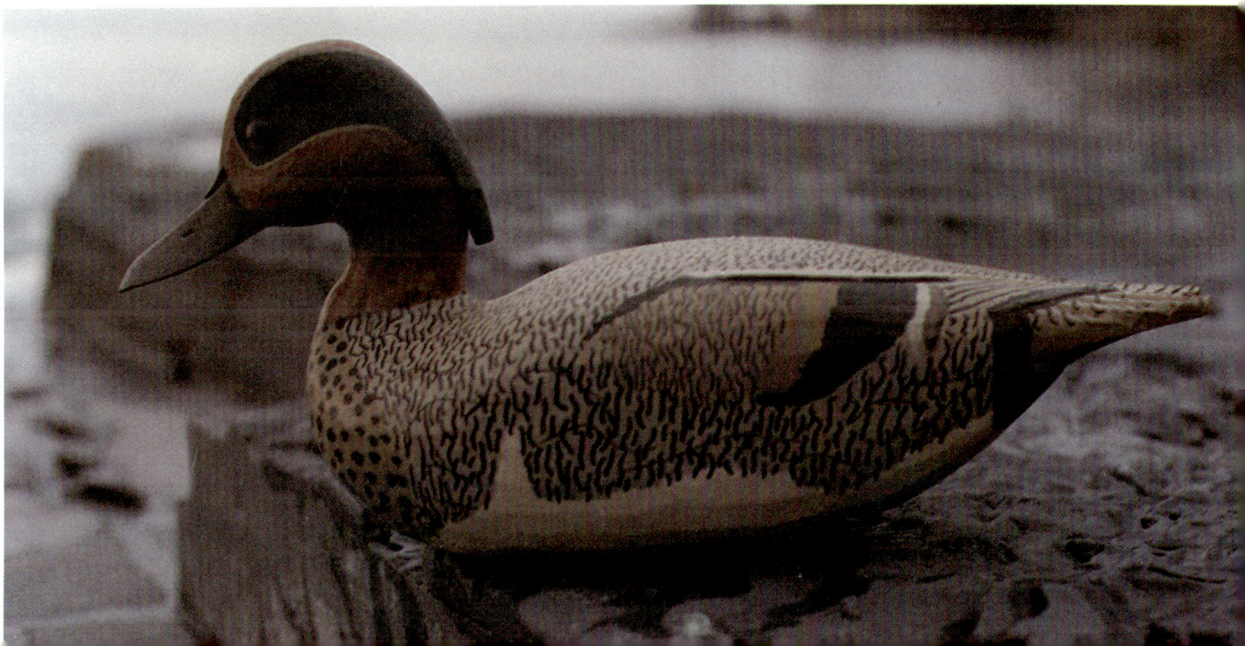

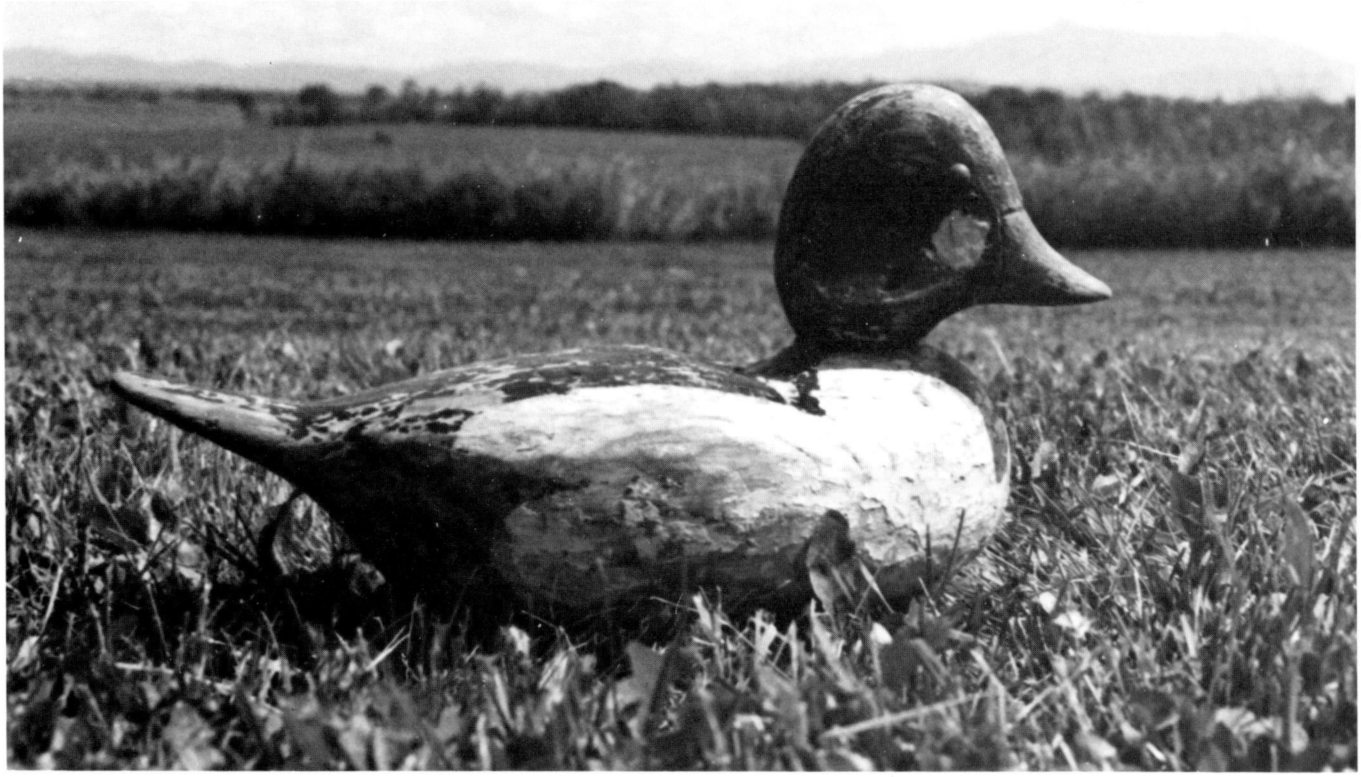

Goldeneye by Gerald Tremblay ca. 1940. Tack eyes. Collection of A. Toutant.

Whistler hen by Gerald Tremblay ca. 1942. Over four hundred of these decoys were purchased from Tremblay by the Beaulieu family during the 1940's.

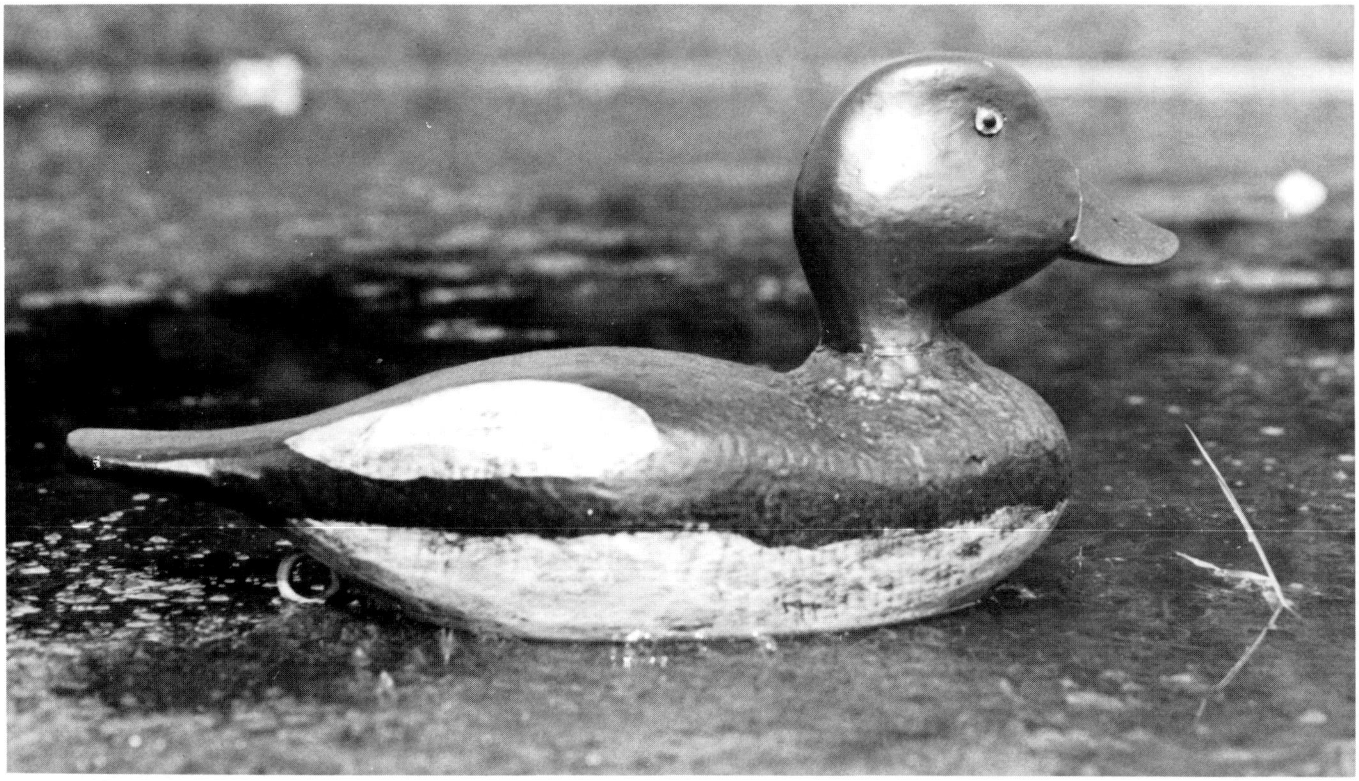

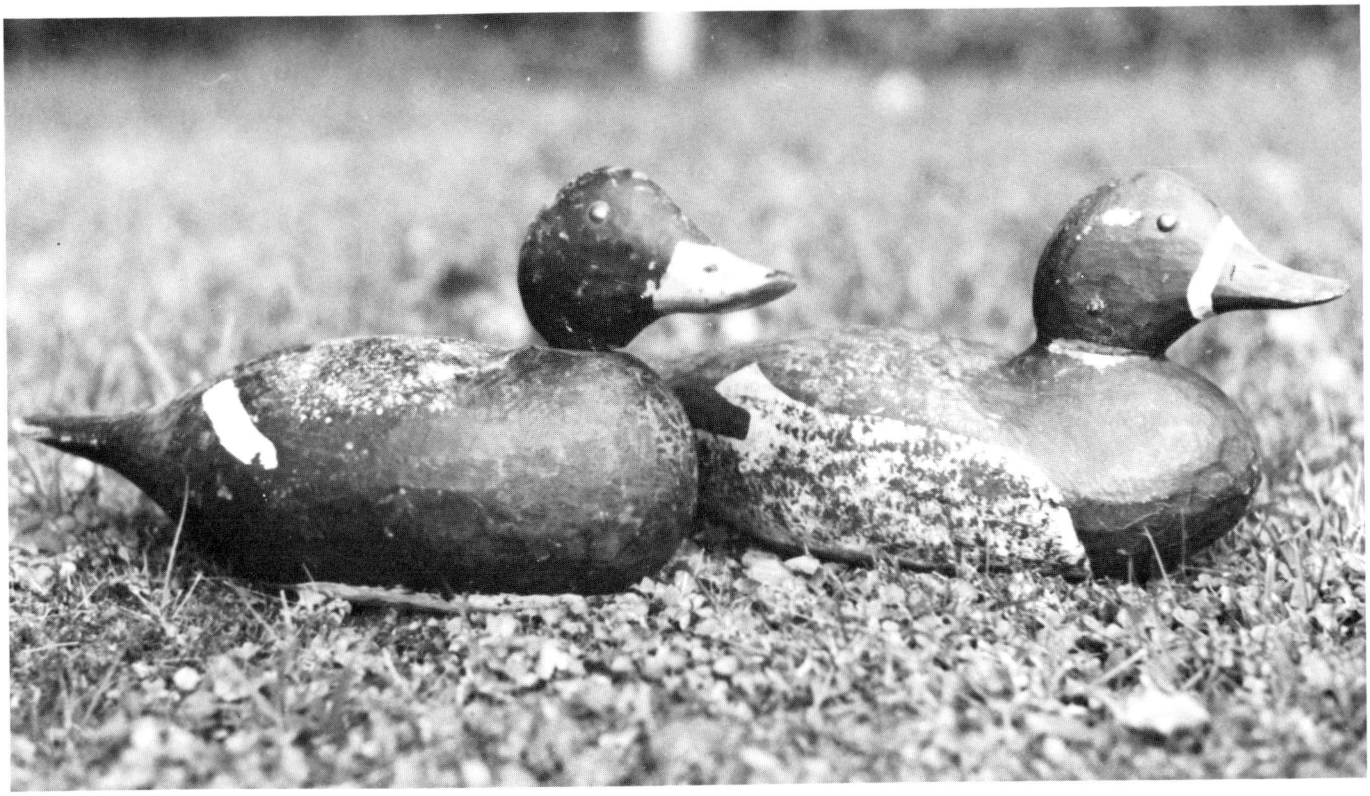

Pair of G. Tremblay bluebills. Tack eyes. Ca. 1950. Collection of Daniel Beauregard

Goldeneye by Gerald Tremblay ca. 1939. Old repaint. Tack eyes-from rig of Daniel Beauregard.

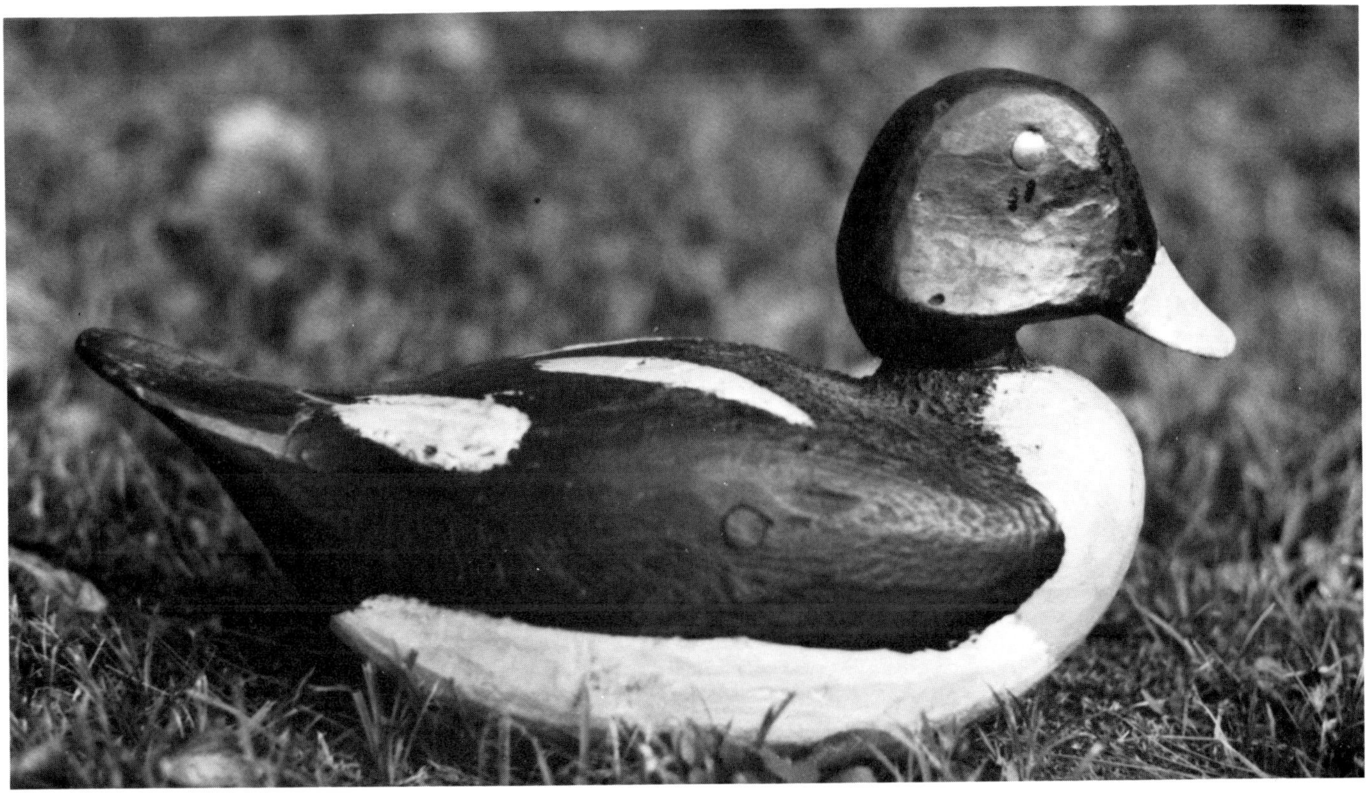

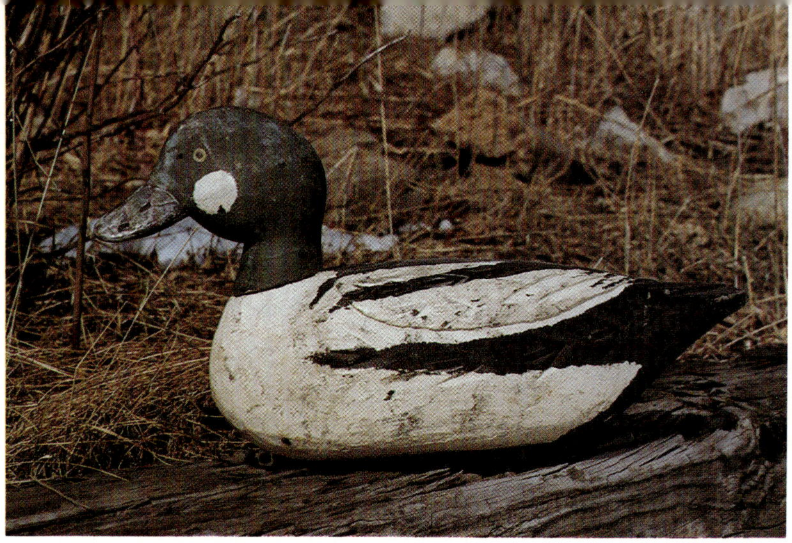

Goldeneye drake by Gerald Tremblay ca. 1944. Branded "G.B." From the collection of Marie Bohannon.

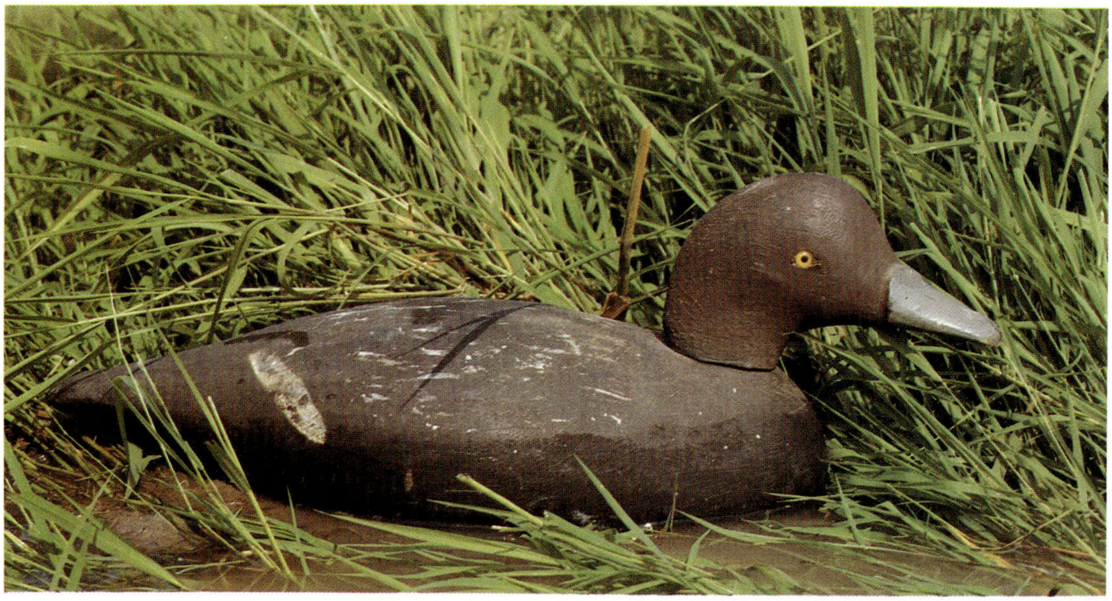

Redhead decoy attributed to Dr. Abernathy, Belvedere, Vermont. Ca. 1945. From the collection of Herbert Prakelt.

Pair of Canada goose decoy floaters from St. Albans, Vermont. Ca. 1940. Collection of David Hoag.

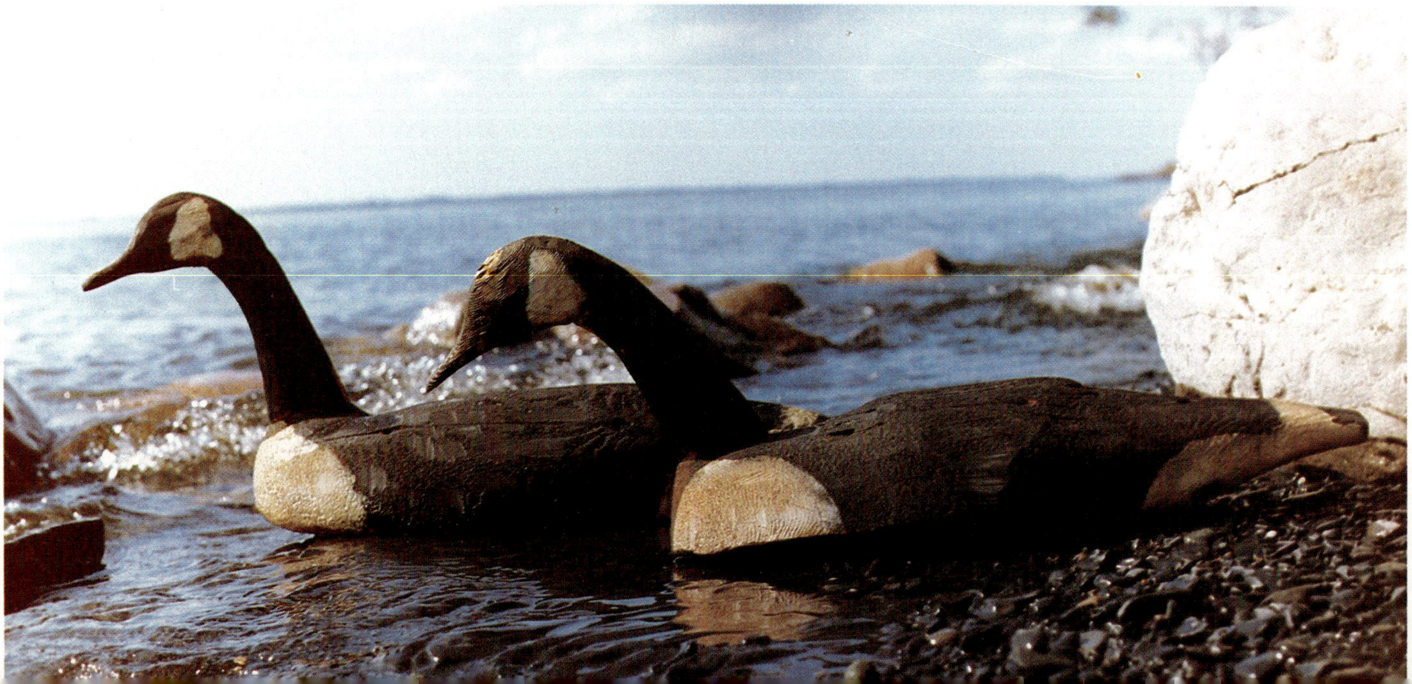

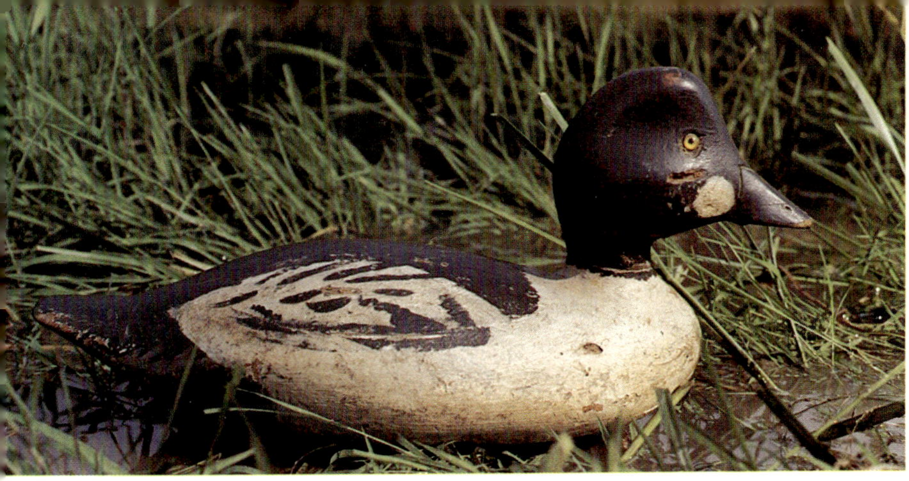

Goldeneye decoy from Henry Salls, Frank Gage rig. One of twenty three decoys found in Gage home, Burlington, Vermont. Included were decoys by Mason, Bacon, Gus Wilson and Frank Owen. This decoy is signed A.G. Fournier. Ca. 1910.

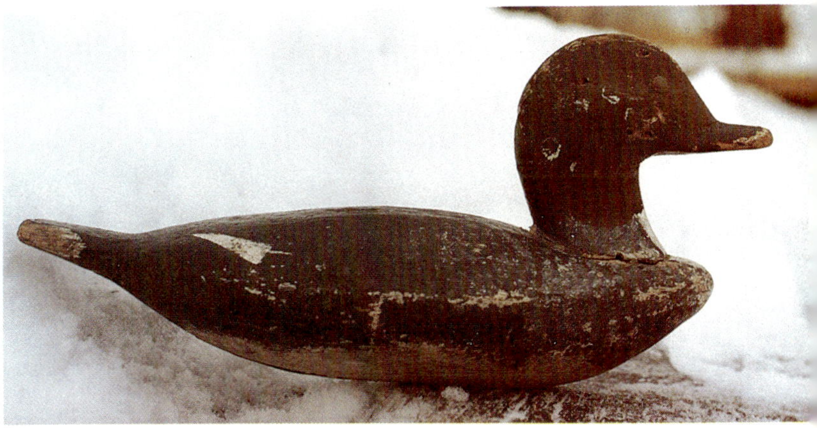

Goldeneye hen from the "Islands" ca. 1910. Original paint, tack eye. From the Paul Casson collection.

Bottom view of Mason bluebills ca. 1890. All marked "W.S. Phelps Sporting Goods". Phelps was located (ca. 1888-1900) on Church Street, Burlington, Vermont. (A truly wonderful find).

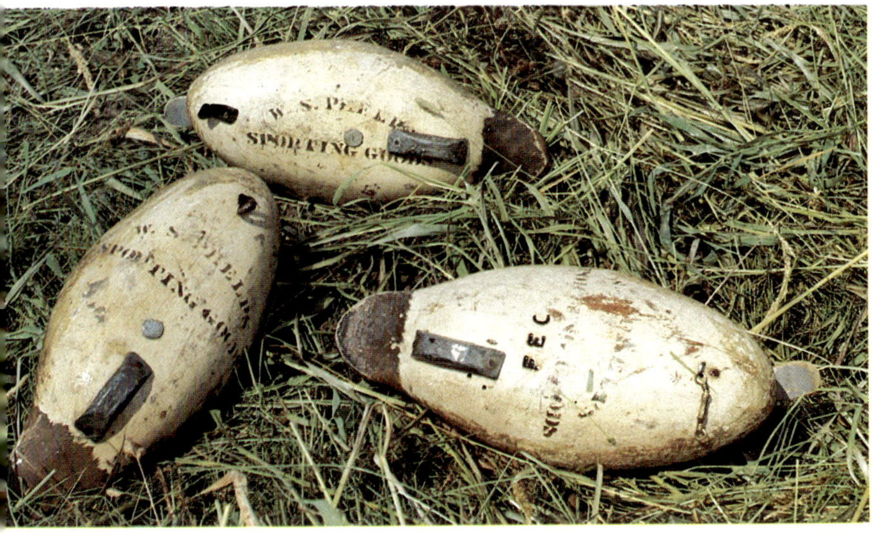

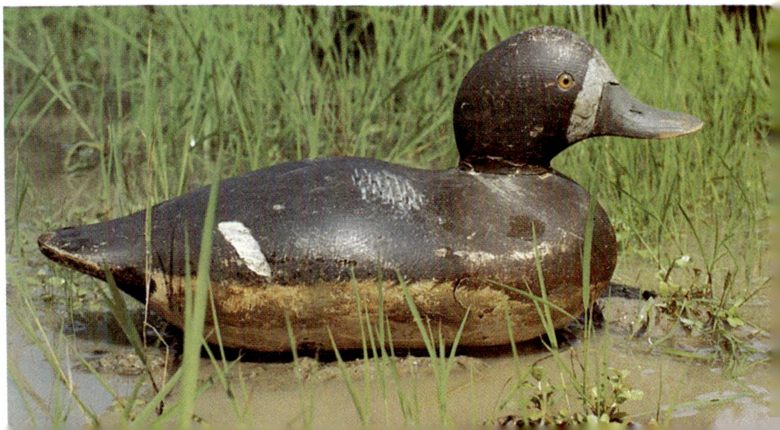

Mason challenge grade bluebill. One of three found with Frank Gage rig, Colchester, Vermont. These are early (ca. 1890) slope breasted style. Each are marked "W.S. Phelps Sporting Goods". Collection of Loy S. Harrell III.

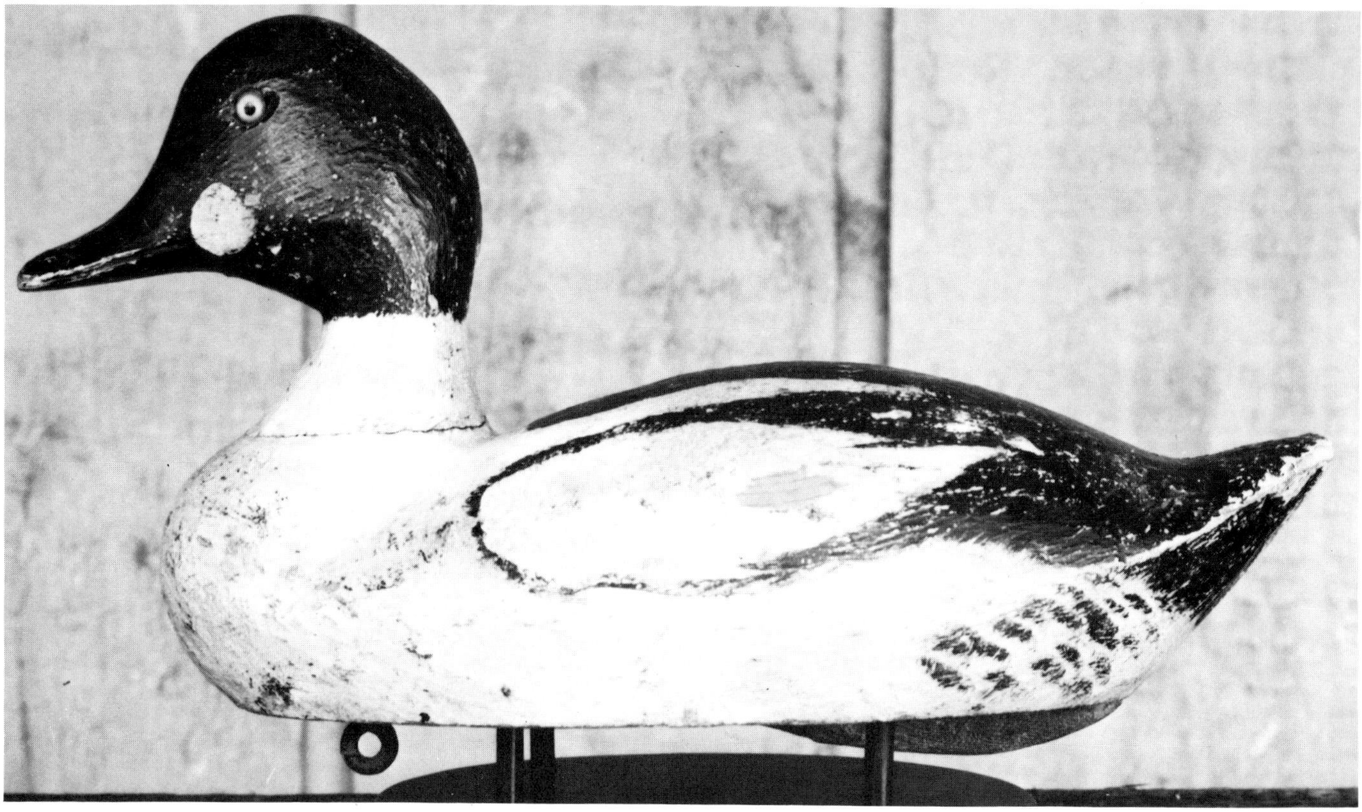

Goldeneye drake, original paint. Part of Henry Salls rig. Ca. 1910. From Swanton, Vermont area.

Whistler drake purchased by George Spear "from a woman in Burlington, Vermont". One of a rig carved by her husband. Ca. 1945.

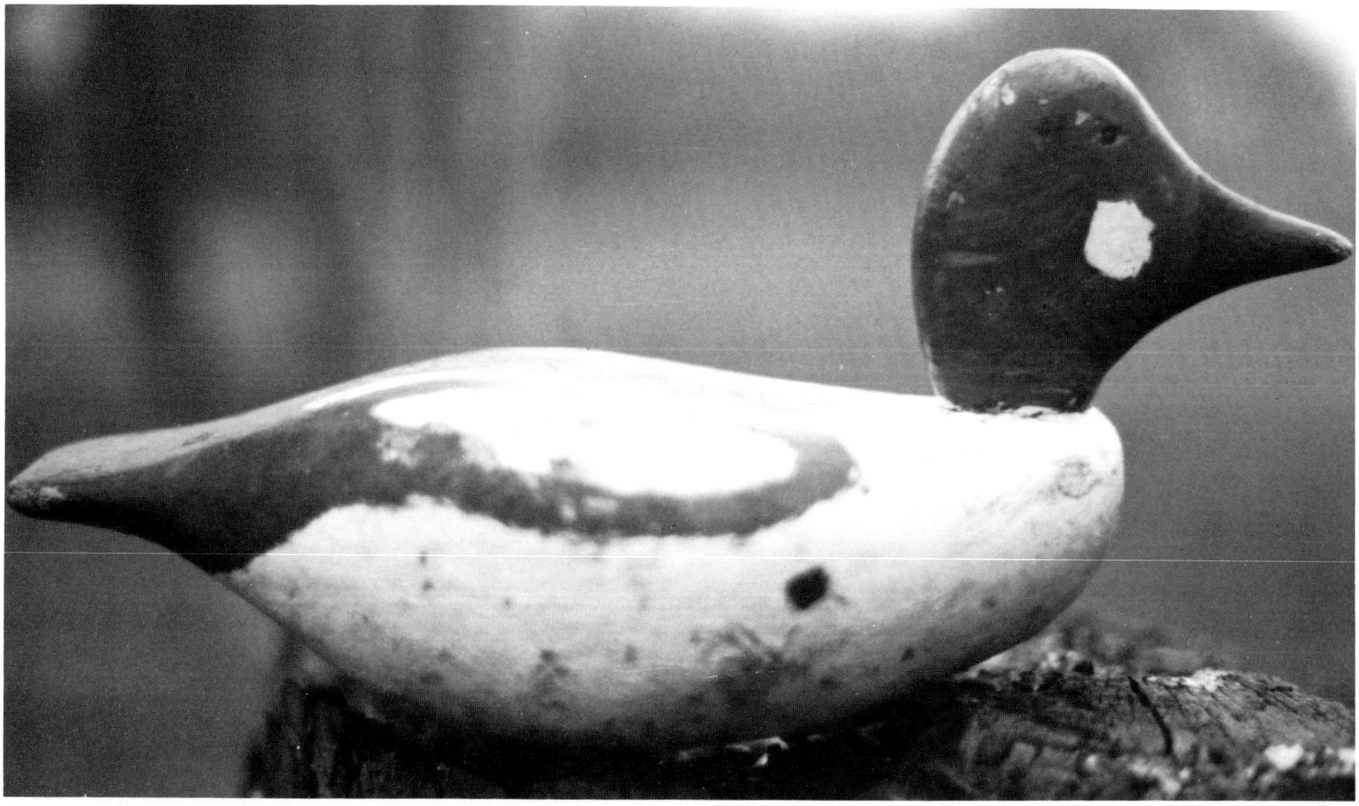

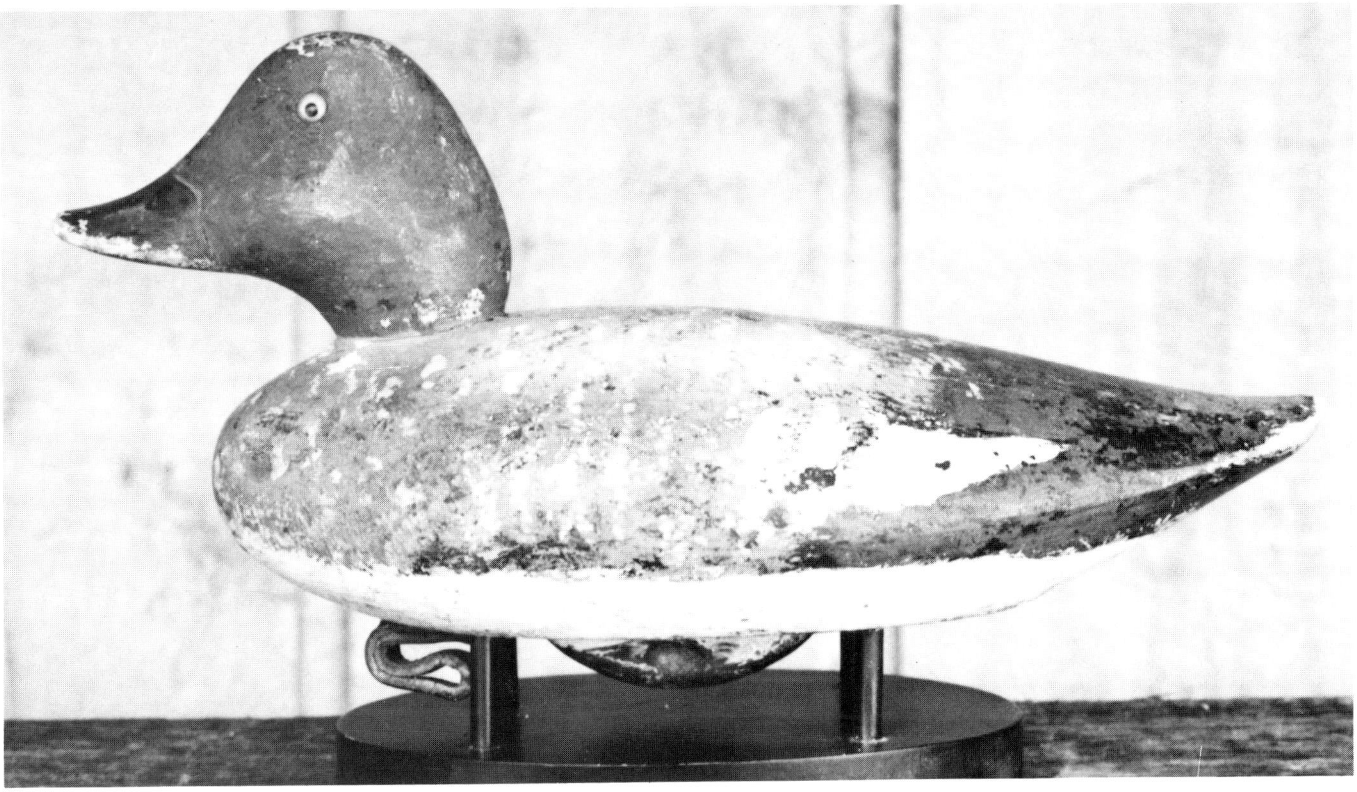

Goldeneye hen from rig of Henry Salls and Frank Gage. Branded "C.E. Irving". Paint is very likely by George Bacon. Ca. 1915.

Goldeneye drake from the rig of Daniel La Pointe, Burlington, Vermont. Purchased from his estate in 1941 by Eugene Luck, M.D. These decoys were painted by George Bacon and are Masons. They were no doubt restored by reshaping the bills and repainting. All the weights are stamped D.L.P. Note the "Bacon" profile.

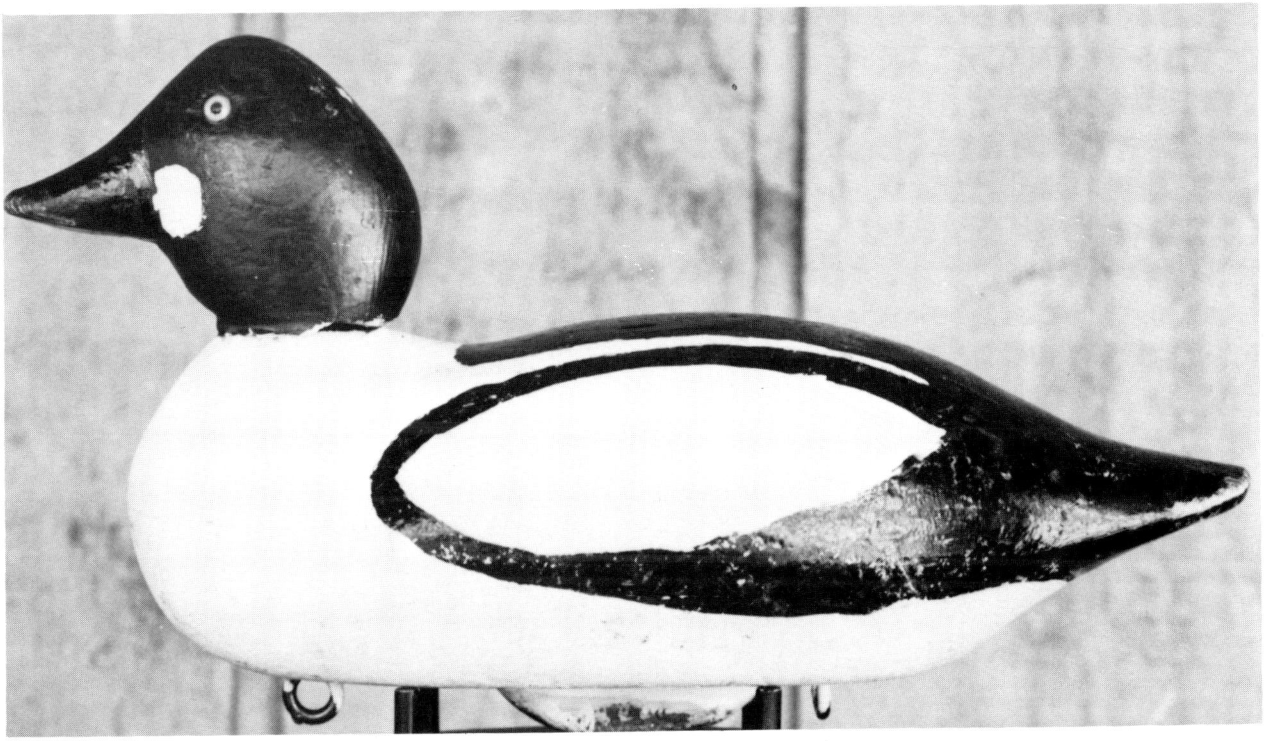

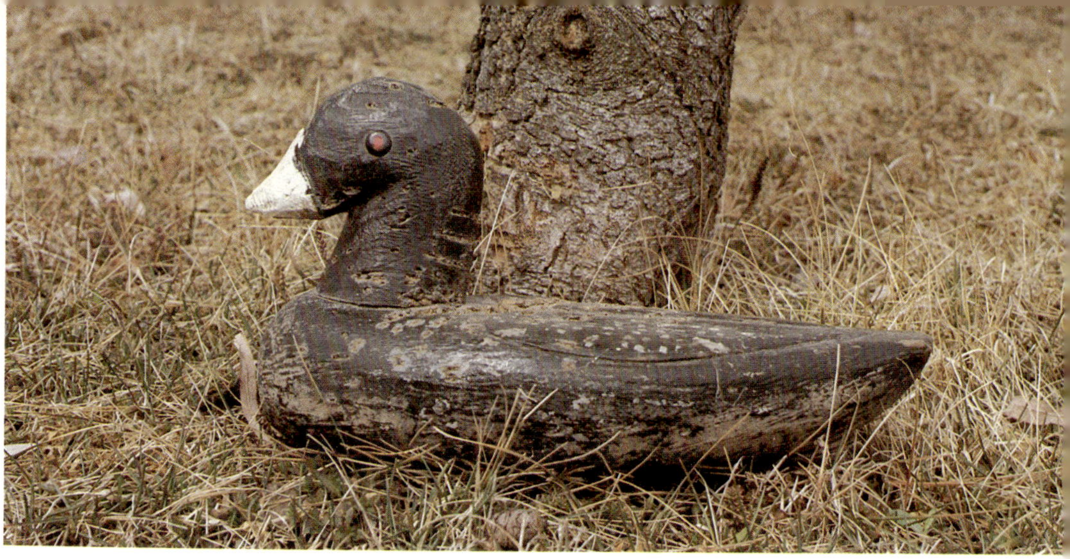

Coot decoy. Ca. 1915 from the Westport, New York Yacht Club. Tack eyes, hit by shot. Rare decoy from the collection of Clarence White.

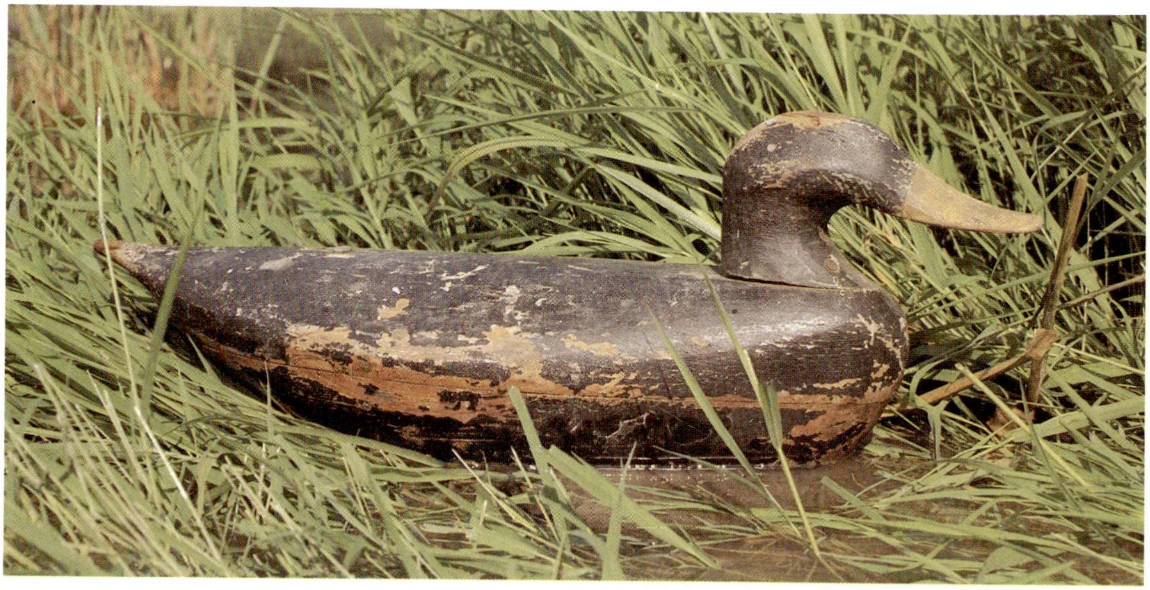

Redhead decoy ca. 1900 found at the Westport, New York Yacht Club. Original worn paint, carved eyes. Hit by shot.

Black duck decoy from Frank Gage rig. Found in 1940 at mouth of Otter Creek, Vermont. Decoy is hollow and held together by two dowels. Original paint.

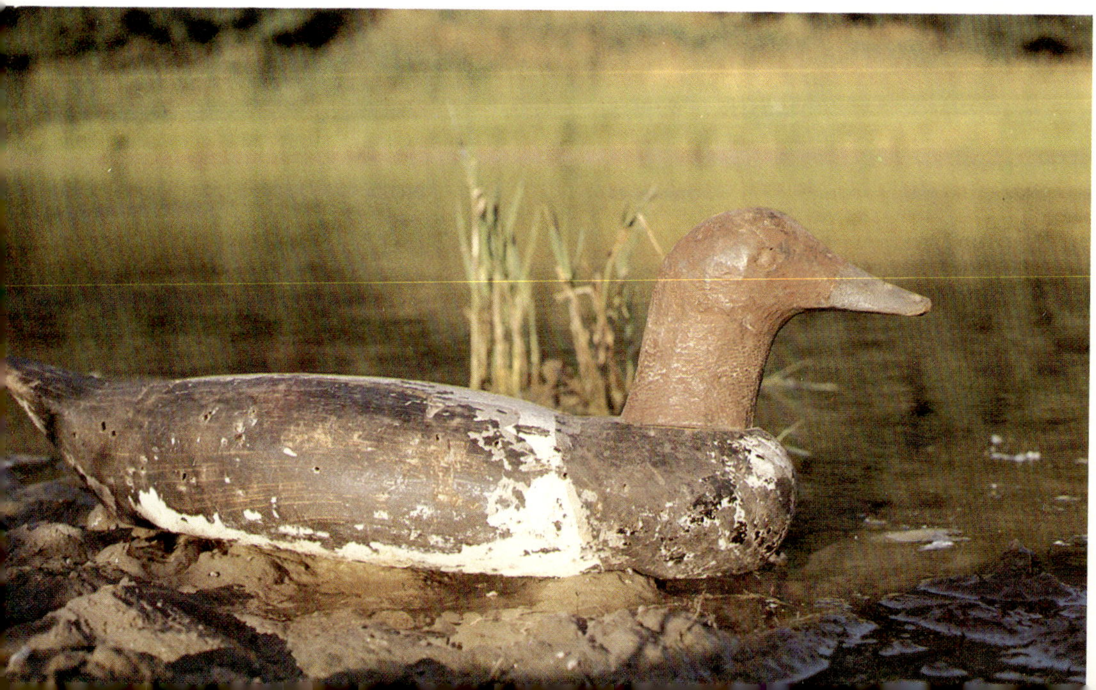

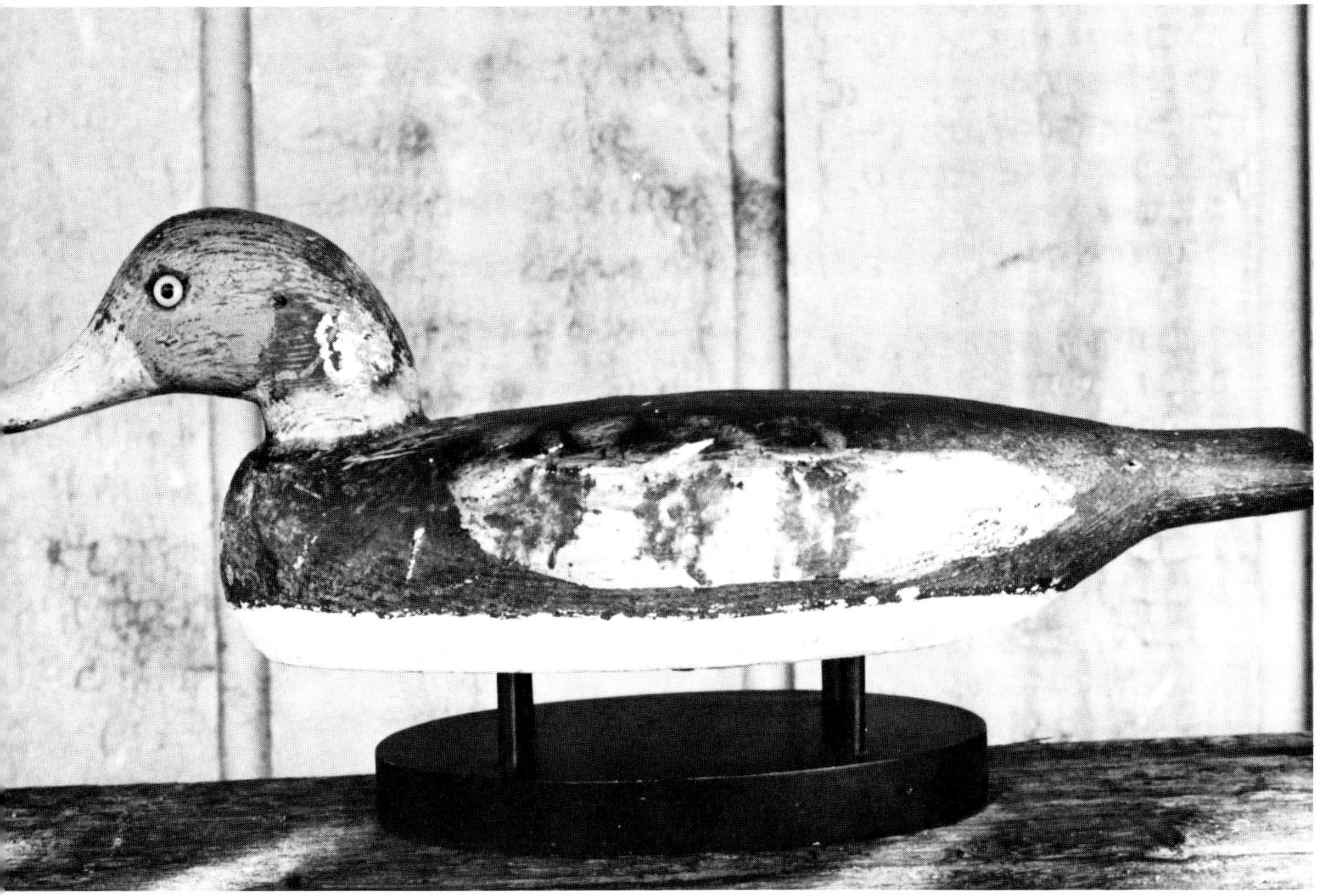

Bluebill decoy found in Charlotte, Vermont. Head resembles Bacon's work. Ca. 1920.

Goldeneye hen by Merritt Vantine, Grand Isle, Vermont. Ca. 1935. Collection of David Hoag.

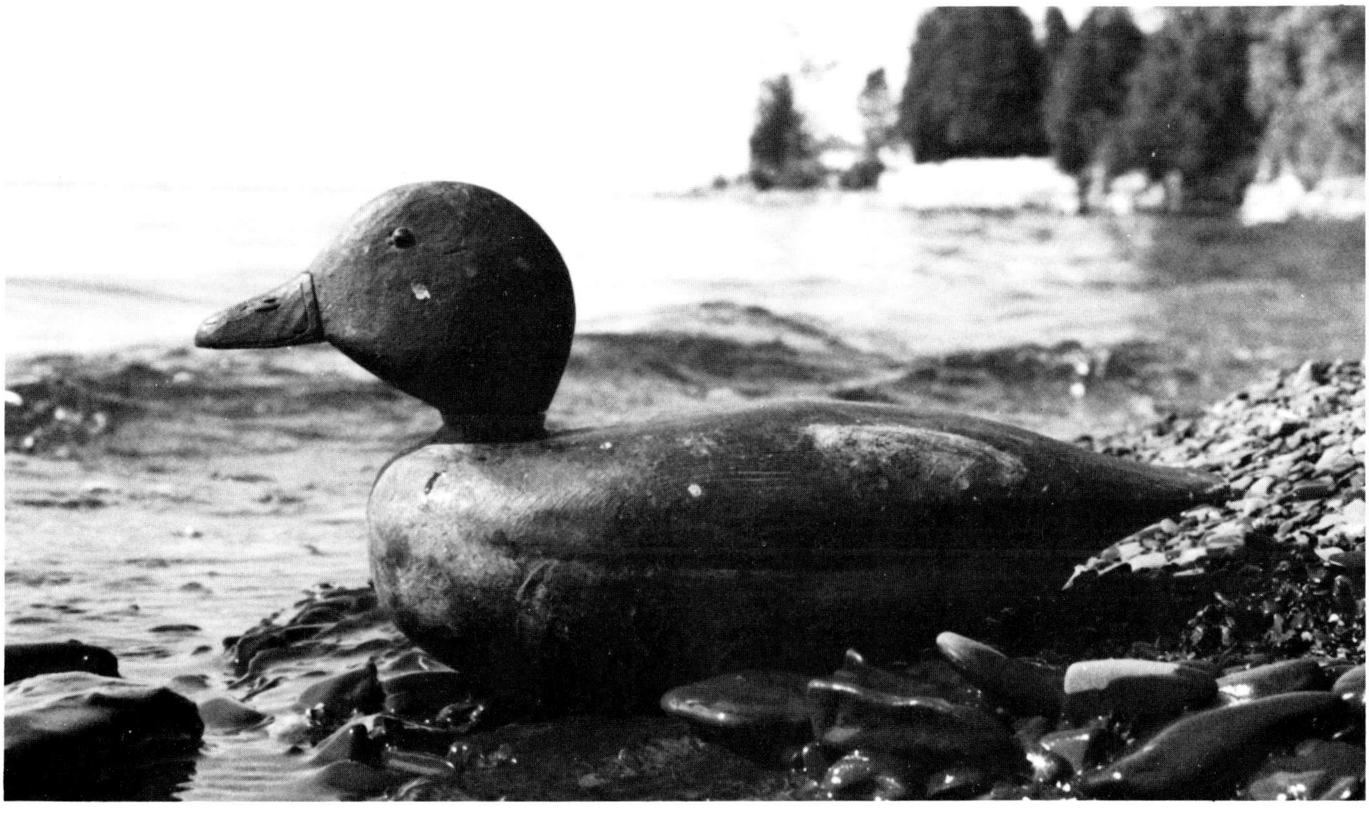

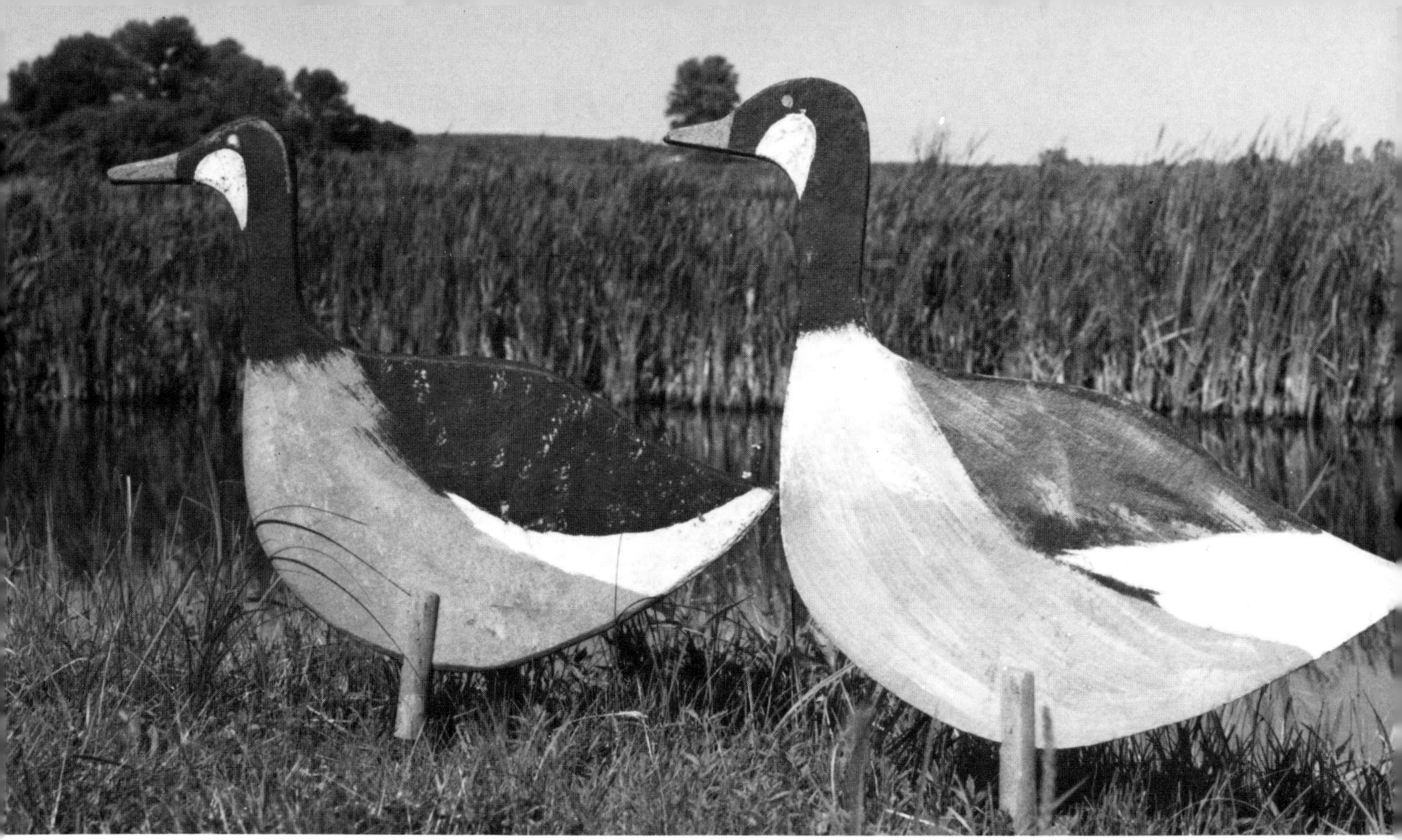

Canada goose decoy silhouettes by Arthur Ladd Way 1893 1965. Photographed on family marsh, North Hero, Vermont. Collection of Winston Way.

Goldeneye hen by **Ernest Way** 1893-1970. North Hero, Vermont. The island mailman, Way hunted and carved decoys in the tradition of his father, Amasa. Collection of Helen Way Kenny.

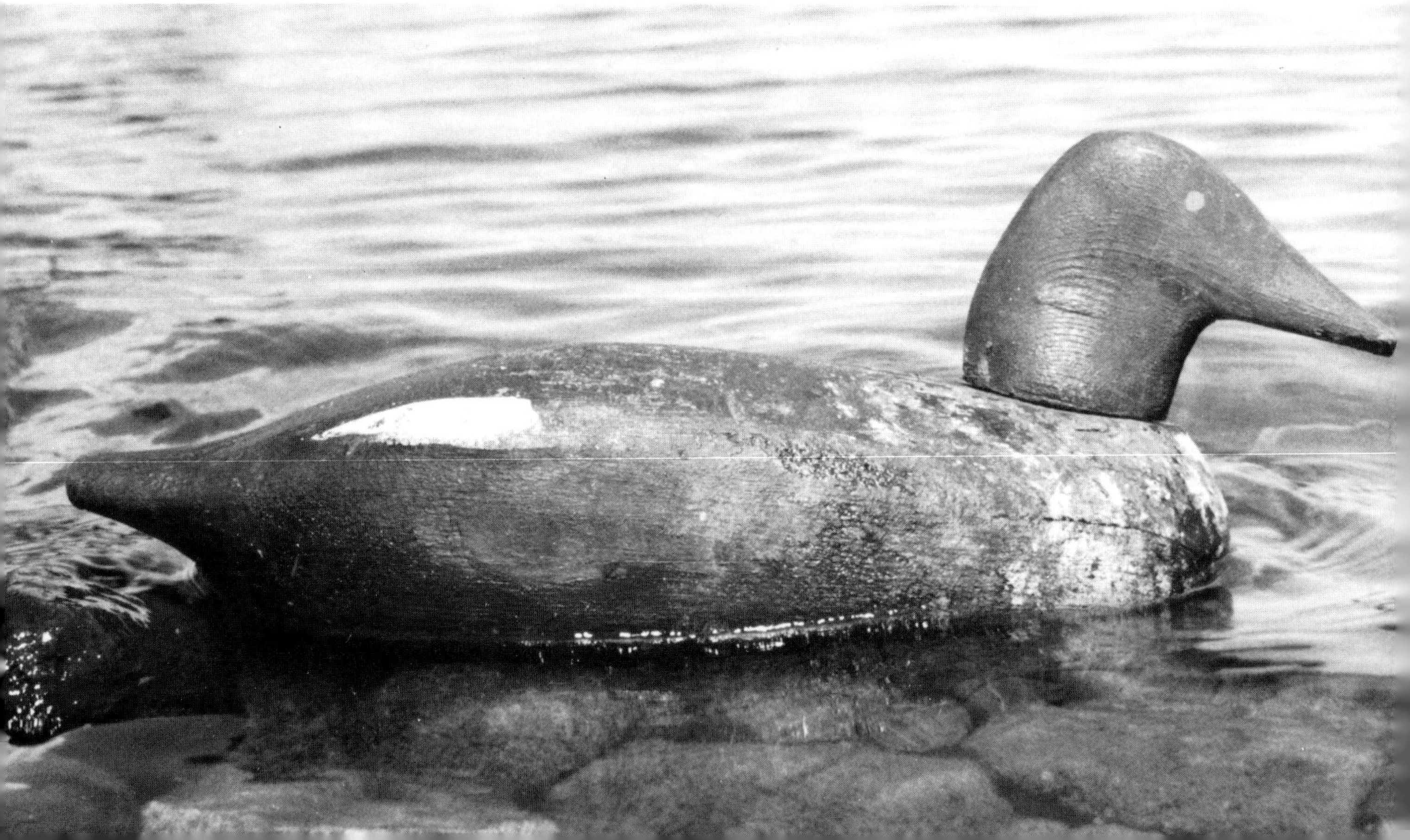

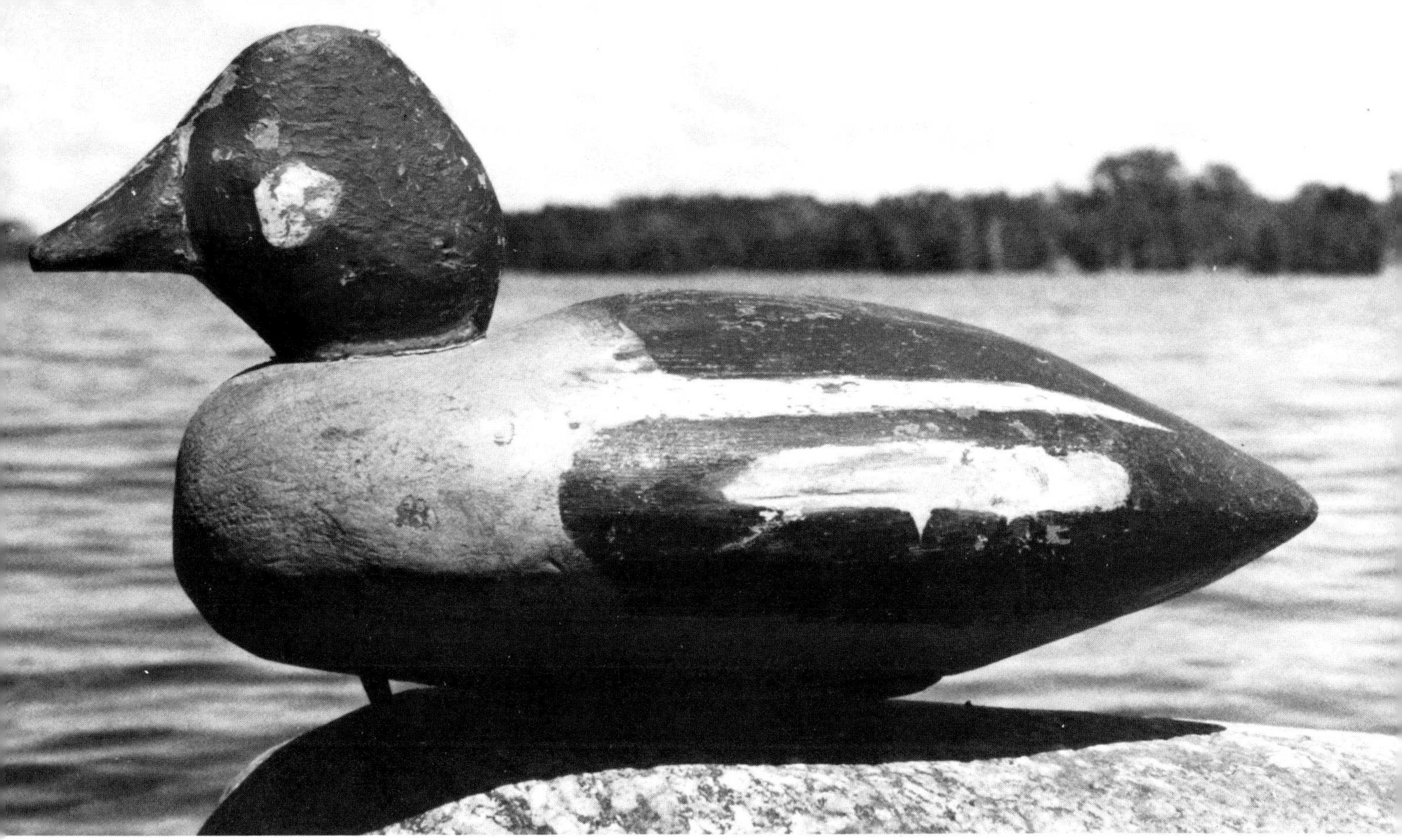

Goldeneye drake by **Amasa Way** 1861-1944, North Hero, Vermont. Way was a farmer and commercial fisherman on Lake Champlain.

Goose decoy by Issac Wells 1840-1910. Milton, Vermont. Hollow with bottom plate, used on St. Albans Bay by Wells who was a commercial hunter and fisherman. Collection of Duane Merrill.

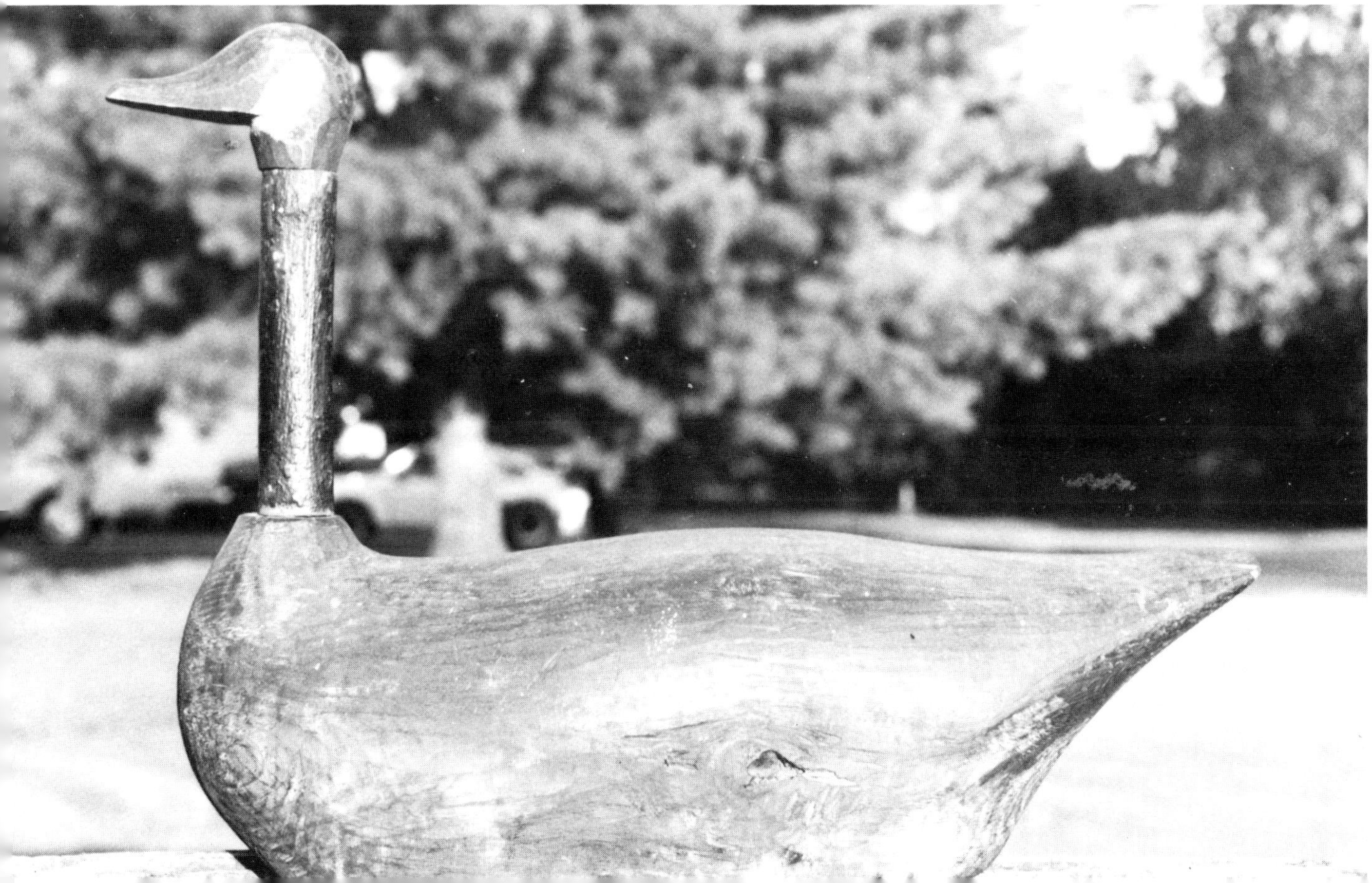

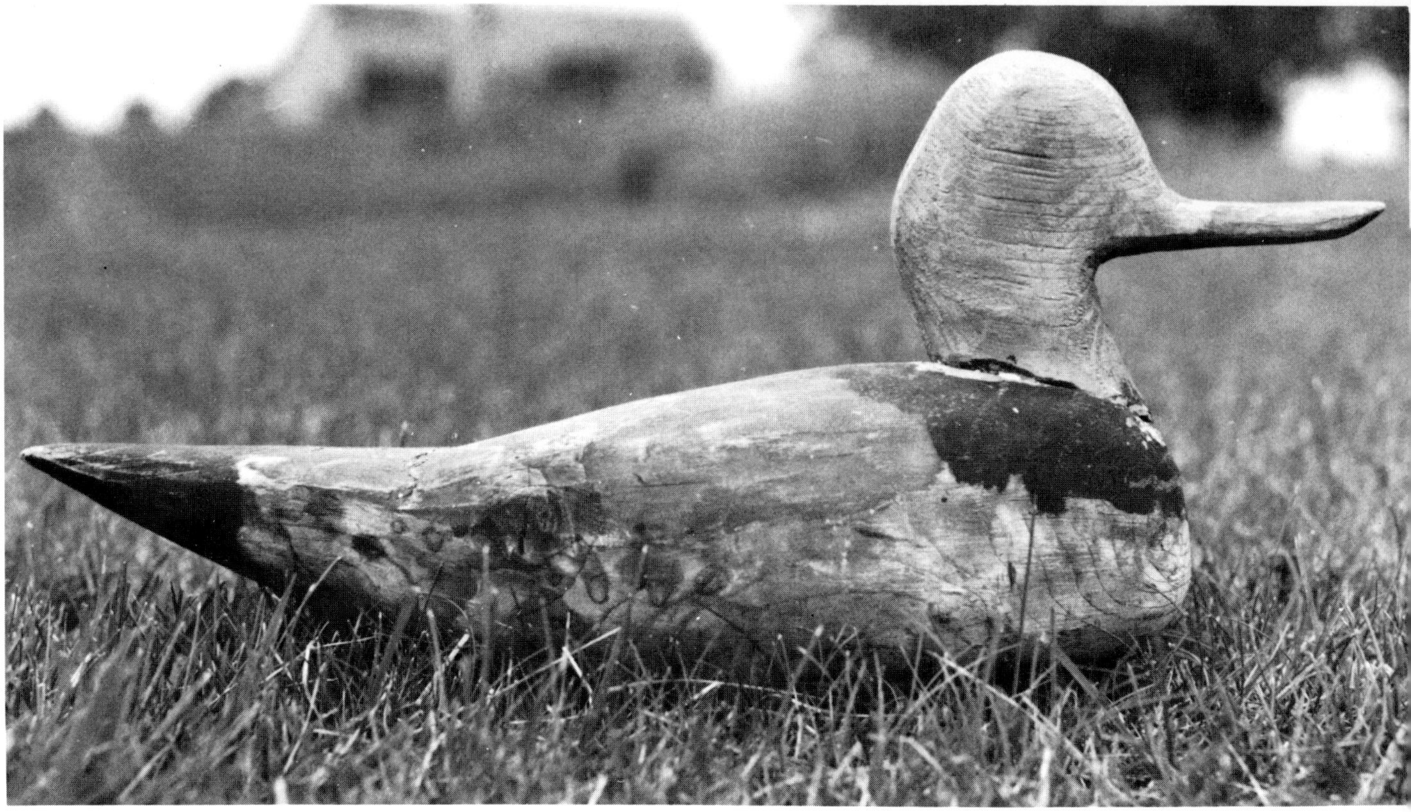

Goldeneye by Albert Willett, 1870-1945, Mooers, New York. Ca. 1905. Hunted at Rouses Point, New York. Collection of E. Rabideau.

Lawrence George Wright 1900-1982, Underhill, Vermont. A businessman and pilot, he carved over fifty decoys starting in 1936.

Working bluebill decoy by Lawrence George Wright. Collection of William Coates.

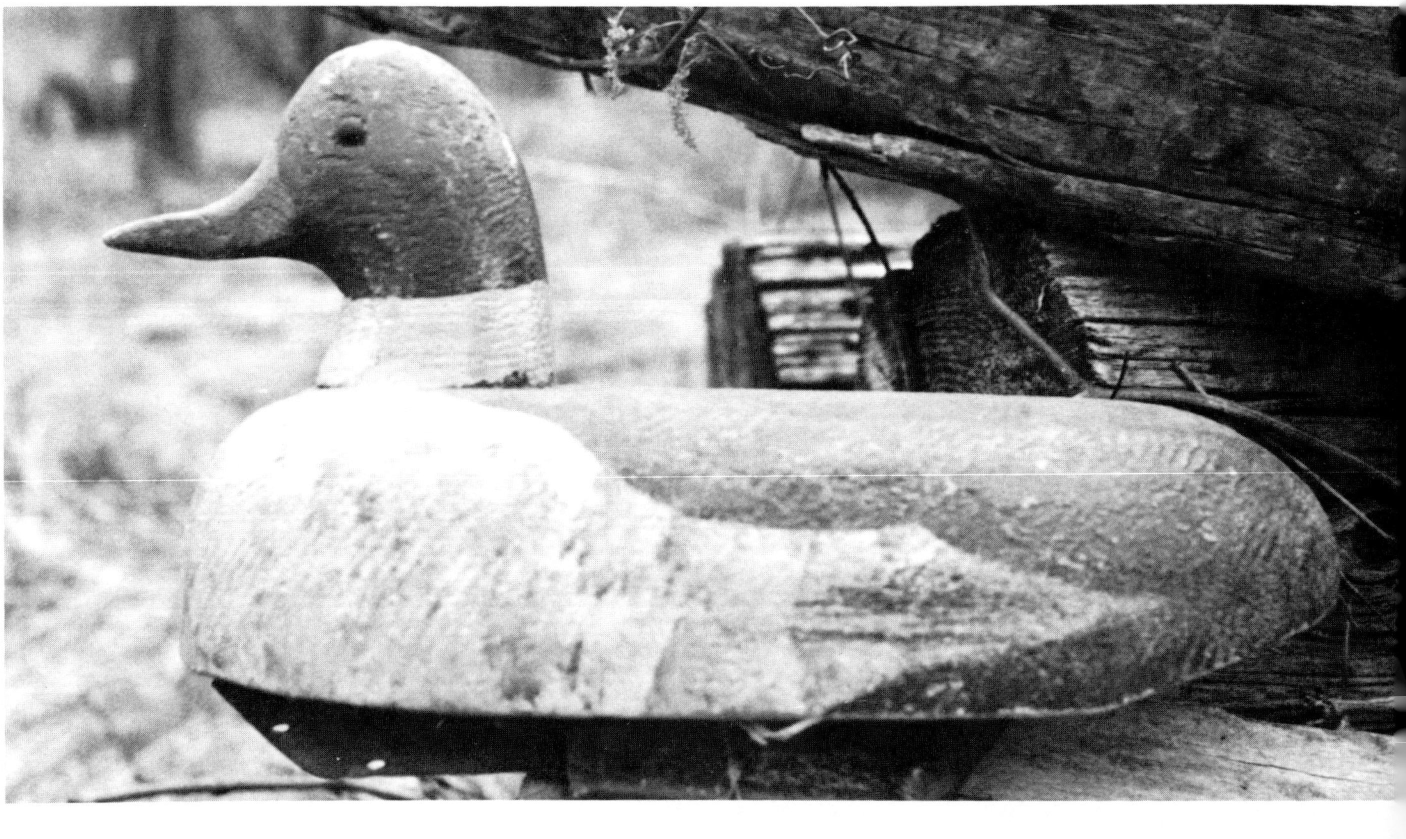

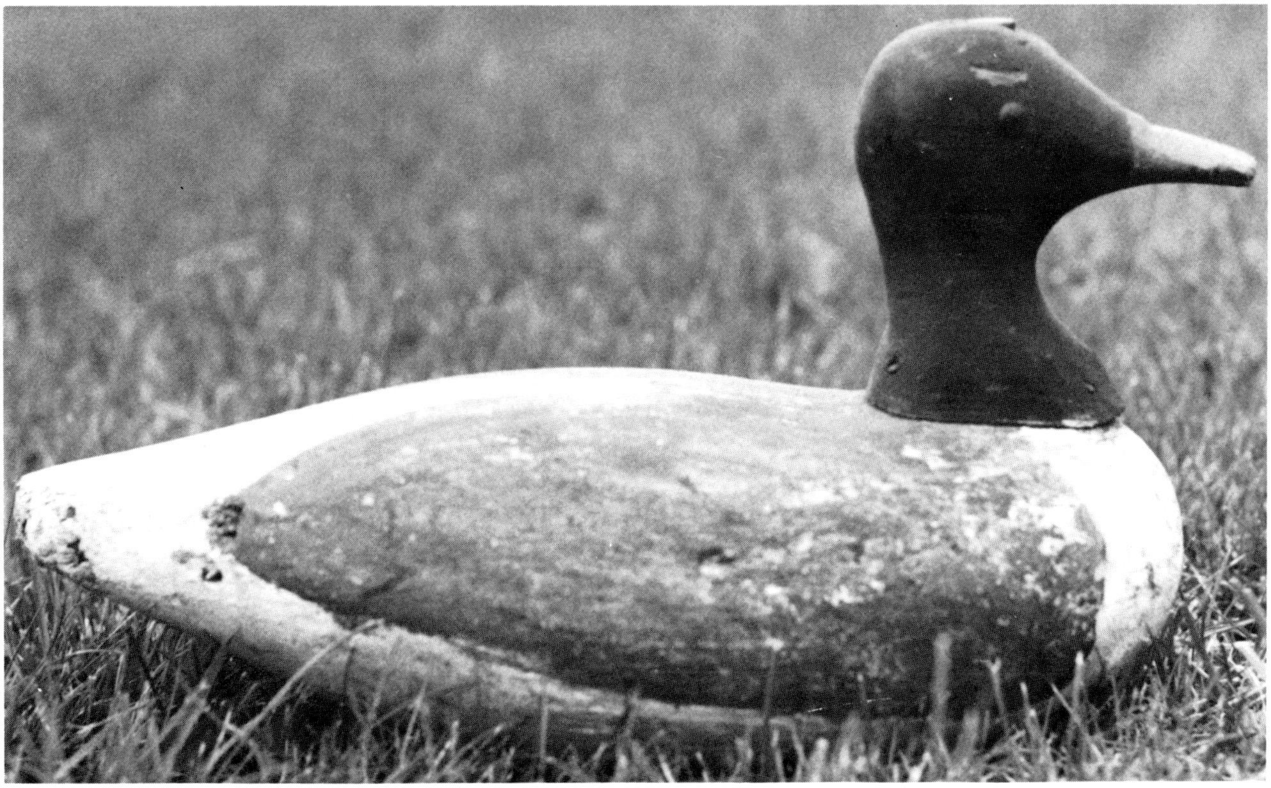

Working decoy by Joseph Willett 1894-1967, Mooers, New York.

John J. Wright 1857-1941 South Hero, Vermont, was one of the founders of the Lake Champlain Ferry Company and a boat captain. Besides farming he built wooden, cedar boats used throughout the islands. Wright also owned Sawyer's Island off the west shore of South Hero. His hand whittled, folky decoys were used on blinds at the edge of the island.

Bluebill hen by **John J. Wright**, South Hero, Vermont. Hand whittled with tack eyes and old repaint. Collection of Hillary and Rebecca Harrell.

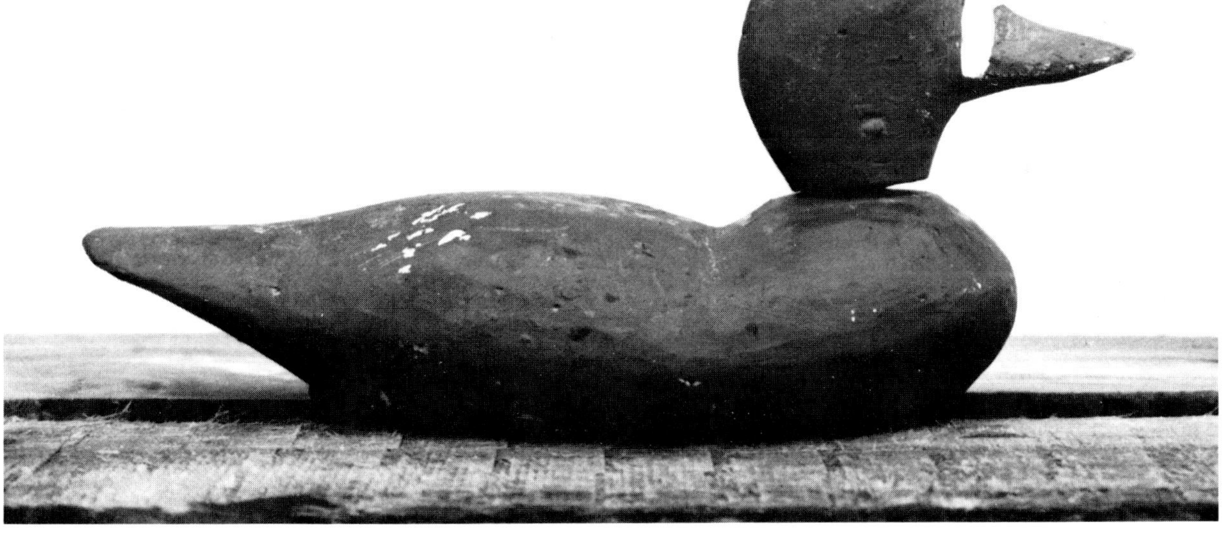

Index

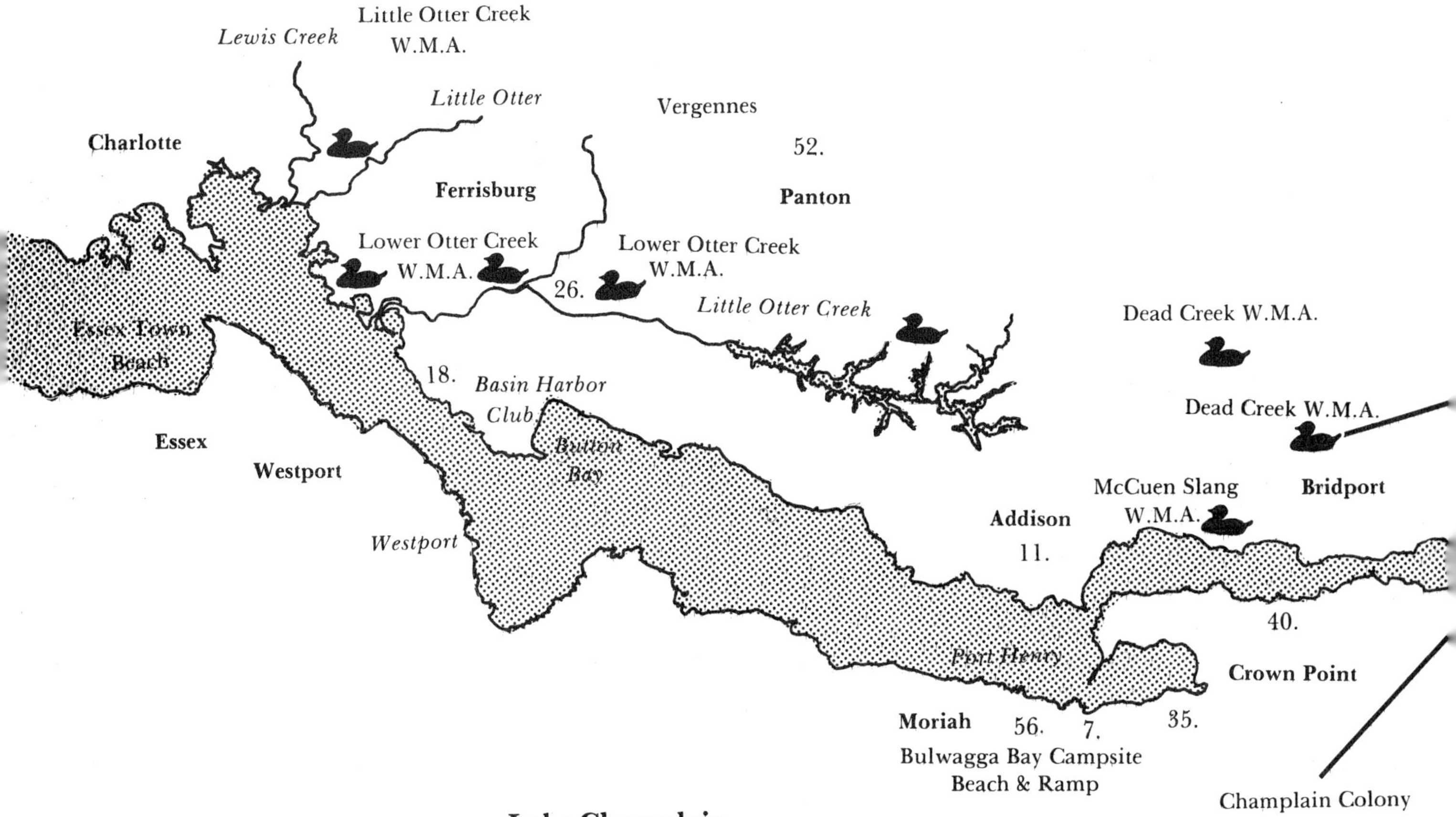

Lake Champlain

Carvers of Lake Champlain

1. J. Adams
2. J. Aiken
3. W. Aiken
4. S. Averill
5. G.H. Bacon
6. F. Baraby
7. B. Beaubriand
8. E. Benway
9. R. Blow
10. R.C. Booth
11. A. Bodette
12. G. Bohannon
13. W. Bruley
14. W. Carpenter
15. P. Choiniere
16. A. Comolli
17. P. Costello
18. R. Curler
19. K. Dolbeck
20. E. Dubuque
21. L. Durbrow
22. L. Duval
23. D. Fasking
24. D. Field
25. P. Gregory
26. E. Griffith
27. D. Harrington
28. J. Holly
29. W.A. Hill
30. D. Hoag
31. C. Holloway
32. A. Jacques
33. C. Kirby
34. R. King
35. E. Long
36. R. Lasher
37. J. Lyman
38. W. Maxfield
39. A. Maxwell